❧ UNVEILING ❧

The Inner Journey

To Stacy —
with and wonderful — with much
appreciation for how you are unfolding
your own "Inner Journey."

— Alay'nya —

(Alianna J. Maren, Ph.D.)

yours,
Alay'nya

ISBN: 0982901305

ISBN-13: 9780982901304

LCCN: 2011928014

THIS BOOK IS DEDICATED, WITH love, respect, and admiration, to the teachers and facilitators who have inspired, coached, and made possible my own "inner journey." These include, most significantly, my master teachers Anahid Sofian and Elena Lentini, and also, in alphabetical order, it is dedicated to wonderful teachers (in martial arts as well as in Oriental dance) and facilitators with whom I've studied: Artemis Mourat, Cassandra, Dalia Carella, Eva Cernik, DeShara, Margaret Devaney, Kathryn Ferguson, Delilah Flynn, Robert Fusaro Sensei, Petite Jamilla, Ruby Jazayre, Medea, Morocco, Pilar, Peter Ralston, Diane Richardson, Suhaila Salimpour, Ron Sieh, Suzanna del Vecchio, Joe Williams, and Zandra. My dear friend and "wise woman," Kathy Carroll, has been an inspiration and teacher on this wonderful life-journey, and this *unveiling* would not have been possible without her!

Advance Praise for *Unveiling: The Inner Journey*

"In *Unveiling*, Alay'nya takes women on a journey to the true *Fountain of Youth*. She unveils how to love and appreciate who we are through the roots of our fascinating womanhood. Alay'nya just may be a goddess of our time."

Julie Marie Rahm
"America's Mindset Mechanic"

"I love your analysis of *The Flame and the Flower* (*Chapter 3*) – [it was the] first romance I ever read!

Maha Najeeb
Oriental dancer

"Alay'nya has beautifully captured the elements of feminine evolution and blossoming in this engaging and powerful book, *Unveiling*. She uses her knowledge of dance as the metaphor for personal growth and discovery – the exploration of finding oneself in both the physical and psychological/spiritual dimensions. Alay'nya shares personal anecdotes of self-understanding which most often have been learnt through pain and suffering. She has taken risks by writing with honesty the intimate details of her search for self and her journey of exploration into the depths of her heart. Both men and women will be empowered by joining Alay'nya on this journey."

Kathy Gillette-Mallard
Administrator, University of Virginia

"It is a wonderful manuscript, but by no means a "casual read." By that I mean that it is not something to read in the little stolen moments of the day. Rather, it is something to explore in meditation and contemplation, with a cup of tea, away from the demands of children and husbands. And then not to read all at once, but section by section with time for reflection between readings… The parts I have read have resonated with me and given me validation for the things I feel and do that don't always fit with society's expectations for me, and given me ideas for how to further mold my life path."

Nimeera
Oriental dance performer and teacher

Acknowledgements

THIS BOOK HAS COME INTO being aided by the insights and wisdom provided by many teachers, colleagues, and friends. My first and greatest thanks are to my primary master teachers in dance: Anahid Sofian and Elena Lentini. Their grace, beauty, passion, dignity, and unswerving commitment to evolving Oriental dance to its highest artistic level have inspired me for decades. I am grateful to them not only for their teaching and guidance, but also for their review and comments on various portions of this manuscript. Dalia Carella, Suzanna del Vecchio, and Robert Fusaro Sensei, with whom I've studied at various times, have each given me insightful and lovely interviews. Both Dalia and Suzanna took time to share their experiences and perspectives just as each was about to begin teaching a week-long workshop; their generosity of spirit is most special. Artemis Elizabeth Mourat, Cassandra, Eva Cernik, and Peter Ralston each graciously gave inputs via email, which were very helpful.

Many thanks go to many wonderful dance teachers with whom I've studied during workshops, in private sessions, and through distance learning. In addition to Anahid Sofian and Elena Lentini, these include (in alphabetical order) Artemis Elizabeth Mourat, Cassandra, Dalia Carella, Eva Cernik, Deshara, Margaret Devaney, Kathryn Ferguson, Delilah Flynn, Petite Jamilla, Ruby Jazayre, Morocco, Pilar, Suhaila Salimpour, Suzanna del Vecchio, Joe Williams, and Zandra. My sisters in dance, particularly Amustela and Nimeera, have been not only supportive but also inspirational. Thank you, dear ones! Of course, my deepest thanks and gratitude go to Medea, my first teacher in this beautiful art.

There have been wonderful men who have been my teachers in the equally beautiful and vibrant traditions of martial arts. My thanks and great appreciation go to Robert Fusaro Sensei (7th Dan, Shotokan karate), Ron Sieh, and Peter Ralston. I am particularly appreciative of phone and email interviews with Fusaro Sensei and Peter Ralston. Diane Richardson, a mind-body integration specialist, was a great influence and coach to me; she facilitated my initial *unveiling*.

I link to all of my teachers and healers through the *Unveiling* website; please visit www.theunveilingjourney.com/teachers-and-healers.htm.

Kathy Carroll, my dear friend and "wise woman," has over many years continuously taught me how to seek Source, and to see the good in all people and situations. I am immensely grateful to her coaching and teaching, and for always encouraging me – both in undertaking my personal journey and in writing. I could not have written this book without her!

My understanding of the *Heroine's Quest* grew as I wrote this book, most significantly during the last few months of chapter rewriting and editing. Katherine Hanna provided me with a valuable lead by noting that the movie *Labyrinth* (discussed in *Chapter 6*) provides an example of a young woman's *Heroine's Quest*. She later reminded me of a similar *Quest* taken by heroine Lyra in *The Golden Compass*. Nicole Cutts, Ph.D. added to my understanding of how we can each write our own "mythic history" by sharing her evolving story of Princess Isabelle, as found in *Many Paths, Many Feet*.

Several people have been enormously helpful as I researched various archetypes, ranging from humankind's most ancient stories to relatively recent innovations. Jacqueline Magness, Ph.D, and Elizabeth Roslewicz, Ph.D., the Co-Founders of Light Works, Inc., and experts in Psychological Types (as expressed using the Myers-Brigg Type Inventory, or MBTI), shared their unique insights and experiences with me, and graciously reviewed and provided useful feedback on certain chapters. Diane P. Thompson, Ph.D., helped guide my understanding of the Inanna myths, both at the inception and in the final editing of this work. I'm deeply appreciative of her friendship and wisdom, extended over many years. Diane Wolkstein and Betty De Shong Meador have each further helped me understand the Inanna story. Donald Michael Kraig, a friend of many years and author of *Modern Magick: Twelve Lessons in the High Magickal Arts* as well as several other seminal works, gave several useful insights, for which I am very appreciative. Dr. Karl H. Pribram greatly facilitated my deeper understanding of brain processes, for which I am enormously grateful.

The idea of having an *integration pathway*, in which we bring together our core feminine archetypes, would have remained an academic concept if there were not real people who illustrated this in their very real lives. Journalist and writer Jonathan van Meter, author of the forthcoming *Ladies' Man*, graciously allowed me to use excerpts from his in-depth profile of Hillary Rodham Clinton, and gave me further useful insights during a phone interview. The deep understanding and appreciation that he cultivated of Mdm. Clinton's complex personality helped me use Mdm. Clinton as an excellent example of personal integration. My dear friend, Maestro Dingwall Fleary, Musical Director of two substantive orchestras, was extraordinarily gracious and kind in giving me an interview, and showing how a man can complete his very similar *integration journey* – including cultivation of all three of his feminine archetypes together with his masculine ones!

Rabbi Harold White, of Georgetown University, shared his insights on the role of ritual in women's lives, and has further clarified my understanding of classical archetypes, particularly with regard to the Kaballah. Father Richard J. Curry, S.J., Ph.D., also of Georgetown University, expressed an enormously helpful view into the spiritual "asceticism" of being a parent during one of his sermons at Holy Trinity Church. Special thanks go to Belita Karima of Baton Rouge, who reminded me of "The Wife of Bath's Tale" from *The Canterbury Tales* by Chaucer, which gave shape to the first chapter of this work. My dear friends Joe Williams and Julie Rahm shared with me useful insights and stories from their own lives, for which I am enormously grateful. Stella Grey's insights, which she has shared in various discussions over the years, as well as through her website and blog, have been both informative and inspiring.

Dear friends and family have supported me both physically and pragmatically, as well as with ongoing encouragement, during the long months and years of bringing this work to fruition. My special thanks go to my sister, Ann Marie McNeil, for her emotional and practical support, especially during the final two years of completing *Unveiling*. My niece, Rachel O'Reilly, has also been enormously kind, helpful and supportive during the last two years of manuscript preparation. My father, Edward J. O'Reilly, Ph.D., inspired my early love for science, and my late mother, Jean Ann Carpenter O'Reilly, was enthusiastic in her support for my early dance studies; she was a profound teacher, and a great mom. She is dearly missed. I am indebted to my maternal grandmother, Ann Carpenter, for her love, wisdom, support, and guidance, and also to my much-loved graduate-school surrogate parents, Jean and Elmer Hiebert. Artie Briggs has generously shared his insights and wisdom over several decades, and I am forever grateful.

Gerson Kuhr has been a friend and supporter of the Oriental dance community in the Greater Washington Metro Area for many years, and has coached me and other fine dancers to greater levels of physical fitness. In addition, he has graciously been a Master of Ceremonies at our many events and shows.

For the past several years, Dr. Dennis Sievers, a gifted chiropractor and healer, has kept me in vibrant good health and energy while I've completed this manuscript and developed new businesses. Anna Gordon, an extraordinary massage therapist and intuitive healer, has been a consistent support at multiple levels. Linda Heflin has encouraged and helped me greatly in matters of nutrition and various supplements; I owe much of my continued well-being to her as well. Other people have, over time, been a source of great healing and comfort as I went through the life transitions that have contributed to this book's richness. Dr. Marilyn Everett, a gifted chiropractor, and Joni Johnson, an extraordinary neuromuscular massage therapist, helped me with my "first stage" breakthroughs. My dear friend, Nader Rafigh, has kept me gorgeous with his mastery of all things relating to hair.

Members of my constantly-changing household have been extraordinarily kind and gracious while I've written and rewritten the final manuscript. My special thanks go to Peter Bradford for many fine meals; there were so many evenings where I had neither time nor inclination (or energy) for cooking. His kindness has been exemplary.

I am greatly indebted to Debra Smyers, my dear friend and a gentle, insightful, and gracious coach and facilitator to both artists and arts organizations, for an early manuscript reading together with detailed and helpful suggestions, and also for many useful conversations as the work came to fruition. I am also deeply grateful to Kathy Gillette-Mallard; her positive feedback as this manuscript came to completion was greatly encouraging.

Robert T. Quinn, entrepreneur and business coach, gave me many useful introductions, suggestions, and referrals as I concluded rewriting major portions of the manuscript. Morris and Sherry Zamora, Kishore and Pamela Carey, and other members of The Life Group kindly supported me with both prayer and practical gifts during a crucial development stage. Likewise, Kim Murray lifted my spirits during the last editing stages.

During final manuscript preparation, Katherine Hanna not only edited the entire text, but also provided useful style pointers and performed detailed checks on all references. This work would not have come together so beautifully without her! In addition, Melissa Brooker, Paul Dwyer, and Alice Peerenboom each provided me with an excellent and detailed set of edits, for which I am greatly appreciative.

Many students and friends within dance have all helped me grow; their positive support, encouragement, and appreciation over the years have made this effort not only worthwhile, but also possible. In addition to the martial arts teachers whom I identify by name, some extraordinary men have also influenced my life. They are described in various places, most notably in *Chapter 23: In Praise of a Few Good Men.*

Finally, I would like to thank both publishers and authors who have graciously consented to have their work reproduced in *Unveiling: The Inner Journey.* Specific authors and publishers are included in the *Credits* at the end of this book.

Medical Disclaimer

CERTAIN MATERIAL CONTAINED IN THIS book is made available with the understanding that the author, publisher, and printer are not engaged in rendering medical, health, psychological, or any other kind of personal professional services. Rather, the information contained is designed and intended to provide useful information regarding women's overall health and well-being, and should not be considered complete with regard to any medical or health-related situation or condition. All suggestions for exercise, and/or for therapeutic care (whether chiropractic, massage, or other), are not to be taken as a medical prescriptive. The material in this book should not be used in place of seeking appropriate medical advice for any condition that warrants attention. Readers are advised to seek medical, health, or otherwise competent professional guidance before undertaking any of the practices offered in this book.

The author, the publisher and the printer for this book specifically disclaim all responsibility for any liability, loss or risk, personal or otherwise, which is incurred as a consequence, directly or indirectly, of the use and application of material presented in this book.

Author's Note

THE SITUATIONS AND STORIES PRESENTED in this book are exemplars of situations that many of us have experienced. To protect personal privacy, the names used in this book are fictitious names and are often composites, with identifying details changed. However, I identify all teachers, healers, licensed therapeutic professionals, researchers, and others who have contributed in a substantive way (as identified in the Acknowledgements) by their full professional or stage names. Where appropriate, I provide their websites in the *References*, and links to their websites and published or available works are also on the companion website to this book; www.theunveilingjourney.com.

While I have made every effort to verify and obtain permission-to-reproduce quotations from various sources, the opinions and insights presented here are my own.

Online Resources

THE COMPANION WEBSITE TO THIS book is www.theunveilingjourney.com. It contains all of the references given here, including direct links to websites as well as to sites where books can be ordered or read online. Further web-based discussions expand on some of the more technical materials found in *Chapters 7, 11,* and *31*, dealing with archetypes from both the Jungian (MBTI) and Major Arcana or Qabalistic perspectives. Additional links illustrate different dances and dance styles. This site will be continuously updated.

Table of Contents

Introduction

I BEGAN MY OWN JOURNEY following the only path that I knew; the *Hero's Quest* — the classic masculine archetypal journey first described by mythologist Joseph Campbell.[1] Of course, as a teenager and young adult, I didn't know that this was what I was doing. Instead, I was responding to gut instinct and intuitive leaning. From childhood on, I was fascinated by the power, the beauty, and the energy-richness of the martial arts. As soon as I could find teachers, I began to study: first judo and ju-jitsu, then the various forms of karate, ranging from Tae Kwon Do to Shotokan. My choice of art depended on where I lived, and who was available as a teacher. Over time, I was able to study with increasingly well-known and established martial arts teachers; men who truly were "masters."

At the same time, I followed the *Hero's Quest* in other areas as well. During my teen-age years, I became fascinated with the potential of our minds and brains. I wanted do scientific work enabling us, as human beings, to make the most of our innate capabilities. "If you want to work in science as a researcher," my father told me, "you need your 'union card.' You need to get a Ph.D. It doesn't matter what field you get it in; you just need to get one." My father, a professor of chemistry, had his Ph.D. in physical chemistry, focusing on the mathematical aspect of chemical systems. I likewise had a gift for mathematics and abstract thinking. After considering other alternatives, I followed a path similar to my father's. During my undergraduate years, I studied math, physics, and chemistry, with a smattering of foreign languages, other sciences, and engineering. Then, I plunged directly into a physical chemistry graduate program.

Five years later, I had my doctorate. Having pushed martial arts into the background while completing my dissertation, I resumed studies; first with a local Shotokan karate teacher, and later (when I moved to a different city) with his teacher, Robert Fusaro Sensei (then 5th Dan, and who as of this writing is 7th Dan, or seventh-degree black belt). Fusaro Sensei, who is one of my favorite "Leading Men," founded a martial arts academy in which women were given excellent opportunities to advance. Two of the teachers with whom I studied in Fusaro Sensei's Midwest Karate Association dojo were Mary Brandl Sensei and Anita Bendickson Sensei, who were 1st and 2nd Dans when I studied with them. They are now 4th and 5th Dans, respectively.

It was while watching a regional martial arts competition, where leading contenders performed *katas* (choreographed movement sequences), that I realized that even though the advanced *katas* were powerful and beautiful, they were not for me. These *katas* were being performed by the best martial artists in the region, and were unquestionably exciting and challenging. However, my sensibilities were shifting. I was feeling drawn towards a different *kind* of body art; one that had a more feminine nature.

I found an opportunity to study T'ai Chi Ch'uan. Over time, I migrated from the beautiful (although linear) Shotokan style to the more rounded forms of T'ai Chi and its sister arts. These were all considered "internal" martial arts; my teachers in this area all did "energy work" as part of their practice and teaching. (Envision, if you will, some of the classic Kung Fu movies and television shows with the various "powers" that the masters possessed. This is the kind of "energy work" that these teachers included in their training – in a much more realistic manner than is portrayed in the movies, however!) Over time, I began studies with Ron Sieh, and when I moved from the area, with Ron's teacher, Peter Ralston. Both of these men are widely regarded as exemplary martial artists and master teachers. It was around this time that I had my first breakthroughs in being able to access and use my own internal energy, or *ch'i*. (I tell this story in *Chapter 29: Pragmatic Esoterics*.)

T'ai Chi Ch'uan satisfied my desire to practice an energy-rich body art that included *ch'i* use and cultivation. Still, I felt that something was missing in my personal quest. I simply needed a more feminine expression. I was inspired, in part, by reading John Grey's now-famous book, *Men are from Mars, Women are from Venus*.[2] If "Men are from Mars," I reasoned, and "Women are from Venus," then there would have to be an *Art of Venus*, or a "Venusian path," that did for women what the martial (Mars) path did for men.

This was more than an artistic longing, and more than an intellectual quest. As a child, for reasons ranging from immediate family dynamics to observations of our cultural patterns, I had decided that the "daddy job" might not be wonderful, but it was much, *much* better than the "mommy job." Beginning when young, I "male-identified." Adding to this, in my teen-age years, I had a self-image of being ugly and socially awkward. Many of us go through this stage when young; mine was probably not much different from that of most teenagers. The way that I dealt with this, though, was not to build girlfriend relations and learn about men through the time-honored practice of "dating and dishing." Rather, I withdrew into my intellect.

I emerged some fifteen years later. With Ph.D. in hand, a fair ability as a martial arts beginner, and a brief marriage and divorce behind me, I had a stunning realization: I didn't know the first thing about men. I didn't know the first thing about interacting with them as a woman. I didn't know the first thing about being in a *female* identity, having barricaded myself behind the ivory tower of my intellect for a lengthy time. I realized that I'd missed something – perhaps a very *important* something. I was ready to learn.

A gentleman friend introduced me to one of his friends, a beautiful and powerful dance teacher named Medea. Through her, I found my starting point for this *Venusian path*, which we call Oriental dance. (It is also, variously, known as Mid-Eastern dance or simply "belly dance." The term "Oriental dance" references back to the overall genre of what we call "Orientalist art"; romanticized interpretations made by the late 19th century European writers and artists who traveled to the Near and Middle East.) Over time, I transitioned from the martial arts to this more *Venusian art*; I let go of the "fighting" mentality that underlies all martial arts, and embraced the warm and womanly sensuality of Oriental dance.

During this time, my work as a scientist took me from one city to another. Usually, I could find a good dance teacher. A new position brought me to a relatively small city; one where there was no teacher of Oriental dance. I realized that the best way to learn from that point onward was to open my own studio and start teaching. (As the old saying goes, "We teach that which we need to learn.")

To continue learning, I went to a great variety of workshops, each of which featured a different guest instructor. Over time, I found two teachers with whom I resonated the most: Anahid Sofian and Elena Lentini, both based in New York City. I adored Anahid's combination of precision and fluid softness; her dance vocabulary range is possibly the greatest among dance teachers today. I was in awe of Elena's controlled passion and deeply moving choreographies. As often as possible, I would travel to New York to spend an intensive weekend of practice; attending their regular classes and following up with private sessions. In addition, I continued attending various workshops, worked out with videos, and hosted master classes for which I would bring one of my master teachers in to teach.

Still, though, I longed for a guide – a teacher or a book – who could show me how this dance form was part of something deeper. Intuitively, I felt that such a *pathway* could and actually *did* exist. Finding it, though, was another matter. I was feeling an increasing conviction that Oriental dance could be more than the physical corollary to martial arts. To realize this potential, though, I needed the other aspects; the emotional and psychological, and the energetic as well. I read Dan Millman's book, *Way of the Peaceful Warrior*.[3] In his youth, Dan was tutored by Socrates, a martial artist and "life teacher." Using a *Star Wars* analogy, Dan had found his Obi-wan Kenobi; his own Yoda. I longed for the same. Despite having wonderful teachers and healers of various types, there was still something missing. I continued searching for a guide; one who would not only help me learn Oriental dance, but coach me on connecting this art to my overall life.

I did indeed find help, from several sources. Diane Richardson, whom I describe in *Chapters 14, 15* and *16* (*Locking Our Minds, Softening,* and *Releasing Resistance,* respectively) was a great facilitator. Without her, I would not have made the breakthroughs that were crucial to my linking the body art of dance to my psyche. However, being a bookish sort, I was still looking for a book, if not an in-person "life teacher."

After a while, I realized that no one teacher, book, or guide was going to "magically" appear. If I wanted a book, I would have to write it myself. At this point, I realized that my own personal *Unveiling* journey had not only begun, but had been part of my life for many years. I had by then been studying martial arts, and then dance, for well over fifteen years. It would take me yet another fifteen years to discover the *Unveiling* secrets, and to complete this writing.

Finding that our physical *pathway* was embedded in Oriental dance did not, of course, fully reveal the whole *path*. This was like finding one strand of a multistranded, severed cord, where the various strands had been pulled far apart. I needed to find the other strands of our lost women's *pathway*. For thousands of years, our Western cultures have done their best to obliterate the original *pathway* of the sacred unfolding within women. Our society is heavily biased to view the world through a masculine-oriented lens. However, our feminine path is so intrinsically different from the masculine perspective that it has been very difficult to simply perceive this; to "re-member" it as a *pathway*. We often simply don't know yet how to remove the filter of masculine values from our minds, in order to perceive something inherently well-suited to women.

My first inkling of how our *pathway* might be found came from reading Dr. Toni Grant's *Being a Woman*.[4] In this book, Dr. Grant described how she had found her answer (to the same question that I was asking) when she came across Antonia Wolff's fourteen-page pamphlet on the *Structural Forms of the Feminine Psyche*.[5] As a scientist, my "discovery-antennae" began quivering. I knew that I had found another "strand" of a woman's *pathway*. This one had a more intellectual and theoretical content. It could also lead to deciphering some questions that I had about my own psyche, and that of women in general. Finding Dr. Grant's work, and through her, the link to Antonia Wolff's, was equivalent to finding a personal Rosetta Stone. It let the discoveries begin.

Just as finding Oriental dance opened up a starting point in my physical practice, finding Dr. Grant's (and Antonia Wolff's) work made the conceptual starting point available. However, the insights presented by Dr. Grant were simply another place-of-beginning, not the end of the journey. Much work lay ahead.

Over the years, I had trained myself to think by writing. Thus, I attempted to write – and complete – *Unveiling* many times. Each time, I came up against a wall. Each "wall" was different. Sometimes it was a life issue. (To be blunt, there were a whole mélange of life-issues; not all of them are fully resolved.) These emerged in the early drafts of *Unveiling*; they made it sticky and gooey with too much personal "stuff." There was not yet enough value to others. Over this fifteen-year timeframe, I would pick up *Unveiling*, work on it, and then realize that I was still not ready to take it to completion.

Most of the time, I put the book aside and concentrated (with varying degrees of success) on working through the "issues" themselves. However, in addition to working through life, I had to learn a whole new approach to writing. I had been trained as an academic, and my writing style was still too abstract; it was not yet relevant to anyone. Not to me, and not to you. I had to learn how to write from the heart, and to teach using stories – most often, my own! (Usually, they were painful and embarrassing. Through all of this, I kept reminding myself, "We teach that which we need to learn.")

In the midst of all of this, I carried on with "life." I honed my ability as a scientist, and became more of an inventor and entrepreneur. I continued studying dance, and built (and rebuilt, many times) my dance school. I organized and hosted dance events, and moved from one place to another as my career required.

After several more years (and the rise and fall of a corporation that I co-founded), I began writing again. This time, I was guided by an intuition that completion was at hand. I collected and revised the various chapter drafts, and realized that this book now had coherence. It now held reasonably useful, clear, and potentially even valuable communications to other women.

By this time, I was listening much more to my own intuition than to the voice of corporate structure. My lover had left me several months earlier, and while I still missed him greatly, and was grappling with simple survival challenges every day, my mind was much more lucid and clear. I was more open to internal wisdom, as opposed to devoting myself and my thoughts to him.

Listening to this "inner nudging," I was guided to attend two different dance workshops. The first was with Petite Jamilla, who taught a veil dance that had great emotional content. In fact, she had devised the dance as a means for her own inner healing. The result was a dance of subtlety, beauty, sensitivity, and passion. Learning this dance from Petite Jamilla was an emotional "re-awakening." I had gone through so much in the previous several years that I had stopped feeding my psyche with the deeper levels of the dance. Learning this single new dance from Petite Jamilla was like opening up a very cherished – but locked away – aspect of my inner being.

Almost immediately thereafter, I was guided to reconnect with one of my master teachers, Elena Lentini. Immersed as I had been in various life challenges, I had not been keeping up with her workshop schedule. To my surprise, she was scheduled to teach a dance workshop in New York City the following weekend, and she graciously invited me to attend.

Elena has been using her dance, for decades now, to progressively embrace a more direct experience of being. Her dances embody mystical elements, and they are increasingly a means of accessing a deeper aspect of our psyches. I felt that the particular dance that I learned from her that weekend could be interpreted as a dance-expression of a shamanic journey. This touched me in a manner similar to the dance that I had learned just a few weeks prior from Petite Jamilla. Petite Jamilla's dance re-awakened my heart, and Elena's dance re-awakened my spirit.

These two dances, taken together, answered a question that I didn't even know I had been asking. After years of grueling business ventures, I had come into a fallow time in my own dance expression. I had reached a certain level of initial mastery; one that I had originally set out to capture. At this point, adding yet another choreography to my repertoire, or mastering one more technical skill, was no longer of interest to me. I was looking for, and actually needing, something deeper. Yet, I didn't know what that was.

The two dances that I learned, from Petite Jamilla and Elena Lentini, brought me back to the healing and the sacred-journey aspects of dance, respectively. They revitalized me, and gave me a new sense of purpose and direction. I knew, from that point, where I was going to go with dance. Within days, I realized that I was ready – for the first time, *truly* ready – to complete *Unveiling*.

Being *ready* to complete a task, especially one as comprehensive as this, is entirely different from actually bringing it to completion. Over this past year, as I revisited each chapter, a series of new insights came to me. Each of these insights, although emerging with a "flash" of coming into focus all at once (much as the insights for my various patents have come together rapidly), required substantial research for fleshing out and substantiation. My studies, over the past year alone, have taken me into areas ranging from the Qabalah to Jungian psychology, from neurohormonal chemistry to history, and from Western esoteric traditions to Taoist sexual energy practices.

During this last year, one factor emerged with great importance. As women, we have a very different neurochemistry from men's. In all human (and mammalian) brains, the way in which information is processed is partially a function of neural structure and connectivity. It is also a function of the chemical environment within which this neural connectivity operates.

Many years ago, I had the opportunity to spend a year attending the lectures of Karl Pribram, one of the world's most eminent brain scientists. During this time, I was able to form a deeper understanding of how the neural structures in our brains process information. This was an important time in my life, as I had recently devoted myself to learning about artificial neural networks, which were computer programs and even hardware implementations that attempted to process information in a manner analogous to how the brain operates. The simplistic view, one that many lay-people and even scientists adopt, is that information is transmitted via connections between the axons and dendrites of one or more neurons to another. Of course, temporal encoding and other factors are important.

Studying with Dr. Pribram gave me an opportunity to broaden my understanding of the areas where he is widely acknowledged as one of the greatest researchers today. Dr. Pribram's discoveries have including functions of the limbic systems and the relationship of the frontal cortex to them; certain sensory-specific "association" areas in the posterior cortex; the discovery (with others) of the fact that the motor cortex encoded targets, and what he calls "images of achievement," which is how the brain represents to itself a desired complete motor task such as picking up a cup or braking a car. Dr. Pribram has also introduced significant theoretical elements, and has been heralded as inaugurating the cognitive revolution in psychology.[6]

My brief year of study with Dr. Pribram paved the way for my later appreciation of the overall dendro-dendritic connectivity of the brain, together with the role of its chemical environment, including how the various neurohormones (particularly dopamine and oxytocin) influence our mental processes. Over recent years, we have become much more aware of the extent to which women's attention and emotional states are influenced by our brain chemistry – particularly by the neurohormones released when we fall in love, experience intimacy (of any sort), and bear children.

I was surprised and very excited to find, during this last year, that the brain chemistry of intimacy correlated with what I had previously identified, from Antonia Wolff's work on *Structural Forms of the Feminine Psyche* (discussed in *Chapter 7*), as one of the major feminine "modes." Finding that at least one of our "modes" has a neurohormonal correlation suggests that the complexity of women's psyches may be related to distinct, measurable factors, as well as to psychological and sociological interpretations. This insight further supported my earlier intuition that a woman's *path* did exist, but that it would be very different from what men regarded as a *pathway*. As women, we would need a very different model. We would need a *pathway* that encompassed the complexity of who we were, and which would give us a sense of continuity throughout our different life-stages.

In writing, I would envision sitting next to you; we'd be having a cup of tea or a glass of wine, and talking about what is really important in our lives. We'd put together what it is that really works, to create a useful, functional, meaningful *pathway*. We'd talk about archetypes, and what they mean practically in our day-to-day lives. We'd talk about men, about sex, and about "getting juice" – that wonderful, life-giving experience that we have when we learn to start cultivating and directing our internal energy, or *ch'i*. Envisioning these conversations with you, and putting them into final form, became my own *Heroine's Quest*.

Naturally, I had many helpers along the way. There were periods where I needed to be very reclusive, focusing on the insights that I was receiving, and getting them down into useful form. Many times, the books that I've referenced heavily throughout *Unveiling*, and indirectly, the authors of those books, were my friends and guides. Also, practically speaking, many people helped me with simple, physical survival, while I deferred traditional corporate (and even academic) roles to focus on completing this book. As I described the "allies" that a *Heroine* calls into her life (*Chapter 6*), I realized that I was following the classic path.

My final step in this particular *Heroine's Quest* has not been to complete the book. Rather, it has been to write my author's biography, together with rewriting my resume and entire life story. For the first time, I am "integrating" three main areas of my life. Previously, my life as a scientist was separate and distinct from that as a dancer, which was also distinct from having an inner quest or vision together with personal investigations into energy work or *ch'i* use and cultivation. As many women do, when they start studying Oriental dance, I had taken a stage name – Alay'nya – within my first few months of studying dance. I had begun writing this book under that name. I had intended – for a very long time – that even publishing this book would belong to a separate "life," apart from that of my "daytime" persona as a scientist, inventor, and entrepreneur. Even when research-ing and finishing this book became the full focus of my daily activities, I still maintained the notion that when this was complete, I would go back to my "real" life, and my "real" identity.

I finally realized that in writing about personal growth and *integration*, the time had come for me to put into practice what I was preaching.

I have found that women actually do have a *Heroine's Quest*, and that it is distinctive and different from that of the *Hero's*. This has become the subject of *Chapter 6*; a chapter that was originally about the *Hero's Quest* alone. Earlier, my intention was to posit the existence of a *Hero's Quest*, and to state that we did not have (although we needed) a comparable one for the *Heroine*. It came as a complete surprise to realize (during the final stages of editing, no less) that we actually *do* have a classically-themed *Heroine's Quest*, which we often tell as a young woman's coming-of-age story.

One defining characteristic of the *Heroine's Quest* is that we don't, typically, do a battle-unto-death with a single antagonist. Bluntly put, we do not define ourselves by whipping out, à la *Star Wars*, our lightsabers and having a duel. Our defining moment comes when we say to that which confronts us, as did the young heroine Sarah in the movie *Labyrinth*, "You have no power over me." *This* is what makes our journey complete.

To complete my own *Heroine's Quest*, I am sharing my full life-story, inclusive of all of who I am as both scientist and dancer, and also a practitioner of various energy disciplines. In doing this, I'm stepping out of the cultural boundaries that say, "You can be any one of these, but not a combination of any two or three. Further, if you want to function in the male-identified world of science and technology, you must hide anything that speaks to your core identity as a woman." To these boundaries, and to the people and beliefs behind them I say, as did *Labyrinth's* Sarah, "You have no power over me." I am finding the courage to bring all of who I am into one person, in the face of corporate cultures that validate us only insofar as we follow the masculine *pathways* of academia or business, staying within the confines of intellectual and cognitive knowledge alone.

Standing up to cultural norms has not come, and does not come, without cost. In my earlier years as a scientist, one boss disdainfully referred to the dance art as "This belly dance bullshit." His words were echoed, to the letter, by one of my business colleagues, many years later. Men appreciate *eros* in women, so long as it doesn't interfere with their need for compartmentalization. (I am using the term *eros* to refer to an operating principle or energy, as distinct from the Greek god Eros.) Men, because they compartmentalize so much, are often threatened when women start bringing together all aspects of who they are.

Not all men are like this, to be certain. In fact, as this book comes to completion, I'm finding that the men who show up in my life are like something drawn from chaos theory; they are either exceptionally wonderful or exceptionally awful, with little in between. Which brings me to the following: *A Tale of Two Men,* or a study in contrasts.

I was on a first date with a certain gentleman, the CEO and founder of his own up-and-coming company. We had met twice before, each time in the context of a business meeting. He had been introduced to me by another business colleague, a man whom I hold in high esteem. During the second meeting with this new person, we had talked at some length about our respective business ventures. In particular, I talked with him about how I was becoming a "product company," even if I was still an "army of one." He seemed to think that I'd offered him good ideas, and told me during our second meeting that he was incorporating the strategies that I had described during our first meeting. Thus, it came as a welcome reprise when he emailed me, asking if I was ready to "come up for air." Yes, I was happy to do so, and he invited me to join him at noon the next day.

In the next email message, he suggested that we take in a matinee. This seemed good to me; I love movies, but hadn't seen one in a theater in a very long time. Then, he suggested that we meet there, as opposed to his picking me up and taking me to the theater; he pleaded the case of an out-of-town appointment, from which he'd just be returning. This was a little against how I like to do a first date, but I agreed.

We met at the appointed time, and took our seats. He wanted to sit up high in the theater, far from others, so we could be "naughty," as he put it. This seemed to be pushing things just a little, but I didn't object to the prospect of a little kissing and cuddling.

The lights dimmed. In no time at all, he took my hand and put it on his crotch. "First date," I told him, as I moved my hand away. This was a little direct, I thought, but at least he was making his priorities clear. He repeated the gesture. I once again removed my hand. I simply wasn't ready for his "escalation" of what I thought comprised a "first date." A few minutes later, he took my hand and guided it again. This time, he had undone his zipper, and was in full flagrante. "Impressive," I murmured, "but this is a first date." And once again, I removed my hand. A short time later, there was a distinctive odor. "Thirty seconds," he whispered in my ear (as if I should be honored). I couldn't really believe what I was sensing, but yes, my mind told me, he had indeed done what he'd just done.

By this time, I figured, he had accomplished his mission. I wanted to accomplish mine; by now I wanted to finish seeing the movie! On the way out, I told him, "According to the *Kama Sutra*, no man gets a woman into bed without a lot of talking. You might want to re-read." "I'm not much for words," he said. "I'm an aggressive kind of guy, and I like to go for what I want." How modestly unassuming!

Later, "30-second Jack" emailed me. "As a follow up to our meeting today, when would you have any time to offer some detailed suggestions on how [his company's name] can institute 'Blogging'? ..."

Excuse me, but that was a *meeting*?

In contrast (I told you this would be a *Tale of Two Men*), Marcus, a dear friend and business colleague, took his two-week summer vacation. He spent it in a Latin American country, where with other church members, he did carpentry, electrical wiring, and plumbing on behalf of a local congregation. Marcus and his wife, Shirley, have adopted a baby from a foreign country. They brought her in as an infant, and Marcus was often the one to get up for the 2AM feedings! Together, they host weekly bible studies in their home.

Both Marcus and "30-second Jack" are exceptional businessmen. In 2009, during the year after the Lehman Brothers collapse, Marcus achieved over 700% of his business development goals. He operates by introducing people to each other, focusing with care and attention on what they need, and structuring his plans to provide them with greatest benefit. He was a godsend in my life when my former lover, Theo, left me over a year and a half ago. (Theo found my personal financial crisis too at odds with his desire for elegant and gracious attention.) In the ensuing months, Marcus opened up his database and personally introduced me to the best in his relationships circle; these included bank presidents, entrepreneurs, and various other "movers and shakers."

I have just now returned from a meeting with Marcus. We've set up a follow-on meeting; he's thinking that I can be a business mentor and coach for a woman that he and other community leaders are sponsoring; she's been through some tough times and needs to connect with someone who has both a business sense and some comparable life history. Over the past two years, I've gone from being someone whom Marcus has introduced to others – in the sense of opening opportunities for me – to being someone that he brings others *to*, so he can open opportunities for them. I'm honored!

In terms of core archetypes, the subject matter of *Chapters 7* and *11*, Marcus is a pretty integrated man. He's brought his spiritual self into his daily business practice. Marcus has built up and strengthened each of his three core masculine roles or archetypes. He is a *Magician* (creative visionary), an *Emperor* (builder of strong, solid systems), and a *Hierophant* (a teacher and coach).

Marcus has also built up and brought in each of his three core feminine archetypes. Specifically, he has integrated his *Isis/Mother* essence. This archetype is not necessarily about being a physical mother; it is about nurturing. This is as important for men as it is for women. Marcus is a nurturing father to his child, and is constantly doing what we would all call "good works," both within his church and his community. He is constantly building relationships; this is one of his greatest business strengths. He has some of what we'll come to call our *Hathor* essence; this is the part of us that is light-hearted and which loves to play.

But perhaps the most important aspect that Marcus brings in from his feminine side is his *High Priestess* archetype. This is the quiet, spiritual, receptive aspect within each of us.

If any of us, man or woman, is to come to know and honor the *Sacred Feminine* within, we do so through accessing our inner *High Priestess*. Men who have truly become complete human beings have done so; this shows up in the way that they treat women, and in the way that they have a deep sense of integrity and wholeness in their lives. (Those of us who may find the *High Priestess* concept a little at odds with a Christian or other doctrinal mindset might substitute the phrase, *Bride of Christ*, anytime they see *High Priestess* in this book. This is still a feminine mode; it is still receptive and still oriented towards spiritual wisdom. Alternatively, we can replace the term *High Priestess* with the notion of opening up to an inner *Sophia,* or wisdom. Another possible substitute term would be *Abbess*, connoting the leader of a women's monastic order who has cultivated her spiritual awareness through years of quiet contemplation.)

The contemplative spiritual dimension is as important to men as it is to women. When we look at someone like "30-second Jack," we see a man who may have all three of his masculine archetypes activated. He may even have an *Isis/ Mother* aspect; "30-second Jack" has founded a business that supposedly offers other businesses important high-level resources. Presumably, there is an element of caring for clients within his business. He may also have a strong *Hathor* (light-hearted, pleasure-seeking) component; he certainly has no problem seeing to his own pleasure! However, this is a person who is devoid of a sense of the sacred. He is unable to honor a woman, either as a colleague or a friend. (Oddly enough, he didn't want to be seen having me touch him on the way into the theater – he thought that one of his employees or business associates might notice and "comment." It is just possible that Mr. Jack has a wife or steady girlfriend; in that case, he is not honoring *her* either.)

I believe that we're at a crossroads in human evolution. We have a very, *very* short timeframe within which to get ourselves together, as a planetary species. I'm speaking now as a scientist, as well as a global citizen who's observed many of the huge ecological and social disasters that we've had recently, with more on the way. If we attend to the ever-increasing growth of not only technology, but also to

PART I:
THE AGES-OLD QUESTION
❦

CHAPTER 1:
WHAT DO WOMEN REALLY WANT?

THE *WIFE OF BATH* WAS a saucy lady. As she tells her story in *The Canterbury Tales*, we note her feisty and independent spirit, and find her as interesting today as did people during Chaucer's time. She held her own among fellow pilgrims when, on the road to Canterbury, they held a story-telling contest. Her story harkened back to the days of knights and dragons, of spells and sorcery, and of damsels in distress.

In the days of King Arthur, a lusty young man came upon a beautiful maiden and promptly raped her. There was a hue and cry at this misdeed, and King Arthur sentenced him to death. The ladies of the court, however, felt this sentence was too harsh. They pleaded for his life. Finally, King Arthur gave this young man over to the Queen. His life was completely in her hands. If she decided that he was to die, he would die. If she decided he could walk free, he would walk free.

The Queen thanked King Arthur, and made her decision. "I will grant you life," she said, "if you can tell me what thing it is that women most desire.[1] She gave him a year and a day to find out, and to return to her with that answer.

On his honor to return, he left her company and the court and wandered for a year, seeking the answer. Many women suggested many things: Some said riches, others said honor, others said pretty clothes, and yet others said "pleasure in bed." Every woman, it seemed, had a different answer.

With a heavy heart, the young man made his way back to King Arthur's court, ready to receive his fate. On the day before he was due back, he saw a group of beautiful young women dancing together at a forest's edge. "Surely," he thought to himself, "in a group such as this I might get an answer!" He drew near, and was surprised to find all the women vanished, save an ancient and ugly crone. "Tell me, by your faith, what you seek for," she said to him.[2]

The forlorn young knight, returning to what he knew would be certain death, told her about his quest. She struck a bargain with him: "Give me your promise," she said.[3] She vowed that if he would do as she asked, she would reveal to him the answer that he had fervently sought for an entire year.

With renewed hope, and with the old crone at his side, the knight returned to King Arthur's court. That night, the Queen assembled her maidens, her ladies-in-waiting, and particularly her widows (because they were so wise). She would judge, with their counsel, the words of the young knight. He gave his answer in a voice ringing with confidence:

"My liege lady," he said, "generally
women desire to have dominion
over their husbands as well as their lovers,
and to be above them in mastery;
this is your greatest desire, though you may kill me;
Do as you please, I am at your will here."[4]

Throughout the assembly, there was not one who contradicted him. To a woman, they agreed that he had answered the question. For successful completion of his task, they said, he should be allowed to live.

At this point, the old crone jumped up, and begged the Queen to witness that she had given the young man his answer on his promise that he would do as she asked. What she asked for, then, was that he would marry her. The knight pleaded; he offered up of all of his property, to no avail. What she wanted was to marry, and to marry him.

They married the next morning, and all that day, the knight hid himself. That night, after they had entered the bridal bed, he refused to make love to her. He refused even to look at her. She chided his lack of civility, and offered him a choice. Either, she said, she could stay ugly and old, and be a "faithful, humble wife," or she could be young and fair – and he would have to take his chances with other men trying to woo her.[5]

The knight was greatly discomfited by having to make such a decision. Finally, he responded as best he could: "My lady and my love, and wife so dear, I put myself under your wise control," he told her.[6]

> "Then have I got mastery over you," said she,
>
> "Since I may choose and rule as I please?"
>
> "Yes, certainly, wife," said he, "I consider that best."[7]

In that moment, she became young and beautiful. The spell of ugliness cast on her was broken, and she and the knight lived out their years in contentment.

৶৶

Over the centuries, male philosophers and poets, pragmatists and politicians, have asked themselves (and occasionally us), "What do women want?"

Men are not alone in asking that question. Now, more than ever, with longer lifetimes and the opportunities to do more with our lives, we women are asking the same question of ourselves: "What do *I* really want?"

If we go with the *Wife of Bath's* answer, we've just discovered a "bottom-line" truth about ourselves; one of our deepest motivations. According to her, we want "mastery" over the special man in our life. As much as we have other, "socially acceptable" motives – such as wanting the best for our children, and to be in loving relationships – we also want power. Specifically, we want *erotic* power. We want power over men.

But is this the whole story? And is this really the fullness and complexity of who we are, and what we desire in life? Let's look a little more closely.

There is no simple answer – because we are not simple beings! We are complex and multifaceted. Thus, even as we create a foundation and a framework for our answer to this wonderful question, we know that whatever the answer is, it will be like us; complex and multifaceted. This does not mean that we can't get the answers, though. We most certainly can. We can understand ourselves, and our deepest core desires, at a new level. More than that, we can take on certain processes – let's collectively call these processes *pathworking* – that will help us enrich our lives considerably.

This, then, is the core and purpose of this book. Some of us may indeed begin with desiring "dominion over [our] husbands as well as [our] lovers." As we'll find out, though, this is just a starting place – both culturally, and within our lives. We will see that as we women have created greater control over our lives, we are far less dependent on men to provide us with the security that we desire, underlying what Chaucer expressed as our desire for "dominion."

We will also find that our desires change over time. As we go through our *pathworking*, or life-mastery and integration processes, our desires as well as our priorities shift. This is not just a function of hormones, child-rearing, and other life stages. If we are taking on our life-journey at its deepest level, our sense of what is important evolves substantially.

In any area of our lives, as we begin to manifest reality according to our desires, we take note of what we are creating. We make adjustments; we do fine-tuning, and sometimes we decide that we'd rather have something entirely different! Let's call this a desire/manifestation/refinement cycle. We do this in many areas of our lives. We very often create exactly what we desire, and then decide to "tweak" things a little bit. Sometimes, we make big, sweeping changes!

Suppose that we were creating a garden. After the first season, we might say to ourselves, "Oh, that was good! But really, I want the cosmos and daisies here, not there, and I'd like a rose arbor over this walkway, and I'd like a series of hanging baskets, laden with flowers, along that wall." We observe our results, and we tap into our *feelings* about what we've brought into being. We check in with our previous and newly emerging desires. We use all of this as feedback to generate a modified (or even brand-new) set of desires or intentions. Then we start manifesting our desires, or creating, all over again.

The most wonderful thing about being a woman today is that, more than ever before, we have sufficient time to do this desire/manifestation/refinement cycle multiple times. Simply put, we live long enough. Many of us also have more resources than ever before. We can select from all sorts of things that inspire longings and desires within us; these can include pictures, stories and news items, and even seeing something that we'd like. We can connect with a huge range of people and resources. We have mobility and knowledge. We are in a prime position to do superb reality creations!

Due to research in neurophysiology, we can understand ourselves – and our complexity – much better than ever before. Recent discoveries about how our (specifically *female*) brains work help us understand the biological underpinnings of our desires and actions. In addition, we also have a range of archetypes, drawn from sources as diverse as ancient goddess personas and more recent psychological typing. We can use these to identify different modes, or ways-of-being, within ourselves. We can begin to note not only which mode we are in, but when and how we shift from one mode, or archetypal essence, to another.

We have one more thing that will help us to *unveil* our inner selves. This comes from our direct, physical experience as we practice one of the oldest and most intrinsically feminine body arts: Oriental dance (often known as Mid-Eastern dance or "belly dance"). By observing how our bodies and our psyches interact as we dance, we gain insight into our own nature. We also get a great way to express ourselves!

In the *unveiling* process, we know ourselves at increasingly intimate and deeper levels. Let's return to the analogy of creating a garden. We might start off simply with a desire to connect with nature, to have a lovely place in which to sit and be surrounded by beautiful flowers and warbling birds. Suppose that we create this garden, and enjoy it fully.

Then, over time, our relationship with our garden grows, and we become more observant. We see the birds come and go with the seasons, and notice the little animals that visit. We might decide that we want more than simple natural beauty; we now desire to create a nature sanctuary. We not only fill the birdbaths and birdfeeders in winter, but we do a little research and plant some shrubs that may not look as beautiful as the others, but which provide valuable food during the coldest months. When we clean up the garden in the fall, instead of hauling off the twigs and broken branches, we mound them into a long burrow in the back. It might not look "finished" in the sense of a picture-perfect garden, but the little animals can hide from the predators in these twig and leaf-covered bramble piles. We may even replace some sections of lawn with various sedge grasses, giving both food and shelter to the little denizens of our sanctuary.

Our relationship with our garden has matured as we gained more insight and understanding; as we spent more time with it, and gained intimacy. In the same sense, our *unveiling* process gives us intimacy with ourselves. We are our own garden. The more that we nurture and cultivate ourselves, the deeper our relationship with ourselves becomes. Most of all, we gain a greater sense of how to live in a way that is deeply nourishing to our essence; to our core.

Thus, we return to Chaucer, and to his answer that women desire "dominion." Superficially, this is a good answer. We want "mastery over men." But is this all?

There is a little hidden something here. The crone who provided the answer started off as "ugly and old." When her husband yielded control to her, she became "young and fair." But her husband was not yielding control in all areas of his life, and she wasn't really interested in controlling his entire life. Instead, he was honoring her wishes in the one area that was vitally important to her; how she would appear. He gave her kindness and consideration in the realm that mattered most *to her.* What made this transition possible was that the woman's husband trusted her to make the wisest decision for herself. He *honored* her. The courtesy that her husband gave, in addressing her as "my lady and my love, and wife so dear" – when she was *still ugly* – was what allowed her to become fair![8]

We will find, in the forthcoming chapters, that we have many modes or ways of being. In one, we are armored; we are *Amazons.* In another, we are the ripe, succulent *Goddesses of Love,* rich with juiciness and sensuality. Both of these are good, and both are valuable. But when we take on the masculine mode of achievement, and enter our *Amazon* state, we often find ourselves trapped in this state. Then, it is difficult for us to find our softer aspects.

In the *Wife of Bath's* story, the young knight had spent a hard, long year seeking to understand women. He had gone from being a man who would casually rape a woman, simply because he desired her, to being a dedicated student of the feminine. He had spent a year listening to, studying, and paying attention to women – as if his life depended on it. (Literally, it did!)

Finally, he realized that for all his searching and study, he didn't know the answer. He was ready to yield his life – because he had given his word. In this state of humbleness, and yielding up his ego, he was ready to honor the woman who came into in his life. Yes, he tried his very best to get out of his commitment. (His ego was battered, but not yet dead!) But after a year of really listening to women, he was ready to be tutored by his wife. With her wisdom guiding him, he accepted her and gave her honor. He did this regardless of her physical appearance and regardless of how happy (or not) he was about his marriage.

His courtesy and consideration created the trust that his wife needed. She was able to let go of her hard edge of ugliness, and become soft and beautiful – in the safety and security of his care.

As we *unveil* the truth about ourselves, we must always remember to look a little more closely. Our first insight, the most immediate answer, might not be the deepest truth. What we want may *not* be "mastery over men," or even the knowledge that we can entrance them with our beauty. Rather, we may desire that they love us and honor us enough so that we can release to that aspect within ourselves that allows us to be beautiful. Beyond that, we may even have further desires.

The *Wife of Bath's* story leaves us pondering. Superficially, this is the old "battle of the sexes." Superficially, this is about ego and control.

When we look closer, though, the message of the story is about going *beyond* ego, about *giving up* control. Specifically, it is about giving up control in a situation where we have created enough trust and caring so that we can go beyond the appearances. Moreover, the story is about being able to trust that someone else will look out for us, even as we also treasure and care for that other person. Only within this degree of safety can we truly surrender ourselves.

As author David Deida writes, in *The Way of the Superior Man*:

> **If you want your woman to be able to relax into her feminine and shine her natural radiance, then you must relieve her of the necessity to be in charge.**[9]

> If you refuse to offer your masculine gift ... then she will have to learn
> to depend on her own masculine capacity... She will refuse to surrender
> to you even sexually, because she hasn't been able to relax and trust you
> all day; you haven't offered her your masculine clarity and perspective,
> so she has to be her own man and give it to herself.[10]

So now we have a conundrum. According to Chaucer, speaking through the *Wife of Bath*, we desire "dominion" over our men, and to be "above them in mastery." According to Deida, women desire being able to be "relieve[d] of the necessity to be in charge." Which is most true? Are they both valid?

To find the answer, we need to go deeper. This time, we look not to the masculine perspective, but to the feminine. We'll start by observing *ourselves*; not so much in what we say, but in what we *do*. So onward, my dear one. Let's explore the nature of our selves together!

PERSONAL PATHWORKING:

1. This is a journey, dear sister. The landscape that we will traverse will be inside ourselves. Gather up the equipment that you need for this journey. Find a comfortable journal (I simply use a letter-sized lined pad, kept in a simple binder), and select a comfortable pen. Find some little patches of time in which you can write.

2. Start writing. We're going to begin with the *Morning Pages* exercise first proposed by Julia Cameron, in *The Artist's Way*.[11] Three pages of long-hand, every day. Anything and everything. Allow yourself to clean out the contents of your mind – the superficial stuff, whatever comes up for you – just empty it out on paper. Don't worry about reading what you've written, and certainly don't share it with anyone. Simply start releasing your daily "stuff" onto the page. More thoughtful analysis and specific exercises will come later. Remember, to the very best of your ability – three pages. Long-hand. *Every single day*.

CHAPTER 2:
WHO ARE WE, *REALLY?*

IN THE LAST CHAPTER, WE answered Sigmund Freud's (and most men's) time-honored question of "What do women want?" with the answer created by Chaucer, a great student of human nature. We agreed with him on a superficial (and somewhat humorous) level, but we also suspected that there might be a good deal more.

Before we go further, though, let's do a "truth test" on what Chaucer has said, through the *Wife of Bath*. If we do indeed desire "dominion" over our husbands and lovers, or over men in general, we should expect to see tangible signs — *evidence* — that this is so. Thus, we can look into our daily lives for patterns that either confirm or disconfirm this claim.

The easiest pattern to assess lies in our advertising. Advertisers and marketing people have unraveled our psyches. They know what we want; they know our secret fantasies. With superb precision, they play to our imaginations and our desires. Haven't we all heard, "Sell the sizzle, not the steak"? If we decode the "sizzle" that is being sold to us, we'll learn our own hidden programming. We can figure out the lifestyle fantasies that appeal to our deepest psyches. This is what we are *really* buying; not the banality of the product itself.

We already know the answer, at least superficially. As many of us have said, when we observe certain advertisements, "Sex sells." But is that all there is? Or is there just a bit more? When advertisers sell to men, what do they use? Typically, a picture of a beautiful, alluring woman. And when they sell to women, what do they use? Again, they use a picture of a beautiful, alluring woman. But sex and allure sell in different ways. Men and women respond differently. And so, of course, the message is different when advertisers use sex to sell to a man, versus selling to a woman.

When advertisers use a beautiful woman in selling to men, the message is, "You can have this woman. You can attract a woman like this, by buying this product." When they market to women, the message is, "You can be like her. You can be attractive to men, by buying this product." Because advertising is about what works, we learn that what we want, almost desperately, is to be beautiful.

Many of us women give extraordinary attention to our beauty. This, in itself, tells us that being beautiful is a survival issue for us. This is no big news. Any woman who puts on cosmetics before she goes out of the house, or whose idea of dressing up includes thigh-high stockings, *knows* that one of her personal priorities is being sexually attractive. But what is a little surprising is the *extent* to which we are programmed, at a very deep level, towards being as attractive as possible.

When we get up in the morning, what do we do? For most of us, sometime after the shower and before breakfast, we put on our makeup. (Even that word, more common in our language than "cosmetics," tells us a lot.) This is one of those things that we do so automatically that we don't even think about the significance of what we are doing.

Let's take a closer look at exactly what happens when we put on cosmetics. Specifically, let's look at the biological symbolism of what we're doing. First, many of us use foundation, under-eye concealer, and a variety of other cosmetics and skin-care treatments to make ourselves look younger. We seek the "fresh, dewy" look of youth. We make our eyes seem larger – and our lashes longer – by using eyeliner and mascara. In this way, we look more like a wide-eyed child or teen-ager than an adult. We often fluff, tousle, or curl our hair. (Note that hairstyles communicate a whole complexity of messages; the more we go up the corporate/political/community ladder, the more we tend towards controlled and structured hair. But that's a different story.)

In addition to these steps, we also use color. We put on eyeshadow, blusher, and lipstick. There is a reason for this. When we are sexually aroused, the fine skin capillaries around our eyes receive more blood, and they dilate. This gives our eyelids a darker look. Also, when we are aroused, our cheeks are flushed, and our lips become pinker. Our cosmetics mimic these physiological changes.

It doesn't stop there. We paint our fingernails and toenails. There is a great deal of erotic charge on those toenails, and when we paint them — well, it's rarely a muted blush! Bright, vivid red is our frequent choice. Similarly, we all know the impact of a pair of sexy, high-heeled red pumps or red strappy sandals. There is a significant difference between wearing, say, a pair of black high-heeled shoes and the same shoes, in red.

Women in our culture are not unique in using red on the fingers and toes. Women in India and the Mid-East have, for thousands of years, used henna to decorate their hands and feet. In particular, a bride will have her hands and feet decorated with beautiful red henna patterns for her wedding. Why all of this? Because, when we are sexually aroused, our fingertips and toes change color. They become pinker.

Grooming is important; it can explain why we wash and comb our hair, but not some of styling. It can explain why we file and buff our nails, but not the bright red nail polish. The bright red — whether it's lipstick, nail color, or a pair of shoes — is an unabashed sexual signal.

The fact that we are sending out a very strong signal is even more pronounced when we consider how limited our "expressive palette" is in other ways. Our cultural concept of appropriate body adornment is both strict and limited. Tattoos and piercings are still statements against our cultural norms. Our jewelry is typically restrained. At the office, we are usually careful not to wear too much print or too much plaid. In fact, the corporate office colors have been described as "machine colors": grays, black, blue, and beige. Anything else is a shock to our social system; think of the bright pink wardrobe in *Legally Blonde*!

In our shoe selection, shape as well as color gives an important sexual cue. There is also the well-known impact of the high heel. Men say that they like women in heels because it makes the calves look shapely. As they bring their eyes upward, they notice that the curvature of our legs is enhanced. And continuing this gaze upward; well, we get the point. All true. This more "shapely leg" created when a woman wears high heels may connote a more direct biological cue, however. As Alison Lurke notes, in *The Language of Clothes*, "an extended leg is the biological sign of sexual availability in several animal species ... [producing the] 'courtship strut.'"[1]

We notice that the effect of wearing high heels is just as strong, maybe even stronger, if all that we see is the foot itself. (I noticed this in a fashion spread that focused on shoes. In a picture that showed just the model's beautifully pedicured foot, arched in an elegant high-heeled sandal, there was a definite sense of *eros*. It had nothing to do with legs, or "moving upward." The charge was right there, in the foot.)

Feet are marvelously expressive, even though we don't think of them that often. Most of the time, they're shod in serviceable leather, and they get us where we want to go. When we gesture, it's usually with our hands, not our feet. However, feet are tremendously important in our overall body sense. There are a huge amount of sensory receptors in the soles of our feet. Feet are complex; as complex as our hands.

So what happens when we're aroused? Not only do our fingers and toes change color, but we also arch our feet. We press down on the balls of our feet, and curl our toes upward. This is very much the same shape that our foot is put into when we wear high heels. In fact, the more we let our feet respond during orgasm, the more we exaggerate the arch. And which is sexier? The two-inch pump or the stiletto heel? Aha! We begin to get some understanding.

To summarize: Before we go out in the morning – sometime between that first cup of coffee and going out the door – we put on cosmetics and select accoutrements that shout to all the world that we are in a state of great sexual arousal. Because what we wear is so emotionally restrained, when we relook at our cosmetics and certain accessories, we get an extra jolt. We are doing a great deal, in a very well-researched and carefully practiced way, to project a message of being sexually "on." We do this even when our thoughts are as far as possible from sex!

So why are we doing this? The most banal answer would be that we want to attract the interest of men. Even if we are happily married, or with a long-term lover, we feel this is necessary. However, we do this both in presenting ourselves to our lover or mate, and for presenting an image of ourselves to the rest of the world. In short, we rate ourselves, and feel as though the world rates us, on our sexual desirability.

But this is too simplistic, and we know it. We *know* that our cosmetics-based physiological cues are those of sexual readiness, and we *also* know that we are — most of the time — not only *not* sexually ready, but not even sexually interested.

We need another interpretation; possibly several other interpretations. Let's consider possibilities.

One possibility is that we are playing a little social-positioning game; with ourselves, with men, and with other women. We are tribal creatures, and we are often members of multiple "tribes." These can be at work, with our families, at church, and even just "going out with the girls." For each different "tribal experience," we dress and present ourselves differently. Through all our different "tribal experiences," though, one thing is consistent. We desire to present ourselves as being vital and energetic. We desire to present ourselves as being healthy, vigorous, and in charge of our own lives. We present this message with our grooming. Being well-groomed is the sign of a "healthy animal." It is only a sick animal, or one in very dire straits, that does not keep its coat well-groomed. We desire to *be* healthy, and so one thing that we do is to *act* healthy, and one way that we do that is to attend to our grooming.

This can be a message to *ourselves* as much as to the rest of the world. When we take the time to make ourselves as groomed and as beautiful as possible, it is a way of telling ourselves that we are feeling good, that we are in charge of our own lives. We tell ourselves that no matter what else is going on, we still care enough to put some effort into our appearance.

Let's take it up one more notch. In human tribes, as opposed to other animals, even primates, we decorate ourselves. It takes time and attention, and often money, to create a polished "look." We know that having the resources of time, attention, and money to devote to ourselves correlates directly with social status. The more resources that we have, the more that we can devote these resources to expensive stylists, time at the gym, and simply to our overall appearance, as opposed to focusing on simple, brute survival. Thus, there is a social dominance component to how we present ourselves.

So what is it that we really want? Clearly, we're not looking for sex, *in and of itself.* As Ann Landers found in her famous informal survey of 1985, most of the time, in intimate situations, men want sex. So what do women want? Most of the time (about 70%), we'd be just as happy with cuddling.[2]

The dynamics are simple. In August and September of 1996, *GQ* ran a two-part article on "What Men Want." Stephani Cook hosted a panel of men, and within minutes, they got down to basics. "We just want," said Jerry, one of the panel participants. "Want what?" asked Stephani.

> "In a word? Sex. That's what we want, and we'll do anything we have to do to get it. As soon as women understand that, then they're in control... If a woman is screwed up, it's because she doesn't understand that her control is to grant sex - or not."[3]

It is not that we don't want sex. We do, although our sexuality is more complex than men's. (We will get to what we want sexually a bit later, right now we're following the breadcrumb trail of cosmetics and their cues.)

If we put together all the factors we've discussed so far (plus a few others), we can make the following connections. First, in business, military, or "formal" power situations, both men and women project power with their clothing choices. Padding throughout the shoulders and chest of a jacket suggests a more muscular physique, which further connotes physical and/or social dominance. This is true in a well-made women's jacket as well as a man's. If we go back to the *Dynasty* TV era, we can recall a time when padded shoulders were even more important in women's suits than in men's! Thus, both men and women don the psychological equivalent of armor before going in to work.

However, the messages are very different. Men simply put on their suits and go! We women, on the other hand, present a more complex message. Even while wearing our "power suits," our cosmetics project physical cues of being sexually aroused; in fact, near climax. These cues are so strong, and make use of so many exaggerated physical features, that the only equivalent we could imagine in male dress would be overt phallic symbolism. And of course, this symbolism actually *is* embedded into their corporate clothing.

Some cultures are bit more extreme in their power and phallic symbolism than others. The well-known zoologist and ethologist Desmond Morris has noted that in New Guinea, "some fiercely traditional tribal males still display their extraordinary penis gourds, an ancient custom that sees them walk about completely naked except for a long golden-yellow gourd-sheath ... decorated with tassels and shells."[4] In most countries, we don't have so extreme a custom. However, Alison Lurke succinctly describes, in *The Language of Clothes*, how masculine accoutrements embody multiple sexual cues. Once we've read her summary of the phallic symbolism in men's ties, correlating cues to size, shape, and color, we can't help but be amused during our next staff meeting![5]

In contrast to the simplicity of men's presentations, though, we women are communicating two messages simultaneously; one reflecting our *Amazon* natures, the other our inner *Love-Goddess*. Our "mixed messages" suggest that we possibly have two or more agendas. Or perhaps it is not so much that we have different, conflicting agendas, but that at any given time, we are *coming from more than one modality*. We have more than one "way of being." This is not new, and it is not confined to women only. Men also have different roles at different times. What might be unique to us as women, though, is that we may move from one role or mode to another very rapidly. We may do this several times throughout our day, interleaving our various roles or modes.

This does not necessarily mean that we are having some inner conflict. It may instead mean that we are skillfully and adroitly weaving together the distinct needs and expressive signs of multiple modes. In short, this may be a very appropriate and useful strategy for who we are and what we are doing, and not at all a sign of "dysfunction." Rather, this may epitomize an extraordinarily high degree of "functioning."

The different modes, their blending, and the underlying desires of each way of being – this is a realm that we still need to explore.

It used to be that we associated our ability to attract a mate, and to keep him, with our survival. In the "good old days," our mate would take care of us, and we would take care of him. We would receive our status in society from him, just as we received his surname. Our children would inherit his genes, as well as the status of his family name. They would also have his protection as they grew up.

To a large extent, despite having made our *Amazon* gains over the past decades, we still live in a *Pride and Prejudice* world. When we think of a man in terms of marriage potential, we consider his ability to care for us. We desire the best quality man that we can possibly attract into our lives. No matter how successful we may be, when it comes to the realms of love, marriage, and potential child-bearing, many of us want to know that our mate can be a "good provider."

Karen Karbo, writing in Hilary Black's *The Secret Currency of Love*, identified this as a "girl's prerogative." She identified this as a belief that women may have in thinking that they have the "choice" to make money or not.[6] Karbo goes on to portray the veil of "magical thinking" that she suggests that some of us have: that "money matters less than love and romance."[7] According to Ms. Karbo, this notion of "choice" depends on the underlying supposition that we realistically have "options" – that we can live either in a world where someone else takes care of us, or in a world where we can *choose* a job or career.

Sometimes, we *do* have the choice. Sometimes, we don't. We know, of course, that money is important. Survival is important, and money is often the key to both security and survival. This is why so many of us have become *Amazons*; we have taken on a masculine focus, centered on work and achievements. Too often, though, we are judging ourselves very harshly if we are not in *Amazon* mode all the time, throughout our lives.

We are tracing "clues" about what we really want; about our values and priorities. We are seeking the "what is really so" about our desires. The next "clue" comes from another essayist in the same book as in which Ms. Karbo's work is presented. Abby Ellin states that she was not surprised (although she was "saddened") to realize that she had expectations that a man would "take care of her."[8] Ellin goes on to cite Louise Story's now-famous 2005 *New York Times* survey article, focusing on how a group of Yale University undergraduate women anticipated that they would handle the work/children challenge.[9] About sixty percent of these high-caliber undergraduates planned to either stop working or go to part-time work during the years when their children were not yet fully in school.

These young women were all smart. They were going to an excellent school. They were young *Amazons-in-training*. They were also aware enough to know that as soon as their biology kicked in – as soon as they went from *Amazon*-mode to *Mother*-mode – they would be under the drenching influence of a rich, yummy oxytocin-induced state.[10] This neurohormone is triggered by intimacy, and when released in our brains, it will further foster intimacy and bonding. (This is not to say that the Yale undergraduate women knew about this pregnancy and lactation-induced neurohormone *per se*, but they had seen the effects of motherhood on their sisters, cousins, and friends. They knew what happened when "Mommy brain" took over.)

Wisely, they prepared for the inevitable.

In discussions with many of my male colleagues, I've learned that they've observed that the young women joining their companies are much more driven and motivated than their male counterparts. The reason is that the women know that they're operating within a limited timeframe. Most of them will dramatically shift their priorities as soon as they have their first baby.

A dear woman whom I know is an excellent financial planner. She has exceptional analytic and research skills, and superb financial intuition. Her clients are very happy campers! She has also recently had a baby, and has scaled back her office time to the absolute minimum. "All I want to do is be with my baby," she says. That's "Mommy brain."

The reality, of course, is that not all women quit their jobs once they've had the first (or even second or third) child. Many stay with their jobs, through both preference and/or need. However, a number of women with young children find themselves "forced out." Sometimes, the work environment itself is so inhospitable to women's needs that it becomes too difficult to maintain both corporate and motherhood roles. This has clearly been one of the toughest situations for women over the past several decades, and continues to be so now.

Being a mom is a full-time job. Being an *Amazon* in the corporate world is a full-time job. We know of relatively few men who manage two full-time jobs at once. Thus, it's very demanding of ourselves to expect that we can do this, especially for prolonged periods of time. Even women such as Mika Brzezinski, currently a co-anchor on MSN's *Morning Joe* and author of *All Things at Once*, have at one point found the combination of parenting and a high-powered job to be too much. In Mika's case, a fall down the stairs, while she was holding her four-month-old infant daughter, was a turning point.[11] She later regrouped, with more household help. She also was clear that maintaining both roles was important to her, even though the price was lack of sleep, lack of time for herself, and lack of sufficient time with her children. Even though she was laid off from one position, and endured a grueling job search, she quickly made her way back into her professional realm, managing (as her book title suggests) "all things at once."

In short, the "real world" evidence seems to contradict the intentions voiced by the Yale undergraduates, as cited by Ms. Ellin. For some of us, once we get a taste of the validation, the confidence, and the sense of identity that we find within our careers, we are reluctant to let these roles go. Others of us find that we are unable to maintain both family and career commitments at the level that we would have previously envisioned.

We seem to have two alternatives: The first option is to get our education, and prepare to someday have a high-powered career, even though we will devote ourselves to our children while they are young. This "choice," if it is available to us, depends on our partner bringing home sufficient income to allow us this option. Also, embedded in this "choice" is the supposition that we can, at a time of our own choosing, rejoin the corporate world and somehow regain the "lost ground" that we would have ceded to the young men who worked through solidly, and to the young women who either did not have children, or who somehow kept their careers going while they had their babies.

In *Opting Out*, by Pamela Stone, we have an opportunity to see how life has really worked out for the young women who have selected this first alternative. They were the ones who took "time off" when they had young children at home. Stone found that, contrary to the illusionary option of choice, the women whose stories contributed to her book were faced with a "choice gap." That is, they confronted a lack of real, viable choices once they were ready to rejoin corporate ranks. This "gap," according to Ms. Stone, resulted primarily from work conditions that seemed best described as an "anachronistic time warp."[12] These women found it difficult (and sometimes impossible) to simply pick up where they had left off. They were often faced with inventing a new career path for themselves.

The other alternative for young women seems to be to carry through both commitments at once. If we choose this alternative, then we somehow manage to keep our careers going full-tilt, no matter what our hormones and heart-wrenching feelings tell us, as we leave our child with the sitter or nanny, or drop the child off at day-care. This is "life à la Mika"; which is a realistic option for some of us, and a necessity for others. (We note that the prices that Mika paid were both financial and emotional. She and her husband brought in substantial extra help, at substantial extra cost. Even with the extra help, she still did not get to spend desired "quality time" with her children.) Many of us have seen cases where the one thing that lets a young woman pursue her career ambitions is the commitment from one or more family members (often of the parent's or even grandparent's generation), who provide loving, trustworthy, and dedicated child-care. This then allows the woman to follow her *Amazon* calling. While this is often a great blessing for the young woman, it comes at the cost of significant time contributions from her family.

It seems as though the appearance of "choice" may simply be that: an "appearance." A choice between a rock and a hard place is not really a choice. Either way, the "choices" are inserted into a culture that is still dominated by and oriented towards a masculine mindset. Karine Moe and Dianna Shandy note, in *Glass Ceilings & 100-Hour Couples*, that our work world is still set up to support a career-focused man who has his needs provided for at the home front.[13] This is not to say that we can't make it work. One way or another, many of us do, as described by Carol Evans in *This Is How We Do It*.[14] We also need to acknowledge the many wonderful men who take on their husbanding and fathering roles with great conviction and dedication. Men, however, still are not often put in the position of "choosing between." We women are still faced with a difficult decision, and either "choice" has serious drawbacks.

Summarizing the career/motherhood challenge, it seems that for young women today, the simple ability and opportunity to have a career is polarized by the demanding requirements of young children. Further, despite whatever gains we've made, we still live in a world oriented towards the male viewpoint, where all is subsumed by and organized towards facilitating a young man on his career-quest. We can emulate the masculine career-focus with relative ease, so long as we do not have children. Once we bring children into the picture, the stakes and the dynamics escalate.

We have developed our *Amazon* natures, not just because we like being in our *Amazon* roles (and many of us do), but largely because we felt this was a survival necessity. In prior times, when we had limited opportunities, we also had limited power. While "choosing between" (or managing a combination of) career and children is difficult, the lack of even an *appearance* of choice is untenable. Thus, we are still in an awkward situation. I offer no easy solutions.

To make a personal aside, my choice really was the "easy way out." I decided not to remarry after an early marriage. I decided not to have children. Instead, I took that "childbearing" time of life, and became not just a very good scientist, but a good *inventor*. I found that inventing something required that I immerse myself with total focus and dedication; it was almost like entering an "altered state" that might last days, or even weeks at a time. (Without the aid of drugs, I might add.) Probably all creative people do something similar; I strongly suspect that composers use such an approach when creating new music. For me, this kind of mindset was somewhat akin to creating a delicate piece of experimental apparatus, except that it was all in my head. At times, even someone saying a casual "hello" would break my concentration, or my mental "construct" of this creative state. This would be like shattering the apparatus! I got much better at maintaining my creative visionary mindset, along with handling interruptions, as I got older. During my best childbearing years, though, I was busy learning how to do different things with my mind. I knew that I wouldn't be able to both attend to children and an invention simultaneously. Instead, I focused on developing my inner *Amazon*.

However, I still had nurturance-longings; a part of me craved being in *Mother* mode. I found that I could relate well to young women. Thus, I followed one of the time-honored alternate paths for women: teaching and mentoring. I became a

Big Sister (in the Big Brothers/Big Sisters program), and I mentored a few young women as they worked to get their advanced degrees. Also, I began teaching dance. I found that with fair regularity, various young women would join my studio whose mothers had died, or who had experienced difficult relations with their own biological mothers. I found enormous satisfaction in being "there" for these women; this continues to be a great source of personal happiness.

This sums up what might possibly be the greatest challenge facing many women today; the time crunch of trading off care for others (which may include elders as well as children) while still keeping up with professional and work responsibilities. There is possibly just one thing that is our saving grace: *We live longer now.* Whatever trade-offs and decisions we make when young, if we simply live long enough, we will have a chance to make other decisions.

Many of us take good care of our bodies. We are more able and adept than we have ever been, throughout history, at managing our health, energy, and overall vitality throughout menopause and beyond. Thus, we are much more likely than our mothers, and certainly more likely than our grandmothers, to have second and even third "chances" to make "choices." Our longer lifetimes, more than anything else, are what we pivot about as we examine our various roles and archetypes, and consider how to design and redesign the rest of our lives.

Our purpose in this chapter has been to lay the foundation for understanding ourselves – for knowing what we want – regardless of how "nice" (or "not-nice," or how politically incorrect) the answers may be. This may not be the way that we would like to see ourselves. Sometimes, though, we need to see scientific evidence to show us clearly a truth that we may otherwise prefer to avoid. Thus, we conclude by taking a look at documented results from paternity studies.

If "biology is destiny," biology is also sneaky. We may think that we're after a monogamous relationship; we desire that one-on-one bonding that will give us the ultimate security. But at the same time, it seems that once we've achieved relationship security, we're willing to look a little further afield for genetic material.

According to recent research described by Matt Ridley in *The Red Queen*, and also summarized by Jan Havlicek and others,[15] it appears that we have a secondary "relationship" strategy. We may get into a steady, apparently monogamous relationship with one man, but are willing to have affairs with a more dominant man *when we are fertile*. As Havlicek puts it, "... a mixed mating strategy may have evolved in females: they prefer genetically superior males as short-term or extra-pair sexual partners while, at the same time, they seek males who are more willing to invest in their offspring as long-term or social partners." (Note that these authors are themselves summarizing the research of others; there is now fairly substantive support for this argument.)

In short, we are genetically programmed to first find security, and then find the best possible sperm donors. Not the other way around!

The relationship-realm is an ever-changing landscape. We probably can't put our finger on any single pattern or dynamic and say, "This is it; this is what is consistent across the board." So let's note that what we have here is a starting point. Although this may not be the only one possible, we have now established a position from which we can move forward, as we decode the complex factors underlying the ages-old question: "What do women want?"

Let's summarize what we've found so far. We've noted that through a combination of dress and cosmetics, we seem to project a complex set of messages. Through our clothing, hair, and cosmetics choices, we communicate an overlapping set of desires, rather than the simpler statements communicated by men's attire. We devote time, care, and attention to projecting ourselves as being healthy, youthful, vigorous, and sexually "ready," even though we may not be particularly interested in sex at the moment. We desire status and security, as well as survival. We want the best possible genetic material for our offspring, but we will get security first. Some of us (not all, but definitely some) will then select someone who is not our husband as our breeding stock.

We have learned to take charge of our personal and financial destinies, through becoming *Amazons*. We still face great challenges as we figure out how to balance (and even whether or not to keep) our *Amazon* roles when we are young *Mothers*. At the level of our deepest desire, we would often rather have someone else take care of us from time to time, particularly when we are *Mothers*. We may feel ashamed of this, and deride ourselves when we speak the truth about this desire. At the same time, we relish the validation (and financial independence, with its implications for our future) that we get from our *Amazon* roles. This is so even when we're *Mothers*; when — at least at some level — we would prefer that someone else would take care of us so that we could devote ourselves to mothering. Just as often, though, we really don't want to give up what we've gained in our *Amazon* mode, simply because our *Mother* mode is also competing for our (of course, full-time) attention.

None of this is politically correct. In fact, as an "operating agenda," this seems horrifically selfish. We would like to think better of ourselves. However, by combining scientific research and direct observation, we have a "what-is-so" about ourselves that, if not very flattering, is possibly accurate.

As our next step, we seek validation of this complex set of motives and drives that seemingly describe our natures. Once again, we'll examine ourselves. This time, instead of looking at our external behaviors, we'll get inside our own heads. That is the function of the next chapter.

PERSONAL PATHWORKING:

1. Refine your journaling, simply by taking note of your day. How much are you in your *Amazon*, or your *Mother* modes? To what extent are you in your *Love-Goddess* mode, doing anything that honors your sensuality, or gives you pleasure? Are you ever in the deepest aspect of yourself, when you are quiet, introspective, or meditative? (If you're a mother of young children, and working, you already know the answer to the last question.)

2. To the best of your ability, start journaling your life-timeline. When did you start entering your *Amazon* mode? When have you been in *Mother*? When have you been in love, or giving time to yourself, and your focus was on your inner *Love Goddess*? When have you been in two modes at once, and how did that feel? (This could get complex. Take your time, return to this as new insights come to you.)

3. As you examine your different modes, look at how you support each. Do you have different clothes for different modes? (Of course you do! Work clothes are different from date clothes, which are different from play clothes, etc.) Take a look at what you have in different categories. The proportion of clothes may suggest how much time you spend in each.

4. Start noting down what has drawn you to different men, at different times in your life. What qualities did they possess? Were they offering sperm quality or security? (Did any offer both?) Please do this without judging yourself. We have enough shaming and disapproval already, not to mention tons of other social conditioning. So try to be as calm, objective, and loving with yourself as you start to take note. Write down what you can; what you're willing to admit right now.

CHAPTER 3:
BEDTIME STORIES

"BODICE RIPPERS"; THAT'S WHAT WE call them. We find them by their covers. The beautiful heroine, swooning in Fabio's arms, is about to burst out of her ever-so-revealing décolletage. There is a standard, stylized plot to go with these stories. Carefully analyzed by Janice Radway in *Reading the Romance,*[1] the plot is readily summed. The heroine, while being good, virtuous, and ignorant of her power to charm, causes a harsh, unyielding, and "alpha" male to fall in love with her and to devote himself to her. There are many twists and turns, of course. A good romance novel embellishes the right ones.

Something about these novels compels us, in moments of weakness, to read them. We read them again and again. We treasure and savor the ones that we like best, because we know they will "feed" us in a certain way. They meet our cravings and needs. Often, the fiction is more satisfying than reality.

Sometimes, we feel that we should denigrate or "pooh-pooh" these romance novels. Certainly, we'll agree that they are not high literature. But their very enduring power, and their widespread attraction for us, tells us something about ourselves. *These novels give us feedback about our psyches.* Along with our use of cosmetics and our dressing cues, and the way that we market to ourselves, our romance novels give us another insight-window into our core desires.

There is something we can note about how these novels are created, compared to movies – another common media. Movies are important, not just for fun, but also because they are part of our society's myth-making and myth-telling. However, movie-making takes a large budget. A commercially-oriented movie with a highly-rated cast will incur up to hundreds of millions of dollars in production costs. Movies require intense collaborative teamwork.

In contrast, a romance novel is typically written by a single woman, at home, alone. The only budget that she requires is for her computer, printer, and paper. Because a woman can write a novel all by herself, these romance novels are a very direct form of woman-to-woman communication. The ones that survive – that are cherished, read, and reread – are those that communicate the best.

A romance novel survives by appealing to our deepest fantasies and desires. If we attend to what we are telling ourselves that we want in these novels, we learn a great deal about ourselves. Janice Radway asked exactly that question in *Reading the Romance*. "Why is it," she asked, "that so many women read these kinds of books? What do they get out of this novel-reading?" While finding the answers, she interviewed a group of dedicated romance readers: the Smithton women.[2]

One of the first things that she learned is that readers hate to be interrupted. When readers read, they are moving towards a point of deep emotional gratification. Ms. Radway polled the Smithton women about their favorite novels. Their favorite, by far, was Kathleen Woodiwiss's book, *The Flame and the Flower*.[3] *The Flame and the Flower* is indeed a well-wrought, emotionally appealing story. We can read it, as we do with many such novels, on two levels. At one level, we're simply swept along by a "good read," where the author skillfully pulls our emotional strings. At the other level, we have a dialogue with ourselves; perhaps even a self-critical one! We might ask of ourselves, "How did I get sucked into this thing?"

How, indeed? Let's look at *The Flame and the Flower* in some detail.

The Flame and the Flower succeeds so well because it most perfectly matches our greatest psycho-social dilemma. This dilemma is: *How can a woman succeed in winning a high-quality mate* (preferably the highest quality that there is), *using her sexual appeal?* Furthermore, *how can she do this and remain totally ignorant of and disassociated from real knowledge of her sexual allure?* In short, how can she win and at the same time, disavow all knowledge of and responsibility for her winning?

Woodiwiss's novels are so satisfying, and have obtained such an enormous readership (over 36 million copies in print[4]) because she managed to tap into this core question directly. Her novels, and other successful romance-genre novels, provide an emotionally (although not intellectually) satisfying answer. So, without judging ourselves – or the novels – let's dive in!

There is enormous consistency in the better (meaning, more widely read) romance novels. In fact, there is a deeply-rooted template that, once discovered, is almost shocking in its repeatability across many novels. This consistency is not only throughout the novels of romantic fiction, but is also common to many of their predecessors: the grand, classic fairy tales!

One remarkably common theme is: *There is no mother.* We can reflect on this. Have we ever, in our lives, read a romance novel in which the heroine could go home, or call home to mom, and say, "Hey, I just met this guy, and this is what's going on, and this is how I feel." Never, right? There is only one romance series (of which I'm aware) where mothers do exist: the works by Nora Roberts.[5] In the first two novels of a trilogy situated in Ireland, *Born in Fire* and *Born in Ice*, the protagonists do have a mother.[6] However, the mother is so bitter and emotionally damaged that she is more of a thorn in their sides than she is a source of nurturance. In another novel by the same author, *Hidden Riches*, the heroine Dora also has a mother.[7] In that case, the mother is so flighty and airheaded that she also cannot offer her daughter any useful emotional support. Dora is the solid, grounded, and mature one in her family.

We think this through and identify the implications. Isolation from maternal nurturance, and often even from a female support network, is an essential factor in these novels. This is because a prime requisite for these classic romance novels is that the heroine must be emotionally alone. There is no mother, no grandmother, and no "wise woman." There is no counsel from the *maternal generation*. Typically, the heroine has no close friends. (However, evidence that this dynamic is changing shows up in more recent works, such as most of Roberts' novels from the late 1990's and onward.) In the "classic" romantic fiction, the heroine's father, if alive, is emotionally, and often physically, distant. It is almost a cliché that the heroine is, emotionally if not physically, an orphan.

This doesn't mean that we have a death wish on our parents. However, the opening for each of these novels has the purpose of causing us to emotionally identify with the heroine. She is alone, defenseless, and frequently overwhelmed. While many of us have living and loving parents, and wonderful support circles of caring friends, when we read a romance, we tap into our feelings of similarly being defenseless and even overwhelmed. (Sometimes, an ordinary workday is enough to bring on these feelings.) While reading a romance novel, we identify with a heroine who can act out the emotional challenges that we feel. Her life reflects ours, except that her situation is more extreme. Her role is to let us identify the feelings that we normally suppress, and to turn up the emotional intensity of these feelings. This lets us tap into the part of ourselves that the heroine represents; the part that feels alone and defenseless in a challenging, and perhaps even hostile, world.

In *The Flame and the Flower*, the heroine is Heather. She is orphaned, and spends her days slaving away under her Aunt Fanny's tyrannical control. Although she has an uncle, he is weak and does nothing to support her or to save her from Aunt Fanny's viciousness. Heather is shy, fearful, and naïve. She is also, of course, exceptionally beautiful. This is the classic Cinderella-story opening.

After a series of preliminary misfortunes, Heather is raped by the American sea captain Brandon, who mistakes her for a prostitute. He further mistakes her naïveté and sexual reluctance as the clever wiles of a woman who feigns innocence and outrage to obtain a greater price. Heather flees, but has become pregnant. When Aunt Fanny learns of her niece's condition, she sets out to find Brandon and force a marriage. Unknown to both Heather and Aunt Fanny, Brandon is also searching for Heather.

Brandon is outraged at having his hand forced. (We are given to understand that he might have married Heather, so great was his attraction to her, but being forced into anything offends his manly sense of dignity and honor.) Heather, newly married, is put aboard Brandon's ship, where they set sail with a load of valuable cargo for the "Colonies." Although she has had her first sexual experience, she is still an emotional "innocent." She has no sense of herself as a sexual being, and has no real awareness of her power of allure.

If we step back to watch Heather's character develop, we notice something interesting. In the opening stages of the novel, Heather rarely gets more than fragmented and momentary glimpses of herself, using a discarded mirror shard. We are to understand that she truly *is* innocent, not only sexually, but even of knowledge of her beauty, and its potent effect on men.

Early in the novel, a scene brings Heather's awareness of her own beauty into sharp focus. Aunt Fanny conspires to have Heather placed in a brothel owned and operated by Fanny's brother. Heather is brought there under the guise of being taken to a "girl's finishing school." When she is left alone to change into a beautiful dress, she sees herself for the first time in a full-length mirror. Heather is allowed a brief moment during which she recognizes her own beauty before she escapes, wanders the streets, and is taken to Brandon. The only time after that when she sees herself in a full-length mirror is just prior to her wedding.

These vignettes heighten the emotional chiaroscuro, or "light and dark" effect, in the plotline. They symbolically represent the fact that a "good girl" has knowledge of her own sexual allure only in relationship with one specific man, and that has to be the man who has "ownership" of her sexuality. If a woman knows her own power in her own right, independent of a man, she is out of bounds. These scenes, plus the many instances in which Heather reproaches herself for her fear and cowardice, reinforce the fact that Heather is a "good girl."

Once aboard Brandon's ship, Heather begins her journey, both symbolically and physically, towards womanhood. She and Brandon begin dialectic. (It is far too premature, at this point, to call it a relationship.) In his rage against a forced marriage, Brandon promised Heather, on their wedding night, that he would neither approach her physically nor offer any form of nurturance or love. This, then, is the real challenge of the novel. Heather now has to woo Brandon over to her side, and to cause him to literally "forsake all others," without appearing to do so. Given Brandon's rage at his confinement in marriage, and his previous history of many light amours, this is a daunting task.

At a symbolic level, though, this is precisely the challenge that many women feel that they face. Even when their husbands are the ones who propose, our whole cultural ethos is that marriage is a trap for men and a victory for women. The situation in which Heather finds herself simply exaggerates the tension (and perhaps the anger) that some men feel about the constrictions of marriage.

Of course, the day-to-day proximity between Heather and Brandon heightens the tension considerably. While Brandon remains overtly cold and abrasive, the story tells us that he has at least the potential for caring: he ordered warm clothing made for Heather before they left on the sea voyage, in addition to an extensive and expensive trousseau.

Heather still must "win over" her man. To do this, she has two strategies. One is conscious, the other is unconscious. We note that there are only a few strategies that are "allowable" in a good girl's fight to win her man, because ground rule number one is that she can't appear to be fighting for her man. She must appear to remain ignorant all the while of what she must really accomplish if she is to survive.

Heather's first strategy is that she gains allies. Her first ally is George, Brandon's manservant. He feels great remorse at having brought a beautiful and virginal girl to such an unhappy fate, and feels responsible for her. His care does more than just offer support for Heather physically and emotionally. George provides Brandon with a role model for caring.

Heather's second strategy, the "unconscious" one, is that she falls ill. After a fight with Brandon, she asserts her independence by staying all night in a cold and wet window seat, rather than sharing a bunk with him. Naturally, by morning, she is greatly ill. Brandon feels remorse, and cares for her single-handedly while she has a high fever lasting for several days. This fever is a major turning point, because it allows the main characters to do things that they each must do, but could not in their normal roles.

During her fevered delirium, Heather recounts her experiences. Brandon pieces together enough of her story to understand her perspective. By being ill, Heather gets Brandon to listen to her and care for her, without taking responsibility for confronting him. She gets what she wants and needs, and can still be "innocent." After all, she was ill and semi-conscious.

After she recovers, Heather is both surprised and embarrassed to learn of the extent of Brandon's intimate attentions. The balance has shifted. We can now hope that since Brandon has realized her value (and that of her unborn child) enough to care for them in extreme duress, he will continue to do so in the future.

The second major turning point in the novel comes when the couple arrives at Brandon's home just outside Charleston. There is a moment of huge emotional release as they drive around the bend and the beautiful house comes into view. As Heather espies the large and stately home, complete with "huge doric columns" and a "wide veranda," she notes the "huge antlers of some great buck of the forest" hung from the veranda's center.[8]

The symbolism could not be more overt. Not only does Heather get the mansion, and all that it connotes, but there, hung on the exterior wall for all to see, is *prima facie* evidence of the male prowess at hunting. Clearly, this implies, Heather will never go without meat in the winter. She and her child will be well fed.

The role of a home within many well-loved romance novels is not insignificant. As Connell Cowan, writing in *The Art of War for Lovers*, states: "Keep coming back to a man's primitive psychology: his caring grows out of *sustained sexual interest* (while for women, sexual interest grows out of *sustained caring*).[9] [Italics his.] We crave this "sustained caring" in the form of security; this often (at least in our fantasy world) means a home. Thus, it is not at all surprising that in many of our most-beloved novels, the house itself is a *dramatis persona*. Think, for example, of the house that heroine Geillis Ramsey inherits in Mary Stewart's *Thornyhold*,[10] or of the huge, gorgeous house (deeply in need of restoration, repair, and love) in Danielle Steel's aptly named book, *The House*.[11] A quick glance through our collections of favorites will show that securing a physical place is on a par with securing loyalty and love.

The strength of our desire for lovely, supportive, wonderful homes is borne out in another area where we women are avid readers: magazines. A quick glance at circulation figures shows that in 2009, *Better Homes and Gardens* had a circulation of over 7.6 million, whereas *Cosmopolitan* circulated at about 2.95 million, and *Glamour* and *Allure* were at about 2.4 and 1.1 million, respectively.[12] This is a ratio of about 2.5:1, reflecting our greater interest in the results (*better homes and gardens*), versus the means of obtaining those results (worldly sexuality, along with *glamour* and *allure*). In contrast, the top-selling men's magazines are *Maxim* and *Playboy*, at a little over 2.5 and 2.3 million, respectively. Other forms of masculine play garner about half as much interest; *Motor Trend*, *Golf Magazine* and *Field and Stream* circulated between 1.1 and 1.5 million each. The means by which men *get* their favored pursuits, e.g., *Forbes* and other business magazines, have all suffered a severe drop in advertising revenue,[13] and counted their 2009 circulation as less than 1 million each.[14, 15] As a simplistic summing-up, women put attention on security versus sexuality (as the means of getting that security) at a ratio of about

2.5:1, and men put an emphasis on sexual experience versus their means of getting this experience at about the same ratio. (Credit for this observation goes to Warren Farrell, author of *Why Men are the Way They Are*; this simply updates his results.[16])

This brings us back to *The Flame and the Flower*, in which Heather's unstated (although primary) goal is to gain security, in the combination of a wealthy and devoted husband, and (certainly not least) a fine home.

In fact, Heather's introduction to the house marks a significant development in the story. On the way there, Heather has met a new enemy: her husband's former lover, Louisa. Before Heather fully comes into her adult role as Brandon's wife, and chatelaine of his large estate, she must defeat her enemy's efforts to lure Brandon away, fight off another who would take her away from Brandon, and gain her husband's trust, confidence, and love. However, it is when Heather meets the "house" – the place where she will feel secure in having and raising her child – that we, as well as Heather, are convinced that things will work out just fine.

Introduced to the community as Brandon's wife, and the mother of his unborn child, Heather has immediate status and privilege. She derives these instantly by being Brandon's mate, and Brandon is, of course, the most "alpha" of the "alpha men" in the community. She has claimed her position at this point, and now she has to secure it. That is the remainder of her story.

Our "romance" stories offer solutions to a major conundrum: How do we get what we want without appearing to either want it, or actively strategize to get it? In the previous chapter, we came face-to-face with how much we are programmed to get the best we possibly can, both in terms of security and sperm (and in that order). That's challenge enough. Now, the message is that if we are a "good girl," we go about getting this without acknowledging it, and heavens forbid that we should have some sort of strategy!

Rather, we are to be continually "immersed" in a state of not knowing: not knowing ourselves, not knowing (and certainly not owning) the power of our allure, and most of all, not knowing how to bring what we desire into our lives. According to these novels, what we desire should simply fall into our lap, because we are good, innocent, and (most of all) beautiful. (If we paid attention to our childhood fairytales, ranging from *Sleeping Beauty* to *Cinderella*, we'll note that this storyline began centuries ago, and began for us personally when we were children. This theme of being "awakened" only in response to a man is consistent throughout both fairytales and their current evolution: the romance novel.)

We ask ourselves: Why do we persist in telling ourselves these stories? Why do they feed us so deeply? We notice that when we allow ourselves a good, cathartic romance novel reading-treat, we are indulging in something akin to an emotional narcotic – or at least the emotional equivalent of hot chocolate with a dollop of something "extra"!

We should keep in mind that our selection of these novels for ourselves is not the conditioning of a "patriarchal society." *We* write these books, and *we* buy them. *We* are the ones who read them, again and again. There has to be a reason, and it has to be a good one. Too much is at stake to let this slip by. We're not going to pass this off as simple "social conditioning." But rather than offer an answer just yet, let's hold this as a question, and move on.

We will return to this point. However, we will do so *gently*. It is easy, very easy, for us to ridicule ourselves about this. This is where we should slow down and pay attention. The point that we should note is not so much that we desire to be cared for. Rather, the point that deserves our attention is that we desire most to be cared for when we are seeking to release our *Amazon* personas and move in a direction that is more feeling-oriented. This pertains as much to the emotional realm as it does to our physical surrounds. We need to feel safe and secure if we are to let down our *Amazon* guard. This means that we need to trust that who-ever is caring for us has our interests at heart. There is something that touches our hearts tenderly in the biblical passage describing how we are to be led by the Good Shepherd; when it says that "he will carry them in his bosom, and gently lead those that are with young."[17] It is this sense of *caring* that is one of the most important factors in how we evaluate men.

This is especially true when we start having children. We are biologically programmed to release into a soft, dreamy oxytocin-induced state when we have a new baby, and we are only *safe* to go into that state if someone else is in full protector-mode.[18] Masculine strengths provide safety if we are going to be biologically incapacitated for a while.

The previous chapter was challenging enough. We realized that, when we "dress up," we present a complex combination of *Amazon/Love-Goddess* cues. We project at least two messages at the same time! Now, we are layering on a new level of complexity. This is that, according to our deepest desires, we desire not only to be cared for by a very strong and capable person, but that we desire to be selected and cared for without having to actively "strategize" this experience. At the same time, of course, we'd like to develop our careers, in whatever manner we've defined our professional ambitions.

It seems, at least superficially, that we're simultaneously pointing in all directions at once! If we adopted a "masculine" (or typical goal-oriented) way of thinking, we'd be strongly advised to pick a direction – *any* single direction – and go with it. But when we check in with our "inner compass," this singular focus often just doesn't feel right. (This is true even if our "inner compass" points to multiple "true norths" all at the same time!)

Recently, while starting up a new business, I ran out of funds. I asked my lover, a wealthy and powerful man whom we'll call Theo, to help me. He did, briefly. He also left when it became clear that I would be more focused on the new business start-up than on going for the security of a job. Clearly, I was going to be "financially challenged" for some time. He wasn't interested in sharing his knowledge, his connections, or his influence, and demonstrated that with his absence.

My mentor at the time berated me soundly. She pointed out that for all my education, prior achievements, and professional ambitions, I had succumbed to a 1950's template of male/female relationships. According to her, I had completely let go of taking responsibility for myself.

She was right. I *did* want to be cared for. In fact, I wanted several things: the opportunity to play the elegant, intellectual *Aphrodite* to my lover's sophistication and worldly knowledge. At the same time, I also wanted to be the *Amazon* warrior in starting my own new business. And at a deeper level, I had "yielded," for the first time in a long time, to a man whom I believed was truly "superior." I wanted to care for him as much as I wanted him to care for me. I sought to be in a nurturing role as well.

Did this work? Horribly not! On our last date, Theo brought along a book on American art and a newspaper article reviewing the work of the late artist Andrew Wyeth. He made it clear that the most important use of my time, in his regard, was to learn about American art so we could have intellectual discussions on this subject. The fact that all the business "deals" and "opportunities" I had been cultivating had fallen through, and that I was simply without funds, was something that he preferred not to address.

I survived. Not prettily, and not easily. And I endured several rounds of brutal chastisement from my then-mentor. For the rest of our relationship, she rubbed my nose solidly in how ungrounded my decisions had been. "It was *your* life, and *your* problem," she said. "You shouldn't have expected him to come in and fix it for you!"

She was right, in many ways. And yet, is there something deeper?

I played out this little personal-life drama after this book was largely written, but before putting it into final form. (Obviously, because you're reading about it!) Did I simply fall off my horse? For all that I have been teaching women, for years, how to empower themselves in many ways, did I simply forget (as my mentor said) all the basic lessons?

Or is there something else?

In my case, I was (for the first time in many, many years) dealing with multiple and conflicting roles and desires at the same time. Previously, although I've wanted many things (all at once, of course), I'd been able to manage – to "time-splice" – among my different desires and ambitions. During the relationship with Theo, though, I'd succumbed to "being in love." I felt the gooey wash of oxytocin and dopamine that suffuses a sixteen year-old girl in her first romance! I lost my usual *Amazonian* clarity and focus.

Naturally, Theo's departure, coupled with simple survival-needs, quickly washed those lingering feel-good neurochemicals from my system. I focused on pragmatics. There were a couple of truly awful months. As I regrouped, family and friends, and small miracles, saw me through the worst stages. Within a relatively short time, I was making new inventions and moving into a new technology. When I got my first program in a new computer language to run, I rejoiced. "This," I told myself, "is better than many dates with Theo!" The uniquely *Amazonian* feel-good rewards that come from achievement, rather than bonding, were emerging once again.

This experience gave me a personal insight into the challenges that many other women have in dealing with multiple roles and "modalities." Having not been a mother, I didn't have first-hand the bonding experience with a newborn. Having not had a special man in my life for a long while, I had forgotten how totally destabilizing it could be to "fall in love."

As I pulled back and regrouped, and gained the insights that allowed me to complete this book, I realized that this sense of being pulled by multiple desires – multiple passions even – is not inappropriate. It is not wrong. In fact, it might be part and parcel of our uniquely feminine psyche.

We desire many things, often all at the same time. Without denigrating the insightful work of the well-known psychologist Abraham Maslow, our desires do not appear to be a "hierarchy of needs," with one stage neatly following another.[19] It seems more as though we have multiple "dimensions" to ourselves, and there are compelling desires unique to each dimension or role. What is more, we have only just begun to identify all of these dimensions!

That will be the focus of the next two chapters.

PERSONAL PATHWORKING:

1. Applying these insights to ourselves, to our own "inner landscape," takes
    both courage and hard work. But start around the edges. "Swiss cheese"
    your approach by looking at yourself indirectly rather than head on. Go
    through your collection of books and movies, and note who and what you
    watch on TV. What have you read or watched more than once? Who are
    your icons? What about them appeals to you? Can you identify them as
    appealing to any one (or more) "dimension(s)," or different aspects of your
    personality?

2. These different dimensions to our beings are not always linguistic, and
    don't always come out in journaling. But one or more aspect(s) *may* come
    out much more by responding to pictures! Start assembling a poster board
    with images of your heroines. If they are movie characters, you can probably
    download a picture. If they are characters from a novel, you can probably
    find an image that suggests the character. (You might get a second copy
    of the novel, as an inexpensive used paperback, just to use the cover for
    your image board.) Spend a little research time; download and print out
    pictures – maybe with the size of the picture relating to how important
    the person-icon is to you. Assemble on a corkboard or poster board. (Note:
    I've painted the edge of my corkboards in various colors, and sponged them
    with gold and other metallic paints. And I've put on luscious, gorgeous
    background paper – burnished gold Christmas wrap, or gift wrapping
    paper showing Oriental rugs or gorgeous art. Other boards are completely
    covered over with collage. Why not?)

3. Are there any other female figures with whom you resonate? Are there any
    images from magazines – ads or articles – with which you feel a strong
    kinship? Add them to your board. Do you have pictures of women from
    your family tree that you want to add? They may be of an ancestress.

They may be of a sister or an aunt — or even a favorite younger cousin whose spunk you admire! (Note: I not only have poster boards — lots of them! — but also collections of pictures in sleeve protectors, kept in three-ring binders. This is a great way to tap into the visual side of our brains. See if this works for you.)

CHAPTER 4:
PLAYTIME FOR GROWN-UP GIRLS

"WRITE ABOUT VEILS," MY FRIEND Sue Ellen was saying to me. It was late afternoon on a warm September day, and we were sitting comfortably on her back porch. Sue Ellen had just read through several early chapters. "Write about dance, and using your colors, and making a veil."

"Veils are for dancers," I protested. "Why would the women who read *Unveiling* be interested in making a veil?"

"I still have my veil," she answered. "And I use it. Not when my husband is around, but when I have time for myself, I take out my veil, put on some music, and dance around the house. I still dance, and I still use my veil — even though I'm not taking belly dance lessons anymore."

"Every woman needs a veil," she continued. I sat there, considering what she said. We all need to be the "fairy tale princess" from time to time.

Sue Ellen was right. Each of us needs a veil. Veils are marvelous play toys, and they let us play out fantasy roles the way nothing else will. During improvisation, or "dance play," this happens again and again. We find that our veil becomes a marvelously expressive tool that lets us act out different moods. Deliciously floating our veils, we glide about with gossamer wings at our backs. Then, our veils let us be mysterious, peeking out at the world from behind the folds. And then, our veils let us be wildly, outrageously seductive: "Now you see me, now you don't." When we dance, veils became an extension of our personalities.

In the previous three chapters, we examined layers of our core desires. We set the groundwork to begin answering the ages-old question, "What do women really want?" We're starting to get answers, and one thing is clear: What we want is really rather complex! It's not just one thing, it's a meshing of several different things, all woven together.

Not only did we start to get some clarity on our core desires, but we also gained a bit of perspective on how much we are conditioned to denigrate, to put down, these desires. It is as though, now that we've won the right to express and exert our *Amazon* aspects in full, we don't allow ourselves to be anything else! (Other than being mothers, of course. Socially, motherhood is always an acceptable role.)

As we explore our psyches a bit further, we uncover our desire to have true, honest-to-God, for-real *playtime.* Or more accurately, we desire to allow ourselves our full range of emotional expression.

Let's think of ourselves as a beautiful Steinway piano. We are capable of a great range of emotional experience, and we would love to have many ways of expressing our full selves. The desire is there. It's just that, most of the time, we don't know how to express it! For most of us, our lives are consumed by our *Amazonian* work-modes, and also by our *Mother* mode. (We can be in *Mother* mode in the office as well as at home, and sometimes we have to bring our *Amazon* natures into our mothering tasks.) All too seldom do we get time to discover and play with our other "ways of being." When we do, these other aspects are so rusty from lack of use, that we often don't know what to do!

We need something that will help us express those modes or emotional "ways of being" that we typically don't access during our task-filled days. We need a toy! And for the price of three yards of chiffon, each of us can have a "grown-up woman's play-toy." More than a toy, this is something that invites the little girl inside each of us to come out and play.

Women have worn veils throughout history. Sometimes, a veil has been a symbol of modesty. This is sometimes taken to an extreme, where some Islamic cultures decree that all women should be covered head-to-toe in heavy veiling. The thought of going through summer heat wearing layers of black is not at all attractive to me, but we can respect the women who do this, especially those who do this by choice.

Dancer's veils are different. They are light, ephemeral, and wonderfully freeing. Not only that, they create new options for our party wardrobe, so we can rationalize the purchase, if we must.

We can let our minds wander back to some of the images we've seen of our mother's time, or possibly, of our grandmother's. These were the days in which women wore hats. Back then, a woman was simply not "dressed" if she were without a hat, as it gave a sense of completeness to her costume. A woman's hat literally "topped things off."

Now, we remember also that some of those hats also had veils; little veils of black net that came down over the eyes. We think of the icon: gorgeously made-up eyes, deep red lipstick, and that cool gaze looking out at the world through a veil. What a marvelous power to seduce and entrance! If we think of it, veils (or veil substitutes) have given women seductive power throughout many cultures and time periods. Fans are a veil substitute, and have been used successfully by women ranging from Japanese geishas to French courtesans to Southern belles.

This is not to suggest that we should wear a veil on our next date. (Although, if we are so inclined, there are some interesting possibilities.) The suggestion is more that we should get a veil, play with it, and see where that play takes us emotionally. We will each learn something about ourselves doing this, and also have fun. Then we can take this new level of self-knowledge into our relationships.

Let's start with the veil. Let's assume that you're going to a fabric store, although you can also purchase one ready-made. If you want to buy fabric, though, no sewing is necessary! You might *choose* to hem the edges, but *you don't have to*! If you don't see anything that you like in your local fabric store, you can order a veil of your desired length, weight, and color from online resources.

Color is the most important aspect of your veil. You are going to be wrapping yourself in your veil, and it will play up your skin. You want something that makes you look gorgeous. To do this, you want a veil that is in one of "your colors." If you've had a color analysis done, and you trust the results, then use your color swatches or chart when you purchase your veil. If you haven't had one done, then get a copy of a color analysis book, such as Carole Jackson's *Color Me Beautiful.*[1]

Even without the book, you can quickly identify (or confirm) your color profile at home. Start by looking at the skin on the inside of your wrist. Do you have a cool (blue) undertone on your skin, or a warm (yellow) undertone? If cool, then wear mostly cool colors: shades of blues, purples, and purple-reds. With this coloring, you would wear silver, pewter, and white gold; and accentuate with white pearls and moonstones. If you have a warm tone to your skin, then you'll wear mostly warm colors: shades of warm reds and peach, golden tones, and even olive or moss green. With this, you'll wear gold, brass, or copper jewelry. If in doubt, ask your friends to help you out.

Another way to get a good handle on your colors is to go to a cosmetics counter in a good store; one where they break down the products into different color groups. Ask them to type you. Of course they will try to sell you something afterwards. However, they will also give you knowledge that you can use in selecting your veil, as well as in your future wardrobe and cosmetics purchases.

In addition to color, the texture of your veil is also important. You will be handling your veil as you move around, turn, and do special "veil moves." It helps to find a fabric that has enough texture so that you can easily keep it in your fingers while you are doing all of this. For this reason, I suggest staying away from the cheapest chiffons; the ones that are slick to the touch. Be willing to pay a few dollars more per yard for something that has a bit of "cling" to it, so that it will stay in your hands easily.

Silk is by far the best material for your veil. Other materials can be used as well, but you want your veil to both *flow* and *float*. Silk is a delightful material, and either silk chiffon or china silk (very lightweight silk, often used for lining fine clothes) will work beautifully. Some polyester fabrics will work also; there are some lovely polyester chiffons. (Again, be certain that you get something where the fabric has a little texture; you don't want something so slick and shiny that it slips out of your hand!) One acceptable polyester option is a type of "iridescent chiffon," woven using two colors; this gives the material a subtle variance in the way that it reflects light. This fabric is heavier than the silks, but drapes beautifully and is sometimes less expensive.

The "standard" length for a veil is between two and one-half yards and three yards long. If you are above 5'7", buy at least three yards. If you are between 5'3" and 5'7", think about three yards. You might cut your veil back a bit; you might not. If you are under 5'3", then two and a half yards, or perhaps two and three-quarters, will suffice. Most fabrics come in a standard width of 45 inches, which is ideal for many of us.

Once you've bought your material, try this simple method to find the veil length that works best for you. Pick up your veil by the lengthwise edges and drape it over your shoulders so that it covers you like a shawl. Arrange your veil so that there is an even length on both your left and right sides. Grasp one of the lengthwise (long) edges lightly between your thumbs and forefingers. You want at least a foot or so draping down beyond your fingertips on each side. Move the veil about a bit. Does the length *feel* right? It's better to have it just a little long, so that you can trim it back, than to cut it too short. If you must trim it, cut it back just an inch or so at a time. You may find yourself "growing into" a longer veil than you thought you originally wanted. For most of us, longer is better.

If your veil is polyester, you can finish the edges by "candling" them. Light a candle, and take up your fabric, holding sections of the cut edge between your two hands. Then, run the edge, a little bit at a time (keeping it very taut), just at the edge of the flame. The candle flame should melt the edge, just enough so that the little threads fuse together. Silk and all natural fibers can be hemmed or left unfinished. If you want to hem your veil, turn over a narrow fold, press, fold again, and press again, so that the raw edge is hidden. You can machine-stitch or hand-stitch the hem. If you choose to hand-stitch, this can be a relaxing way to spend an evening. However, you don't need to hem your veil; your veil is for you, and for your personal playtime.

Now that you have your veil, play with it! First, find a "safe" time and a "safe" place. A safe time is one when no one else is around. This is time for you, and you are probably trying something new. You don't need comments or "helpful critiques" from anyone. You need to get your feedback directly from *yourself*; from how *your* body feels, and what emotions *you* are feeling. A safe place is one with enough room to move and try a few things, such as veil swinging, without fear of knocking lamps and vases onto the floor. If there is no room like that in your home, get creative. Will a friend let you use her great room? Can you get into a fitness center at a time when few people are there, and use the aerobics room? Take along a little CD player or your iPod. Get yourself into whatever you use for exercise or play clothing, get your music, grab your veil, and go!

How about the play itself? First, put on some music that inspires you. Then, without worrying about technique, or how you are "supposed" to do things, just try things out. You don't have to have specific "belly dance" music; music by Loreena McKennitt, Enya, and others works wonderfully.

Try wrapping yourself in the veil, and slowly reveal different parts of yourself. (This is best done when watching yourself in a full-length mirror.) Hold your veil behind your back, and pull it with your fingers so that the top center of the veil rests snugly against the back of your neck. Try twirls and swirls, just moving and spinning around the room. Drop the veil to the floor, hold it with one hand, and "snake" it along. How do you feel, playing with your veil these different ways?

Anahid Sofian, one of my master teachers, is fond of what she calls the "Turkish turtleneck." Lay your veil out lengthwise, and find the center. In this center area, fold your veil lengthwise into accordion pleats, where each pleat is only a couple of inches wide. Now, carefully lift your veil in the pleated area, and place this against your throat. Criss-cross the two lengths behind your back, and let them drape down along your fingertips. Take hold of one of the (lengthwise) selvage edges (making sure it is the same selvage edge on both your right and left sides), and pull this veil edge taut to create "wings." Adjust your veil so that the "wings" are even on each side. (About a foot or more will trail behind you on each side.)

To open your veil, drop the wings, take hold of the selvage edges across your neck, and slowly unfold. You can lift your veil up to cover your face, or lower it down; it is your call! Try twirling and swirling again, and learn how it feels. Just run across the floor with your "angel wings" floating behind you. With some good music in the background, this can be a real return to your "fairy princess" days as a child!

Finally, do you remember the classic "belly dancer pose" – the one that we've all seen in the movies? The dancer stands in a suitably exotic and sultry manner, with both arms raised above her head. The wrists are crossed, fingers pointing up, so that the two palms are flat against each other. (Yes, "real" dancers do this during "real" dances). Go ahead, try it with your veil! Hold your veil in front of you this time. Bring your hands up slowly, along each side of your body, and move into this classic and beautiful pose while holding your veil. Look at yourself in the mirror. Your face is now beautifully framed in the drapes of the veil. Try little rippling motions with your hands, and then slowly bring them down your sides. Play with this, bringing your veil up into this position and down again. How does this feel? You might want to journal about your experiences.

Keep your veil someplace where you can see it, and let it inspire you to take it out to play every so often. Note how your confidence increases the more that you play. You begin to feel, "Yes, this is also me." Your imagination suggests new things to do, and you get a sense of your body tempos and rhythms. A part of you, in the back of your mind, begins to incorporate a new concept of yourself; you are now capable of being the "mysterious, veiled woman," instead of merely wishing from time to time that you were she!

PERSONAL PATHWORKING:

1. Turn your "veil hunt" into a mini "vision-quest" for yourself. Before you go out, set aside some time to be open to receiving images and ideas about who you are and what you want. Send a little message, or "prayer," out to the universe about what you want. Make a clear statement of intention, so that the universe can support you in giving you the experiences that you desire – and more! What emotional qualities do you want to feel when you hold your veil? Do you want to feel passionate, or playful? Powerful or sensitive? Romantic or bold? Or do you want to let the universe surprise you? You may want to find pictures that speak to you about the qualities that you want. Put them in a special folder, and meditate on them the evening before you go hunting.

2. On the day that you go looking for your veil, take time to make it a special occasion – even if you have to squeeze the veil-hunting in along with other chores. Wear something pretty; something that makes you feel good. Put on special perfume – the one that you reserve for your very best dates. Do your hair, and find a flower to put into it. Find music that inspires you, and play it as you get ready to leave, and on the way there.

3. Let your friends (your trusted, loving friends) in on what you're doing. They can be a source through which the universe blesses you with abundance. You'll be surprised at how many have lengths of material, beautiful costume clothes, outrageous fantasy jewelry – and even veils and other belly dance gear – that they simply long to give to you! Accept graciously; this is the universe's way of supporting you in your new venture.

4. Go through your jewelry chest, and find all those wonderful playthings that you simply can't wear to the office. (Too much jingle, too much color, too much of anything.) They speak to you – at least an aspect of you, or you wouldn't have them there. Find a pretty bowl or basket that will let you display them, and put them where you can see them near your veil. Let them inspire you to put them on and dance.

CHAPTER 5:
CREATING STARDUST IN OUR LIVES

THERE IS SOMETHING THAT MANY of us crave, but which we often don't know how to put into words. We don't want it all the time, but when we do, we want it dearly. I'm not talking about sex, or power, or even survival, which is the most basic of our cravings. I'm not even talking about play, or exploring our "emotional range."

None of these. Rather, I'm talking about something that slips up sideways and gets a hold of us every so often. When it does, it is both compelling and disorienting to our regular way of life. In the wake of this craving, this need, often comes a sadness and sometimes even frustration – a frustration with life, with "things as they are," and most of all, with ourselves.

Picture a dark, blustery, wet day in late March, and although the tulips are blooming, it's cold outside. We are sitting together, you and I, close to the fireplace. We are fortified with a cup of hot chocolate. In this very quiet moment, with just the two of us together, we can each admit something that we rarely share with others. We each want something that we, as grown-up adults, feel that we "should" have outgrown a long time ago. *We want some magic in our lives.*

We desire a feeling of transport, of "something special." *We want a feeling of stardust in our lives.* We want the magical, the make-believe, the feeling that something extra-special really is possible. We want the feeling that we lost when we were, perhaps, about seven years old.

This craving for a bit of magic gets shamed out of us before we become adults. It is okay for little girls to play fairy princess, but as grown-up girls, with partners and careers and duties and commitments, we're supposed to have outgrown that kind of feeling. Even our playtime is supposed to be "adult." Fun: yes. Fanciful and magical: no. Even our fun should deal with the real "here-and-now," not some make-believe. And in our society, as things are today, it would be so much worse to actually believe that some kind of *stardust* really *could* come into our lives. We are conditioned by the time we put into our *Amazon* modes to be ruthlessly cognitive and oriented towards tasks in the "real world."

Nevertheless, we have a *stardust calling*. We see this evidenced in our books, our movies, and even our various role-playing games. This *stardust calling* is represented by more than just Tolkien stories. Laura Esquivel gave us the beautifully surreal novel, *Like Water for Chocolate.*[1] Laurell K. Hamilton has introduced us to her sublimely exotic and erotic world of vampires and were-beasts of all natures.[2] Without question, "magical realism," along with the fantasy genre, has emerged as a significant literary force.[3]

The evidence of this desire surrounds us. The *Harry Potter* book series has sold more than 400 million copies.[4] As of this writing, the *Twilight* series, started more recently, has topped 100 million copies.[5] These books, and our desire to experience something beyond the "Muggle" world, are not anomalies. Rather, they represent a questing within; a desire to go beyond what seems to be a banal world filled with increasingly homogenized products.

Perhaps most compelling (and reflecting of our own desires) is that some of our favorite romance authors have been introducing a "magical" element. We have seen this trend grow steadily in the works of Nora Roberts (the *Key Trilogy* is a good example), as she has gone from tentative brushes with to all-out immersion in those worlds where the "magical" meshes seamlessly with daily experience.[6]

As children, we watched cartoons and read comic books filled with action-adventure heroes, most of whom possessed powers far beyond those that you or I possess. As adults, our super-hero desires become sublimated, but they're still there. We watch the *X-Files* instead of the *X-Men*. (OK, maybe we watch both.) The point is, the desire for something beyond the everyday is vigorously repressed, but in many of us, it is still there. It's just that we don't dare talk about it. Instead, we play "pretend."

Some of my younger dance students live out their *stardust callings* by participating in "Live Action Role-Playing" (LARP) games. These take earlier, more imaginary role-playing games (*Dungeons and Dragons, Vampire: The Masquerade,* and others) into full-fledged weekend experiences, complete with costumes. Many women who study Oriental dance are drawn by the allure of an exotic "alter-reality," taken more from fantasy than from any existing culture. This is how most people satisfy the urge for *stardust* — for magic and a dash of glamour — when they go after it vicariously.

Yes, we women want a magical experience, which is a certain *quality of experience*. To create that, our cognitive mind simply has to let go. We need to shift control to our "other self." This is difficult for us. In fact, the more "successful" we are — the more that we've created a "role" for ourselves in the upright, logical, day-time world — the more challenging this is.

It suffices to say that whatever tools we normally use to create success in the cognitive (rational, everyday) areas of our life will *not* be the tools that we use to create a different kind of experience. This is the kind of thing where our "project management" mindset will not work on our behalf. To experience this not-so-cognitive, and not-so-rational, kind of experience, we need to *shift state.*

Our first step is to name and own our desires, and to do so in a slightly different state from our normal, cognitive, "to-do" list selves.

We know this. We know this to be so. We are taught this in Rhonda Byrne's *The Secret.*[7] Joe Vitale presents a similar lesson in the *Attractor Factor,* and many, *many* others start with this as a basic premise.[8] Yet, in this particular area, our desire, even our craving, for a bit of *stardust* makes us exceptionally exposed. We are greatly at risk.

The reason is that by naming this as one of our desires, we are stepping outside of the realm that is permitted by our society. We are going into a different *state.* We are letting down our hair, both figuratively and (as often as not) physically as well. We are not just speaking, we are singing. We are dancing. We are creating a lush, luscious, juicy, erotic power within ourselves.

At the same time, we also desire a quality that goes beyond this. We desire something that at its root, at its very core, goes beyond language, and even the desire for outward expression. Something that is quiet, and holy, and very still.

Within the stillness, there is a sense of pull, or draw. This is not simple passivity. Rather, there is a sense of being receptive. It is this receptivity itself that exerts the "drawing" power, much like a force of magnetic attraction.

When we take this "magnetic" power into our conscious selves, and begin to play with it, we find that we are dealing with something that is well-known in our culture. We have words to describe this; very old and powerful words.

We desire — we truly crave — the powers of *glamour*, *charm*, and *allure*. We crave them so much that two top-selling women's magazines carry these potent names. Also, it is no accident that *Charm* is not a magazine; it originally was, and then was merged with *Glamour*![9]

There we have it. *Glamour*, *charm*, and *allure* are words that have typically described a feminine form of magical power; a power of "attraction." We sometimes use these words in a much more banal setting, as in "She was absolutely charming," or "Movie-star glamour!" The origin of these words in fact speaks to the ancient power of their earlier meanings. The word "charm" originally referred to a magical spell; a "good-luck charm." Similarly, the word "glamour" also carries the connotation of true magical power. According to the Merriam Webster online dictionary, the original meaning for the Scots word "glamour" was that of a magical spell.[10]

The truth is that these words carry a deep cultural resonance. Because they originally, and still, refer to a "magical" attractive power, they also remind us of the fear that men (and even some women) have of this inherently feminine way of being. Women have been tortured and burned alive for even the suspicion, or allegation, that they possessed such powers. Our society has, for over four thousand years, been so vehemently antagonistic towards women's innate intuitive and attractive abilities that we have largely eschewed anything that resembles them.

Instead, we have taken refuge in our "to-do" lists and our day-planners, in the vast offerings of media, and in activities. We have crowded our lives to overflowing. And yet, at times we still feel a yearning. We vaguely sense a deep, unmet desire. Whether our professional and personal lives are on track or not, we still feel the tugging at our psyche that is best described, for now, as a *stardust calling*.

It's time to answer that calling. *Our first step is to honor our intention for bringing ourselves to this journey.*

This really is a journey; it is simply being done within ourselves, as opposed to going someplace physical. If we have been following through with the **Personal**

Pathworking suggestions of the previous chapters, and this one, we have been preparing for this journey. *Our journey begins in the next chapter.*

PERSONAL PATHWORKING:

1. Do you "cue" yourself to be in a certain mode? For example, do you use a certain song to get pumped up for a day at the office, or for work on a special project? Do you use certain scents? Cast a glance over your life, right now, before we start to go deeper.

2. Start a journal dedicated to your "stardust calling" alone. Think of it as a "laboratory notebook." You are now a scientist; an independent investigator. Seek to write your experiences relating to your sense of "stardust" quality in your life; however you may define or interpret these experiences. (You may use this as an excuse to buy one of the beautiful, elaborately-decorated bound journals available in most bookstores.)

3. Independent of your journal, assemble a personal chronology, or life-history, of your experiences so far. Pay particular attention to those times when you seemed to experience this "stardust" quality in your life. You may have been a child, playing make-believe. You may have been in love. It might help you to break your life into four- or seven-year segments, or segments of time when you were in a certain school, job, relationship, or specific "place." As you go along, identify not only those times when you had some sort of "stardust" experience, but also begin to fill in the space around those times. What was going on? What allowed you to have experiences then that might be different from how your life is now? This may take time. Plan to revisit this exercise, and fill in details as your memory brings moments back to you. (NOTE: You may want to do this journaling in graphical free-style form, drawing little "bubbles" of experiences, or "connecting the dots" in some manner. You may want to use colored pens or pencils, or glitter pens for those "stardust" times. Use whatever works for you, and maybe several things will work.)

4. Are there any times in your life where you *did* feel that you were opening up to a greater range of internal experience? What happened then? Did you, for any reason, shut this down? Why? What happened then? (NOTE: It is important for you to remember, to "re-member," the totality of your experience in this area, if you desire to bring it back; this time safely, and under your control. This may require you to visit some very tender times in your past. Again, repeat this exercise gently but persistently over time. Allow memories to come back to you. Write them down.)

5. In addition to your journal, begin to characterize your "stardust" essence. Perhaps you want to revise the way you've been collecting images. Notice that it may not be any one specific picture, but rather the amalgam that speaks to you. Consider collecting objects also: small statuary, shells, whatever speaks to you. Give yourself permission to acquire these items, even if they seem nonsensical. We are after the not-so-sensible part of your being here! Allow yourself to purchase a magazine if there is even one picture that really speaks to you about how *you* desire *your* "stardust" feeling in your life.

PART II:
A WOMAN'S PATH

⊰⊱

CHAPTER 6:

THE HERO'S QUEST — AND THE HEROINE'S AS WELL!

IN *STAR WARS*, THE YOUNG hero Luke Skywalker receives a charge to go on a quest. What could be more compelling for a young man, particularly a very gifted and very bored young man, than to be told that the fate of a beautiful woman, and possibly the civilized universe, rests on his actions? To accomplish his mission, he must first seek out a teacher: the retired Jedi knight Obi-Wan Kenobi. Luke trains with two different teachers; first with Obi-Wan, from whom he learns how to use a universal energy field called the *Force*, and from whom he receives his father's lightsaber (a laser sword). Later, Luke trains with Yoda, from whom he learns arcane secrets and further mastery of the *Force*.

Luke does deeds of derring-do, fights personal duels, and has tremendously compelling realizations. (The evil Darth Vader turns out to be his father, and the beautiful Princess Leia turns out to be his sister.) He finally saves the universe from the Emperor and his robot-like minions.

Why do we love *Star Wars* so dearly? Why has it become such a mainstream cultural fixture? It's not just the special effects. Those were truly wonderful, and we will enjoy them whenever we see the movie, no matter how long we live. But special effects were not what made *Star Wars* so appealing and satisfying, for so many, many people. Nor was it the acting. No discredit to the actors, who each did well, but this was not a movie about great acting. So what was it then?

Star Wars is a classic, absolutely complete, no-detail-missing reenactment of a myth that has been with us as long as there have been human beings on this planet. This myth, whose cross-cultural structure has been identified by Joseph Campbell, is called the *Hero's Quest* or the *Hero's Journey*.[1]

There are key, absolutely essential components to this myth — to this archetypal story — and the writers and producers of *Star Wars* were simply savvy enough to include all of them. That was their genius. In short, *Star Wars* succeeded as brilliantly as it did because it faithfully gave us the storyline that we needed. In this, it was very similar to Kathleen Woodiwiss's *The Flame and the Flower*. Both delivered emotional gratification.

Just as we learned a lot about ourselves by looking, really *looking*, at *The Flame and the Flower*, we can learn a lot about ourselves by looking, really *looking*, at *Star Wars*. At least, we can learn something about men, and the classical masculine quest.

Here's how the *Star Wars* plot goes. (Note: this is the plot of the classical masculine quest story, and is therefore not exclusive to *Star Wars* or any other particular book, movie, or play.) The young man, the hero, the "protagonist" (as our English teachers would say) is called upon to take on a *Heroic Quest*. Without his knowledge, he has been ready for this calling. He is restless, and there is some buried, unresolved conflict in his past. He needs to confront and resolve this conflict in order to know himself and come into his own power. Also, he is at the stage where he needs to become a man. He needs to see the world, and slay a few dragons along the way.

A crucial part of the mythological story is that our hero must find a teacher. Think about this. In the stories with which we resonate the most, the element of "transmission" – of receiving special training and knowledge, perhaps even a quest or a charge from a teacher – is an essential part of the story line. Think not just of *Star Wars*, but also of *The Karate Kid* (either as the original 1984 or more recent 2010 version). When really pushed to the wall, "life circumstances" can take the place of a real, physical teacher. However, in the most vivid and classic retellings of the *Hero's Quest*, the "teacher" role (the role of guru, guide, and mentor) is a necessary archetypal component.

The *quest* itself is, of course, the central theme. This *quest* must be sufficiently compelling, dangerous, and challenging to be a real transition experience for the young man. It must tax the hero to his utmost; he must draw upon inner resources that he didn't know that he had. This is how the boy becomes a man.

A woman must be involved. She must, of course, be beautiful. However, the story need not end with him "having" her. She is less important as a person, and more important as an ideal; she expresses the moment where the hero meets the "Goddess." (This explains why Princess Leia is able to spend days in the hands of her captors, run up and down the corridors of spaceships, and go through garbage dumpsters, while her lovely white gown stays far cleaner than what you or I would experience, going through the same thing! She's not a person, she's an *idealization*.) The woman's role, when she is not being a goddess, is to be in desperate need, and to be unable to save herself.

The young man also needs one or more sidekicks, or "faithful companions." Their role is to keep the man company on his long *quest*, do odd chores now and then, and serve as comic relief. The robots C-3PO and R2D2, as well as Han Solo and his Wookie companion Chewbacca, provide the essential comic components in *Star Wars*.

Of course, there is also "that which needs to be overcome." As with the teacher, it is best if this is a person, or some group of people. It is best if there is one person in this group who represents the "negative pole" – that which Jungian psychologists would call our "shadow self." That is, the hero has to come to recognize that whatever qualities he finds abhorrent in the opponent are actually within him. The most compelling dramatic moment is when the hero confronts and conquers *himself*. He may be conquering some external thing or person at the same time, but if the drama is done right, we all know that what he is defeating at the moment of victory is the "enemy within."

The story completes rapidly. By conquering the evil or the fear within, the hero gains the prize or the goal. He also gains access to the beautiful young woman. (In the case of *Star Wars*, Luke gains Leia as a sister, not as a bride. However, Princess Leia as the "goddess" personification becomes incarnate in his life.) The most important factor is that our emerging young hero crosses a threshold. *He becomes a man.*

Well and good for the hero involved. Now, what about the woman? Her role is pretty much laid out for her. Her job is to be in distress, and of course, unable to do anything but plea for help. (A good friend, on reading an early chapter draft, reminded me that Princess Leia took down her fair share of villains. Pointed granted; think *Princess Bride* along with *Star Wars*.) To give a (tongue firmly-in-cheek) summation, the "Princess" is to wear a white dress; a symbol of her purity, her innocence, and (most important) her unavailability. And she absolutely must not let her lipstick get smudged, no matter how many garbage dumpsters she goes through!

This is not exactly an inspiring role. It is especially not inspiring if we figure that we will have to support our husband while he goes through medical or law school, ourselves and our children after the divorce, and ourselves once again after our husbands have died and we've retired. Like the young men, we ask: Isn't there something more? But unlike them, we are not presented with a strong, cohesive, useful role model.

Let's look at this once again. There seems to be something about the male psyche that demands feats of derring-do. At a deeper level, there is something that demands a single point of confrontation, in order for a "boy to become a man." This is such a deeply embedded cultural archetype that we can't begin to argue with it; it is simply "what is so" about men. If a young man can't save the universe, then he will, intent on his journey of manhood, take on whatever *quest* he can find. He will join the Marine Corps (if he's strong), go to graduate school (if he's smart), or take up rock climbing, or do *something* where he finds mastery. Ultimately, he finds mastery of himself.

So what is it that we women do? Do we have a comparable need for a *quest?* If we can identify how men claim their identity, then what is it that works for us? Before we go into women's experience, let's look at one more (yes, again) male *Heroic Quest* story to more closely examine the female role.

Mozart's opera, *The Magic Flute*, is the story of a young man's heroic initiation into a sacred order.[2] The young hero, Tamino, seeks not only to know and understand the deeper mysteries, but also to attain a level of personal mastery. There is a subplot; in so doing he receives approval and (it is assumed) the "mantle of leadership" from the High Priest Sarastro, who, unbeknownst to him, is his father.

Tamino is accompanied on his magical *quest* by two other persons: his true love, Pamina, who accompanies him on his *quest* up until the time he undergoes the trials of initiation, and a person dressed in feathers, Papageno, who functions as Tamino's comic servant.

Tamino is successful in mastering all of his trials, including one in which he has to traverse a passageway while responding to no one. He doesn't know at the time that he will have to ignore the pleas for recognition by his true love. (At this point, we might wonder who is undergoing the greatest trial; Tamino or Pamina. Tamino at least knows why he has to ignore her; she is left in the dark until the whole opera is almost over. And what, we may ask, is more demonstrative of a man's whole-hearted commitment to his path than that he is willing to ignore the pleas of the woman who could possibly distract him? The implication is clear; if he can do this once, during initiation, then he can do it again in his life, when "duty demands.")

Naturally, being a Mozart opera, the situation ends happily for (almost) everyone involved. Tamino is initiated into priesthood and is united with Pamina, who has been sufficiently purified by her suffering to be allowed initiation along with Tamino. (This is in contrast to Masonic tradition, which held that slaves, women, and immoral men – in that order – were not eligible for initiation.) The High Priest Sarastro, who serves the Sun God, welcomes in his new acolytes. The evil Queen of the Night is rendered powerless, and is served her comeuppance in that her daughter, Pamina, has gone over to the side of the Sun (the true, the wise, and the good).

In *The Magic Flute*, there is a single great exception to the classic male-myth storyline. It is that Pamina, as well as Tamino, goes through initiation. Here's where the truth comes out about gender differences. The young man goes through ordeals because they are necessary for him to attain mastery. They are required for initiation.

Pamina, on the other hand, endures these ordeals because of love, not because she wants to prove herself or "get mastery." All she wants to do was is accompany her great love on his *quest*. This sounds familiar, doesn't it? As young women (and perhaps as more mature ones), it is not just that we are taught to invest ourselves in relationships; this is often what is most natural and "right" for us.

This is not to say that many of us, whether young or old, don't take on *Heroic Quests* ourselves; at least for a while. We do this because we have our own ego needs; we are complete human beings. We have our own mountains to climb; our own thrills, our own challenges. We, as much as men, want to "be all that we can be." And sometimes, we take on this role simply to survive. We become heroes not because we desire self-aggrandizement, but because we have no other choice.

We have enough of a desire for our own thrills, challenges, and survival to have our own "movie cult" about this aspect of ourselves. After the original (1984) movie, *The Karate Kid*, was milked for all it was worth, producers finally made the *The Next Karate Kid*, featuring a teenage girl as the acolyte. We've had *GI Jane*, and various Lara Croft movies. We had the wonderful Emma Peel in the 1960's TV show, *The Avengers*, followed by *Charlie's Angels* in the 1970's and by many more. In short, we've created an exciting cult of the "dangerous woman." (And it is true – the *femme fatale* has been with us as archetype for a very long time. Sometimes our *femme fatale* persona appears as an action hero in her own right, and sometimes as the siren. We can be dangerous in many different ways!)

For all that we have fun with this, and sometimes spend years (and perhaps even most of a lifetime) on various accomplishments, the realm of accomplishments does not fulfill us as deeply as it does for men. Very simply, we are more complex creatures than men are. We may feel the call to some sort of "path" – something akin to our own *Hero's Quest*. Even when we take on our own *Heroine's Quest*, though, our journey is different from men's.

We find that there actually *is* a pattern to the young woman's *Heroic Quest*. We notice that in our cultural storylines, a young woman takes on this *quest* after puberty, but before her attention is caught up by marriage and children. As we saw in *Chapter 3: Bedtime Stories*, once we have the first baby, our opportunities for *questing* are severely limited. Moreover, our priorities are different. We are more interested, not just in taking care of our babies, but simply in *being* with them. Once our children leave the nest, our hormones shift once again, and so do our priorities. We consider how a mature woman takes on her crucial *inner journey* during the last five chapters of this book. For now, we look at a young woman's parallel to the *Hero's Quest*.

Maureen Murdock was asking about our own *Heroine's Quest* when she wrote *The Heroine's Journey*. When Ms. Murdock was studying this issue, she was dealing with this question in a very personal way. She was asking how she could come out of her formerly male-identified life, into something which honored the feminine aspect of her being. During this process, she talked with the renowned master of mythology and archetypes, Joseph Campbell. She was trying to find out what he had to say about a "path" for women. His reply to her was essentially that a woman did not need a path. "'In the whole mythological tradition,'" Mr. Campbell told Ms. Murdock, "'the woman is *there*.'" [italics hers]. He described the notion of a woman seeking her own *Heroic Quest* as being "'pseudo-male.'"[3]

We can certainly agree with Mr. Campbell, and with Ms. Murdock, that we are all better off without being pseudo-male. But that does not really address our issues. Neither does the wave-off of saying that we should just be "there" satisfy us. Being "there" may sound good, but how does it relate to healing the schisms that have developed in our life? How does it relate to balancing our inner needs with our outer commitments? How does it give us a sense of experience that we can return to and resonate with; something that becomes a touchstone of sanity and wholeness in our lives?

One of the biggest reasons that we have not found a single type of *Heroine's Quest* is that we have not just one, but rather, several. This is because each of the different adult stages of our lives, if lived in "classical" order (puberty/adult initiation, motherhood, and then a vital, new landscape beyond that), has a different type of vision-fulfillment. These correspond to not only to our personal situations, but also to the type of neurochemicals that govern our brain chemistry during each timeframe, and through them, to our life-priorities.[4] We thus have different sagas for our experiences as young women coming-of-age, but not yet enmeshed in desire for our husbands and children, versus our time as young brides and mothers, versus our time of mature *questing* after our children (and often careers) can stand on their own.

We begin by looking at stories depicting our individuation-journey; our *Heroine's Quest*, which we undertake while we are on the threshold of adulthood. As a starting point, we begin with Dorothy's journey in the first Oz story, where the mythic aspects were pointed out by Caroline Myss in *Sacred Contracts*.[5] Comparing Dorothy's journey (and that of other young heroines) to the classic *Hero's Quest*, we can identify three key ways in which the *Heroine's Quest* differs from the *Hero's*.

A first crucial difference between the masculine *Hero's Quest* and the feminine *Heroine's Quest* is that while both protagonists often set out to save or rescue some entity, the masculine focus is often grand, glorious, impersonal – and ego-gratifying.

The young man "saves the world"! In contrast, the young woman embarks on her quest to save someone whom she already knows, and with whom she already feels not only a personal bond, but often a sense of personal responsibility. Often mixed with this is the need to "return home." Such is the case with Dorothy, who must get both herself and Toto back to Kansas. In the movie *Labyrinth* (1986), fifteen year-old Sarah travels to a mystical land to rescue her baby half-brother.[6] In the book (and later the movie) *The Golden Compass*, the young heroine Lyra travels from home to rescue her best friend Roger (as well as other children) from the Gobblers.[7] A key theme in the *Heroine's Quest* is one of taking responsibility for a family member, in either a personal or extended sense of "family." This presages how the *Maiden* will later become the *Mother*, and later the *Crone*, whose wisdom watches over her family and community. Thus, even though we as *Maidens* may go adventuring, our focus of "saving someone" is much more personal than is the classic masculine *quest*. As a side note, our journey, as often as not, is through an inner, or "mythic," landscape. In the cases of Dorothy, Sarah, and others, each heroine enters an "alternate world." This suggests that our journeys are often through our own psyche, rather than necessarily being "in the world."

A second difference between the *Heroine's Quest* and the *Hero's* lies in how we, as the *Heroines*, are accompanied by allies, just as the young *Heroes* are accompanied by their companions. First, we *perceive* our companions differently. We perceive those whom we select as complex beings. Whatever "face" these persons present to society, even if wounded in some way, our new allies are never simply comic relief. Second, we not only perceive our allies differently, we take an active role in their healing. Dorothy, for example, releases the Scarecrow from being affixed to a pole. She finds an oilcan and helps the Tin Man to become mobile again. Further, she does these actions simply as the preliminary steps, well before the "deep healing" takes place!

Dorothy's journey involves first strengthening, and then integrating, multiple inner aspects.[8] Here we see a key difference between Dorothy's journey and the classic *Hero's Quest*: Dorothy gains healing for her comrades; the Scarecrow, the Tin Man, and the Cowardly Lion. Each represents an aspect that Dorothy very explicitly develops during her journey. Toto, her little dog, represents being grounded in simple, physical reality. (He is one only one that doesn't need something special to complete him! Also, in the end, Dorothy and Toto return to "ground"; the Kansas that they left.)

The Scarecrow longs for intellect ("If I only had a brain"), the Tin Man needs a heart, and the Lion seeks courage. In the Lion's case, the courage that he craves represents not so much the heart as it is does resoluteness and will. We have, in order, *body* (Toto), *mind* (the Scarecrow), *psyche* or *emotion* (the Tin Man), and *energy* (or direction of energy through will; the Lion). Thus, Dorothy's journey is one of healing and integration for her comrades (and implicitly for these aspects of herself), as much as it is one of discovering her own courage and perseverance.

We might think that this is a singular example, but similar retellings of the *Heroine's Quest* emerge in other stories, such as *Labyrinth*. In the course of her quest, Sarah finds allies in Hoggle, a curmudgeonly dwarf, in Sir Didymus, a chivalrous, fox-like knight, and in the gentle giant Ludo, whom she rescues from the goblins. In each of these creatures, she recognizes a capacity for heroism that has gone unnoticed and unacknowledged by others.

Thus, our *Heroine's Quest*, if we tell it in completeness, has some elements in common with the *Hero's Quest*. At the same time, it also has much greater complexity. We can see a pattern emerging from these examples. First, our journey tends to be more internal than external; even if it is one of "individuation"; separating ourselves from our family. Also, our initial impetus to go on this journey is to save someone (or something) that we love. Second, in each case, as a *Heroine*, we not only find allies, but help our allies to each find what they need. This is something that rarely, if ever, is found in the *Hero's Quest*. We may even go so far as to say that one aspect that makes the *Heroine's Quest* distinctive is that the heroine helps to heal others, or at least she recognizes their worth and gives validation.

With this as a pattern, or template, we see examples of the *Heroine's Quest* in other stories. In a mythic storytelling under development by Nicole Cutts, the young heroine, Princess Isabelle, finds allies as she goes about her *Heroine's Quest*.[9] What is crucial is that Isabelle identifies her allies as "goddesses," incarnate in various forms. Many of Isabelle's goddess-companions need the healing that comes about as they find common cause and meaning in joining Isabelle's *Quest*.

A third crucial way in which our *Heroine's Quests* are different from the *Hero's* lies in how we resolve the final conflict. We typically do not have the dramatic dual that signifies the *Hero's* ascendency to power. Rather, we save the ones who are dear to us, and reframe how we experience life. For example, Dorothy not so much defeats the evil Wicked Witch of the West, as she saves her companion, the Scarecrow. The Witch's "dissolution" in the water that Dorothy uses to put out the Witch's fire on the Scarecrow is accidental, rather than the result of a dramatic dual. Dorothy has to find her courage in this confrontation (as she later has to find courage to see the "real" Wizard), but her task is finding inner courage and taking appropriate action, not to engage in a dual. Similarly, in *Labyrinth*, Sarah resolves her conflict with the King of the Goblins by recalling the one line from the play that she is learning that always seemed to elude her grasp. "You have no power over me," she finally claims. With that, she is able to take her baby half-brother and return home.

The key, for the *Heroine*, is to reach the point where she recognizes that the "evil other" has *no power over her*. She relinquishes the social conditioning of being a "good girl," and claims the right to think and act for herself.

We can now use these three distinguishing features as guidelines to discover when we are taking on our own *Heroine's Quests*. We take note of situations in which we are rescuing someone or something dear to us, when we are calling on others to be allies (and helping them to heal in the process), and when we are reframing our world-view so that we can say to whatever it is that we found threatening, "You have no power over me!" This is how we recognize that we are on a *Heroine's Quest*.

For example, my dear friend Kirene, as I write, is engaged in a *quest* to reclaim the family house and estate. An elderly relative died, and the will – written when he was aging and ill – gave almost all of his estate to a caretaker couple. Kirene, together with her sister and mother, is now engaged in a *Heroine's Quest*. In seeking to reclaim not only the estate, but also the house where she has many fond memories, we see that Kirene's *Quest* meets the first criterion; she is saving something personally dear to her.

To accomplish this task, Kirene has called upon friends to be allies, providing both strategic and emotional support. She has also reached out to find new allies. In one case, someone who is providing crucial advice and guidance is between life situations; Kirene's validating his insights and guidance is a source of healing for him.

Finally, the primary means by which Kirene is reclaiming the family estate is to work within the legal system. She, her mother, and her sister have all done a great deal of research and investigation. They have put together a compelling case, working with multiple lawyers and other specialists. They have done all of this within and according to the "law of the land." Nevertheless, their approach – their taking action – is a means of reclaiming power in the face of persons who tried to make off with the family fortune, the lawyers who set up the will that allowed this, and the legal system itself. In this, they are saying that the legal system has "no power" over them; they are creating their own power by acting appropriately *within* the system.

Like Kirene, we can apply the signposts of the *Heroine's Quest* to many moments in our lives. Although Dorothy, Sarah, and Lyra each take on their *quests* when young, we may find ourselves taking on a *Heroine's Quest* at different times, no matter what our chronological age may be. The key factor is the calling; the need to rescue or claim someone or something. The resolution always comes about when we rebuke whomever or whatever has held us in thrall, by challenging its authority, taking responsibility, and finding the power that we've had all along.

Quests can also be to claim (or re-claim) an aspect of ourselves; bringing that part of who we are into completeness. When we are *questing*, we are typically in *Amazon* mode – and we often don't have time for anything else! For example, we are *questing* when we are getting an advanced degree, preparing for a martial arts exam or for a dance or musical performance, or doing anything else that has *claiming* something (e.g., a degree, a performance, a new "belt color" in karate) as a result.

As we examine our lives, we will find that we have many instances of a *Heroine's Quest*; these are alive and well within our cultural mythology and our own lives. Valerie Frankel's book, *From Girl to Goddess*, brings together many retellings of the *Heroine's Quest* across diverse cultures.[10] In our own lives, our *Heroine's Quests* may be successive and even build on each other. For example, in Kirene's estate-claiming *quest*, she drew on the experiences and confidence that she gained in an earlier *quest*, reclaiming her professional "identity" that was threatened during corporate maneuvers. Our various *quests*, conducted as emerging or mature *Amazons*, give us the skills, insights, and pragmatic knowledge that we need – as well as self-confidence! They do not speak against those times when we are seeking to move into our other modes; they do not mitigate our desire to be cared for when we go into our caring and nurturing *Mother* mode. However, they give us a complementary way of being. In fact, our *questing* times are often those when we come to know and cultivate our *Amazon* natures.

As Kirene expresses it, "If little girls were exposed to the female *vision quest*, and learned early on that life is full of victories and obstacles that must be overcome using teachings from our mentors, and [if they learned] to not be afraid, but rather to embrace the challenges with a pure heart, then girls growing into womanhood would be better able mentally and emotionally to navigate … turbulent waters and resolve the perceived insurmountable."[11]

Clearly, *quests* are an important part of our lives. However, as adult women, we have both *quests*, which are specifically-focused, and the more long-term process of *pathworking*. It is via *pathworking* that we *integrate*, and it is via *quests* that we gain specific skills, confidence, and networks. As adults, our life-journeys encompass both. By clearly identifying what comprises our *quests*, we can more confidently characterize and understand our other inner work; that which constitutes our *pathworking*.

We are now "re-membering" our own sacred journey. Very fortunately, the pieces that we need to "re-member" for our *pathworking* are available to us. We have done sufficient work, across sufficient related disciplines, for long enough now, to know the *essence* of our path. There is also much more scholarship, together with depths of historical resources, upon which we can draw. From this point, let's move on to discover what our *personal path* might really be.

PERSONAL PATHWORKING:

1. Once again; continue journaling. Consult with your personal timeline. Where and when have you gone on your own *Hero's* (or *Heroine's*) *Quest*? (You probably have, many times.) How did it feel; as you did the *Quest*, and after? What did you do next?

2. Find some of the men in your life who have gone on a *Hero's Quest* similar to yours. How did they do it differently (to the best of your knowledge)? How did they feel when they achieved their goals? (You may want to ask some of them.) What did they do next? Similarly, can you find women in your life who have done their *Heroine's Quests*? (The kind that we have described here are those that they possibly did when they were young.) What are their stories?

3. As you completed more and more of your own *Quests*, how did this "sit" with you? Did you feel complete, partially complete, empowered, saddened, jubilant, calm ... what did you begin to notice about yourself?

CHAPTER 7:
A REAL WOMAN'S PATH (REALLY *DOES* EXIST!)

IF YOU WERE A YOUNG man living in China about 600 ACE, and if you felt a desire to follow a *body/mind integration path*, the choice was obvious. You would have traveled to the Shaolin temple in the Henan area, and devoted yourself to studying martial arts and practicing meditation.[1]

If you were a man living in Europe, from the mid-1100's through the end of the 1200's, you could similarly have satisfied your need for a *quest* by joining the Knights Templar.[2] And if you lived "a long time ago, in a galaxy far away," you might have joined the Jedi Knights.[3]

Throughout history, if you were a man, there was often (not always, but often enough) a *pathway* for personal growth. This *pathway* involved gaining mastery in physical, intellectual, spiritual, and even "energetic" dimensions. During the course of your studies, you would have had tests and initiations. It was by passing these tests, and surviving the initiations, that you had confirmation that you really were advancing on your *path*.

While the work would have been challenging (in fact, it would have been designed to challenge you to your utmost), you would have had one great security throughout your journey. This security was in knowing that your *path* was already defined. You had master teachers who would guide you on your way. Yes, you had to work hard. Sometimes, you had to figure things out. (Figuring out riddles, or interpreting the meaning of an initiation challenge, was part of the task at hand.) However, you didn't have to invent the *path*; the masters had already done so.

If you were a woman, and had comparable desires, what could you have done? Was there a temple at Avalon to which you could have gone? Perhaps. The existence of such is more myth and legend than recorded historical fact. Was there an order of priestesses where you could have learned sacred rituals and sacred dance?

Where you would have learned the use of herbs, and how to heal both body and soul? Perhaps. There is some evidence that such temples existed, before they were destroyed as being too challenging to the notion of a singular, and masculine, God.

So throughout recorded history, if you were a woman, what would you have done? By and large, no matter what you desired, you would have married and had babies. And you would have spent your life being pregnant, nursing, caring for children, and taking care of your husband. If you were very lucky, you survived your many childbirths and lived to reach menopause. Then, if you were fortunate enough to live in a culture in which you didn't have to throw yourself on your husband's funeral pyre, or were not burned as a witch, you might have been able to join the women elders; the "wise blood."[4]

With the rise of the Judeo-Christian-Islamic religions, knowledge of a feminine *pathway* for *body/mind integration* has largely been destroyed.[5] The best that we have had, over the past two to four millennia, have been various women's religious orders. These have been home to great women saints and mystics, such as Hildegard of Bingen[6] and Julian of Norwich.[7] These orders, however, were housed under the auspices of "Holy Mother Church." This has put constraints on women's experience.

As a result of the dedication, sacrifices, and hard work of generations of women preceding us, we've now achieved significant victories. We have the option to marry, and the right to get a divorce. We can vote and run for office. We can own property, drive a car, and wear whatever we want. We can have careers and still mother our children. (In fact, we often do both.) The main considerations are often pragmatic ones: time, logistics, and money.

The biggest three changes in women's experience are now converging. First, we have control over our reproductive experience, and – most importantly – our children usually survive. We no longer need multiple pregnancies and childbirths to produce just a few children who will live to adulthood. Second, we have education and legal rights that were previously unavailable. These combine with our increased avenues of communication, making us a more potent force than ever. Third – and this may be the most important – we live longer. Many, many more of us safely reach menopause, with our health, our vigor, and our teeth intact. Instead of fading away (or being persecuted), we have the time, energy, vision, and money with which to determine what we will do next in life. Many of us take this as a time for new adventures.[8]

Specifically, women from all parts of the world, and all walks of life, have been re-igniting the question of feminine spirituality. In the powerful book, *The Feminine Face of God* by Sherry Ruth Anderson and Patricia Hopkins, Ms. Anderson describes a dream that initiated her quest:

> ... Melchizedek answers, "We are celebrating because you, a woman, have consented to accept full spiritual responsibility in your life. This is your initiation as one who will serve the planet."
>
> As I wonder what this means, he continues, "And you are not the only one. Many, many women are coming forward now to lead the way."
>
> "But who will be our teachers?" I protest.
>
> "You will be teachers for each other."[9]

This much is encouraging. And yet, we are in the position of having to be our own "Grand Masters," without much training or lineage. We have to figure out what our *pathway* is about, taking into full account the realization that all the "templates" that have been infused into us for so many lifetimes, for so many women, are all variations of the patriarchal theme.

So how do we discern our uniquely feminine *path*? Clearly, we need an understanding of our own psyche that allows us to know ourselves in a useful and meaningful way. As the social psychologist Kurt Lewin once stated, "There is nothing so practical as a good theory."[10] Fortunately for us, our necessary "theory" already exists.

For this inspirational work, we are indebted to Dr. Toni Grant, whose book, *Being a Woman*,[11] is still available. In fact, it was a best-seller shortly after being published in 1988. Dr. Grant was on the same *quest* that we are pursuing here; the challenge of knowing our true selves, at the deepest possible level.

Dr. Grant's studies took her through a great deal of research, spanning many years. Finally, she came upon a little fourteen-page booklet; more a pamphlet or article than anything else. When she read it, she knew that her search had "come home." It took her a while, but she built a whole book explaining what she had learned, putting it in context, and giving us practical guidelines. The booklet that Dr. Grant had found was *Structural Forms of the Feminine Psyche*, written by Antonia Wolff, a protégé (and later the lover) of Carl Jung.[12]

Dr. Grant, and before her, Antonia Wolff, identified four major archetypes that, *taken together*, describe our full feminine core. These four aspects, according to Grant and Wolff, are the *Amazon*, the *Mother*, the *Courtesan*, and the *Madonna*.

According to Wolff's original concept, when we are in our *Mother* aspect, we dominantly relate to people.[13] However, we can reframe this archetype as one in which we show any kind of caring or nurturing behavior. This can include caring for animals, and even for groups or organizations. We can support this mode with recent neurophysiological research summarized by Shelley Taylor, Ph.D., in *The Tending Instinct*.[14] Thus, as a starting point, let us think of the *Mother* aspect within ourselves as not just physical or even surrogate "mothering," but the full range of "mending, tending, and befriending" behaviors (using Dr. Taylor's phrase). Collectively, these behaviors have contributed to female and group survival during human evolution.

As described by Dr. Taylor, and also by Louann Brizendine, M.D., in *The Female Brain*,[15] these nurturing and care-taking behaviors release oxytocin; a soothing, feel-good hormone. Oxytocin is both triggered by intimacy and itself will trigger intimacy and bonding feelings. Two other neurochemicals come into play; estrogen and dopamine. Dopamine stimulates the pleasure-inducing areas of our brain. Estrogen, which girls begin to generate in greater quantities with the onset of puberty, increases both dopamine and oxytocin production. Thus, as girls pass beyond puberty and enter into pair relationships and become mothers, their brains become awash in the potent oxytocin/dopamine mix, which stimulates their drive for intimacy. Concomitantly, these two neurochemicals also reduce stress, which is why women use the "tend, mend, and befriend" strategy for stress-reduction.[16]

When we are in our *Mother* role, regardless of how we express it, we are dominantly influenced by oxytocin. We can get our "oxytocin fix" from holding our baby, and looking into its eyes. We can also get a similar neurochemical reward (not as intense, but still satisfying) by petting a cat or playing with a dog, or by cuddling with our loved ones. Dopamine intensifies our pleasure-seeking behaviors, and we get a huge dopamine release during orgasm. But the way that it interacts with oxytocin in our brains is complex, as discussed by Marnia Robinson and Douglas Wile, Ph.D., in *Cupid's Poisoned Arrow*.[17] Drawing on neurological research, they suggest that we can create a good overall mix of these neurochemicals in our brains, and have better (and much more enduring) love relationships. We can do this by emphasizing oxytocin-releasing behaviors, such as touching and cuddling, and minimizing our urge for orgasmic completion.

Many of these insights are relatively new, and so getting a good map of our complex neural landscape is still an ongoing process. Further, we are just beginning to get good strategies to help us manage our own neurochemical balance. As described by neuroscience researchers Tracey Baskerville and Alison Douglas,[18] studies of the complex oxytocin/dopamine interactions show that they participate in a "much larger neural network comprised of multiple neurochemical pathways and intricate circuitries." Clearly, more detailed knowledge will be forthcoming. For our immediate use, though, we'll make a simple and direct correlation between the *Mother* archetype, as identified first by Wolff and then by Grant, with a state-of-being that has a neurochemical correlate.

Our *Mother* essence, with the assistance of our "bonding" neurochemical oxytocin, has been essential to our cultural progression, enabling us to domesticate animals. The entire shift in human ecology from hunter-gatherer to farmer-herder became possible through animal domestication. Consider the "simple" act of milking a cow. Even though a lactating animal can produce milk, she will not "let down" and let her milk flow freely unless she is relaxed, and trusts the one who is milking her. Our oxytocin-based "bonding system" let us cultivate empathy with animals to such a degree that they would trust us enough to release their milk, as described by Meg Olmert in *Made for Each Other*.[19] This was a huge step in our cultural emergence, as human civilization grew out of our transition to being farmers and herders.

Likewise, many other "grazing" animals became sufficiently domesticated for us to herd them. Certain wolves evolved into the dogs which became our intelligent and essential hunting partners, and who also provided us with a natural "security system" through barking. While men certainly played their role in animal domestication, it was the bonding nature of the *Mother* archetype that allowed all humans – male and female – to connect with animals and make animal husbandry (notice the original meaning of the word) possible.

This gives us a reasonably full sense of our *Mother* archetype; we know that there is a biological basis for this mode in us, whether or not we are actual mothers, and whether our children are young and dependent or full-fledged, thriving adults. We know that we transform our *Mother* archetype over time, but its essence lies in nurturing and caring.

In contrast to how we inhabit our *Mother* archetype, in which we focus on meeting the physical and emotional needs of others, when we take on the *Amazon* archetype, we are focusing on ourselves; on our achievements, on our self-definition.

Our *Amazon* role is important. The entire Women's Movement of the latter 1900's created the space in which this role could emerge. Even before then, the women's suffrage movement in the late 1800's and early 1900's laid the foundation.[20] We don't want to dismiss this aspect of our lives; our *Amazon* qualities are what help us to achieve our personal, professional, and community goals and visions. This aspect of our psyche lets us create our physical and financial independence, and fight fiercely on behalf of those who need our assistance.

When we set *Amazon*-style goals for ourselves, we strengthen our ability to call our own shots, run our own lives, and do as we please. This can be tough at times, but there is much value in doing something challenging, and realizing that we can accomplish our goals.

Many of us who have had significant *Amazon* times in our life may recall that at the extremes of our *Amazon* moments, we experienced an identifiable "state-of-being." We know now that our *Mother* role has a distinct neurochemical basis. The early *Mother* stages are characterized by a dreamy feeling of contentment, induced by oxytocin.

In contrast to this, my experience of being a young *Amazon* was that I was a bit adrenaline-driven. This may be true for many of us. I've noticed that many women in their late teens and early twenties are attracted to martial arts, and to other activities in which they can "test themselves" against various challenges. Since we already have some neurochemical support characterizing our *Mother* mode, it would be interesting to see if there are neurochemical correlates to our other modes. This is a complex task, as we would seek to correlate neurochemical and neurophysiological processes with brain functions, and those functions with behaviors, and then collections of behaviors with an overarching "mode" or "state," which we would then identify as connoting a certain archetypal essence. Research in these areas will continue to evolve over time.

The more that we learn about how our neurochemistry is influenced by both behaviors and experiences, the more that we can take steps to create both better self-knowledge and a better quality of life. For example, we know that when we are under stress, we create more cortisol and adrenaline in our systems. If we are under long-term stress, too much of these neurochemicals can result in "adrenal burnout," or a suite of symptoms that includes chronic fatigue.[21] By learning to balance our internal modes, or at least recognize our need for accessing each of them, we can potentially mitigate some effects of overdoing one at the expense of the others.

In North America and in many European countries, and very possibly worldwide, many of us women have adopted lifestyles that put us largely in our *Amazon* modes. We may, in fact, have overdeveloped our *Amazon* aspects. Or rather, in our pursuit of our *Amazonian* dreams and conquests, we perhaps have lost touch with the other aspects of ourselves. What we are seeking now (especially for those of us who have some conquests, and defeats, to our credit) is a certain sense of balance, and even *integration*, in our lives. We are often seeking to identify and reconnect with those aspects of ourselves that we have pushed to the side while devoting ourselves to our *Amazon* and *Mother* callings.

We have an esoteric underpinning to our culture. Our symbolic foundations have had recent attention in novels such as Dan Brown's *The Lost Symbol* and *The Da Vinci Code*.[22] Underlying our cognitive world-view, we have a felt-level understanding of personal journey as a life-metaphor. We express this understanding in our myths and legends, and these motifs provide the basis for the "grand sagas" of our society. Thus, movies such as *Star Wars* are much more than entertainment.

They speak to us on a powerful and symbolic level. As we deal with *pathworking*, it is useful to employ such symbols to focus our understanding.

The Tarot deck, in a manner similar to the archetypal stories in movies, has a meaning that goes beyond the superficial one of fortune-telling or divination: it captures the archetypes of our world. Of the seventy-eight Tarot cards, fifty-six are known as the Minor Arcana. These became our current set of playing cards. The remaining twenty-two cards are called the Major Arcana. These are our deep cultural archetypes; the major elements of our life-journey.

In any human society, we organize our world-view around a set of symbols or themes, through which we interpret our experiences. In the early 1960's, Allen Newell and Herbert Simon, both pioneers in artificial intelligence and cognitive psychology, suggested that all intelligent thought rested on manipulating a "physical symbol system."[23] The elements of such a system could be a number of things, ranging from algebraic entities such as "+" and "*" operators to things in our physical world, such as a "dog." This chapter rests on the proposition that the Major Arcana form a "physical symbol system" on which our North American and antecedent European culture is based. If we were in China, our understanding of the world, and how we interpret life, would be governed by a different symbol system. This would similarly be true if we were brought up in any other very different part of the world. Within our North American and European cultures, though, the "symbols" of the Major Arcana permeate both our culture and our mental predispositions for interpreting our lives.

There are additional "symbol systems" that we will use in this and succeeding chapters. For example, we will take into account not only the Major Arcana, but also Carl Jung's theory of Psychological Types.[24] Any of us who have learned to think of people in terms of whether they are "introverted" or "extroverted" is using Jung's symbol system. A major purpose of this chapter is to relate both the Jungian and the Major Arcana symbol systems to the simpler one proposed by Antonia Wolff, described earlier in this chapter. This integration across symbol systems will give us much greater completeness for understanding both ourselves and others.

There is particular value for us in using the Major Arcana as a symbol system, simply because these concepts are pictorially represented. We often say that "a picture is worth a thousand words." Pictures condense a great deal of meaning into something that our minds readily grasp and store. In particular, we are especially good at interpreting pictures of people (or people-like beings). The Major Arcana frequently uses such pictures. When the pictures are not of people, then they are of events with strong emotional content. Our brains are greatly attuned to understanding, interpreting, and applying pictorially-related archetypal depictions such as those found in the Major Arcana. Although many artists have produced different versions of the Major Arcana, this book will refer to those originally painted by the artist Pamela Colman Smith, under the guidance of renowned esoteric scholar Arthur Edward Waite, and first released in 1909. This is commonly referred to as the "Rider-Waite deck."

There are several ways in which the Major Arcana can be organized. However, one that makes a great deal of sense divides the Major Arcana into three sets of seven, plus the initial card. Each set of seven cards represents a crucial stage in a person's adult development. This organization into three sets of seven cards each is described by Rachel Pollack in her book, *Seventy-Eight Degrees of Wisdom*.[25] Author Sallie Nichols, in *Jung and Tarot*, uses the same organizational approach in correlating the Major Arcana with a Jungian interpretation.[26] Corrine Heline, in *The Bible & the Tarot*, again uses the same organization in describing the Kabbalistic origins of the Tarot.[27]

Our brains are designed so that we can hold a limited number of independent thoughts in our head at one time. George Miller, a pioneer in cognitive psychology, described this as the "magic number seven, plus or minus two."[28] When we are holding a single "train of thought," such as remembering a phone number, a grocery shopping list, or people on a committee, we can easily remember up to about seven items. Then our short-term memories start to "wobble."

Thus, grouping the Major Arcana into three groups of seven cards each makes sense in terms of how our mental processes can hold "sets" of thoughts at a given time. We will focus in this chapter on the first seven Major Arcana and how they relate to the "feminine archetypes" intuited first by Antonia Wolfe, and then re-introduced by Dr. Grant. This will give us a deeper understanding of our feminine archetypes; we'll be able to draw on a richer "symbol system."

The Major Arcana "zero" card is the *Fool,* or *Wanderer.*[29] The *Fool* typically shows a young man setting off on life's journey, carrying the sum of his worldly goods wrapped in a kerchief, tied to a stick across his shoulder. He is so lost in his exuberant daydreams that he's about to step off a cliff! A little white dog yips at him, trying to warn him of danger. He is young, innocent, and carefree; albeit a little too lost in his adventuring daydreams rather than paying attention to the actual journey. The *Fool* represents our excitement and enthusiasm, and our youthful naivety, as we embark on a new quest or venture.

Using Rachel Pollack's designation, the Tarot's Major Arcana first seven-card sequence (after the *Fool*) is called the *Worldly Sequence.*[30] It defines the basic human archetypes of our culture; the building blocks. If the *Fool* were to meet the various people described in the first five of these cards, he would encounter, in order, five persons: the *Magician,* the *High Priestess,* the *Empress,* the *Emperor,* and the *Hierophant* (the leader of an esoteric or knowledge order). These are encounters with clear, well-defined archetypes. He then encounters a pair of *Lovers* (Card VI), and then his first experience with putting what he has learned into action; the *Chariot* (Card VII),

Surprisingly, both the *Lovers* and the *Chariot* archetypes have been degraded over time. (Several cards have been morphed to lose their original feminine/goddess associations.) If we go with the original interpretations as provided by Gareth Knight, in *Evoking the Goddess,* eleven of the original twenty-two Major Arcana cards showed feminine or goddess figures![31] This suggests that the earliest Tarot system may have been much more even-handed in its gender treatment than more recent versions would indicate. It also affords the possibility that it was a *pathworking* guide for women as well as men.

In particular, we note (with Mr. Knight's help) that in the earliest version, the *Lovers* card was depicted as the *Goddess of Love,* with pairs of lovers receiving her blessings.[32] Mr. Knight suggests that the procession of pairs of loving couples became too complex for the woodblock artisans of the time to reproduce easily. Thus, artisans simplified the image to a single pair of lovers, along with Venus, the Goddess of Love. Venus's son, Cupid (*Eros*), hovered overhead as the Goddess gave her blessing to the young couple. Over time, the interpretation of this card became muddled, so that in later woodblocks, the image became that of a young man who was undecided about two different women. These ladies later became known as "vice" and "virtue." However, if we go back to the earliest versions, we see that the card focuses on the single *Goddess of Love*, Venus, or to an "implicit" *Goddess of Love*, wherein a couple is being "brought into love" by the arrows of Venus's son, Cupid.[33]

Just as surprising, the *Chariot* has also been transformed over time. In current and recent historical depictions, the *Chariot* is shown as an armored warrior driving a triumphal chariot, drawn by two animals — variously shown as sphinxes/lions/horses. One is white, the other is black. In some cards, the *Charioteer* holds reins. In others, he directs through the power of his mind alone. He uses his will to direct all of who he is to achieve his goals.

In the earliest versions, though, the powerful, masculine *Charioteer* was originally female! Knight describes the original rendering as one where the *Charioteer* (as the *Winged Victory* goddess) was shown from the side, with the wings fully displayed.[34] When the woodblock artisans modified the original design, for simplicity in their reproductions, they turned the *Charioteer* so that the person appeared face-on. When this happened, the *Charioteer* (the original *Winged Victory* goddess) suffered a sex change. She became a masculine character![35]

One more note will help us position the first seven Major Arcana cards in time, space, and cultural context. We've just noted that *Winged Victory*, the seventh Major Arcana, shows the goddess in her beast-drawn chariot. In the second century BC, ancient historian Lucian wrote a detailed eyewitness account of his visit to Hieropolis, literally, the "sacred city." Hieropolis contained, at that time, the largest and most magnificent temple structure in the world. It was a city dedicated to the reigning goddess-religion. In short, it was the Vatican City of its time.

Lucian starts his narrative by noting that the Hieropolis temple followed both an architectural and spiritual pattern drawn from similar, and earlier, holy sanctuaries in Egypt."[36] Speaking of the Mother Goddess, or Moon Goddess, who was honored in this temple, Lucian noted that she was depicted in her chariot, drawn by two lions, symbolizing Earth.[37] The connection between *Winged Victory* and the Mother Goddess of the Hieropolis central temple is probably not coincidental!

Just as the original *Winged Victory* depiction references a very common, although ancient, archetypal concept, there is a similar connection for the *High Priestess*. The *High Priestess* (Major Arcana Card II) is shown sitting between two pillars. While the Rider-Waite depiction is itself of relatively recent provenance, the configuration of the two pillars flanking the *High Priestess* is not a new idea. This "twin pillar" symbolism has been well-known through ancient Judaic mystical studies, and has been essential to the Kabbalistic and later Qabalistic formulation.[38] It is also not a coincidence that these "twin pillars" are positioned with the Major Arcana's *High Priestess* (Card II). The Major Arcana depictions are replete with numerical symbolism in addition to pictorial. (Think of the "phallic symbolism" inherent in depicting a single pillar. The *Magician* (Card I) holds a rod in his upraised hand. The "twin pillars" of Card II are a form of "vaginal symbolism," and are associated with the first depiction of a female archetype.) With these as just two of many examples, we see that the concepts underlying the Major Arcana archetypes may greatly predate our earliest known Major Arcana card decks themselves. This suggests that even though our earliest extant Tarot decks come from about the 15th century,[39] the traditions and mystical studies underlying the first known decks may go back hundreds of years earlier.[40]

We see that masculine and feminine archetypes within the first six Major Arcana (the *Worldly Sequence*) are well-balanced; there are three of each gender. For the masculine, the archetypes are the *Magician* (ability to create through focused power of will), the *Emperor* (authority and order, power and control), and the *Hierophant* (induction into the mysteries; although well-structured and ordered; somewhat akin to entering a Masonic order).

For the three feminine archetypes, we begin with the *High Priestess*, an expression of wisdom and calm knowing. (This archetype is the one most closely related to *Sophia*,[41] or knowledge.) Next, and right after the *High Priestess*, we have the *Empress*; an expression of life and fecundity. Then, following the *Emperor* and the *Hierophant*, we have the *Goddess of Love*.

These three Major Arcana feminine archetypes map directly onto three of the four postulated basic female archetypes that were intuited by Antonia Wolff and later adopted by Dr. Grant. The *High Priestess* is an earlier form of what Dr. Grant called the *Madonna*, and what Antonia Wolff originally denoted as the *Medial*

Woman. The *Empress* is the *Mother* archetype; she is the source of life. And the *Courtesan*, a more limited version of the *Goddess of Love,* is represented as the sixth card. Our *Amazon* archetype is not one specific female-centric card. Rather; when we adopt her mode in our lives, we are really bringing into ourselves a combination of all three major masculine modes; *Emperor/Magician/Hierophant*.

Winged Victory, as the seventh and concluding card of this first sequence, represents bringing together opposing forces. These may include each of the basic archetypes presented in the previous six cards. She represents the first step towards *integration*.

Society has always supported our being in the *Mother* mode. Depending on culture and time, there has also been support for our being an *Amazon*. In fact, any time that we are dominantly in our cognitive and ego-states – when we are living in the context of our goals and ambitions, our day-planner and "to-do" lists – we are in our *Amazon* mode, or in a mixture of *Mother* and *Amazon*.

Let's give our attention to the remaining two feminine archetypes, and figure out where they are in our lives, and how we inhabit these roles. Of these two, the easiest one to understand is the *Courtesan* archetype. Dr. Grant explains this as being a "man's woman" – a woman who exists to please men, and who has created herself in the image of what they believe an attractive woman should be. In short, she is not so much herself, as she has become a projection of male desires and fantasies.[42]

Let's stay, just for a moment, with Dr. Grant's interpretation. At first glance, we might think that being a *Courtesan* is shallow. And even worse, we might worry that by developing the *Courtesan* aspect of ourselves, we would not be our "authentic self." Before we pass judgment on this, let's consider how some of the world's most luminous and intriguing women have used their *Courtesan* role as part of their complete being.

Our *Courtesan* role balances the "severity" of our *Amazon* mode. Throughout history, all great and powerful women have used their sexuality – their *allure* – as part of their seductive power. This power is not always applied to simple physical seduction, of course! Gaining ground in a business deal or cultivating international relations was more often their focus. Think of Cleopatra, of Catherine the Great, and of Queen Elizabeth I. Eleanor of Aquitaine was a complex and fascinating woman. Author Desmond Seward described a key to her personality as her "thirst for power."[43] However, she was also renowned for her beauty, generosity, intellect, and charm. Seward describes her as being worshipped by men when she was young, and for far more than beauty! Her intelligence, liveliness, and passion for life made her a compelling person. When she was older, her children revered her. Her court in Paris fostered not only intellectual advances – a resurgence of interest in classical scholarship and the mediaeval Latin lyric – but also sponsored the troubadours, with their love songs and their epic *chansons de geste*. Eleanor fully used at least three of her modes: *Amazon, Mother,* and (most notably) her *Courtesan*. It was the latter that helped her win the devotion of her husbands and sons.

Throughout history, our *Courtesan* mode has enabled us to break free of many social confines and expectations. The greatest real-life courtesans of history were brilliant as well as beautiful. With their charm, zest, and joie de vivre, they assembled salons which fostered the highest cultural moments of our greatest civilizations. Aspasia, in ancient Greece, created a salon in which genius flourished.[44] Similarly, intellectually powerful women sponsored salons in the 16th century in Italy,[45] and in the 17th and 18th century salons in Paris.[46] These stimulating environments encouraged and stoked the vital creative flames that spurred new ideas. Women, as *salonnieres*, not only made their own intellectual contributions, but created the environments in which the creativity of others could be expressed. What an exciting combination of *Amazon* (intellect and discernment), *Mother* (nurturing), and *Courtesan* (allure)! Men have been endlessly fascinated with such brilliant and scintillating women. Betsy Prioleau, in *Seductress*, tells us that men have found intelligence in women to be a strong aphrodisiac![47]

Delightful though this *Courtesan* aspect is, though, it does not seem to be complete. What causes us to seek a deeper interpretation of this archetype is our "gut sense" that a core archetype for women would *not* be identified simply in terms of masculine projections. This just doesn't make sense! So we look for a deeper meaning; one congruent with the singular integrity of each of the other archetypes.

Finding that the original design for the sixth Major Arcana card was the *Goddess of Love* is a major breakthrough, as we correlate the Major Arcana with the core feminine archetypes. We can now "pivot" our understanding of this *Courtesan* archetype. We go from something that is masculine-centric to an archetype that is whole and wholesome unto herself. We find that, in one form or another, the *Goddess of Love* has shown up in almost all cultures. She was denoted Aphrodite (ancient Greece), Venus (ancient Rome), and Hathor (ancient Egypt). So, instead of calling this our *Courtesan* archetype (which is too male-focused), or the *Goddess of Love* (which is too impersonal), let's reframe this as our *Hathor* archetype.

Hathor was the ancient Egyptian goddess of fertility, of beauty, and of love. She was seen as the embodiment of all those things which made life joyous and happy. She presided not only over love and romance, but also those arts that gave sweetness to life: perfume, alcohol, music, and dance.[48] In short, *Hathor* was the original party girl! If we were to meet Hathor today, she would absolutely be the person with whom we'd love to get together – or better yet, to *be* – when we want to have a good time!

This *Hathor* archetype is much more "unto herself" than the *Courtesan* concept. Iris Stewart, in *Sacred Woman, Sacred Dance*, cites a hymn to Hathor, describing how people ascribed "jubilation" to her, along with dance.[49]

At the same time, to give balance, let's also reframe our *Mother/Empress* archetype using the Egyptian goddess *Isis*, who was the goddess of fertility and nurturance.[50] (Yes, *Hathor* represented fertility also; but we have to make a distinction someplace.) *Isis* and *Hathor* complement each other, which is why we benefit from selecting two goddesses from a single culture.

Let's move on to the last role; the *Madonna*. This is the archetype that we've already associated with the *High Priestess*, and it represents the most quiet, internal state of our being. Our *Madonna* essence is like having a deep well inside our psyche; this is where we refresh ourselves, and when others come to us, they are also refreshed.

Our *Madonna* self is not necessarily anti-sexual. Please, let's not have any vestiges of "Holy Mother Church's" concept of "Mary, ever-virgin!" It is not so much that our *Madonna* is not sexual, it is simply that her essence is not as *emphatically* sexual as is our *Hathor/Love Goddess/Courtesan*, or even our *Isis/Empress/Mother*.

The *High Priestess* archetype embodies stillness and inner knowledge. She is a counterpoint to the "active," or *yang*, principle of the *Magician*. Because this archetype is so basic, we don't connect it with a goddess-personalization. Rather, Knight has associated the *High Priestess* with internal qualities, including wisdom at its "deepest level."[51]

It is this "still" essence that Joseph Campbell was referring to when he was interviewed by Maureen Murdock for *The Heroine's Journey*, saying that "'In the whole mythological tradition the woman is *there*'" [italics hers].[52] Campbell, like other insightful men, readily focused in on one of the most unique essences of feminine nature. However, he was too simplistic in his treatment. He disregarded both the complexity of our psyche and the complexity of our environment; he did not address the multiple demands on us and the various roles that we play. That is why his answer, if taken alone, is so unsatisfying. Nevertheless, we can acknowledge that he correctly identified the nature of deep feminine wisdom: our *High Priestess*.

Thus, our springboard for creating a real "woman's path" is to ***identify and integrate all our core archetypes***. This brings us back to the last Major Arcana card of the first seven-card sequence; *Winged Victory*. As we come to know each of our inner archetypes or essences, we can draw on just those aspects that we need to meet each situation. Thus, one sign that we have mastered the lessons of the first sequence is that we comfortably draw upon, and *integrate* (blend and use together), the various essences that we need for any purpose or situation.

From our jumping-off point of Wolff's and Grant's four feminine archetypes, we have refined our understanding of these modes by mapping them onto the symbolically-represented archetypes of the Tarot's Major Arcana. We have made a one-to-one matching of three of Wolff's archetypes with the first three feminine Major Arcana archetypes, and correlated Wolff's single masculine-oriented *Amazon* archetype with the remaining three masculine Major Arcana archetypes

Now, we are going to take one more step. Over the past several decades, the work of two exceptional researchers and innovators, Katharine Cook Briggs and Isabel Briggs Myers, has given us a widespread awareness about Personality Types. During the World War II, they extended Carl Jung's foundational Psychological Types[53] by developing a questionnaire that led to type-profiling. Based on Jung's original work defining the Psychological Types, these Myers-Briggs Type Inventory (MBTI) profiles came to be known as Personality Types.[54] The fundamental components of the Personality Types were four "continuous" dimensions: Extrovert/Introvert, Sensing/iNtuition, Thinking/Feeling, and Judging/Perceiving.[55] There are a total of sixteen different possible "combinations" of these four dimensions.[56] We have already related our four feminine modes to the six core human archetypes within the Major Arcana. Clearly, we're not going to get a one-to-one match with the Jungian-based Personality Types! Even so, we can get some correlations.

The value of these correlations is that the MBTI is already well-known, and many of us both know our own Type and are becoming increasingly adept at "typing" our intimate partners, our children, and our colleagues, bosses, and clients. This knowledge gives us a strong set of "tools" for understanding ourselves and others, and for framing communications. So, if we can connect our six Major Arcana archetypes to the MBTI, we have yet one more context for understanding ourselves, especially as we seek to integrate the full spectrum of who we are into our daily experience. We are using the Major Arcana as our base, because it gives us the three core masculine archetypes as well as the three core feminine ones; we need all six to make the correlation with Jung's Psychological Types and their current incarnation as Personality Types. This means that instead of "typing" our inner *Amazon*, we note that our *Amazon* refers to three distinct masculine archetypes, and we'll correlate these with the Jungian Types.

We begin by making two great simplifications. For purposes of this work, we will ignore the Extrovert/Introvert distinction, even though it is important. We will also identify the "Judging" (come-to-closure) dimension with the masculine archetypes, and the "Perceiving" (open-ended) dimension with the feminine. (This is not inappropriate as a broad distinction; men are more often Sensing/Judging types, or SJs, than are women.)

Focusing on the three feminine archetypes of the Major Arcana, we identify three candidate matches to the Jungian Types, giving us:

➤ *Isis/Empress/Mother*: iNtuition/Feeling (NF),

➤ *Hathor/Love-Goddess*: Sensing/Feeling (SF), and

➤ *High Priestess*: iNtuition/Thinking (NT).

To expand on this: we associate our *Isis/Mother/Empress* archetype with the Jungian iNtuition/Feeling (NF) dimensions; this archetype is the one most sensitive to the feel-good neurohormones associated with caretaking and bonding. In this mode, we are noticeably Perceiving; open-ended and possibility-oriented. We are iNtuitive about caring for others, and we are very attuned to Feelings. We can be Extroverted or Introverted; ENFP or INFP (Extroverted or Introverted iNtuition/Feeling/Perceiving).

We connect our *Hathor/Love-Goddess/Courtesan* archetype with the Sensing/Feeling (SF) dimensions. In our *Hathor* mode, we are again Perceiving; open to various possibilities. We are attuned to fun and pleasure in the world around us; we are Sensing. We are oriented toward our Feelings, using them as a guide to what will please us the most. We may be Extroverted or Introverted. It is interesting that MBTI specialists most often describe the ESFP (Extroverted/Sensing/Feeling/Perceiving) Psychological Type as "playful." Could anything possibly be more descriptive of our *Hathor*?

Finally, we connect our *High Priestess* with the iNtuition/Thinking (NT) dimensional combination. In the *High Priestess* state, we are in our quiet mode. When we are in this state, we notice and attend to an ever-widening set of possibilities; this is definitely a Perceiving, not a Judging, state. This state is very internal, so let us say that it is more often Introverted rather than Extroverted. We know that this state is very iNtuitive, rather than Sensing-specific. Finally, though this is not a state in which we do "cognitive" thinking, it is a state in which we are definitely not focused on relationships. Imagine someone who is a nun in a monastic order as an "idealization" of this state. We enter our *High Priestess* through prayer, contemplation, meditation, or tasks that allow our minds to disconnect and simply be in a "state of awareness," rather than focused on problem-solving or "doing."

We have not assigned the Perceiving Sensing/Thinking (ST) type-combination. The Perceiving ST combinations would be the Extroverted and Introverted STPs (ESTP and ISTP). According to MBTI expert David Keirsey, a psychologist who encapsulated the sixteen Types into four Temperaments, these ESTP/ISTP Types are promoters and crafters; modes oriented towards tangible production.[57]

It is possible that these two modes combine to form a "rest" state for women; we may be in this state when we do gardening or crafts, or when we tend house.

This state may be nurturing for us; it can also be a "transition state" by which we enter other modes. I personally find that the meditative state produced by hand-sewing, gardening, or even cleaning helps to induce my *High Priestess* mode. The directive, "Wax on, wax off," from the original movie, *The Karate Kid*, illustrates the value of simple, repetitive motions in leading us to a calm mind.

To complete our matching between the Major Arcana and the Jungian Types, we turn our attention to the three masculine archetypes. Just as we assigned the Perceiving mode to the feminine archetypes, we will assign the complementary Judging mode (coming to closure; desiring completion) to the three masculine ones. A reasonable association between the masculine archetypes and the MBTI Types is:

> ➤ *Magician*: iNtuition/Thinking (NT),
>
> ➤ *Emperor*: Sensing/Thinking (ST), and
>
> ➤ *Hierophant*: iNtuition/Feeling (NF).

To expand on the correlations for the masculine archetypes: The *Magician* mode is very oriented to creating new things in the world, but can be internally or externally-oriented in how these creations are made. (This is a very "active" archetype and is a complement to the *High Priestess*.) The Magician is iNtuitive and a Thinker (NT), and wants to make his envisioning "real" in the world; he wants to come to closure. He is a Judging type. He can be Introverted or Extroverted (INTJ or ENTJ). The *Magician* is the company founder, or the scientific or technical "brains" behind a company's core inventions and intellectual property. He is also the Chairman of the Board, with a gift for strategic, visionary thinking.

The *Emperor* likes to build structures and empires; he believes in order. He deals with real, tangible things more than he deals with "visions" for what he'd like to create; he is more Sensing than iNtuiting. As with the *Magician*, he is Judging, and can be Introverted or Extroverted (ISTJ or ESTJ). According to Keirsey, ESTJs are natural leaders and guardians, and ISTJs are upholders of law, duty, and order. A company's CEO, CFO, and COO are all likely to have the *Emperor* as their dominant mode-of-being. Project managers typically are in *Emperor* mode. Even if we personally are not dominantly *Emperor*-types, we may enter into an *Emperor* mode when we do our taxes, set a meeting agenda, or coordinate our children's activity schedules. Our *Emperor* mode, more than any other, thrives on "to-do" lists, and loves to check off completed tasks!

The *Hierophant* coaches, mentors, and teaches others about how to live and thrive within a known order. His ability to be iNtuitive about people and their dynamics makes him ideal for working within complex social structures. He is people-focused, and more Feeling than Thinking. As with the *Magician* and the *Emperor*, he is also Judging (an NFJ), and can be Introverted or Extroverted (INFJ or ENFJ). In Keirsey's observations, ENFJs are often teachers, and INFJs are natural counselors.

As with the assignment of the three core feminine Major Arcana archetypes to the Jungian ones, we still have an unused Type combination; the Introverted and Extroverted Sensing/Feeling (SF) types that are also Judging (the ESFJs and ISFJs). Keirsey described these persons as closure-oriented care-givers and nurturers. We would connect these Types more with the with the *Hierophant* archetype than any other. This is the most "feminine" (caring-oriented) of the Judging Types. We may personally align this mode as supporting our inner *Isis* or our *Hierophant*.

As women, many of us have overworked the *Amazon* aspects of our being. In doing this, we have combined one or more of the masculine archetypes – *Magician*, *Emperor*, and *Hierophant* – to create our own inner *Amazon*. Even though we may have a strong *Mother* role, we can now see that the *Mothering*-aspects that relate to teaching people (who may be our children) how to live and work "within the system" are really picking up on a masculine archetype, the *Hierophant*. Thus, many of our mothering activities are really more within our *Amazon-Hierophant* realm, and not within the open-ended, feeling-oriented archetypal *Isis/Empress/Mother*. For example, when we teach our children, "Look left, then right, then left again, and now we'll cross the road," we are acting within the Judging mode; we are seeking closure on a behavior that we want to teach our children. This makes us – when in that mode – more *Hierophant* than *Isis*. On the other hand, when we are playing with our children, or singing to them, or telling them a story, we are more likely to be in *Isis* mode. We women may transition between modes so readily that we don't always notice when we are making a shift!

We've now simplified (for our purposes) the sixteen Jungian Types to eight, and correlated six of these remaining combined Types with the six Major Arcana archetypes. Through the first six Major Arcana (archetypes I – VI), we then link back to the four "feminine" archetypes originally envisioned by Antonia Wolfe.

This brings us back to the question of why we would use the Major Arcana in the first place. The rationale may be more evident if we understand why the Major Arcana would have been invented. Specifically, we can get some insight if we understand how and why the Major Arcana's developers may have made their selections. At first, we might think that they had to winnow from a huge range of possible choices down to the crucial six (three masculine, three feminine) archetypes that became the first Major Arcana sequence.

If we envision them picking and choosing from among the huge pantheon of god and goddess figures available, the process would seem potentially a bit hit-or-miss. Earlier cultures (Egyptian, Indian, and others prior to them) were replete with a variety of gods and goddesses, each of whom offered a unique personality "niche." How would the original Major Arcana developers know that they were selecting, from among all possible options, those archetypes that most substantially reflected the needed components in a grown person's psyche?

If, however, we think of the Major Arcana's developers as building out both the Major and Minor Arcana from a very formal symbol system, drawn from the Qabalah, then we arrive at a different interpretation altogether.[58] The Minor Arcana elements correspond to suites in our playing cards today. The ten numbered cards and four "face cards" of the four Minor Arcana "suites" have devolved to give us the ten numbered cards and four "face cards" within each suit of our card decks today. However, the ten numbers relate historically to the "centers" (Sephiroths) of the Qabalistic "Tree of Life." Each of these "centers" corresponds to an aspect of God, or an "emanation" of divine energy.

According to Qabalistic (and earlier Judaic Kabbalistic) teachings, there are twenty-two defined "pathways" connecting the various centers. (Clearly, not all centers connect to each other.) Each Major Arcana card corresponds to a distinct "pathway." Part of the Qabalistic teaching is that a person can advance in their level of consciousness by traversing between the different "centers." To do so, they must follow the identified "pathways" in an inner journey of conscious experience.

The fact that there are twenty-two Major Arcana cards, twenty-two letters in the Hebrew alphabet, and twenty-two identified "pathways" between the Tree of Life "centers" is not a coincidence; this linkage between the Hebrew alphabet letters, the Qabalistic "pathways," and the Major Arcana is well known in esoteric circles. Thus, one reasonable possibility is that both the Major and Minor Arcana were invented as tools for use in the "Mystery Schools" to teach acolytes about their life-journeys.[59]

The Tarot, especially the Major Arcana system, was thus possibly a condensed form of curriculum. Further, because it was pictorial in nature, we can think of it as something like an ancient "Powerpoint™ deck"[60] capturing key curricula elements. While the earliest known Tarot decks were circulated in the fifteenth century, the connection to Qabalistic history suggests that they may have a much earlier provenance. There is reasonable evidence suggesting that the Qabalah (in the form of the Judaic Kabbalah) was known prior to the time of Christ.[61]

It is possible that in the "Mystery Schools" of earlier times, acolytes (think "graduate students") would be shown, not simply a Major Arcana card, but a life-sized depiction. This could have been a living vignette, or perhaps even an enacted scenario. Minimally, there would have been a grand-scale painting. I am inclined to think that the "revelation" to the acolytes, for each step, would have been as dramatic as possible, in order to achieve maximal emotional impact. At the appropriate times, with full ritual, the priests and priestesses (think "graduate faculty") would bring acolytes to the next scenario. "This is what you'll be studying next," would be the message of each presentation.

Thus, just as we store our Christmas decorations – our "Jesus, Mary, and Joseph in the stable" manger scenes, and our life-sized Santa and his reindeer – our forebears possibly had closets where they tucked away the costumes and accoutrements with which a faculty member (or member of the relevant priest or priestess order) would "enact a role."

If this were the case, then the Tarot's Major Arcana became a "shorthand notation" for the set of full, ritually-ensconced archetypal presentations. They also became a way that researchers could discuss various aspects with each other, or travel with a "pocket version" to another school. In addition, they also would have served as (essentially) stage manager's directions. All the important elements of each card would be presented, as much as stagecraft could allow, for each appropriate occasion.

Once again, we turn our attention back to the Jungian Types, and take note of how work in this area is evolving. To get a sense of perspective, let's first briefly take a look at the history of Psychological Types. Although various theories of Psychological Types go far back in time (to Hippocrates in 370 BC, and to Galen in 190 AD),[62] Jung introduced his crucial Extroversion/Introversion distinction in 1921. However, the idea of distinct Types was largely banished during the era of behavior psychology. The importance of Types was only brought back into the mainstream by the work of Isabel Myers, who worked with her mother, Kathryn Briggs, to develop the Myers-Briggs Type Inventory (MBTI). This did not get widespread adoption until the latter half of the 1900's. Myers and Briggs used statistical analyses to back up their questionnaire and its results. The kinds of statistical methods available at the time caused them to "linearize" their Types. It also resulted in what seemed to be a sort of permanent "Typing." The earliest MBTI work suggested that a person was more-or-less confined to one of the sixteen specific Types throughout his or her life.[63]

However, as suggested by MBTI specialists Drs. Jacqueline Magness and Elizabeth Roslewicz, the apparent simplicity indicated by MBTI type-profiling does not fully convey the richness of Jung's perspective. Rather, his theory indicates that "we are born with specific preferences and keep those preferences throughout life. As one matures, however, he/she can develop more skill using non-preferences, so MBTI scores may reflect that maturation. Jung believed, though, that we kept the same preferences throughout life."[64] Jung's work indicates that we have preferences, but are not rigidly typed.[65] Newer interpretations are much more in line with Jung's idea that people *develop their personalities* over time.[66]

We get a similar insight – that personalities develop over time – by studying the first seven Major Arcana. They suggest that our first major adult life-journey is to *integrate* across the archetypes. In essence, the life-task of an adult woman is one of integration, wholeness, and completeness. This is in contrast to the simpler

Heroine's Quest done by a young woman. Since *integration* is often an ongoing process, and not a single *quest journey*, I refer to this as *pathworking*.

We often spend our early adult years developing both our *Amazon* and our *Isis/Mother* roles. By the time that we are in our forties or fifties, these roles consume less of our attention. We ask ourselves: What next? (Or, as one friend has put it: What now?)

Our life-journey is now to *integrate* in our other core feminine archetypes. Thus, to complete this life-stage, our tasks are to know and bring into our lives both our *Hathor* essence (Sensing/Feeling/Perceiving) and our *High Priestess* qualities (iNtuition/Thinking/Perceiving), and balance these with our *Amazon* and *Isis* modes. This may be something of a challenge.

We can create our transitions, and we can even do *integration*. However, we need some practical methods. The remainder of this book focuses on these pragmatics.

PERSONAL PATHWORKING:

1. Return to your first exercise from *Chapter 2*, noting when you've been in different modes. Now, with greater clarity, how do you spend your time? Use your day-planner to verify how much time you spend in each.

2. Have you taken an MBTI questionnaire? If so, what Type are you? Does this match to how you sense you connect most with the different archetypes? (There are various online versions available; find one that seems to work for you.)

3. What happens when you attempt to "switch" modes, especially to your *Hathor* or *High Priestess*? Do you encounter some internal resistance? (I still do!)

4. Consider the women whom you most respect; women whom you'd most like to emulate. How do they integrate the various modes in their lives? (Or, have they sacrificed – or seem to have sacrificed – one or more modes for the sake of "fitting in" to cultural norms?) How do you feel about this? Are there any women whom you know who seem to have created some kind of balance or integration? Can you talk with them about their personal journey?

CHAPTER 8:
THE ESSENCE OF STILLNESS

IMAGINE THIS: YOU HAVE BEEN selected, from among all the women in your city, to be brought into the ruler's harem. You enter this harem along with hundreds, possibly thousands, of other young women; all as lovely and fresh and nubile as you. And from this select group, you are chosen. You are "the one." The king prefers you to all the others.

You are given the place of honor in the harem, and a title. Servants are at your beck and call. The king gifts you with jewels and precious baubles. Your wardrobe dazzles your mind and delights your eye. Your living quarters are swathed with silk, and adorned with precious tapestries and delicate inlaid mosaics. Other women curry your favor.

Even more than this, you have had the heady, intoxicating thrill of making love with the most powerful man in the world, and knowing that he is besotted with you. Without question, you have become "the chosen one."

Now dwell on this scenario just a little bit more, and add in the "reality factors." You were pulled from family, friends, and home when you were selected for the harem. What friends you made since your entry are distanced from you now; your high position precludes intimacy. Many of the girls to whom you opened your heart earlier have succumbed to harem intrigues. You've learned to keep your heart and your voice to yourself.

You don't taste a morsel of food, or drink a sip of juice, unless it has been tested and approved by your poison taster. This is not a joke; you've seen too many women perish in this manner. (Your children are not immune to assassination attempts, either. What more expedient way for an ambitious woman to remove a rival to her own son's prospects?) The harem is a pressure cooker of political intrigue; the women are often both brilliant and shrewd. Every word you say — every conversation, each glance — is endlessly dissected.[1]

Although you exchange messages every day, you have not seen a male member of your family in years. It is simply not allowed. There are many freedoms and simple pleasures that are now forever denied to you. You will never again walk to the market to buy fresh figs when they are in season. You are a prisoner in a gilded cage. There is no way out, and there never will be.

The only males that you see are either children or are castrated, or — every so often — the royal lord himself. But even though you still occupy the "place of honor," you are not called to the king's bed as often as you once were. Other favorites have been chosen, discarded, and new ones have been found, in an endless cycle since you became the "chosen one." And even though your position is formally secure, you see the measuring, aspiring looks of the newcomers. You see the former favorites, and the hope-to-be's, the clique leaders and the gossip mongers, all watching you out of the corners of their eyes; always measuring, always waiting.

So you hold your head high, and smile graciously at every one, and say a kind word when appropriate. By now you've learned, the hard way, that any outrage, any lapse — even a momentary failure to act kindly — can cause a ripple with major repercussions. The smallest look or gesture impacts lives.

And once a month, every month, you all go through it together. Everyone has cravings at the same time. Everyone is on the verge of a screaming, crying tantrum. Fights break out, women are disciplined, small things are magnified out of proportion, and you would give anything, absolutely anything, to run free. But there is no escape. So you hold your head high and smile graciously.

One of the worst things, in this situation, is the enforced passivity. Whether queen or slave, the title makes no difference, if we do not have control over our own lives. Yet it was in just this kind of situation that Queen Esther, of biblical fame, was able to save the Jewish people.[2]

How did she manage to go from village life to queen? The Bible is remarkably obscure on this point, except to say that "she found favor." (Well, wouldn't we all like to know *how*?) Yet we *do* know that at the time that she saved her people, she took an enormous risk. She entered into King Ahasuerus's presence without being specifically invited to see him. This was an offense punishable by instant death, unless he chose to grant clemency. Fortunately for her, and for her people, he did. But she had no way of knowing that as she walked into the throne room.

All that she knew, as she walked down the long expanse towards the king, was that she had no other choice. Her people were slated for near-term destruction. She could not rely on any regular "pillow talk" with the king; she had not been invited to see him for over thirty days. She still had her official place and title in the harem; she was still queen. But she was no longer favored with regular summoning to the royal bedchamber.

Can you imagine how scared she must have been, walking alone down that long aisle towards the throne? The king had deposed his former wife for an act of disobedience – what if he had decided to be sterner in the future? At any moment, a glance from the king to his executioner would have meant sudden death. She had no way of knowing how the king felt about her; if he was just dallying with a temporary fancy, or if he was truly bored with her and simply didn't care anymore. Thirty days is a long time to wait for the summons to the royal chambers!

Scheherazade's story has similarities.[3] She volunteered to go to the king's chambers, knowing he was in the habit of bedding a virgin each night and having her beheaded the next morning! Right or wrong, he was absolute monarch, and his word was law. To stop the cycle, Scheherazade had persuaded her uncle, the Grand Vizier, to allow her to be the king's next selection.

Scheherazade, who was as intelligent and courageous as she was beautiful, had a plan. She insisted that her sister accompany her to the king's chambers, telling the king that for years, she had told her sister a story each night. After their lovemaking, she had her sister called in, and began telling her sister that evening's story.

The king was intrigued, and when the cock crowed just before the high point of the story, he granted her a day's reprieve. She would conclude her tale the next evening. They repeated this cycle for another one thousand nights. At the end, the king relinquished his intention of executing the young woman who was his lover, and similarly granted life to whomever else he would bring to his bed. Scheherazade's courage, and her ability to draw out the story, was what saved a generation of women in her kingdom.

Esther employed a similar tactic. When the king extended his scepter to her, granting her life, she did not immediately ask him for what she wanted. No, she invited him (and his advisor — the one who had schemed against her people) to dinner. At dinner that night, she invited him to dinner again the next night. And then, she invited him to dinner once again.

The king knew that she had something on her mind. Clearly, she did not put her life at risk in order to invite him and his advisor over for a little dinner party. But she drew out the dramatic tension of her request.

Scheherazade similarly drew on dramatic tension. Night after night, pitching each story to reach its climax just before dawn, she built the drama and expectation. Once again, her king knew that this was happening. Yet he never said, "Hurry up, get to the end, so I can have you executed!"

No. He wanted the tension, the interest, the dramatic experience to unfold. He wanted to be brought to a point of arousal; not so much sexually (that was easy), but intellectually. He was curious. He *wanted* to be kept waiting.

How did Esther and Scheherazade each cultivate the personal discipline that let them carry through these challenges? This self-discipline kept Esther from falling apart in the midst of harem intrigues, and from blurting out a bald and panicked request when she first saw the king. This same self-discipline allowed Scheherazade to artfully time each story, so that the most essential part would come just as dawn arrived. If we have ever had a hard time telling a joke at a dinner party, the social gaffe of our missing a punch line is nothing compared to the possibility of losing a storyline focus, with the executioner just outside the door!

Of these two women, Scheherazade is fictional, and Esther's story is apocryphal. But each of these two women — whether "real" or not — has as much power within our psyche as any other woman's story. Esther and Scheherazade had more than an ability to "keep it together" under stress. They each had not only personal discipline and emotional self-control, but also spiritual depth.

At their very core, in each of these two women, we see the *essence of stillness*.

Esther had this. She was already deep into her spiritual practice, because when the challenge arose, she didn't fuss or flail. She didn't go into emotional spasms, or consult with her advisors. Instead, she meditated, fasted, and prayed. (According to the story, she not only went without food for three days, but without water as well! This pushed her to the limits of human endurance.)

In crisis, we women will do what we've trained ourselves to do. We will act as we have trained ourselves to act. We will behave as we have trained ourselves to behave. We use the "little things" in life to train ourselves for the big ones. This is why we have fire drills. This is why we have "dress rehearsals" before any show.

One of my gentlemen friends tells me of the time a corporate crisis hit. The call came at 3AM, and within hours he was boarding the corporate jet. But he didn't have to "make plans" or "figure out" how to deal with the situation. As Corporate Vice President, he had already built a "risk mitigation plan" to describe how the company would deal with all sorts of crises. This was a crisis; he acted as he had trained himself (and his company) to do.

When we deal with a predefined challenge, one that fits into our "contingency plans," we know what to do. However, most of life is not as clear-cut or so well-defined. Often, we encounter challenges that we have never anticipated. Then, we have two basic choices. We can flail and thrash about, calling up all of our friends and creating drama. Or, we can opt for *stillness*. By becoming quiet within, we allow the answers to emerge. At the very least, the inner peace that allows us to deal with a situation will manifest itself.

Esther opted for *stillness*, along with fasting and prayer, when she had to decide how she would respond to the annihilation threat to her people. Then, once her answer emerged, she took action. The situation was similar for Scheherazade. We don't see the *stillness* part of her life, while she was preparing. We don't observe her as she took the situation into her heart; as she felt the trauma of the many young women who knew that they were going to their certain death. We see her only as she's found the solution. She's built on her natural gifts of imagination and story-telling. She's spent years researching, building up a mental "treasure trove." And she's practiced; telling stories to her younger sister every single day. By the time that she convinced her father, the Grand Vizier, to allow her to be presented to the king, she was ready.

She had to be. She had to come up with a different (yet very intriguing) story; every single night. She had to get the character development, the setting, the plot intricacies, and the "interest factor" (along with the timing) precisely right; every single time. There was no let-up; no reprieve. There were no "nights off." And the executioner was always waiting.

Could any of us have done anything like Scheherazade's feat, without a strong spiritual core? Remember, if she failed, not only would she die, but her sister as well (after being deflowered by the king), and the endless progression of sacrificing other young women would resume. So night after night, she had to be witty and charming, light and amusing, and totally present in the moment. If she let doubt, confusion, or worries interfere, all was immediately lost!

The means by which we deal with not only big life crises, but a whole range of challenges, is to is to develop our spiritual core. This includes challenges that pragmatically arise as we cultivate our *High Priestess* life-integration. Our solution, in advance of these challenges arising, is to *practice stillness in our souls*. Then our "outer expression," whether our inner energy is fully evoked or carefully subdued and banked, becomes powerful and effective. This is because our "outer expression" resonates against a backdrop of stillness.

Esoteric Judaic studies revere the feminine presence of God as *Shekhinah*.[4] This was carried into the Gnostic tradition of Sophia.[5] While revering the feminine aspect of God has been devastating to many (the annihilation of the Cathars is one example, the Inquisition which followed is yet another),[6] honoring Mother God is still common throughout the world,[7] and is the oldest form of religion within our European-based culture.[8] Nevertheless, in our Judeo/Christian/Muslim cultures, we have only limited access to a tradition honoring the *Divine Feminine*. And thus, we are rarely brought into the stillness that comes through knowing Her.

Our *High Priestess/Madonna*-self is perhaps the most important aspect of our psyche, because it is through this aspect that we become quiet and centered. As we come into ourselves, and gain the ability to be present inside ourselves, without always thinking or reacting, we develop the core from which our attractiveness emerges. This is an extension of the "attraction dynamic" that has become so well-publicized lately. This is why we study the "essence of stillness" first, before we dive into cultivating our juicy *Hathor* natures!

Many years ago, I began using Oriental dance as a means to integrate the four feminine archetypes. It was relatively easy to find lots of *Hathor/Courtesan* examples in Oriental dance. (Not always well done, but at least there were many attempts.) However, it was years before I found my first experience of the *High Priestess/Madonna* archetype in this dance form.

One teacher who influenced me here is regarded, world-wide, as one of the greatest masters in Oriental dance. I've been able to study with her for nearly twenty years. Elena Lentini has always embodied a quality of inner stillness.

Over the years, I made every effort to study with her, despite the fact that she lived in New York, and I lived in various towns and cities that were, at best, hours away. A turning point came when she invited me to participate (albeit in a very minor role) in a dance production. I worked with her instructions, practiced diligently at home, sent her videos of my work for her review, and flew to her city in time for the single show.

The performance was set in an old synagogue; a crumbling remnant of what had once been an extraordinary space that was now slated for destruction. Its only use was as an occasional rental hall for unusual arts productions.

The two opposing interior walls, to the left and the right of the seating area, were divided into little alcoves, heavily decorated with deep carvings. As a prelude to the main choreographies, each of these alcoves contained a dancer who held "poses." Slowly, ever so slowly, each dancer would shift from one pose to another. We (the corps of dancers who created these "freeze-frame" images) represented *odalisques*; a French expression for the pleasure women of the harem.

Elena's dance, the last work in the show, built on the dynamic tension that had evolved through a succession of dances by her corps. She capitalized on this tension. For the first few minutes, she did nothing. *Absolutely nothing.* She was simply a meditative presence on the stage.

Slowly, she began to move. Slowly, she worked into a dance of great exuberance and passion. But – and this was *the essence of her dance* – she began from a place of stillness.

Have you ever studied with a great teacher, and heard them say the same thing time and time again, and yet not heard them? All of a sudden, you "hear" what that teacher is saying on a particular topic. And then you realize that they've been saying the same words for years, but up until that moment you simply weren't ready to hear what they had to say.

That is what had happened to me. I had been hearing Elena speak about stillness for years. I had flown to her city, and participated in a performance where the most powerful aspect was those few moments of stillness, and I still had not gotten the lesson. It wasn't until a few years later that I truly heard what she had to say.

I was in New York again, this time for a week-long intensive class with her. She taught us movement patterns, techniques, choreographies, and zill (metal finger cymbal) rhythms. Two of the choreographies stood out in my mind, not just because they were beautiful (they were), but because each of them was preceded by a period of meditative "presencing." In each case, the music had a long prelude. Elena's instructions were to simply *be there*, and be *present*. Finally, during this experience, I began to "get it" about stillness in dance. Then, I remembered that she had been teaching this for years.

When I got home, I began to look for stillness in other ways within the dance. I began to search for a sense of stillness between the movements, much like a traditional Japanese painting is composed of the bare minimum of brush strokes on paper. I also began to seek a greater quality of stillness in my life.

I found that this discipline was not only valuable, it was necessary. The opportunity to study with Elena, and to put into practice what she taught me, came in the midst of a very turbulent and stressful transition. This continued for over a year after I had the "stillness" insight. I was attempting to strike out as an entrepreneur, and resources were tight. I would wake up every morning in a state of panic, and that panic would continue all day, for weeks on end. It would diminish only when I worked on a specific, focused task.

Over time, my entrepreneurial (*Amazon*) role began to take shape. I built a business that rose and then fell; due to a combination of events and influences. During this time, I had new insights in solving tough technical challenges. My colleagues and I built a product based on one of my inventions, although we were not able to take it to market. Then I started a new company, under almost the same circumstances as the first.

The challenge of creating yet another business venture was enormous. At the same time, there were big transitions in other areas of my life. My lover, seeing that I was in some distress, discretely distanced himself. In the midst of these changes, I was still attempting to bring my new inventions into existence, as well as manage an ongoing crisis of pure, financial survival.

My "wise-woman" friend, Kathy Carroll, guided me through this time, as she had during the first round. "Seek Source," she counseled. "Source, or God, provides. It is not one single person, or one product, or one situation [that provides or cares for us]. Source can provide for you through many channels." She went on to say, "We live within pure, positive Source energy – but we always interpret it. Our mind wants to keep us on the "outer." Our *pain-bodies* [a term created by Eckhart Tolle[9] to describe "an accumulation of old emotional pain"] cause us to distort what we see and experience. But going back to Source is everything." Kathy encouraged me to practice gratitude for the many ways in which Source did continue providing for me.

In starting the next company, I used my *Amazon* archetype to envision a new business, write business plans, call and set meetings with both new and known people, and start developing a new technology base. I used my *Isis/Mother* role in nurturing others, realizing that we were all human, and all of us had challenges, no matter what was going on in our professional lives. I used my *Hathor/Courtesan* aspect, being charming and attending fully to the interests of others. But it was the *High Priestess/Madonna* archetype that gave me peace and solace.

PERSONAL PATHWORKING:

1. How do you connect, right now, with your inner *Hathor*? With your inner *High Priestess*? As you journal, notice those things that work best for you – do you need connection with family or friends, or with nature, or with your pets? Do you need to do something artistic and creative, or nurturing? When you access your *Hathor* mode, do you like to dance or go to a party, or do you prefer soaking in a hot tub while reading a book? *Both* are good, although they are different ways of being in this mode!

2. Can you invoke your *Isis/Mother* mode to discern whether you need a bit more *Hathor* and/or *High Priestess* time? That is, can you turn your nurturing *Isis* aspect towards nurturing *yourself*? Can you invoke your *Amazon* mode, right now, to pull out your day-planner and schedule both *Hathor* and *High Priestess* time?

3. Explore what other women have done to create time-away. For example, read May Sarton's *Journal of a Solitude*[10] and Joan Anderson's *Year by the Sea*.[11] See what they have offered that you can interpret in small (perhaps weekend-size) doses.[12]

4. Consider the possibility of going on a retreat. This may be at a yoga ashram, an art or dance camp, or an honest-to-God(dess) retreat, at a real retreat center. (Not all retreats, even those hosted by religious orders, are necessarily "religious-dogmatic." Many are designed for persons of diverse beliefs and faiths. I've gone to the Dominican Retreat House in Northern Virginia[13] and had wonderful experiences.) Find something that is simpatico with your needs and close to where you live. If you can't afford a formal "retreat," see if a friend will let you use her spare apartment, guest room, art studio – whatever is available – for a weekend. Get books from the library, gather food and supplies, and "do it yourself."

---

5. Explore the world of sacred dance. Read Iris Stewart's *Sacred Woman, Sacred Dance*.[14] Do an online search for dance performances in your area that might fit this interpretation; they may be classical Indian dance, liturgical dance, or women's "dance circles." Keep talking with your friends, find and email the teachers at various dance schools, and your best sources will come up!

6. See if you can add "moments of stillness" to your everyday life. Perhaps the simple act of making a cup of tea can become a moment in which you can center yourself and breathe deeply.

PART III:
RIGHT HERE, RIGHT NOW

⚬⚬

CHAPTER 9:
THE ART OF VENUS

I HAD JUST FINISHED GIVING a project briefing to over a dozen officers from the U.S. Marine Corps. It wasn't just me alone, of course. On this trip, I was accompanied by Rocky, the vice-president from the company where I worked. Rocky was gregarious, with a warm, hearty laugh and a gorgeously muscular body that he kept up with weight lifting and cardio workouts. As a former U.S. Navy Navigator/Bombardier, he had flown many missions that had him launching from and returning to a carrier deck. Rocky had great leadership ability, a superb sense of humor, and cared about the people on his team.

The two of us, with some others, had teamed up on a new project. We had done an outstanding job, and we knew it. By the time we were through with the briefing, the Marines knew it as well. It was time to relax and unwind. The officers had listened carefully, despite having this briefing added to their already demanding day. They had given us positive feedback, and told us what we could do to help them. The day's work, for all of us, was done. Now, they were forming little groups, and making plans for the evening. The mood was good, the time was right.

I took off my suit jacket and laid it gently over the side of a chair. Instead of a blouse, I was wearing a form-fitting ribbed silk sweater underneath. It was dark aubergine, matching my suit, hose, and shoes, which were (of course) the highest heels that I could walk in without falling over. Very slowly and deliberately, I took the pins out of my hair and shook it loose. Being the superbly disciplined creatures that they were, the Marines pretended not to notice. Being the superbly disciplined creature that I was, as well as a dedicated tease, I pretended not to notice them pretending not to notice me. Ah, erotic power! Such a wonderful thing!

I haven't always been able to do this. For me, this has been a learned skill – one that I began to develop well after I got my chemistry Ph.D. A couple years after getting the degree, and having had my head in a study cubicle for many years, I realized that I didn't know the first thing about men – but that I wanted to learn!

My early self-image of *not* being attractive gave me even more motivation to learn. As a child, I would walk by the sorority houses near the university campus; I would look at the pretty coeds sunning themselves on warm spring days, and think to myself, "I will never be like them." To hide from the pain, I took refuge in being intellectual. On the night of my high school's junior prom, I stayed home, and spent the evening reading a book on tensor mechanics.

Since then, I've gone from geek to gorgeous. This has been more than a physical transformation. It has even been more than a life-style change. Over the past dozen years, I have "re-created" myself from the inside out, and am now very different from where I was many years ago. In short, I've learned to develop my *Hathor* essence!

Earlier, when I was still exclusively in my *Amazon* mode, this dream seemed totally unrealistic and out of reach. Now, it's my reality. It's not just that the quality of the men in my life has improved. I've also increased my ability to attract all sorts of things: people, events, even life situations. In short, I've become an *attractor.*

If this is something that I can do, then you can do this as well. I've seen many other women do this; women with different personalities, different figures, different charms. Over the years, I've realized that if any woman wants to become attractive (in the very literal meaning of the word), so that she is *attracting* into her life whatever she desires, then she can.

This is not just a matter of working out, doing a physical makeover, and shopping for some new clothes. Of course, there's nothing wrong with these things. Most of us, if we are serious about developing our inner *Hathor,* will do something of this nature. But what I'm talking about is much more. It is more than self-confidence, more than simply looking great and feeling great. It is a matter of creating a new reality, and creating ourselves anew within that reality.

This is a vital part of our *pathworking.* Most of us have our *Amazon* and *Isis/Mother* modes down very well. To cultivate our fullness, we now seek to cultivate our *Hathor/Love-Goddess* and *High Priestess/Madonna* aspects. And one way in which we do this is with the most ancient, sensual, and feminine of all art forms: Oriental dance, often called belly dance!

I observed this transformation in Lucinda, one of the senior dancers in my dance studio some years ago. Lucinda was confident, intelligent, and pretty, with a very open and fun-loving personality. There were times that I'd envied her natural outgoing warmth. She was certainly one of the more delightful women that I knew, both physically and personally.

On a long drive to a dance party, she confided that she had just recently begun to feel beautiful. Of course I was surprised, and asked her to explain. "Men have always told me that I'm beautiful," she said, "but I just didn't believe them. I didn't feel beautiful back then – and now I do."

"What has made the change?" I asked.

"Belly dance, actually. Now, when I see myself dance in front of the mirror, I look at myself and know that I'm beautiful. I move in a beautiful way, and feel that way also."

Lucinda had made the breakthrough that most of us want to have. She still looked pretty much the same. Granted, she toned up her belly and hips; almost all dancers do in their first year. But there was no outright, dramatic change in her physical appearance. Nevertheless, she had created the confidence to get up before dozens of people and do an improvisational dance, moving in a very slow and sensual manner, while using her veil for increased emotional impact.

This breakthrough in how she *felt* about herself had a profound impact on how she experienced the rest of her life. At the time of our conversation, she had recently gone through a breakup with a man whom she had hoped would be "the one." (After hearing her story, I and all her other friends had concluded, "You deserve better." But nothing really eased the immediate pain.) Earlier, she would have been devastated. She would have wondered what she had done wrong; where she was at fault.

Now, following her realizations, Lucinda was secure in the knowledge that she was more than beautiful; she had become *attractive*. Her "attractiveness" had become an alive, operating force! Yes, the recent breakup hurt; it hurt a lot. But we all saw her go through this being far more secure and happy with herself, with *who* she was, than she (or any of us) would have been before this kind of break-through. She had achieved a new level of security and a new level of knowledge in her potent juiciness. She knew that she could, and would, attract another man, and that he'd be a better one for her.

At some level, many (if not most) of us desire erotic power. We want to cultivate that sense of divine allure that has been embodied in all of our *Goddesses of Love*; from the goddesses of myth and legend to the more recent "goddesses of the silver screen." Who among us doesn't wish that she could *be* Marlene Dietrich, when she sang that men would flock around her, like "moths around a flame."[1]

Marlene was erotic. She was more than sexy, more than glamorous; she was *erotic*. In the characters that she played, she was also powerful. Through movies and books, and even through our personal lives, we all know women who are our *erotic* icons. We also know women who are *sensual*, and those that are *sexy*. Though our thesaurus would have us believe otherwise, there is a difference in these words. The difference is subtle, but there is enough of a difference to be worth our attention.

Most of us know how to be *sexy*, at least from time to time. We also know how to be *sensual*. We know how to treat our senses right when it's time to get out of our heads and into direct experience. Most of us, though, feel a little less comfortable when it comes to being *erotic*. We feel a little at a loss when we reach for the fullness of our own *Hathor* essence.

The reason for this is that becoming *erotic* is both deliberate and intentional. At the same time, it is not blatant. Oh, there may be erotic moments that just "happen," but when a person decides to become skilled, or powerful, in this particular area, she learns how to set the stage; how to make *eros* an underpinning of her life, rather than a matter of happenstance. When a woman fully develops her *Hathor* mode, she is cultivating something for herself, not for others!

This sense of having awakened an inner energy primarily for our own fulfillment means that *we* are the center of our own universe; not someone else! Thus, when we observe a woman who is rich in her *Hathor* essence, we get a sense of depth. We sense that there are still some secrets, some mysteries, something yet to be discovered.

The essence of what is *erotic* is *charge*: it is the suspenseful buildup of anticipation. When we are doing erotic play, our intention is not just to attract attention and interest, but to build mutual desire to the maximal level. When we start cultivating our inner *Hathor*, we give attention not only to external matters, such as appearance and physical expression, but also to our ability to work with internal energy. So when we start playing with the kind of *charge* that I just mentioned, we play on multiple levels: the physical, the intellectual and emotional realms, and also the energetic. We blend these together.

The kind of woman who consciously cultivates her *Hathor* essence is usually a "Type T" personality. Psychologist Frank Farley, who introduced the notion of "Type T" people in 1985, described these people as those who live off stimulus and intensity.[2] The "T" stands for thrill-seeking in general. (Personally, I also think it stands for testosterone as well; especially when applied to men.) A Type T person will start his or her own business (several times, if necessary). The Type T person will almost never be the one to retire with a gold watch after "35 years of dedicated service."

Type T people do danger sports. They need the rush in order to feel alive. Type T women, in particular, tend to have intense, dramatic love affairs; the kind of "roller-coaster" ride that fills their lives with ups and downs, with rarely a plateau in between. Type T people *need* to "live on the edge."

It took me a while before I figured out that I was a Type T person. As one of my beaus once told me, "You're a margin player, Alay'nya." He was right; he could identify that trait, because he was one himself. Since then, I've realized that many of the people in the small, entrepreneurial companies where I've worked are also Type T. The dancers in my school who move rapidly from beginner's studies into performance are also Type T. After a while, we learn to recognize each other.

Type T people play in the erotic realm because they need the *charge*. In fact, it is this whole quality of "developing charge" that makes an erotic experience what it is! An analogy comes from the world of physics, where a capacitor is a "charge-storing" device. Positive charge builds up on one surface, and negatively charged particles build up on the other. At some point, when the charge can no longer be sustained, an intense voltage leaps across space, and the charge is neutralized. So it is with creating an erotic experience. Our goal is to bring our experiential *charge* up to the maximal level that we, and our partners, can sustain.

The analogy with the physical device of a capacitor holds in many ways, because erotic play is essentially where we play with our personal energy. We don't have a good vocabulary for this kind of experience, either in our language or in our culture. Because of this, we borrow terms from other cultures; cultures in which this kind of energy development is widely accepted (although still esoteric). Yogis refer to this energy as *prana*, which loosely connotes the "breath of life." Martial artists variously refer to this as *ch'i* and *ki* (for the Chinese and Japanese martial arts, respectively). All the exciting and interesting "special effects" that we see in the various kung fu movies are depicting feats supposedly done using *ch'i*.

Many of us desire a stronger degree of *charge* in our lives. Often, what we really want is a greater degree of internal energy, or *ch'i*, as well as more emotionally intense and compelling life experiences. Not everyone who desires these kinds of experience has the personal discipline, or depth of understanding, to take on full mastery of an art form that will lead to the actual enriched experiences themselves. Many will often resort to paler, more shallow, versions. For example, some people want the *charge* that can be obtained from karate *kumite* (sparring) or judo *randori* (free-play). However, if they don't have the discipline to go to classes and practice, they will instead spend hours immersed in videos and role-playing games, whether live or online. This is not to say that such games are wrong or bad; simply that hours spent in a "pretend" world will never translate to even a few minutes of the "real thing."

Similarly, people who want to introduce greater *erotic charge* into their lives may take on a little role-playing. In the realm of *eros*, this may actually be useful. Many of us have felt the extra "zing" that we get by introducing a little novelty into our erotic worlds. Anyone who has bought as much as a peek-a-boo nightie has played this game. This is one way to get out of the ordinary, and such activities help us to build up a bit of the desired *charge*.

For much the same reason, we may have sex in different places, which adds not only novelty but occasionally the titillating possibility of discovery. We've probably all found that our sex lives are rejuvenated on vacation, or even while at a conference. Others will participate in various forms of more stylized erotic role-playing — with or without the additions of costumes, props, and the involvement of others.

There is a final very common approach to developing erotic intensity in our lives. This is much more common than dress-up and role-playing. Simply put, we fall in love. This kind of "falling in love" is not the same as being in a *state* of love; of wanting the highest good for our partner, whatever that might be. Rather, it is the process of "cathecting." Scott Peck has written a good description of this process in *The Road Less Traveled.*[3] As a brief summary, when we "cathect" something, we put a sense of *charge* on it. We can cathect a person, an object, or an experience.

When we cathect something, we energetically place our *sense of self* on the other. For purposes of conversation, let us say that "the other" is a person, and can be referred to as "he." So we place our sense of "self" on a man, while our conscious awareness of being a "self" remains associated with our physical bodies. In this state, if the person with whom we cathect is not returning energy and attention to us, we feel as though we are, energetically, bleeding all over the floor. Very likely, in that sense, we are!

We cathect for very good reasons, each of us. One (and one that I've used a lot in my own life) is out of fear. Rather than get into a real relationship with a real person, I've "fallen in love" with someone with whom a relationship would realistically just not happen. This has allowed me to feel all sorts of emotional experiences, yet stay in the "safe" realm of never having to be really involved. There are times that we all do this, and if we are Type T, we might even do it a bit more than usual.

Many of us cathect because we know that the person of our choice will continue to be "out of reach." That actually serves our purpose, since our underlying motivation is to go through highly charged emotional experiences. When we do this, we do it because we crave the drama. We want drama more than we want a stable, happy relationship. So we find someone who really is the "wrong person," but about whom we can temporarily say that he is the "right one." Then, we cathect our hearts out.

This may or may not involve any degree of sexual, or even erotic, experience. The point is that the intensity of the experience comes from the insecurity of not knowing if the relationship with the sought-after person will persist. That, when we are honest, is where we are really getting our *charge*; from the tension of insecurity, of not knowing.

Most of us have sampled from these different approaches to increasing both the erotic and emotional intensity of our experiences. Most of us have also been dissatisfied with the results. Marnia Robinson, in *Cupid's Poisoned Arrow*, suggests that there is a biological reason why many of us, after reaching the heights of passionate satisfaction with a lover, become disenchanted.[4] We then long for (and sometimes actively seek out) a new and different partner. Robinson notes that this "disenchantment" is correlated with dopamine, which is released during high-intensity sexual experiences. To build greater long-term bonding, she suggests that we emphasize sexual experiences that build affection (and concomitant levels of oxytocin, the "bonding" neurochemical) without necessarily invoking orgasmic release.

Robinson makes an excellent point. Her approach is somewhat like slow-cooking as compared to char-broiling. However, my sense is that we would like to have the full range of experiences. We desire an approach that will help us build our erotic vitality and keep the long-term attention of our partner. We also don't necessarily desire that either we or they should have to forego orgasms! Yet at the same time, we can acknowledge the possible biological base for desiring sexual variety. Thus, we want something that will take us to a new level.

We each want more. We want *real* erotic empowerment. We want to discover the full range of our *Hathor* essence, and simultaneously (this is important!) to tap into our deeper, richer spiritual self; our *High Priestess* or *Madonna*.

And we can! This *Art of Venus* really *is* a *path*; it is a personal discipline. It can be mastered, just as any of us can master any art; with patience, commitment, and practice. The challenging part is that, because this is an art, it will require all of these characteristics to develop full mastery. As a *pathway*, the *Art of Venus* needs a physical embodiment. We find this through the ancient art of Oriental dance.

As an art form, this "Venusian art" may seem "soft." There may not be the same thrill as sky-diving or competitive sports. (That is, of course, up to the point where we start performing; then there are giddying rushes of adrenaline!) As a personal *pathway*, though, what we are doing is not just a "body-art" or a "dance-art." Rather, it is a "whole-life art." Those of us who cultivate this are truly embracing a personal discipline; one that is as demanding as is devotion to athletics or to achievement in any other dimension.

This *Art of Venus* is even more suitable for us as we become "of a certain age" than when we are young. We have the wisdom, the full-life perspective, and often the financial and time resources with which to devote attention to this *path*. And at the same time, we often have energy and the desire to open up a new personal frontier! At the same time, this art is also uniquely well-suited to us when we are younger; it is especially helpful when we are pregnant and then rebuilding our bodies after we've given birth. World-renowned dancers such as Morocco of New York City and Delilah Flynn of Seattle have each written useful articles, insightfully sharing the role of Oriental dance in women's lives, including pregnancy and childbirth.[5]

One thing that works in our favor is that when we reach menopause, we often gain the increased clarity that comes with emotional detachment. As described by Dr. Christiane Northrup in *The Wisdom of Menopause*, we become attuned to new pathways opening up for us at this time.[6] With the monthly cycle of hormones diminishing, we have a more steady and consistent "baseline" for our self-observations. (Many of us have found value with Bio-identical Hormone Replacement Therapy, or BHRT, as described by Dr. Northrup as well as by Suzanne Somers in *The Sexy Years*.[7]) Also, we know ourselves better. This results from simply living longer; in our bodies and our lives.

As we pull our attention from the needs of others, we begin to focus more on ourselves. Dr. Brizendine, in *The Female Brain*, describes how one of her menopausal patients expressed herself in terms of having a "haze [that] had lifted." She was no longer as compelled to rescue and care for others as she previously had been. This release from the attachment of caring so much for others was part of what gave her new energy. She was able to ask herself about what she wanted to experience next in life.[8]

It is not just that the pull of our *Isis/Mother* essence loosens its grip; we begin re-evaluating our professional lives as well. Much as with men who take on a demanding career, we may not have had much "inner time" until our careers are more established. However, after several years of focused career development, we often reach some degree of professional stability.

Thus, with the prospect of longer lifetimes, we can now look forward, with some confidence, to devoting more time to ourselves. Then, these inner journeys become not only possible, but also much more likely.

⚮

"You ooze sensuality, Alay'nya." This was one of my beaus, speaking to me several years ago. "You drip sensuality," said another.

Without knowing how, yes, I had cultivated something. There was indeed a certain kind of energy that I had learned to access. I was playing with it; experimenting. This wasn't entirely physical, although this new quality did influence how I walked and moved. What I had been developing, though, was more than the physical. It was a hallmark of developing a real *women's path*.

As we progress in our *pathworking*, we become more adept at both calling on and using each of our archetypal modes. Our *Isis/Empress* role is a powerful nurturing essence, and our inner *Amazon* gives us discipline, focus, and (most of all) a strong sense of self; of ego. She helps us define our boundaries when our oxytocin-induced *Isis* mode causes us to focus more on attending to others than on meeting our own needs. Our *Amazon* helps us regroup when our inner *Hathor* falls in love and loses her sense of self, or our internal and deeply knowing *High Priestess* gets too diffuse. Our inner *Amazon*, for example, is what will save us when we've cathected too much or too far!

As part of developing a personal and uniquely *feminine* pathway, it is our job to integrate these four aspects; our *Amazon*, our *Isis/Empress/Mother*, our *Hathor/Love-Goddess/Courtesan* and our *High Priestess/Madonna*. All of these belong to us.

Yet, as we cultivate our inner path, it is the *Hathor* and *High Priestess* modes that we most seek to develop. Our *Isis* mode comes to us from our innate caring and nurturing behaviors, and our *Amazon* mode is by now strongly reinforced – perhaps too much so. Our *Hathor* essence opens up our sense of playfulness and light-heartedness, which we may have lost during our career-building stage. Our *High Priestess* role completes us and balances our inner *Hathor*. By combining these two archetypal qualities, we develop a true attractive power.

As we tap into our *Hathor* archetype, we experience the rich, juicy sensual part of ourselves. This aspect goes beyond such ripeness, even though others may observe and comment on our increased sensuality as we cultivate our inner energy. Yet, wonderful though this experience is, in itself, it is not enough. For full completion, we still need to attend to our inner *High Priestess*.

Now, we want to move forward with this personal *integration*. We want to take both our inner *Hathor* and our inner *High Priestess* into our lives. We desire that our personal *integration pathway* will help us to access each of our core archetypes. It should help us blend and balance them as appropriate, and do so at will. And this, we will find, is not the only task in our *pathway*. But that's for later in this book. Right now, we focus on identifying and accessing the full range of our distinctly different "modes of being."

When we decide that we want to deliberately incorporate more of our *Hathor* and *High Priestess* modes into our lives, we often find huge (although often unrecognized) challenges. One big challenge is that we are so used to measuring ourselves by various "achievement" yardsticks, that it is often hard for us to shift gears into something that is not achievement-focused, either for ourselves or on behalf of others.

Very simply, until we've learned how to access our four primary modes at will, we are often at a loss of what to "do" to create the transition! Yes, we may have some things that we do to relax, or to unwind at the end of a long day, or as spiritual practices. Often, though, we do not have a clear process for *shifting state*.

This is not a fault or a reason to criticize ourselves, although many of us may have given up our earlier attempts. One reason that we have such a difficult time is that we lack the feedback process for knowing when we are "doing it right."

Without knowing exactly how these *Hathor* and *High Priestess* internal states are supposed to *feel*, and without feedback to guide us, we give up on accessing these states, and resolve to start our own company, get an advanced degree, or throw ourselves into a social or environmental "cause." (These are all things we can do in our well-known, comfortable, and familiar *Amazon* mode.)

There is another factor that undermines our efforts to transition to our *Hathor* and *High Priestess* states; one that is both subliminal and yet pervasive. This is our underlying *knowing* – one that all women have – that our movement in this direction is challenging to social mores. Thus, even obliquely or indirectly, we put our lives at risk when we move in this direction.

It is not that we expect to be burned at the stake for taking time for our inner selves. However, history is replete with examples of women who *have* been burned at the stake, for crimes ranging from knowing their own sexuality, to spending time with animals, to having healing wisdom and knowledge of herbs.

The famous Venetian courtesan and poet Veronica Franco (1546-1591)[9] was brought before the Inquisition on the charge of witchcraft. While she was able to save her own life, she lost her reputation as a leading luminary, and died in poverty a little over ten years later at the age of 45. Aspasia (ca. 470 BC – ca. 400 BC), the famous Milesian courtesan and mistress of Pericles, was also teacher of rhetoric and philosophy, and her home became the intellectual center of Athens, hosting Socrates and other great thinkers of that time. She was likewise the subject of slander and was put on trial for impiety, with the added insult of having a comic poet as prosecutor.[10]

Throughout history, the women who have stood out the most in terms of combining their intelligence, sensuality, and empathy were *precisely* the ones most vilely persecuted. In other words, the women who had indeed integrated their *Amazon*, *Isis*, *Hathor*, and *High Priestess* roles were often the subject of greatest attack. (Yes, both Veronica and Aspasia were mothers as well!) We have internalized many of these social judgments. Even as we seek to break free of both mental and practical constraints, we are as readily confounded by our own inner barriers as we are by time commitments.

The real challenge that we have to address is *that we tend to trivialize our deepest selves.* This manifests on many levels, and is very subtle. It is often one of the hardest things to discern in our own thinking, and even when we've come face to face with it, it is often very hard to let it go. Our first step, in cultivating our previously-neglected aspects, is that we must come to believe that we are worth our own attention. We do this by addressing our self-image; the subject of the next chapter.

PERSONAL PATHWORKING:

1. To what extent do you feel that you've developed your *Hathor* essence (your inner *Love Goddess*)? This question has nothing to do with relationships; with whether or not you have a husband or "special other," or if you've recently broken off a relationship, or if you have been single and celibate for years. This also has nothing to do with your actual sex life, *per se*. It is about whether or not you've cultivated your "juiciness" as a state-of-being. Do you feel the sort of succulence that would come about by making *Hathor* a part of your everyday experience? Is pleasure – of all forms; intellectual and artistic as well as sensual – a regular part of your life?

2. To what extent would cultivating your *Hathor* essence be important to you? What are you willing to shift – in areas ranging from beliefs and attitudes to daily patterns – in order to increase the *Hathor* aspects of your life?

3. If you feel that your *Hathor* aspect is a little weak and wan, make a commitment to yourself (put this in writing, please – perhaps as part of your daily journaling) – that you will devote a certain amount of time and energy to this aspect. Treat this like making a date with someone (where that "someone" happens to be an aspect of *you*).

4. Make a list of little things that you can do that will increase the *Hathor*-quality of your life. These can be big and extravagant, such as a week at a spa. They can also be very small; involving only minute amounts of time and money. Look at all the low-cost, low-time, and low-energy ways that you can increase the pleasurable aspects of your daily life. (Fresh flowers, anyone?)

5. Select a few of these options from your list, and put them into your day-planner. Your *Amazon* is now in charge. It's her job to get to the

Hathor-pleasure aspects of your life, just as much as she needs to go to work, pay the bills, and pick up the laundry or dry cleaning. Keep up with the balancing and negotiations, and steadily increase the dosage of *Hathor* pleasure that you squeeze into all sorts of odd places.

6. What sort of books, movies, and (readily available) places can you access that will help refine your *Hathor* sensibilities? What speaks to this aspect the most? Start factoring these in.

7. Sometimes, we need a little spiritual balancing to tap into what we really desire. As much as you develop your *Hathor* aspects, also spend a little time in quiet meditation, and perhaps a regular religious or devotional service. Allow these quiet times to speak to you. What is it that you need now? Perhaps simple quiet contemplation of the Divine will bring some peace and perspective, and even deepen your intuition. Allow your *High Priestess* aspect to guide you as you begin *unveiling* your most private, inner self to yourself.

CHAPTER 10:
IN OUR BODIES

IT WAS ONE OF OUR first "haflas," or belly dance parties. We had scheduled the evening with a local theater and had put together a "mini-show" for ourselves and our guests, complete with lights, a good sound system, a true dance-floor stage, and real theatre seats. Gaia, one of my students, had pulled me aside. "I'd like to make an announcement before the next set, Alay'nya. Is that O.K.?" I nodded. Anything was game.

The next set started, and Gaia stood up and addressed the audience. "We've learned so much by studying with Alay'nya," she began. Of course, I basked and glowed. "One of the things she's encouraged us to do is to practice on our own, at home. At first, this was a little difficult, but then we started getting into it …"

We were interrupted. Some sort of sound was coming over the system. It was a radio, an early morning broadcast: weather and an ad. As soon as I figured out what was going on, I hurried towards the sound system. Other dancers reached out to stop me. "Let it go, it's a part of the show." "But that's a radio announcement," I protested. Just then, the advertisement stopped, and the music began.

"When you're in love …," the singer crooned. The dancer emerged onto the stage. She was in costume, all right, but not like one I'd ever seen before. Her hair was in curlers. She was wearing a plaid flannel nightgown under a tattered chenille robe, and scruffy slippers adorned her feet. She was sweeping the stage with a long-handled dust mop.

"When you're in love …," the singer repeated, as Sue Ellen, one of my former students, executed a series of perfect hip thrusts circling around her mop handle. The audience roared with laughter when, in a fit of ecstatic abandon, she discarded her mop, pulled off her bathrobe, and used it for a series of dramatic veil swirls.

Curlers flew across the floor. The audience rose to their feet with applause as Sue Ellen made her final bows and disappeared backstage.

Sue Ellen stole the show that night, and her piece is the one that we all remember, years later. Also, having seen a few "campy" performances like it in other cities, I still have to say: Sue Ellen's was the best. It was totally unexpected and beautifully done. I still chuckle at the memory.

Yet then, and even now, I've wondered: why is it that sometimes we have such a hard time allowing ourselves to believe that we're beautiful? Sue Ellen was funny; no question. But underneath the humor, a possible different message was: "I'm *not really* beautiful. I can practice this art form on my own, but if I'm going to perform for you, I've got to mock my pretensions for assuming that I really, truly can be sensual and alluring. So if I make fun of myself for doing this kind of dance, then you'll be laughing with me, not at me."

Now let's be honest. Few of us are really drop-dead gorgeous. Most of us, when we get up in the morning, are not yet as beautiful as we will be by the time we go out the door. On the other hand, most of us have the innate ability to create the kind of presence that we want. With the aid of cosmetics, costume, and attitude, we can become almost any character that we desire to be.

Remember Olivia Newton-John in *Grease*? In the early part of the show, she was voted "too pure to be pink"; she was deemed too straight-laced to be part of the ruling clique of girls. In the last scene, though, she showed up in skin-tight black, with tousled hair and red Candie's. She dominated John Travolta during the dance scene. She was more than equal to the leather-jacketed "tough guys."

That is a little extreme, maybe, but it tells us something: We choose what kind of person we want to be. Nothing is intrinsically off-limits to us. If we want to be erotic, alluring, and seductive, we can. This is not so much a matter of acting; it's a matter of *shifting state*. We can be whoever, or whatever, we believe ourselves to be.

So the first question that we really have to face is: what limiting beliefs do we have that constrain us? Second: what can we do to change these beliefs, to open up the possibilities?

Almost all good self-help books these days have us looking at our "limiting beliefs," so this should not be new to any of us. But if we look in this particular area of our lives, we will probably find that our "limitations" are all variations on the theme of being a "good girl." If we step outside our culturally permitted roles, we've gone from being a "good girl" to being a "bad girl." Then, of course, we're afraid of what might happen to us. We might not survive.

As limiting beliefs go, this one has something to back it up. As we have seen, we have huge amounts of cultural conditioning, ranging from our childhood *Sleeping Beauty* fairy tales to their eagerly-sought adult equivalents: romance novels. Our novels, movies, and television shows all reinforce the "morality play" that "bad girls" will get what's coming to them, and that "what's coming" will not be good!

Even now, we are still working with the double standard, which takes no further explanation. We get angry at this, but have been socially conditioned (and to some extent, programmed by our own biology) to deflect or minimize our anger.[1] Is it any wonder that we have turned our anger against these constraints towards ourselves, instead? We particularly do this when we have *internalized social constraints within our own minds.*

Sometimes, as we begin to change our beliefs about ourselves and about the world we live in, we do create enormous risks for ourselves. Our fears can manifest as very real, negative, and scary events. For that reason, many women who would love to cultivate their *Art of Venus* never do! Also, many women who do choose this path of expanding their range of "self" go through some scary shifts, as they redefine who they are. For the moment, it suffices to say that many of us start by creating an *alternate persona.*

Creating an *alternate persona* is a way of doing play-acting. We make up an imaginary character, one who has the attributes that we wish that we had. Then, we become her — at least temporarily. This is a transitional step in cultivating our *Hathor* essence.

One evening, Donna, a woman living near a major East Coast city, and her husband (then her boyfriend) made a trip to a well-known night club (actually a "sex club") with another man. Donna had decided that for that evening she was going to be hot stuff: very, *very* hot. So what she did, before she got there, was to transform herself, *in her mind*, to being a high-class, sophisticated, beautiful call girl. When they got to the club, she went into action. As a result, both men had nights that they'll never forget.

The interesting part of this story is that Donna is overweight; *substantially* overweight. Ever since I've known her, she's been more than a little heavy. But she didn't let that get in her way. When she decided to *shift state*, she changed her body image as well. At the same time, she changed her concept of *who she was* and also what she could *do* and *be*.

Each of my dancers has had to deal with self-image issues. One willow-slender young woman disparaging described herself as having "monkey arms." Over time, she was able to realize that those same "monkey arms" gave her greater reach with her veil; she was able to create more compelling patterns as she moved across the stage. Those same arms also let her frame herself more beautifully; the extra reach allowed her to create a longer "line." In contrast, I've had students with shorter frames and plumper figures; they have often wished they were more slender. They sometimes have longed for the long torso that would let them show off moves such as undulations to greater advantage. Over time, these women also come to embrace the special message that their figures convey; they embody Earth-Mother nurturance. Once they internalize that identity, their audiences feel a deep sense of contentment watching them dance. Each of us needs to both accept and work with our physical presence, and also to create an internal image of ourselves as being beautiful.

I've had to work through my own image issues as well. For example, I have a broad bone structure in my shoulders and pelvis, as well as strong leg muscles. When I'm in top form, my dancers and audiences may describe my dance as being "powerful," but never as "ethereal." I have to work with my own body type. At the same time, by embracing my physical strength, I can do a very convincing sword dance!

When we act "as if" we are beautiful, people treat us as though we're beautiful. When we act "as if" we're successful, people treat us as though we're successful, and we draw to ourselves the experiences of success. Similarly, if we want to develop our sensuality, our *eros*, one first step is to act "as if" we are a totally, compellingly gorgeous and erotic woman. We *are* Mata Hari, or Marilyn Monroe, or our most favorite and compelling style icon, come to life!

Dancers use this mind technique all the time, just as actors do. We use it to get into our stage personas. In fact, if we have different kinds of dance forms, then we may cultivate different stage personas, one for each dance style. Dalia Carella, one of New York's leading dancers, does this when she performs in both her elegant and classic Oriental dance and also her own wild and eclectic *Rom* (gypsy) dance. "I have different personas for the Oriental and the *Rom*-inspired dances," she says. Between the intricate control of the one and the joyful abandon of the other, the difference is clear.

It's not just women like Dalia, who have devoted their lives to the art, who can effectively enter such "alternate personas." Dalia's personas are for stage presentation; many of us use a similar approach to "try on" a different aspect of our own selves. For example, Jackie had been dancing for just a couple of months. She started to practice and perform *Rom*-inspired dance. This was a powerful form of self-therapy, because her daily self was very diligent and responsible. She was an oldest child, and no matter what job she took, she soon found herself in a management role. She had high expectations for herself in all areas, dance included!

Jackie, like many other dancers, was responding to a fantasy-notion or made-up persona that helped her step outside her usual realms of expression. This persona has been represented to us in operas (*Carmen* in the opera of the same name is one example) and in books and movies (Esmeralda in *The Hunchback of Notre Dame* is known world-wide now, thanks to the Disney movie). Each of these "icons" represents someone sensual, free, and outside the normal bounds of society – and in Esmerelda's case, someone who has a sweet and pure heart. For Jackie, tapping into her *Hathor* essence involved taking on a Carmen/Esmeralda "stage" personality; this helped her in "loosening up" her spirit!

In a similar sense, many of us take on fantasy alter-egos as we begin exploring and cultivating previously untapped aspects of ourselves. We may draw inspiration for these made-up personas from sources ranging from Orientalist paintings to movies. Although we semi-situate these personas in different cultural settings, we know that the "culture" that they're referencing is about as real as a Disney movie. This is allowable!

Our culture (as with most cultures, throughout the world) is, in some ways, very rigid in its roles and expectations. If we need to create a fantasy persona as a starting point, then let's do so! Drawing in a fantasy role based on a myth or projection of some aspect of ourselves onto another culture is acceptable, *if we are clear* that what we're doing involves some form of play-acting, and is *not* a serious "cultural" interpretation. (As a note: Many Oriental dancers *do* concern themselves with accurate and precise renderings of authentic, or culturally-inspired, dances; these include a wide range of folkloric dances as well as others. This is different from what I'm discussing; both are valid experiences. We simply need to be clear about what it is that we're doing.)

Thus, when we challenge ourselves to believe that we can be more than what we've allowed ourselves within our current roles, we can find play-acting as a valuable tool for getting "outside of ourselves." Doing this is normally a transition step; it is a way to start accessing a different state of being. As we start accessing the real release from our "daily selves," we need fantasy personas less and less. We begin knowing and connecting directly with our own inner *Hathor*, however we manifest her.

Our thoughts, our mental "states," create reality. This is a far-reaching claim, but is one that we can observe to be so in our lives. In fact, this is *so* true that most of what we can learn about entering a different state (going from *Amazon* and *Isis* to our *Hathor* and *High Priestess*) has more to do with how we create our thoughts and shape our minds than with anything else. This has a very direct and visible influence on how we hold and present ourselves physically. The feeling here is that we can go from believing that we are *potentially* an erotically-charged, compelling, attractive woman into believing that we are this way *right now*, at *this very moment*. This feeling, this belief, changes everything – including how we hold our bodies!

During dance classes, and even during performance, a woman will often *shift state* between being "ordinary" and having a totally compelling "presence." She may do so several times, even in the course of just a few minutes! So how does a woman go from "ordinary" to "erotic," "exciting," and "compelling" – all within seconds? Once she makes the transition, how does she keep herself in her desired state? In fact, what makes the difference between the two states? Typically, only a few millimeters. That, and an attitude.

This often becomes most noticeable as we practice the *Principles* that I've developed and teach to all my dancers. These *Principles* are ones that I've learned and synthesized throughout years of studying with some of the finest T'ai Chi Ch'uan masters and dance teachers in the world.

It's very easy for a woman to use the *Principles*, and very easy for her to align her body. During this portion of class, I work briefly with each student; correcting her posture and alignment. I ask her to change the way she's holding her body in very specific ways, and guide her into the new state. "There, now," I'll say. "Do you *feel* the difference?" Yes, she can. Even I can feel the difference, and so can anyone who is watching her. All of a sudden, in the new body alignment, she radiates poise and confidence, grace and beauty! It doesn't matter what she looks like or how long she has been studying dance. Even if she's forty pounds overweight and has been in class for only two weeks, at that moment, she is commanding the stage. She has a *totally compelling presence*.

I move on to work with the next woman. Too often, when I look back, the woman with whom I've just worked has gone from "compelling" back to "ordinary." Her posture has drooped, just a miniscule amount. She's ever-so-slightly, but oh-so-significantly, lost the "presence" that she had just moments ago.

What's happened here? It's not that the body posture is difficult. The body alignment needs a little holding of muscles in a certain way, but it's not hard. The body posture aspect of being in a gorgeous, awesome, and even erotic state is certainly not the challenge. What is it, then?

With most of the women, it's a feeling, an attitude, a *belief* that each one has about herself that says, "Oh, I can't. Not *me*. I can't be erotic. I'm not beautiful." It's the *belief about ourselves* that is simultaneously the most important limiting, and freeing, factor.

Can we change our beliefs about ourselves and enter into a *state* in which, regardless of our appearance or physique, we can be alluring and compelling? Can we *become Hathor*? Can we move into our inner *High Priestess* at will?

The answer is *yes!* I've learned to do this, and so have many others. Bit by bit, I and others have learned to transform ourselves. Sometimes, it happens slowly. Then this transformation reflects changes in our personal lives as well as in our dance.

This ties in very much with our self-image, and our self-consciousness about our figures. A while back, I was driving back from a day-long dance event with three other women. One of them remarked that she was unhappy with the soft condition of her tummy. Another dancer responded, "Oh, your belly is a very special place! That is where your babies come from." This shows us a way that we can encourage each other to move beyond self-judgment and into self-love.

As part of living in our current culture, we are bombarded with images telling us that a sexually attractive woman is one who has the lean, firm torso of a young woman; one who is just coming into her full sexuality, but who has never borne children. If we have a round belly, then we think that we are not as attractive.

However, when we look at art by some of the great European masters, men whose paintings form part of our cultural lineage, what do we see? Pictures of naked women, of course, but these women have soft, rounded bellies. Maybe we need to take a step in the direction of respecting the beauty of our bodies when they are changed by the processes of pregnancy and birth.

The key factor in learning to *shift state* – to access our inner *Hathor* – is to cultivate a deep appreciation of ourselves. We each need to *believe* that we are beautiful, and then we can experience and project that belief. Maria, a woman with a lean and slender body (not what one would think of as a "typical" belly dancer) developed a hip shimmy of exquisite beauty. The "compelling" aspect of this move might have lasted just a few seconds, but she brought it in, and it was real. Gloria developed an extraordinary ability to "present" herself in dance. It didn't matter that there was more weight on her tummy and hips than she liked; when she combined the *intention* of presenting herself beautifully along with the *Principles* that let her do so, she was absolutely captivating.

Along with learning the *Principles* and the techniques of Oriental dance, my students and I have learned the ability to *shift at will* into different *states. Shifting state* is the subject of the next chapter.

PERSONAL PATHWORKING:

1. Bring to mind some times that you've been in one of your different modes, and desired to *shift* to another. How did you do this? Can you remember any physical actions? (Perhaps you took a shower or a long hot bath, put on a favorite dress or special perfume, listened to music, etc.). Did you talk to yourself in a certain way, or envision yourself "acting as if" you were a different kind of person? How did you know that you'd *shifted state?* (This could be a simple as a mood change, or perhaps you acted differently – you may have had a different posture, or made more eye contact.) More important yet, what cues do you use *now* to trigger your transition into one of your desired *states?*

2. Are there roles that you would like to inhabit, but have not allowed for yourself? Which ones? Imagine what it would feel like if you were to *shift state* into one of those different states-of-being. Play this out as an envisioned scenario in your mind. Should your thoughts detour into a negative thought-pattern (you allow your envisioning to focus on something that you *don't* want), mentally "scrub away" or "erase" that part of your envisioning, and begin again – focusing on the positive experiences and outcomes that you desire!

CHAPTER 11:
SHIFTING STATE

ONE OF THE MOST HORRIBLY embarrassing, relationship-damaging experiences was recounted by my dance friend Alyssa. As she puts it, "This was something that I brought onto myself, completely; I still cringe when I think about it!"

For some time, she'd had a job in a town about two hours from her home, and thus made a weekly commute to work, spending the weeknights in a small apartment. Mondays, she'd get up and be out the door by 6:30 AM. Friday nights, she'd get home late, usually between 10 and 11PM. The two hour commute between two cities gave her ample time to think.

On the trip home, especially, she noticed that the thoughts with which she started tended to build in her mind during the trip. If she could think happy thoughts, she'd arrive home happy; almost jubilant. If she thought unhappy thoughts; well, this story tells it all.

The story actually begins with the weekend before, because she and her beau Kenny had bought a new computer. They unpacked it, and he put the boxes out on the front porch. "I'll put them away later," he promised. Monday morning, when she left in the cold, pre-dawn hours, they were still there. "I bet they'll still be there when I get home Friday," she muttered to herself as she drove off.

Friday night came, and she began the long trip home. Do you know how our minds have this little habit of poking around and looking for trouble? Hers certainly was. Of course, she remembered the boxes on the front porch. "I'll bet they're still there," she grumbled to herself. She began thinking about what a total chaos-making, scatter-things-all-over-the-universe, leave-things-where-they-may-be person Kenny was. (In her mind, this was true!)

Then her thoughts got more negative. She began to not only think that the boxes would be there, but that her house would be in shambles, and there would be a sinkload of dirty dishes. She told herself that Kenny didn't respect her or her property, that she would have to take care of this all by herself, and she still had to prepare for the next morning's dance class. There were more thoughts, but you get the drift! They went from negative, to bad, to just plain awful. So you can imagine her mood, as she rounded the turn to her driveway.

Of course, the boxes were still there. Not only boxes, but a nasty, gray old mattress was leaning against a front tree. There was a can of some sort of liquid, sitting in a plastic bag, in the garden. The place looked, shall we say, not at its best.

She was more than in a snit. She was outraged, as she strode, hatchet-faced, into the living room.

"Hi, honey; what's wrong?" said Kenny as he came out to greet her. She didn't even talk to him, but instead started moving boxes downstairs. She poured the liquid from the can out into the garden, and threw the can into the garbage. She was about to start on the mattress, when Kenny confronted her. The result was not pretty, nor was it fun.

In the end, they got it straightened out. As Kenny tells it, he had been cleaning all day. He was preparing to strip, wax, and polish the wooden floors; something she had dearly wanted done for a long time. The boxes, which he had brought in during the week, were now back on the porch while he cleaned the floors in preparation for wax-stripping. The mattress had come out of his van, which he was cleaning as well, and was going to go back in the following day.

As for the liquid, which she poured over her garden? It was a wax-removing solvent. Kenny had bought it earlier in the day, only to find that the can had a leak. Rather than have it leak inside the house, he had set it out in the garden.

Kenny had been looking forward to having her come home. He had dinner prepared and was eager to see her. Her sense of righteous indignation and self-justified outrage ruined the evening, when it could have been lovely (if she was just willing to overlook some boxes). It took her not only days, but weeks, to repair the damage that her mental state brought on. This experience taught her something valuable, though – something worth the price of the lesson.

This experience was one of the most vivid that she'd ever had of her thoughts creating reality. She expected to see boxes, and they were there. She expected to see signs that Kenny didn't care for her property, and they were there also. She had just demonstrated a superb example of "reality creation." In the process, her "reality creation" destroyed the reality that her beau was trying to create, which was that of having a wonderful evening together, with good food and lots of loving. Making up after the fight was not nearly as much fun as Kenny's original plan, especially since she had to do most of the apologizing.

What she learned from this experience, painful and "in-her-face" as it was, was that her thoughts did indeed create her reality. This is so for each of us, every single day. The challenge that we have is to use our thoughts to create realities that we want to experience, and ones that we also want to share with others. We can, through our own intention and creation, help others to experience delightful things as well!

Medea, my first teacher of Oriental dance, would transform herself from an ordinary, everyday woman into some magical, powerful creature when she got ready to teach dance class. She would walk into the studio, carrying bags of tapes, children's toys, and dancer's gear, with her two-year-old son in tow. A perfectly normal woman, she was like any young mother you would meet on the street; slightly stressed and hassled. She would then slip into the woman's room, and add extra eyeliner and mascara; a bit more color to her lips and cheeks. Returning to the studio, she'd settle her son with some toys, and reach into a shoulder bag heavy with beaded jewelry, hip scarves, and coin-laden belts. Not just everyday dancer's gear, but a wonderful, mood-shifting, treasure-trove of costume items.

"Belly dance gives me the chance to do the things I've loved since I was a little girl," Medea would explain. "Dress-up in costumes, wear make-up, and dance!" As she talked, she would be reaching into her bag and pulling out a triangular hip-scarf, over a yard long from one tip to the other, and bordered with long fringe. She'd wrap this around her hips and add a heavy gold chain belt with lots of little dangling coins. She'd put on heavy gold earrings, and slide golden bracelets onto her wrists and arms. She'd stand up, stretch, align her body, and all of a sudden, she was different. She was no longer the stressed and harried young mother who had entered the room fifteen minutes ago. She was Medea, a high priestess of the Goddess; a woman who could captivate an audience or a man. She was a woman with strength, purpose, and presence. Once she had *shifted state*, class would begin.

What Medea did, what I've learned to do, and what thousands and hundreds of thousands of woman have done over the centuries, is to use *personal ritual* to create a *state change*. Of course, this *state change* is all in the mind, so dressing up, putting on cosmetics, and adding perfume are not in and of themselves necessary. However, when we take the time to enhance our physical appearance, we do more than simply help ourselves look better and feel better. We help ourselves to *shift state*; to move into a different place *inside ourselves*.

Shifting state is a learned skill. However, to some extent or another, it is a skill that we already have. What is most important is that when we *shift* our *state*, we *shift* our *concept* or *belief* about ourselves. Other people respond to this, and they start to believe what we believe.

W. Timothy Gallwey, in *The Inner Game of Stress*, describes how we have two "selves." "Self 1" is the "invented self." This Self lives in the world of concepts and expectations; it labels things as right and wrong, desirable and not desirable.[1] (This is much like the *Predator* described by Don Miguel Ruiz in *The Four Agreements*;[2] both are out-picturings of the *pain-body* described by Eckhart Tolle in *A New Earth*.[3] Throughout the world, current thinkers and ages-old traditions converge to provide the same insights.)

In contrast, according to Gallwey, "Self 2" is the one who is actively engaged in living, and not critiquing that living on a moment-by-moment basis![4] The fascinating thing is that if we can get our "Self 1" out of the way, our "Self 2" knows *exactly* what to do!

One of Gallwey's more stunning examples has been in coaching people to play tennis. Many of these were people who had never played tennis before. Within twenty minutes, though, they were to be playing in a demonstration that would be shown on national TV.[5] The amazing thing is that Gallwey was able to get his clients to *shift state*; from a state in which they were missing their tennis shots (or not doing them as well as they'd like), into a state where they were doing exactly as they desired!

This ability to *shift state* – to become as we desire *instantly* – is something that we can all learn. We can apply it to whatever area of our lives we desire. This is not to say that it is easy, and certainly not to say that it is trivial. However, this is a learnable skill; perhaps much more than we have thought possible.

We can learn to *shift state* when we want to go from one *state* to another, such as shifting from our work-focused *Amazon* to our fun-loving and playful *Hathor.* By becoming more adept with these shifts over time, we begin to gently layer these *states* on top of each other. We move between our different modes more adroitly and easily. This is where we begin *integration.*

We can identify a striking integration example in Hillary Rodham Clinton, who is often in her *Amazon* mode. As described by Jonathan Van Meter in the December 2009 issue of *Vogue,* "her mastery of the issues is dazzling."[6] She has won world-wide respect for her acumen and leadership. At the same time, she has developed her other modes as well. She's connected with her *Hathor.* As Van Meter states, "She's fun. She laughs at herself."[7]

Yet it is Mdm. Clinton's *Isis/Empress/Mother* mode that most infuses her *Amazon,* making her both much more real and much more effective. It's not just that she is a real mother. As Van Meter quotes a Clinton staffer, referencing her time as First Lady, "'Say whatever you want to say about the Clintons, but they [were] poster parents for successfully raising a child in the White House.'"[8] Part of her success lies in how she incorporates her *Isis* mode into her *Amazon*-based work. "I was struck by her tone," Van Meter writes, after listening to her give a speech while on a multi-country tour of African nations. "It sounded like a speech that only a mother could give."[9] The sense of "motherly caring" that infused her speech also let her be very direct and forthright.

Mdm. Clinton also shows her *Isis* mode in how she cares for the people around her. Van Meter notes how she "mothered" him, making sure that he got a hat when they were out in the sun. She had the doctor bring him some medicine when he came down with food poisoning, and followed up by sending a staffer to give him a Sprite and some white bread. Mdm. Clinton demonstrates that she has *integrated* her *Isis* with her *Amazon*. In her *Amazon* mode, she grasps the delicacies, intricacies, and nuances of global politics. In her *Isis* mode, she remembers – and *cares* – about the details regarding very specific people and their needs. Her *Isis* quality helps to soften her *Amazon*, and makes her more effective in establishing rapport, which is essential to her *Amazon* role!

Unlike most of us, Mdm. Clinton has had to do her tough *integration* job in public, under the harsh light of consistent media scrutiny. Faced with such a challenge, I believe that she has achieved more than many of us have – not just professionally, but personally as well. As described by Anne E. Kornblut, in *Notes from the Cracked Ceiling*, it was when she had gone through the actual process of *integrating*, in full public view, that she won a greater level of support from the American people.[10] Any of us who may have felt earlier that she was too invested in her *Amazon* role, as she attempted during the 2008 election campaign to prove her readiness to be Commander-in-Chief, saw Mdm. Clinton shift into a different mode. Simply put, she had an *"Isis* moment."

It happened at a press conference when Marianne Pernold Young, a freelance reporter, asked one of the last questions. Young queried, "How do you do it?" Mdm. Clinton, initially at a loss for words, started her response in her usual upbeat tone. But she slowed down her answer as the personal nature of the question drew a more introspective response. "... I couldn't do it if I just didn't passionately believe it was the right thing to do."[11] As she talked further about her feelings for this country, it became clear that what was motivating her was a sense of relationship with the nation; an urgency of caring. This was her *Isis* side coming through. Her *Isis* nature – her deep sense of caring – was what brought her to spend so much time being an *Amazon*. We could understand this; we resonated. And our respect for her grew.

We see, in Hillary Rodham Clinton, one example of a woman combining two of her major feminine archetypes; her *Amazon* and her *Isis*. Another way to look at how she's accomplished the same integration is from the Myers-Briggs Type Inventory (MBTI) perspective. As described by Ross Reinhold,[12] an expert on Myers-Briggs Types, Hillary Clinton began with a great deal of idealism, as evidenced in her book, *It Takes a Village*.[13] This suggests that her basic Type includes being an iNtuitive Thinker. (This correlates with being an *Amazon-Magician*.) She is also likely to be Judging; she likes to come to closure. In using her Thinking and Judging aspects, she shares much in common with male leaders. (Over 95% of all corporate executives are Thinking, and 87% are Judging.[14]) Over time, we have seen her become very pragmatic and rooted in the specifics of thinking through her various plans. She has integrated her Sensing (concrete, detail-focused, pragmatic) aspects together with her basic iNtuitive sense. In short, she has cultivated her *Emperor* (Sensing/Judging) aspects while also cultivating her inner *Isis* (Intuition/Feeling).

As Mdm. Clinton cultivated her "softer" side in public, we might at first have interpreted her actions as developing her *Hathor/Love-Goddess/Courtesan* mode to gain allies and understanding (as part of what some journalists have called her various "charm offensives[15]"). However, as described by various media sources, this was actually a time when she was focusing on "listening" more than on "charming."[16] She developed and exercised her ability to create rapport. She was more *Isis* (nurturing and attending) than *Hathor* (playful and light-hearted).

This is a common *integration path*. As Mdm. Clinton cultivated her *Isis/Empress* (iNtuition/Feeling) aspect, she also cultivated her *Emperor* (Sensing/Judging) abilities. These are two very different modes, but they function together in a complementary manner. My colleagues, Drs. Jacqueline Magness and Elizabeth Roslewicz, both MBTI specialists, have noted that when a person has used their primary "temperament" to the point of excess, it can sometimes become more of a liability than an asset. When this occurs, an iNtuition/Feeling (NF) person will go to Sensing/Judging (SJ) mode, and vice versa.[17] For example, when your branch manager, an SJ-personality, realizes that his over-emphasis on tight timelines and performance goals has caused the entire team to be in an uproar, he'll switch (temporarily!) into his NF mode. He'll have mini-focus groups with you in the break room. "Tell me how you feel," he'll say. "What can I do to help you feel better?" This lasts until he "senses" that the team is back on track, then it's back to milestones and deliverables once again!

Similarly, suppose that you (as an over-stressed, over-worked NF, *Isis*-dominant woman) feel that your life has gotten out of control. Your tendency to love, nurture, and empathize with others has let the kids talk their way out of chores. You've delayed your own "deliverables" while you counseled others, and stacks of paperwork have piled up – both at home and at the job. Under this stress, you switch to SJ mode. You go from *Isis/Empress* to *Emperor*! All of a sudden, you're barking out orders. Your husband and kids are shocked (only initially; by now they've been through this before), and within a few days, the house is clean, your desk is clean, and you've handed in a beautifully concise and cogent report. You can ease back into a good connection-time with your girlfriends; your naturally dominant NF mode comes to the forefront again.

Similarly, in a manner similar to the NF/SJ switch just described, Drs. Magness and Roslewicz also note that a typically iNuitive/Thinking (NT) person will switch to being in Sensing/Perceiving (SP) mode under stress, and again, vice versa.

What is fascinating about people like Mdm. Clinton is that they don't need crisis to access their "crisis-switch" mode. They've *integrated*, skillfully and beautifully. As a result, they are often much more encompassing in their world-view than are their male colleagues, who typically do not master "integration" as part of their skill-set. (Note that some men do; these are the ones who become superior leaders.)

Another outstanding *integration* example is Madeleine Albright. She, like Mdm. Clinton, is also a conceptual and abstract thinker. On reading any of Mdm. Albright's books, I get a sense of how her high-level understanding of overall dynamics works together with her "intuitive" sense of how various forces and factors interact.[18] She likely spends a great deal of time not only in her *Amazon* mode, but specifically in the *Magician* aspect of her *Amazon*; visionary and creative! Like Mdm. Clinton, she is most likely an "NT" – an iNtuition/Thinking person. Yet at the same time, she has a playful sensibility. She has integrated her SP; her "playful" Sensing/Perceiving mode, or *Hathor*, with her inner *Amazon*.

Although both Hillary Rodham Clinton and Madeleine Albright have each used what the press calls "charm," we see a difference in how each *interprets* "charm." Madeleine Albright has gentled her way through male defenses when negotiating tough situations. She has said: "I was very nice and charming and I'd say I've come a very long way and I must be frank. But I danced. I sang and did all kinds of things."[19] This is Mdm. Albright using her *Hathor* mode.

Most recently, Madeleine Albright has published *Read My Pins*, which shows a very light-hearted and playful way of dealing with situations that normally include not only tension, but testosterone-laced egos.[20] Mdm. Albright lets her collection of jeweled brooches provide a subtext to her verbal message. What a delicate, elegant, and understated way to invoke her inner *Hathor*; her delightful pleasure-Goddess! Wit, as a form of intellectual pleasure, has been a tool of some of the world's most fascinating women. In using her brooch collection, where sparkle delights the eye and both whimsy and versatility delight the mind, Mdm. Albright shows us that our *Hathor* playfulness can be intellectual as well as sensual. As a now-famous example, she wore a serpent pin to a meeting with members of the Iraqi government, after their press had published a poem criticizing her as being an "unparalleled serpent." When questioned, she simply "smiled and said that it was [her] way of sending a message."[21]

Now that we've seen two stellar *integration* examples, we can apply our observation powers to our own lives. We are now setting this kind of *integration* as a goal for ourselves, especially focusing on integrating our two "least used" archetypes; our *Hathor* and *High Priestess*. As a theoretical or conceptual framework, this is a reasonable starting point. What we need now are the pragmatics.

It can be easier to *shift state* in some cases than others. A few years ago, I had to re-ignite my dance practice, and was especially motivated by an upcoming performance. To get started on this practice regimen, I made a list of Saturday morning dance "to-do's." My plan was to warm up, review music, write down notes on music structure and timing, develop micro-choreographies for various sections; the list went on.

Being as diligent (and as driven) as I am, when Saturday came, I went through that list, consciously and conscientiously. I did all that I had told myself to do that day regarding dance. But by the end of that very long practice session, I had to admit: I hadn't been having much fun. There was diligence, and there was discipline. But there was absolutely no joy. I had been in my *Amazon* mode, even though doing a *Venusian* art. I took comfort in the fact that I had at least renewed my dance practice, and went into the kitchen to make lunch.

Switching to *Mother* mode wouldn't have helped. (This is the mode that I use when teaching, or connecting with people.) What I needed was to access my *Hathor*, and this is not the easiest *state-change* for me!

I was standing in the kitchen, assembling a tuna-fish sandwich, when something started to happen for me. Various little themes and motifs from the music I had just used kept popping back up in my head. Little ideas for movements came to mind. I put down the bread, went back into my "studio," and began to fool around with music and movement. To my own surprise and delight, I began to play! Not only did I dance some more, but I danced in a different way. My body was a lot more loose and relaxed. I let myself reach and bend and flow a great deal more. I was much more expressive, and I was actually having fun!

I didn't play for long. I was hungry, and that tuna-fish sandwich beckoned. But I had gotten a taste of the release, the joy, and the expressive freedom that had drawn me into dance so many years before.

My dear friend, Dingwall Fleary, is known to friends and colleagues both as "Dingwall," and – in his professional role – as "Maestro Fleary," when he conducts either of the two exceptional community symphony orchestras that he has formed and led for many years.

By now, I was aware of how I *shifted state* within myself, and was beginning to understand how others did the same. But what happens when we are leading a group, and we need to get an entire group of people to *shift state*; and preferably shift into the *same state*, with a united purpose and vision? I have done this several times – typically in organizing some sort of event, such as a dance concert. However, I don't do this often. I was curious about how someone who had to do this all the time dealt with the challenge.

Maestro Fleary, as with many conductors, has a special challenge. He has *two* full-scale symphony orchestras, each with shows every six to seven weeks during the concert season. This means that every few weeks, he has to get large groups of people into performance mode. Prior to that, there are intensive rehearsals with each orchestra, as well as with the various sections (strings, woodwinds, brass, etc.). How does Maestro Fleary get everyone not only into *state*, but into agreement and alignment with *his* purpose; with *his* vision of how the music should be interpreted and played?

To get his insights, I took him out for coffee.

"When I was young," he explained, "my father [a practicing musician] took me to New York to attend both concerts and orchestra rehearsals. Once, we had an opportunity to sit in on a rehearsal led by [the late] Leonard Bernstein. Between Bernstein, the concert master, and the strings section principals, there were diverse opinions on how a certain passage should be bowed. Bernstein had already explained how he wanted it done, but he let them talk it through – for eight whole minutes!" (As Maestro Fleary noted, given the hourly rates by which musicians were paid to be in rehearsal, and the number of musicians present, this was a *huge* amount of time that Bernstein allowed to be absorbed by this discussion.) "Finally, Bernstein said, 'Ladies and gentlemen, I appreciate the opinion that each of you has offered. However, let me remind you, that *I* will make the decision!'"

And that, of course, was that.

Fleary identified this as "one of the most musically salient moments I had ever experienced in my life." This makes sense. It was a perfect blending of the three key masculine archetypes; *Magician, Emperor,* and *Hierophant*. The *Magician* aspect is obvious. As Maestro Fleary elaborated, "Sometimes some of my senior musicians – those who know me well and have heard me tell this story – will tell me that I'm having a 'Bernstein moment.' That gives us all a good chuckle! But when that happens, I am doing what has to get done in order for us to be on the same page. There is a sense of satisfaction in being able to direct the thinking of a group, so that nobody is unhappy, and so that we can all come together to create a magical moment."

There we have it. The *Magician* is creating magic, in real time.

Of course, to do this, he has to invoke his other core masculine archetypes as well. The "Bernstein moment" is a classic invocation of not just his *Emperor* archetype, but of *both* his *Emperor* and his *Hierophant*. Remember, prior to issuing his "I will make the decision" edict, Bernstein allowed eight minutes (times the number of musicians, times their rate per minute) to be taken up with their discussion.

Had he simply imposed his will without hearing them out, they would have felt unsatisfied and unheard. Although he could have obtained compliance, he would not have invoked their full heart-and-soul alignment with his intention. Hearing others, and giving them the space within which they can express themselves, is the act of the *Hierophant*; one who teaches, within a known and structured order. Teaching is not always about talking-to, or lecturing. Sometimes it is creating the space in which others can come to their own understanding.

So we have, in the case of Maestro Fleary, an example of a man who has integrated all three of his core masculine archetypes. This is excellent, but not particularly surprising. What did surprise me, though, was what he said next.

"The feminine archetypes are also important to me. Sometimes I will say, to someone close to me, 'You have just seen my feminine side.' I not only recognize it [in myself], but am grateful that I can step back and see it."

I asked him how it was that he knew and identified with his feminine arche-types. The *High Priestess* aspect became immediately obvious: he takes long daily morning walks. These are important to his listening-in; this is where gets much of his sense of balance and inspiration. Playwright and creativity coach Julia Cameron, in her book *The Vein of Gold*, recommends a *Daily Walk*.[22] Walking has been adopted by artists, philosophers, and poets throughout the world as a means of getting their heads clear of daily dross, and to be open to inspiration.

Maestro Fleary is also sensitive and compassionate. He has to be; he has to be "tuned in" to not only the music that his orchestra members make, but their state-of-being as they make it. "Each section has a different personality," he says. "Strings are different from woodwinds, which are different from brass." He under-stands that musicians are innately sensitive. Without the full-fledged emotional connectivity and sensitivity to nuance that comes from his *Isis/Empress* archetype, he would not be attuned to the personalities behind the music. This attunement, he says, is very necessary. "Working with [volunteer] amateurs is more difficult [than working with professionals]," Fleary states. "They have to *want* to be with me."

So there we have two of the three core feminine archetypes; his *High Priestess* and his *Isis/Empress*. I asked, "What about the *Hathor* archetype? *Hathor* is not only goddess of music and dance, and all forms of artistic and sensual pleasure, she is also playful. She is all about having fun!"

"Actually, *Hathor*, as a goddess archetype, is one of my favorites," he replied. "[I connect with her] all the time! As I am in rehearsal," he elaborated, "and sometimes in performance, I can feel when there has to be a release from the tension of what I'm asking, what I'm *demanding* – and I look for an opportunity; [one where] we can release and smile." … "I've been told that I'm a master at that, without losing control and [the] focus of what we're trying to create; and when working with volunteers, it has to be fun!"

"It's all about the enjoyment; all about the process," he concluded. That's an exceptionally *Hathor*-like comment.

So here we have a person – admittedly an exceptional one – who has identified and *integrated* all of the six core archetypes within the *Worldly Sequence* of the Major Arcana (which we first described in *Chapter 7*). Maestro Fleary can access each of his archetypal essences, knowingly and at will, and use each as needed to bring about his desired results. He is probably dominantly connected with his *Magician* essence, but has found all the archetypes to be essential. He has cultivated access to and use of each.

Maestro Fleary happens to be a man, but I think his example is useful for all of us. Whether male or female, we are each tasked to know and *integrate* all of our core archetypes within our first personal growth challenge of the *Worldly Sequence*. Because we are all different, we will each have differences in which of the core archetypes we find to be the most comfortable, or "ground states." And of course, the end result – the balancing and blending – will be uniquely different for each of us as well.

PERSONAL PATHWORKING:

1. Who do you know – who can you observe – that *shifts state?* Can you note how they go from one archetypal state to another? Can you interview them? Are they aware of how they do this? (Take note: The more that someone "knows" how to do this, and the more that they are expert at *state-shifting,* the less easily they may be able to explain *how* they do what they do! So to learn from them, we may need to model ourselves on them, and not look for a by-the-rules explanation.)

2. Make a list, or compile a little story, about how you may switch between your archetypal modes throughout the day. ***This is an example of a day upon which you could build a story:*** You open the day with being very organized and structure-focused; getting everyone off to work and school, and making "to-do" lists and calendar notations (*Emperor*). Suppose that, once at work, you block out your first two or three hours to design a corporate strategy or develop a marketing campaign. You are being visionary and creative, with a closed-end perspective (*Magician*). Then, you take one of your young colleagues out to lunch, and coach her on how to "work the system" and develop her career. You are being people-focused and nurturing, but within a very structured and closed-end approach; you are guiding her to work *within* a social system (*Hierophant*). After lunch, another colleague asks you for a closed-door session to deal with a personal problem. You make the time, and are largely in listening and nurturing mode (*Isis*). Instead of going directly home from work, you take a brief walk, then freshen up, put on some extra mascara, blusher, and perfume, and stop by a professional event. You are intentionally upbeat and light-hearted, charming your way through the room. Yes, you have an "agenda," but you work it skillfully and delicately, so that people *enjoy* being with you (*Hathor*). Finally, you get home, and spend a little time with family. (In this little scenario, they have had dinner and cleaned up without you,

and similarly gotten themselves through evening chores and homework in your absence. And yes, this *is* a fantasy-scenario.) You take a bit of a hot soak. Then, you light a scented candle and put on your favorite mood music. You do some slow yoga stretches to unwind. You calm your mind, practice mindful breathing, and start observing your thoughts. After a bit, "quiet spaces" start to appear in your mindscape (*High Priestess*).

CHAPTER 12:
BE, DO, HAVE: THE WAY TO
GET FROM "HERE" TO "THERE"

"How LONG?" THIS IS THE question that I'm most frequently asked by beginner students, once they've worked up the courage to talk with me. "How long before I'm a dancer?"

I try to learn the real meaning behind the student's question. Is this a "performance goal" question? Is she really asking, "How long will it be before I can comfortably and confidently get up on the stage, do a dance, have the audience enjoy watching me, and feel good about my dance?" Or is she really asking about creating an internal experience? Is she really saying, "How long will it take me to have the feeling – the freedom – the expression in movement that I want?"

The answer is: "Instantly. You can be a dancer *right now*, right this minute, right this very second." It is also: "Forever. I've been studying with my master teachers for years, and I don't look like them yet." At the same time the answer is also: "A little bit more, every single day, and breakthroughs do happen!"

So which of these answers is the "real" answer? Of course, they all are. However, I'd like to show you how the first answer, "Immediately! Right away!" can be true. Especially, how it can be true for you.

Very likely, of course, you don't want to be a stage-performing dancer right now. But if you were asking me questions about becoming more *sensual*, and even *erotic*; about entering your *Hathor* essence, wouldn't one of your first questions still be, "How long?" Wouldn't you ask the same question if you wanted to access your inner *High Priestess*? The same answers still apply.

I'm going to use the idea of "being a belly dancer" as an example, because it's something we can easily visualize. Being "erotic," or even "playful" – tapping into our juicy *Hathor* archetype – is more amorphous. The real challenge with an intention such as accessing our *Hathor* essence is that it is an inner change rather than an outer one. It is subjective, not objective. It is a "felt-thing" – an internal shift in how we perceive our lives. It is a shift in how we feel and act, and as a result, there is a corresponding shift in the kinds of experiences that we draw to ourselves.

Learning to create an internal shift, and integrating this into our lives, is not the same as achieving a "performance goal." "Performance goals," no matter how challenging they may be, are easy in one special sense: they are very measurable. You know when you are done. They can range from getting your next degree to putting on a holiday dinner. Because it is so easy to measure a "performance goal," there are endless articles about them: "Lose 20 lb. in One Month!" or "Organize Your Closets in One Weekend!"

When we decide that we want something, our minds usually set up a series of things that we "have to do" to "get there." After we "get there," our minds tell us, we can "be" that which we set out to be. This is true for whatever we want to "be," whether it's being a belly dancer, an astute stock investor, or a playwright. Whatever our goal is, we are heavily "have" and "do" focused. That, in fact, is the exact sequence in which we often think: *Have, Do, Be.* We typically think that in order to *be* something, we have to *have* a lot of prerequisites, and then we have to *do* lots of different things. Then, at long last, we can finally *be.*

Let's go back to our practical example – the notion of becoming a dancer – and see how this would apply. When we decide that we want to *be* a dancer, we often think that we first have to *have* things like costumes and music, private lessons, participation in workshops, acknowledgment and support from other dancers, and the list goes on! We also often think of the things that we have to *do* in order to *be* a dancer. We calculate the investment: years of lessons, hours of practice, and multiple appearances in shows across the country. Finally, we think, someone will look at us and say, "Wow! You're a belly dancer!"

Well, it's true that *having* and *doing* all of these things count. None of them though, not a single one, is the essential core of *being* a dancer. The core is – you guessed it – a state of mind. So, what if you could just go directly into the desired state? What if you could go directly from *here* to *there*, without having to make all the little stops along the way?

"Well, that's cheating," you might say. "I have to *earn* the right to be a dancer (portfolio manager, playwright, etc.)." While your imagination might be attracted to the prospect of instantaneous gratification, your common sense and wealth of world experience would be saying, "That's not how the world works."

What we're talking about, though, isn't a matter of defying reality, or living with our heads in the clouds. What we are talking about are the *pragmatics* of getting, of *creating*, whatever we want, as expeditiously as possible. The way to do this most *expeditiously* is to create reality so that things flow in the direction that we want.

When we are in *have, do, be* mode, we constantly feel that we were laboring; the feeling is somewhat like rolling a big rock up a hill. There is a feeling of effort. When we take this approach, we will indeed create our desired results. However, they will happen surrounded by a feeling of the labor and the effort needed to bring them into being.

Suppose that we reverse the process. Suppose that we create it so that *in our beliefs*, we already *are* whatever it is that we desire to *be*. Then, from that position of already *being* in our desired reality, we do what comes naturally. For example, if I want to *be* an Oriental dancer (or, okay – a "belly dancer"), and then create it in my mind that I already *am* a dancer, then I do what dancers do, every day, as a matter of course. This might mean that I get up early every day to practice before going in to work. It might mean instead that I go to class every night that I can, whether or not I'm in the "mood" that evening. Because I already *am* a dancer, I simply do these things. A lot of the anxiety – the mental effort of decision-making – is released. I don't think about whether or not I will, I simply *do*. Then, as a result, I *have* the desired dance ability. It might take a while for this ability to manifest completely, but the state of mind of *being* in the desired state brings it about as easily as possible.

Think about it for just a minute longer. Those of us who feel drawn to cultivating our *Hathor* essence, or our inner *High Priestess*, already *know* that these modes speak to aspects of ourselves that are denied by our competitive and cognitive daily worlds. Many of us find our day-to-day lives driven by intense performance pressures. There is little time for our "inner selves." No wonder our inner core cries out for something like a very special, "women-only" kind of *path*. We are done with competing with men in games that are defined by men!

At the same time, the pragmatics of our lives often dictate that we do what men do. Thus, we *have* to get up each morning, go to work, and hold ourselves to the same demands and performance schedules that they do. We do this because, in many ways, this is still a "man's world." When we get home, we still have chores. No matter how great the calling, and the inner desire, there is little room in our lives for anything else that requires a great deal of *doing*. Also, we are busy enough with *having* things, whether they take up our time, space, or money. Very realistically, we often *have* enough already.

Suppose, though, that this "inner path" actually takes the pressure off our *having* and *doing*. Wouldn't that be a tremendous release? I had a practical example of this a while back, when I had a "computer-day-from-hell." By early evening, I had only accomplished a fraction of what I'd set out to do in the morning and had foregone my evening dance class with Anahid (one of my master teachers). I was resigned, but not very happy. Later, in the apartment, I made a conscious decision to relax and unwind. There was already some classical music on the stereo, and I turned the lights down low. I found an old candle stub, put it in a wine bottle that hadn't yet been thrown out, and lit it.

I began to do something that I hadn't done in months, which was to just spend some quiet time alone, inside my body, paying attention to how my body felt. I began to spontaneously do the movements that my master teachers had taught me; the undulations that I'd learned from Anahid Sofian and some of the soft *chi kung* movements (a breathing practice related to the Chinese martial arts) that I had learned from Elena Lentini. This didn't come from a program or plan. I did them simply because they felt right.

I realized that there, in New York City, I'd put myself into a *have* and *do* approach to studying dance. Yes, living in close proximity with my teachers was a dream come true. I was studying with them diligently. But in my quest to be diligent, and to follow their path, I'd forgotten that mastery in any art comes from within. In dance class, whether teaching or studying, there is always a part of me that is very cognitive, paying attention to either my students or my teacher. But the real expressive part of dance comes from within, not from counting out the sequence of steps!

I began to reconnect with the feelings inside my body. I experienced again how these wonderful movements are really generated from the inside. I began to get a sense of perspective, not only about the day, but about my entire experience of being in New York. What had been a very stressful day was transformed into a soft, wonderful mini-healing. I felt reconnected again. I realized that I didn't have to try so hard, all the time. My sense of mastery, in dance, and in accessing both my inner *Hathor* and my inner *High Priestess*, would evolve from this state. Not from the number of classes that I took.

The beauty of this approach – the awe-inspiring, soul-satisfying wonder of it all – is that once we create the intention of *already being* in the state that we desire, the universe cooperates massively to deliver this reality to our doorsteps. When we create the state of *already being* where we desire to *be*, things flow in our direction. It is almost as though a river reverses course. Our consciousness attracts experiences and things to us that match our vibrational being. *Our beliefs shape reality.*

As an example, I have seen what happens when women decide that they want to do more than just "study dance," in the sense of attending dance classes once a week. Once a woman makes a decision that she wants to "be a dancer," I've seen other people spontaneously give her gifts of jewelry and clothes that support that decision. Opportunities for study and performance arise naturally and easily. In my own life, the experience of living in Manhattan for several months had been an extraordinary manifestation. I'd wanted to study intensively with my master teachers for years. Being invited to come to Manhattan, having a place to stay, and even being given a one-way plane ticket were all "reality creations" of the highest order. I can tell you that I put no effort into any of them! No effort, just the heart-realization that if I wanted to develop real mastery in dance, I needed to study intensively with those who were already masters.

Sometimes, the manifestation can look as though it isn't serving us. This happened to me several years ago. I moved from a charming, intellectually-sophisticated town to a remote town, hundreds of miles away. As I drove to my new location, I cried. I thought I was leaving civilization behind forever! Moreover, the new job that I was moving to (and it truly was the best job choice for me at that time) was at some distance from any place where there would be Oriental dance groups or teachers. I didn't have funds at that time to travel on weekends and get away to dance workshops and seminars. I felt lonely and isolated.

In that small town, though, something almost miraculous happened. During the four years that I was there, I met two women, Marilyn Everett and Joni Johnson. Marilyn was the best chiropractor I'd ever known. (Up to that time, of course; I've continued to meet comparably wonderful ones ever since!) Joni was the best neuromuscular massage therapist I'd ever met. Both women were, and still are, genius-level in their abilities and gifts. In those four years, I learned (with their help) to release the deep tension patterns that I'd built up. This literally did take four years! Further, that was what I *needed at the time.* I could have studied with the best dance teachers, and practiced ten hours a day, but without the deep release of those tension patterns, I would never have matured as a dancer.

At the end of that four-year period, a new job opportunity helped me move on. I was able to resume weekly Oriental dance classes with a fine teacher, and also to study modern and jazz dance. Intense practice on my own helped me to mature, so that when I moved later to a different town, I was ready to open my own studio and start teaching.

The "lesson" of this story is that when we create an intention; when we set forth our desire to learn, become, have, or do something, or even to *shift* the way in which we live our lives (our relationships, financial security, or health, etc.); then what happens next may seem at first to be a huge detour. However, as we review our lives some time later (perhaps even years later), we see that this "detour" was actually the fastest and shortest route possible to our desired experience.

For me, practicing Oriental dance has been the outward manifestation of my *inner path* of developing internal energy. The special value that this *be, do, have* approach has had for me is in creating an energy state that is *attractive.*

Yes, this helps me be more attractive to men, when I choose to use the energy this way. However, this approach does a whole lot more. It helps me to attract *whatever I need* into my life. Also, it reverses – energetically – the way I go about bringing things (or events or people) into my life. Instead of "striving" outwardly, I now "draw" things to myself.

Of course, there is still the physical and mental attention involved. I won't call it effort, though, because as soon as I start "efforting," I know that I'm going about things the wrong way. The nature of this process should be *effortless*.

Years ago, Peter Ralston,[1] a martial arts master with whom I've studied, had a big realization. He was a young martial artist at that time, and practicing judo. Peter never does anything by partial measure. When he studied judo, he was in class every night, and doing *randori* (judo play) as much as he could in between.

Peter had been trying and straining and working very hard. Then suddenly, it hit him. "It should be effortless," he realized. Once he "got it" about how judo worked, he advanced rapidly. He was awarded his black belt within the year, and progressed to study many other martial arts. He later demonstrated what he had learned by winning an all-arts, all-techniques, full-contact tournament. This was the kind of contest about which martial arts movies are made. In Peter's case, the one in which he participated, and won, was real. He then opened a studio, began to teach full-time, and wrote a book; *Integrity of Being: The Cheng Hsin Teachings*. He later revised and expanded this book; it is now *Cheng Hsin: Principles of Effortless Power*.[2]

This principal – that of being "effortless" – holds true for us as well. If we are seeking to cultivate our *Hathor* essence, then we need to create it in a way that is effortless, natural, and easy. Similarly, if we wish to access the deep wisdom of our inner *High Priestess*, this must especially come about in a soft and gentle manner! In part, because this is the characteristic of real power. And in part, also, this is the only way that things will work most effectively in our lives.

Recently, I needed to make a change. A *big* one. Previously, whenever I worked for, or started, a company, I thought that I needed someone else to be both the marketer and the "business sense" of the company. I felt very comfortable in my role as a scientist and inventor, but felt that I lacked the people skills to make connections; to develop rapport and create clients. As I did more of the *integration* work described in the previous chapter, I realized that I was actually very good at connecting with people. I was perhaps even much better than the men with whom

I'd entrusted this role! But still, I needed to learn how to focus on the business aspects of a company, as well as on the scientific and technically creative ones.

This was a development that I couldn't put off any longer. I knew that certain crucial persons, with whom I'd worked as different business associates, had never really understood the totality my visions. They understand specific, scoped aspects, but not the whole picture. In order to move on, it was time for me to be the CEO of my own firm.

This, however, was my weakest area. I had already moved more into my *Mother-essence*, learning that I was a great salesperson when I pushed myself towards extroversion. I had already accessed the iNtuition/Feeling aspect of my being. However, most CXOs (CEOs, COOs, CFOs, etc.) are Sensing/Judging types; they are detail-focused and very specific. To deal with other business leaders, I had to become more like them. This means that I had to learn to *differentiate* between my various *Amazon* modes.

Being an inventor was like being a *Magician*; visionary and creative. I knew how to be in this mode already; this had been my primary professional expression for years. Teaching, which was being in my *Hierophant* mode, was also safe, comfortable, and familiar. This was true whether the teaching was in a company, in a university, or in mentoring younger colleagues at work. But now, I needed to learn to be an *Emperor*. I needed to become someone who would build structures; structures ranging from companies to products to business plans. I didn't expect to live in this realm forever; there are people who are much better at this than I am. However, I could no longer avoid this role completely.

I immediately began acting as if I were already a CEO. I switched what I was watching on TV during my early morning workouts. Instead of watching the weather and then a home decorating show, I'd watch Bloomberg and occasionally CNN. As a nice little spontaneous manifestation, various old bank and travel "rewards" programs insisted that I use up some points, and offered various magazine subscriptions. Within a few weeks, I was regularly reading *Barron's*, *The Economist*, *Wall Street Journal*, and *Fortune*. Through colleagues, I secured positions as adjunct professor at two different universities, teaching courses that could best be described as "Business Plans 101." As the old saying goes, "We teach that which we need to learn," and I was learning rapidly. Now, I was getting paid to focus on that which was most important, while I still worked on inventions and developing the technology base for my next company.

After all this refocusing, would someone want to hire me as CEO? Certainly not! Bad for me; bad for them. I'm still really not of that mindset. Even though I'm a pretty good *Amazon*, the *Emperor* mode is the still the weakest of my *Amazon* personas. But the sum of these actions, all taken from the position of how a CEO or other high-level executive would orient his or her thinking, has brought me much closer to this kind of work. Also, this has taken place in a very short time frame; several months at the most.

When the time is right for any of us to make a transition, of any sort, we can take similar action. We can jump into the middle of *being* that which we *desire to be*. Then, we *do* what we would normally *do*, *being* who we are now in this new *state*. Then, we watch what sorts of things manifest; this will be our new set of *haves*: new friends, colleagues, partners, romantic interests; even new opportunities. This actually is the fastest way to create something new in our lives!

PERSONAL PATHWORKING:

1. What is the change or transition that you are most seeking to create in your life right now? Can you put yourself in the mental state of already having created this experience? (You might want to do this as a sort of deep "visualization" practice.) As you do so, and you observe your life in this state, how are you living? What are your habits? What are you doing? What comes easily and naturally to you in this new state? Now, seek to maintain that feeling, connect it with your present life, and bring those habits, actions, and feelings into your current state. Note: This exercise and any others that require deep visualization of a different reality or "state-of-being" may require multiple attempts. Keep at it; sometimes it takes a while for our minds to release to this different state.

2. Find someone who exemplifies the qualities that you desire to create. Then, *be* that person. As Peter Ralston, one of the greatest martial artists of our time, has told his students, "*Be* me!" He meant that his students should drop all the judgments and preconceptions, and just take on *who* he was and *what* he was doing. If we take this approach to "modeling" ourselves on someone who epitomizes what we would like to be, then we create a short-cut to their state. I've done this with dance teachers in seeking to learn their style. Just *map yourself onto* the other person. (And yes, imitation is the sincerest form of flattery!)

3. Read what Tony Robbins has to say about "modeling" ourselves on others when we want to rapidly master a new life-skill.[3] Apply what you learn.

4. Find the greatest leaders in your field, even if you can't study with them directly. Research them, and try to emulate how they act. Suppose that you want to become an astute stock investor, and you decide that Warren Buffet is someone whom you'd like to emulate. When you read that he's

made a certain decision, research the facts for yourself, and try to think the way he thought. Are you coming to the same conclusions? Always, *always* study with the masters. Study long-distance if you must, or via "remote" means such as reading their books, watching their performances, and/or studying their creative or intellectual output. Travel if you must (and if you can). But focus, *always*, on the "best of the best." Never settle for less, just because it is more readily available. This sends out a very clear and consistent message to the universe. Over time, your desires will be answered.

CHAPTER 13:
THE GENTLE ART OF RECEIVING

THE DAY AFTER I HAD surgery, my friend Annabelle came to pick me up at the hospital. Instead of taking me straight home, she took me to my favorite restaurant for lunch. After lunch, she brought a beautiful triangular hip scarf out of her purse. It was a deep red silky chiffon, bordered with an extravagant edging of iridescent purple-back beads. "I wanted you to have this, Alay'nya," Annabelle said, "because I think you need practice in receiving."

I fingered the beautiful material and hand-done beading, and thought: "She's right. All my life I've been achievement-oriented. This is not a bad thing, in and of itself. But I've gotten off-center. I've gotten into a place where the only way that I think that I can bring something into my life is to achieve it. There's nothing wrong with achievements, but they are not all of who I am. Especially, they are not all of who I am as a woman."

Over the past several years, I've had more and more lessons in the *gentle art of receiving*. There is something very humbling, and *softening*, about realizing that we don't always have to strive. We don't always have to achieve, and we don't always have to "make things happen." Instead, there are times that we can simply yield to being in a receptive state, and let the universe flow towards us. This is operating from our feminine core.

I'm reminded of a time when my mother watched the growing identification of Bridgette Bardot and other starlets as "sex objects." Nothing new in the identification, but that was the first time that she had heard the "sex object" phrase.

"Sex object," she mused to herself. "What does that mean?" After some serious thought, she came up with an answer. "I have it!" she announced to the family at large, and to my father in particular. "I will be a *love object*. I will allow the world to love me!" My mother had dramatic tendencies, having modeled herself on the renowned nineteenth-century stage actress Sarah Bernhardt when she was young. This time, she had it right. She was the mother of five children, a teacher at a private school, and active in community and church affairs. But her core was now to be a *love object*, and to graciously receive what the world had to offer.

It's worthwhile noting that she achieved this insight in her mature years. She had already had her time of achieving, and had completed the brunt of her duty as caretaker for five active children. She was in a position where she could contemplate what her femininity meant to her. Also, she was spiritually mature; she was able to receive in the finest sense.

There are times that each of us is achievement-oriented, and wants to prove how strong, how smart, how tough, and how adventuresome we can be. This is very human, and even for the most feminine of women, there are times when this is very appropriate. This is when we are in our *Amazon* personas.

There are few things that feel as good as competency; the knowledge that we can do something, and do it well. Generally, the feeling of competency comes about through achievements. We have to learn our skills, and invest the time and effort in gaining mastery.

In a like vein, each of us has times when we go into a receptive mode, which is an important balance to our lives. This is how we both get in touch with our spiritual core and also how we access our creativity. Men as well as women can be receptive. Julia Cameron, in *The Artist's Way*, talks about how we can do this. She describes this as "filling the well" – something important to all creative spirits.[1] Also, when any of us takes on a life-endeavor that is truly more than "who we are" as an individual person, we need to blend our achievement-endeavors with the quality of receiving. We must graciously receive help from others, and from God or Source, in order to create our dream.

A wise and skillful person, a "master," knows that receiving is as important as putting in the effort, in order to create overall success. The "receiving" may often be of an insight needed for the next step. Then, as we identify the insight that we have received, we switch into a more outwardly-focused mode. This is the *yin/ yang* (or *High Priestess/Magician*) balance that we need in our lives.

Receiving, then, is a quality that epitomizes the nature of our feminine energy. It is active, not passive, but it is a quality of drawing inwards to ourselves, rather than thrusting out. (And yes, the similarity to the way each gender has sex is not accidental.)

Along these lines, nurturance (from our *Isis/Mother* archetype or persona) is not necessarily the only area where we find our feminine core, although we have often been taught to believe that it is. Throughout history, one of the main roles that we women have played has been to care for others. Let us just accept that as a "what is so," rather than evaluating it and placing judgments on whether or not it is a good or bad thing. The bottom line is that we have done a lot of caretaking, and that caretaking is generally regarded as a feminine task.

While we often get a great deal of emotional satisfaction ourselves in taking care of others, let's remember that caretaking is in itself an achievement; an accomplishment. It can be a feminine task, but it is not the only essence at the core of our feminine being. This is why many women who are caretakers feel that they are not fully satisfied. It is because no one is taking care of them, and they do not have (or do not create for themselves) the opportunity to access their other essential archetypes.

This is why our *Hathor* and *High Priestess* modes are important to us; particularly our *High Priestess*. Each of these allows us to receive, in very special ways.

Becoming willing to receive is not easy; it is actually a spiritual discipline. This is so because when we receive, we have to give up control. "Control" is an illusion anyway, but we cling to it so tightly that we often forget its illusory nature.

One of the greatest challenges that we have in life is that of developing balance. As women, we have fought long and hard for the gains that the Women's Movement has made. The pioneers in this area often suffered great hardships to win benefits that many of us now take for granted. The rights that we now have are rights that many women throughout the world do not yet enjoy.

The women who obtained these rights for us had to be in their *Amazon* mode most of the time. What they achieved for us were not only the rights to own property, vote and hold office, and to have jobs with equal benefits and compensations. They created a place for us from which we can now regroup and re-assess our overall situations. Because we now have the benefits (as well as the woes) of using our *Amazon* as well as our *Mother* mode, we can start sensing what it is that we are still missing.

During our struggles to gain and to exercise these rights, both as a society and as individuals, we have sometimes lost our sense of balance. We have been particularly susceptible to this loss when we have either focused strongly on achieving, or when we have concentrated on what we do not have and have felt like victims. Either perspective, taken to an extreme, pulls us from our center. In particular, we have often strayed from our center when we have taken the male model of power as the only real concept of power, and applied it to ourselves.

There are times that we do need to spend a great deal of time immersed within our *Amazon* role, for various good reasons. There are times that we need to focus on achievements, and on leaving our mark on the world. There are also times when we need to address and redress injustices in society. However, keeping our focus solely on these issues prevents us from completing our own growth. To invite our own soul-growth, we need to confront that which we, as modern women, fear the most.

This fear is *no longer* that we cannot survive on our own; that we need a man. By now, we are very good at taking care of ourselves. Our real fear, the one that we often don't want to admit to ourselves, is that if we let go, everything will fall apart. We have replaced a belief that we need an *external* man to care for us with the belief that we need to be in our *internal* masculine mode – our *Amazon* – all the time! We're afraid that if we don't control things and "make them happen," then we will not be supported and cared for. By going into our fear, we open up the avenue for tremendous growth.

We are ready to figure out what form our *integration pathway* will take. We have already determined that one aspect of our *path* is to first know, and then access, each of our core archetypes. We need the masculine as well as the feminine, and we need the feminine archetypes that we have most likely neglected. Then, we need to learn *integration*; we need to be able to call on whichever aspects are most needed, at the right time.

However, we know that there is more to our *pathway* than this. We know that we need some form of body art; a physical practice. The Shaolin monks had the martial arts. Yogis have had the physical practices of *hatha yoga* (the positions and poses), augmented by *pranayama* (breathing exercises) and *kundalini yoga* (energy practices).

In addition to the physical aspect, we need a *pathway* that helps us unify our full awareness of body and mind, psyche and spirit. The martial arts have included a mental discipline and a spiritual component as well as the physical movements. However, they are called the "martial arts" for good reason; they correspond to the masculine essence of Mars, the god of war.

We need something comparable. Whatever we select has to involve physical movement, and at the same time, engage the fullness of who we are. We know, also, that our "fullness" is substantially more complex than men's; we are not just interested in ego-dominance and achievements. Testosterone (together with other masculine neurochemicals) does wonderful things for men. (To a more limited extent, it is also useful for us women.) However, our feminine physiology, neuro-physiology, and psychology give us a much more complex, and ever-changing, mix.

It is our *potential range* of emotional experience that should invite our full attention. The overwhelming majority of us go through our days locked into a very tight emotional range; we are being *Amazons* at work and *Mothers* at home. This is like allowing ourselves a single octave, in which we play only the key of C major, throughout our lives! We need much, *much* more. Whatever it is that we use as the physical basis for our *integration pathway*, we know that it must allow us to express a wide range of feelings.

Finally, we know that what we create as a *path* has to give us the *potential* for the ecstatic. We don't expect the highest moments of exaltation every time we do a physical practice, but brief moments of being "beyond ourselves" have to be fully within and encompassed by our *pathway*.

Our ideal *pathway* thus has to at least have the *potential* for invoking our mental attention and for allowing us to express our full emotional range. It also has to give us the *potential* for accessing our spiritual essence. And of course, we need to involve our bodies as well.

In *The Feminine Face of God*, authors Anderson and Hopkins relate:

> **A young rabbi told us, "Throughout Jewish history there have been sacred places for men to study, called *yeshivot* from the words *to sit*. But we women don't need a place to sit, like dead weights! We need a *rikudya*, a place to dance the energy of the holiness in ourselves and to bring though our bodies the sacred feminine Torah."**[2]

Clearly, we need the physical expression even more than men! The realization that our spiritual, as well as our sensual, natures can find release through dance is our key to identifying Oriental dance as the physical embodiment of our *pathway*.

Robert Fusaro Sensei, 7th Dan (seventh-degree black belt) in Shotokan karate, is one of the world's leading martial artists.[3] He was one of my earliest teachers, along with his junior teachers (black belts who were invited to teach classes), when I was able to study in his karate studio in Minneapolis, MN many years ago. Fusaro Sensei respects Oriental dance as a *pathway* for women. He's observed Cassandra, a highly-respected performer and master teacher.[4] (Cassandra taught my first dance teacher, Medea; this makes her my "grandmother" in dance lineage!) Describing Cassandra and her students, he said: "I respect what they are doing ... [they have] control over their bodies and a good mindset; it's just tremendous!" Speaking specifically of Cassandra, he went on to say, "She's like me" [in terms of proficiency in her art form]. Noting that his wife also likes to dance, Fusaro Sensei said "dancing is so good for your health, and [in particular] belly dancing [is about] more perfection of body dynamics and control ... [dancers have a] smooth transition of force, of motion ... individual control [of the different muscles], but also fluidity [in] going from one action to another; the action control is very apparent."[5]

The praise from a martial arts master to a master of the *Art of Venus*, or Oriental dance, shows that these art forms are similar in their complexity and physical demands. In a martial art such as karate, the "improvisational" aspects come about during *kumite* (sparring). In Oriental dance, we learn to do solo improvisations. However, just as karate, judo, T'ai Chi Ch'uan, and almost all other martial arts include "set pieces" (such as the karate *katas*), we also have well-defined, choreographed dances within our art. Each dancer typically develops her own, although master teachers will impart their choreographies during workshops or use DVD or online formats for teaching. Some works, such as those of Suzanna del Vecchio, have an iconic quality; they become inspirational references for us.[6]

Cassandra herself noted that Oriental dance provides a *body/mind/psyche-emotional/energy pathway* that is especially suitable for women. "In Oriental dance, like other dance, the dance movement is all about the energy flow through the body, and the efficient use of that flow to express the emotions the dancer feels from the music. Because the movement is uniquely feminine, it is able to give women deep insight and awareness of their bodies, and the mind/body connection."[7] Similarly, Maria Strova, author of *The Secret Language of Belly Dancing*, describes how dance gives us the means for complete emotional expression. As she puts it, "Its [belly dance's] language gives us a voice in the world."[8]

My dear friend, Stella Grey, has for years been an intellectual force characterizing the true nature of Oriental dance. This is important for us, as Oriental dance truly is an *intimate* art form. This is a dance form that is best both expressed and experienced in a close and personal setting, rather than as a staged performance. As Stella describes it in one of her blogposts, "The [O]riental is a small thing, a bijou, a beautifully cut jewel in an exquisite setting. It is built out of small tender gestures and subtle, precise moves. The tilt of the head, the twist of a hip, the emotions that flicker across that dancer's face: these are where the enchantment lives."[9]

It is *because* of this delicacy and nuance, together with communication intimacy, that our dance form is so distinctively feminine. This is not simply a juxtaposition to the more masculine art forms, such as the martial arts. At a deeper level, the masculine nature is to put forth ego and to assert dominance. (Dr. Louann Brizendine notes, in *The Male Brain*, at a very early age, boys focus on establishing their order within group hierarchies. This attention to dominance hierarchies continues throughout their lives.[10])

In contrast, Oriental dance is an intimate art precisely in that it is an *act of communication*. There is a known and explicit dynamic, ideally between the dancer, the musician(s), and the audience. In the same blogpost, Stella characterizes this interaction: "I believe that the dance is at its best when it is a spontaneous three way conversation … among the musicians, the dancer and audience. The dancer makes the music visible to the audience, the audience's appreciation is heightened and feeds back to the musicians." This conversational aspect, conveyed through the dancer's gestures and the way in which she uses her gaze – a much more complex communication than simple "eye contact" – offers us a realm of human experience that is difficult to access with other, more stylized and staged dance forms.

The innate intimacy of Oriental dance is what allows the art to be so healing for the audience members as well as to the dancer herself. An emotional rapport builds as the dance progresses. A true relationship develops, even if it exists for only a brief moment in time. This relationship – especially if the dancer can "flow" her energy throughout her entire being – is enormously healing and refreshing.

In addition to being a way in which we as dancers connect with our audience, we also use Oriental dance as a way to connect with other women. From ancient though present times, women have used this dance form as a way of celebrating life's joyful moments with each other. Anne Thomas Soffee, in *Snake Hips*, describes how she found a circle of friends and a renewed sense of personal identity through her study of Oriental dance.[11] I have personally found not only camaraderie and support from my sisters in dance; I have been inspired by them as well!

For example, Amustela,[12] one of the leading dancers in our area, recently participated in a dance event sponsored by the Washington Area Mid-East Dance Association (WAMEDA, Inc.[13]), our local non-profit dancer's organization. While Amustela was clearly the "headliner" and the most accomplished and exciting performer, she made a point of being enthusiastically supportive of the other dancers. She made certain that each of the soloists and troupe members felt very positive about their performances. Amustela's hearty applause and the generous and whole-hearted praise that she lavished on each performer was what made the event happy and memorable for each of them. It was not just that they were getting the praise; they were getting it from one of the best dancers in the area!

Similarly, another of my dear dance friends, Nimeera, is also enormously supportive of dancers throughout the area. Her expression is quieter, but no less considerate, kind, and generous. In addition to being a fine dancer and teacher, Nimeera also runs a dance supply business.[14] I've seen her in her "vending" role at a major workshop, and marveled at what a focused and purposeful business-woman she is, in addition to her performing and teaching excellence. In one case, I observed her close-hand during a major vending event, for which she needed several assistants. Everyone who worked with her during that long weekend not only got an opportunity to attend an important dance show, and to receive excellent discounts on what they purchased from her, but they also had quality coaching during a "mini-apprenticeship" with a business guru!

Amustela, Nimeera, and many others like these two have continuously provided leadership for and encouragement to other dancers. Since one of our basic needs is to build relationships and be part of a community, we find that the leadership offered by senior dancers is vital to our happiness and well-being. Within almost every community, we will often find dance leaders who will provide nurturing guidance as we embark on dance as our personal *pathway*.

In sum, we find that Oriental dance provides a complete *pathway* for women, encompassing not only the physical discipline of the body art, but also the means to use our minds, connect with other women, express our full emotion range, and cultivate our internal energy, or *ch'i*. This truly makes Oriental dance a *body/mind/ psyche/energy pathway*.

We don't have to be a "Professor of Symbology," as is Robert Langdon, the hero in Dan Brown's recent novels, to figure some things out for ourselves.[15] We can get considerable insight just from examining the materials that we have at hand, and adding in both our common sense and real-world knowledge.

When we looked, in *Chapter 7*, at the *Worldly Sequence* of the Tarot's Major Arcana, we noted that it closed with the *Chariot*, which I'll now call *Winged Victory* in deference to its original meaning. *Winged Victory* is a feminine archetype. It is a powerful card; one of mastery. Many of us, during our early stages of career-building, resonate with it. However, *Winged Victory* is at the end of a sequence; it is the seventh card in the series. Without knowing what has happened, many of us, in our lives, have already passed through the *Worldly Sequence* into the next one.

This second sequence, or second major challenge of adult personal growth, is the *Turning Inward* sequence, as described by Rachel Pollack, author of *Seventy-Eight Degrees of Freedom*.[16] We have already *integrated*, we have achieved *Winged Victory*, and we are ready to move on.

The second sequence in the Major Arcana begins with one of the strongest metaphorical images in our culture; the concept of gentle *Strength*. As commonly depicted, a beautiful woman, garlanded with flowers and wearing a long, flowing white dress, eases a lion into submission. She is not forcing the lion; she is not wrestling with it. Rather, she is gently easing it to the ground. There is a huge shift in our psyches as we go from *Winged Victory* (Card VII) to *Strength* (Card VIII). We shift from being *The Karate Kid* (or *The Next Karate Kid;* the troubled, teenage *karate girl*) to being the gentle (yet effective) practitioner of *Kung Fu*. We are still achieving our goals, but instead of a direct and linear approach, we use the more "internal" martial arts. As we would in T'ai Chi, we blend with our opponents, and we use their own mass and momentum. We softly bring the world into alignment with our desires, instead of forcing our will onto a situation.

The *Turning Inward* sequence begins with *Strength* (Card VIII) and ends with a mystical and somewhat mystifying card; *Temperance* (Card XIV). Between the beginning and the end of this sequence, we go through a major life transition. For the moment, though, I will focus on the sequence's first and final cards. These two cards give us very different approaches to dealing with life. In the first, we are still ego-driven. We may approach life in a gentler manner than we did in our younger years, but we are still imposing our will on situations. (We may even be imposing our will on ourselves, as well, driving ourselves to reach performance objectives.) In contrast, when we reach the stage of *Temperance*, something very different happens.

Temperance shows us an angel with one foot on land, and the other immersed in a flowing stream. The angel is pouring liquid from one cup to another, but the cups are separated by a horizontal as well as a vertical distance. We know that a liquid normally doesn't flow down "sideways," but in *Temperance*, it does! The *Temperance Angel* has gone beyond the laws of gravity. Further, as shown in some decks, the flow is both from the lower cup to the higher, as well as from high to low. A later depiction of the same card (from the BOTA deck) shows the *Angel* pouring water from a pitcher onto a lion, and simultaneously dripping fire from a torch onto an eagle.[17] (Note that the theme of taming the lion, or powerful beast, is continued.) The eagle is the "higher form" of sexual energy, having been transmuted from the "lower form" depicted as a scorpion. Thus, this alternate depiction of *Temperance* again involves two essences; water and fire. Further, they are being blended.

The eagle in this specific rendering of *Temperance* represents the water element. This is because the "lower form" of the eagle, the scorpion, pertains to the astrological sign of Scorpio, which is a water sign. (Traditionally, each of the various astrological signs is assigned to one of the cardinal elements; air, earth, water, or fire.) Similarly, the lion represents fire. This is because the lion relates to the sign of Leo, which is a fire sign. Thus, the *Angel* is pouring water onto the fire-sign lion, and fire onto the water-sign eagle. Metaphysically, the *Temperance Angel* is *mixing essences*; fire and water. When we bring this quality into our own lives, our *integration* becomes more fluid and natural. In fact, more than easy, this "blending" actually moves us to a new level of practice; our *integration* becomes "alchemical."

The essence of alchemy is transformation. The analogy has always been that of turning lead into gold, or discovering (or creating) the powerful, life-giving Philosopher's Stone. When we see *Temperance* as the end state of one of our life journeys, we foresee a new way of living.

This is huge transition time in our lives. This also points to opening up our ability to receive. We have gone from being the personification of *Winged Victory* to the gentle *Strength Maiden*; we have moved from asserting our will to gentling life's beasts and rough situations. This is our transition from the *Worldly Sequence* to *Turning Inward*. Yet at the end of our *Turning Inward* journey, signified by *Temperance*, we are having much more in the way of magical experience. We begin "blending" various essences within our lives.

For example, we begin bringing the peace and serenity of our *High Priestess*, whether gained from yoga, meditation, or dance, into our *Amazon* lives. We can be enormously helpful to each other as we do this, both in our friendships and through our various forms of teaching.

One of the most important things to note about entering into our *Hathor* and *High Priestess* modes is that we begin to *receive* more. As with the *Temperance Angel*, we are both pouring ourselves out (being in our *Amazon* and *Mother* modes), and simultaneously receiving. We receive insight, love, and support (in our *High Priestess* and *Hathor* modes). In these latter two modes, we are not merely passive, we are actively receiving; there is an energy exchange that goes on, and perhaps even more!

❧❧

One thing that holds us back from fully receiving is that we do not honor ourselves sufficiently. The reason, of course, is that society does not greatly honor the *Sacred Feminine*. It will help us if we can understand that, over the course of human history, this is a recent development.

We need to reconnect with the severed ends of our pathway; with those last known moments in which women were regarded as having connection with the sacred. Margaret Starbird asserts, in *The Woman with the Alabaster Jar*, that the "woman at Bethany" identified in the gospels was very likely Mary the Magdalene (where "Magdala" is reasonably translated as "Tower of Strength").[18] The *Gospel of John* identifies her as Mary, the sister of Martha and Lazarus.[19] Mary's act of anointing Jesus with costly spikenard (an exotic perfumed oil) was not only to foreshadow his coming death, but also to confirm his role as king, where his sacrificial death would redeem his people. In the ancient tradition which she enacted, it was the high priestess's role to anoint the king! In so doing, Mary let us know that she was part of a priestess lineage. (She also signified to all the other guests that Jesus was acting as king on behalf of his people; this was an event of extraordinary significance.)

Though some scholars disagree, the Mary who anointed the feet of Jesus with costly oil was very possibly the same Mary depicted in the *Gospel of Mary*, who was known for being a close companion as well as a disciple of Jesus. Mary's role as priestess is different from her role as both a disciple and a companion, and was not simply due to her lineage. She had an extraordinary depth of spiritual sensitivity and understanding. Throughout the *Gospel of Thomas*, as well as the *Gospel of Mary*, there are many indications that she understood the teachings of Jesus at a much deeper level than any of his male disciples.[20]

Even as Mary honored Jesus with the act of anointing, he in return honored her. His disciples spoke against her for the extravagance of her gesture. In response, Jesus said, "... what she has done will be told in memory of her."[21] Much of the interaction between Jesus and Mary has been lost; some of this at least is due to the antagonism towards her by his male disciples and later followers. We have only recently discovered, for example, fragments of their conversations as recorded in the *Pistis Sophia*.[22] Throughout the past two thousand years, though, the retelling of this one incident – the anointing with oil – has persisted. Only now, however, is the full impact of Mary's role being understood at a culturally-widespread level. She was indeed the *High Priestess*. She alone had the honor, and the duty, of anointing the sacrifice before he was slaughtered.

Mary's lineage, through the Hebrew people (and possibly through the tribe of Benjamin), traces back to Sarah, wife of Abraham.[23] A study of Savina Teubal's detailed book, *Sarah the Priestess*, gives us further food for thought; there are very reasonable indications that Sarah herself was *High Priestess* of a people who honored the Great Goddess.[24] Her marriage to Abram (later called Abraham) was at the turning point of her people's future. In fact, we know what happened to many competing cultures of that time. The ancient Israelites, under direction from their (masculine) God, killed every man, every male child, and every "woman who has known man by lying with him."[25] This was a common practice as the Israelites gained territory through war. Thereafter, they did not "... permit a sorceress to live."[26] In short, they eradicated the goddess-religions, and with them, access to a viable women's *pathway*. (We may note that the trend towards minimizing the role of goddesses was not unique to the ancient Israelites; Tikva Frymer-Kensky's *In the Wake of The Goddesses* points out that even in ancient Sumeria, the role of the Great Goddesses diminished over time.[27])

Jesus himself honored women. However, his male disciples, particularly Peter, were very opposed to the Magdalene, and Saul (later Paul) had views about women's roles that were in some ways still representative of their times; limiting and con-strictive. Women were enjoined to "learn in silence with all submissiveness."[28]

Some four hundred years after Jesus' sacrificial death, the Emperor Constantine adopted Christianity as the official state religion. However, he did this primarily as a political move to stabilize the empire. Over the years, those in ecclesiastical authority used the church as a means to gain both wealth and power. In fact, during the two decades prior to Constantine's conversion, "Holy Mother Church" had accommodated to its cultural (pagan) surrounds to the extent that it became expedient for the emperor to use the now-compliant church to his advantage![29] This meant that alternative paths needed to be extinguished. Hundreds of years later, this trend continued; the Inquisition was just one means by which any fur-ther remnants of a women's *pathway* was obliterated.

Fortunately, current historical research is giving us insights and connections that were not available even a few decades ago. It is up to us to make use of them. There are three steps that we can take. The first can be to honor *Shekhinah*, or the *feminine face of God*, in ourselves, in others, and as She expresses Herself around us. Our second step is to continue with the research, and restoring the connec-tion with our ancient heritage. In other words, we must continue learning what we can and from this, create greater understanding. This allows us to begin some inner healing.

As Starbird states, in *The Woman with the Alabaster Jar*:

> One of the saddest realities in our culture is that the ascendancy of the wounded masculine has led to emotional exhaustion. Where the feminine is not valued, a man has no real intimacy with his counterpart, his "other half." He often cannot channel his energies in a loving relationship, since his partner is not considered worthy... the frustrated ascendant male causes burnout: "where the sun always shines, there's a desert below."[30]

Possibly as important as our learning to honor our *Sacred Feminine* is our third step: the healing our own inner masculine. This is likely to be something that we cultivate as we progress through our *Worldly Sequence* of core archetypes, moving towards our own personal *Winged Victory.* We acknowledge that we need to heal the wounded masculine within ourselves, before we can heal any aspect or person without. Practically, this may be appreciating our inner *Amazon* when she gets up to go to work each day, or stays late at the office to finish a report, or volunteers for an extra committee assignment. We can love and support our inner *Amazon* by attending to her need for comfort as she works; letting her (perhaps even making her) take a break and walk around the room every so often; bringing flowers to the office, and in general treating her as we would treat someone whom we loved. In particular, we learn to treat her as someone whom we love who is doing a hard and demanding job. As we are more loving with our inner *Amazon,* we can be kinder and gentler with the external men in our lives.

Then, as we progress with the healing of our core masculine archetypes (that is, our inner *Amazon*), and by honoring our feminine, we can move towards deeper *integration.* At this stage, our pathway shifts from *Strength* to *Temperance.* In this next realm of our inner *path,* we shift from using force of will to gentleness, and finally learn a form of internal alchemical or magical blending. That means, we bring our various essences together without striving. To us, and to those who watch us, it seems as though things "flow" towards us. They may even, like the magical liquid in the *Temperance Angel's* pitchers, flow upwards to reach us!

An important aspect of this inner healing and *integration* is that as we move from *Winged Victory* through *Strength* to *Temperance,* we become ready to work with our internal energy, or *ch'i.* We can do this energy circulation practice either individually or with a partner. Moreover, we can incorporate energy circulation and direction into our dance, which is a more advanced practice. We address this in the final chapters. For now, we turn our attention to the simple physical pragmatics of re-aligning our bodies and releasing tension. This is an essential prerequisite for any effective energy circulation, or "alchemical union."

PERSONAL PATHWORKING:

1. Simply take note. Start by observing: When or how often are you in your *Amazon*? How much are you pushing? What happens when you let go, and start to receive?

2. Prayer time. Begin to ask God, Source, Higher Power, or whatever aspect you understand to be "greater than you" for the wisdom and grace to stop *asserting* so much, and to allow yourself to *receive* more. This sounds simple and easy, but is one of the most challenging aspects of our journey. Divine grace is definitely in order.

3. While reading the recently discovered and translated ancient documents about Jesus and Mary the Magdalene is useful, we can possibly get a more "felt-sense" appreciation of the time in which they were written, and the significance of Mary's spiritual walk, by reading about these documents and their discovery in the context of a story. I recommend *Resurrection*, by Tucker Malarkey.[31]

PART IV:
IN OUR BODIES

⚜

CHAPTER 14:
LOCKING OUR MINDS OUT OF OUR BODIES

ACROSS THE CROWDED FLOOR, A series of young women swayed like seaweed in the ocean. Their eyes on the diminutive teacher, they followed Anahid Sofian in her graceful yet precise movements. Getting Anahid to come to the Southeast was a rare event, as she was highly in demand for her New York classes. But we had put together a "master class," and dancers from several cities had gathered to study with Anahid, renowned for both her technical mastery and exquisite expression.

The virtue of these master classes was that unlike the larger workshops, in which up to fifty or more dancers would be gathered together, the size was limited enough so that we could each receive individual feedback and correction. And that is exactly what we were getting.

"Leah," she called out to a dancer, "you need to release – right here." She gestured to her own sternum. We were practicing upper body undulations, one of the most beautiful and sensual moves in Oriental dance. "And Alay'nya," she turned, scrutinizing me, "you need to do the same."

Both Leah and I were well beyond the beginner's level. Leah, with long, ash-blond hair and a svelte figure, had been dancing professionally for years in a major Southeast city. I'd been studying for many years as well, and teaching for several of these. Here we were, getting the same correction on one of the most basic moves. "What," I wondered, "is going on with us?"

Suddenly it hit me; one of those "Aha!" moments. Leah and I both epitomized the "young-woman-on-her-own-in-the-world." Having to make it on our own in essentially a man's world, we had taken on the masculine attributes of body armor by using our muscles and ligaments! By stiffening our muscles, and holding them tightly, we created an impenetrable shield; we were "armored" against the world. What we were doing in our bodies reflected more the influence of Athena,

Goddess of Intellect (as well as war; she is the ultimate *Amazon*), than Aphrodite, the Goddess of Love. We were fully in our *Amazon* mode!

Releasing the muscles in our sternum took conscious attention from each of us. It did then, and it still does. The old tension patterns die hard.

A basic biological strategy to help us avoid pain is that we "compartmentalize" our bodies. If we are wounded, and are trying to get to safety, then we override the pain in one part of our bodies, and throw our energies and awareness into the parts that work. We get out of danger as fast as we can.

As a basic strategy, this has helped us survive for thousands of years. However, the sources of "wounding" in our lives are now more often emotional than physical. Despite that, we tend to use the same biological strategy. We compartmentalize the emotional pain into compact places in our bodies, and then lock out awareness away from these areas.

When we do this kind of physical and emotional compartmentalizing, we tend to "lock up" our bodies. We tighten up our bodies so that we can't feel. I see so many women (and men) who have locked themselves out of their bodies that it saddens me. Each of us has seen them, I'm sure. And maybe, without realizing why, we may have felt saddened as well. Perhaps we have each had the thought, "I don't want to end up like that!"

We don't have to. None of us has to end up in a tight, tension-riddled body pattern. But the way that we work through this is not just to remind ourselves to "have good posture." "Good posture" is important, of course. However, when we hold ourselves in a tense or strained manner, it doesn't mean that we're doing the best thing for our bodies. Similarly, if we just "sag," the reason is not just that we're lazy. Usually, there is something going on at a deeper emotional level; this is true whether we're overly tight or too lax in our posture.

When we start to change how we hold our bodies, then we begin to confront the mindset that kept us in the "poor posture" state. This can be a powerful, and sometimes a scary, experience. Scary, in that usually when we've blocked off awareness of part of our bodies, we have done so because we're storing away a feeling that we don't want to experience. The feeling can be fear, it can be shame; it can be a number of things. It can even be a normal, ordinary sexual feeling.

However, if we grew up in a culture that taught us that sexual feelings were bad, then we'll do what we can to block these feelings off. Thus, we use tension – and associated poor posture – to block off awareness of certain feelings. In addition, our habits of sitting for long periods of time in front of the computer (or sitting during meetings, or when watching TV at home) reinforce any postural problems that we may have.

Many of us have noticed that both we, and the people around us, have tension patterns in our bodies. We may, in fact, have noticed three major types of blockage patterns. The first one is very common. We'll see her (or sometimes him) in the grocery store, in the mall, or in church. The woman is often very full-figured, and as she sweeps down the aisle, she seems like a three-masted schooner under full sail. Chest thrust forward, she looks as though she's taking life head-on. But wait, there's more! When you look at her derriere (form a mental picture of someone as you do this; it may even be of someone that you know), it sticks out also. We're not just talking size; we're talking position.

What's going on here? If a person's front and rear are both sticking out, that's not normal posture, is it? Think about it. Our mamas told us to "stand up tall." So how does a person even begin to stick both the front and rear out at the same time?

Well, a person actually has to work at it! This is really an "extreme" posture. To do this thing of "sticking out both ways," someone (let's say, a woman) has to lock her knees. Once she does this, she'll have locked up her pelvis as well. Then, guess what? With her pelvis locked up, it's hard for her to feel what's going in that area! (Maybe that's *why* some people do this.) Now, suppose that someone is actually going to do this kind of posture, and take it to the fullest. What happens next? Well, after locking up her pelvis, she'd have to let her tummy muscles become flaccid. They absolutely have to *sag*.

Now, something has to carry the weight. This means that the muscles in the lower back start taking on the workload. They get shortened, and after a while, they get very, very tight. But once all this is done, the end result is achieved! The pelvis, and the entire torso, is canted forward.

Now, no one walks around in a sort of permanent forward bow. We all like to see where we're going. However, if the pelvis is canted forward (which tilts the whole torso forward), then the only way to bring the head up is to arch the back. This has the effect of jutting the chest forwards.

So really, this posture began down in the pelvis-hip configuration, and the chest-thrust-forward effect is simply an end-result, because the person is trying to see. The overall combination puts tremendous strain on the back. There is strain in the lower back, from the lumbar vertebrae down to the sacrum, and there is strain in the upper, or mid-back, where there is a compensating arch.

After a while, this begins to hurt. And when muscles hurt, they tighten up. But the only ones that will tighten are the ones that are already tight — say, the muscles in the lower back. When a person has this kind of posture, and the muscles in the tummy are flaccid, then they aren't supporting anything. Also, the pubococcygeus (PCG, or "love muscle" — the one that connects our torso, front to back, at the bottom) becomes very weak.

The end result is not just that this hurts. There's more. Throughout North America, the United Kingdom, and several north European countries, lower back pain (and back pain in general) is one of the greatest causes of work absence.[1,2] Posture may play an important role. Hernias can easily result when we have poor posture, because the abdominal muscles are so weak. Also, it is very easy for internal organs to become prolapsed — to lose their place inside the abdomen and simply "fall down." How can they not? There's nothing holding them in place!

So why, and how, does a person get into this situation? Nobody starts off saying, "I want real intense lower back pain, and I want hernias, and ruptured disks, and prolapsed organs." But that is what results. So what is going on that allows a person to get into this horrible situation in the first place?

The answer is: she or he disconnects. There is something going on in the body that the person just doesn't want to feel. What is often going on has to do with real basic, primitive emotions: fear, shame, and sexual feelings. These are feelings that reside in the lower parts of our bodies: the "lower chakras" (energy centers).[3]

If we tighten up our lower backs, lock our pelvic girdles, and allow our tummies to sag, we can get the lower parts of our bodies as far away from our heads as possible. By doing this, we become a sort of "Talking Head"; one where all the sense of "self" is up in the head, and the body is just there as a life-support system.

If we have feelings of fear, of shame, of being "not clean down there," or any other negative feelings that we have connected with sex and survival, then this lower back tension is an effective way of blocking those feelings.

When a person is blocked off, he or she "feels no pain." That is, the person has disconnected from pain on the emotional level. However, the pain comes back at the physical level, due to body distortion. Most of us have the tendency to do this, to at least some extent.

The alternative, something that we often notice in people with a very rigid posture, still produces a similar disconnection. The people who have overly rigid postures, who often have a military background, hold themselves at a kind of permanent "attention." These people might not be letting themselves sag, but they often lock up both their pelvic areas and their diaphragms. The end result is the same: they can't feel what is going on in their bodies. Because of the rigidity and tension in their posture, they are also susceptible to back problems.

Emotional tension produces physical tension. Since most of us experience emotional tension from time to time (often hourly and daily), we all tend to store this tension in our bodies. We can do this out of fear and anxiety. However, tension comes from many sources.

One of the most common causes of our emotional and physical tension is simple physical fatigue. When we have to "override" our body's desire to relax, to sleep, or simply to let loose and run and play, we often do so by "tensing up." When we launch into "overdrive," whether on a big project at work, getting through final exams, or even keeping up with active children when we've been up late the night before, we tighten up. We "soldier through." Literally, we keep our bodies in rigid tightness. Then, we wonder why our necks and backs ache!

When we feel this kind of tension, we tend to "pull in." This leads to a second postural tendency that we often see; one usually found in older people. We might notice a sweet older lady, or a dear little old man, who has a sort of pot belly beginning just under the sternum. Now this does not refer to a *real* pot belly – the one that is gained manfully (or womanfully) after drinking rounds and rounds of beer. What we are envisioning is less about fat, and more about collapse.

When we look closely, we notice that such a person has "collapsed inward," right under the sternum. This is where the diaphragm is located, and the diaphragm lifts and supports the heart and lungs, and keeps these organs from falling into the abdominal cavity. When someone collapses their diaphragm, by just sort of "caving in," then the heart and lungs really do "fall down" inside the torso. The abdominal organs have no place to go but out, so they do. This creates that bulge that starts just under the ribs, and continues down to the pelvic area.

The sad part about this posture is that it's often a very nice person who shows this pattern. Somewhere along the way, though, that person learned to be a victim. He or she learned to "just take it." The result is that they go through life with a posture that looks as though someone just punched them below the sternum. The resulting posture is an attitude of defeat. The two feed each other – the posture and the feeling of defeat – in a cycle that is often hard to break.

There is a third postural problem that we often see: the dreaded "dowager's hump." This isn't just a matter of increasing age and calcium deficiency. It's much more a matter of "hunching over." Partly it's physical; we all wind up with tight shoulders and necks after sitting at a desk all day. Even more than a physical response, though, it's emotional. When we get tense and scared, we "pull in." Literally. We do our very best to imitate a turtle, and suck our necks down into our bodies. In fact, we are culturally conditioned to "pull in" – we are told that we "shouldn't stick our necks out!"

By using Oriental dance as a *body/mind/psyche pathway*, we begin paying attention to how we organize, or "hold," our bodies. By paying attention, we can start making changes. From this, breakthroughs can happen; both little ones and big ones. When we are young, natural life-force, energy, and ebullience often override postural problems. However, past the age of forty, how a person "wears" his or her life begins to show. Around this time, those women who practice a body art, such as dance, begin to look noticeably better than their peers.

This increased level of natural beauty has almost nothing to do with exercise, or physical fitness, and almost everything to do with posture, or "carriage." As mature women, we can learn to carry ourselves with grace, poise, and elegance. Our bodies can remain (or become) soft and flexible, vibrant and open. Certainly, the physical disciplines that we all practice now, such as yoga and Pilates, cardio training and core conditioning, resistance training and flexibility exercises, all contribute to our keeping a youthful and vital body. However, Oriental dance is uniquely effective in helping us to re-create our physical alignment, gain a flexible spine, and cultivate a released and relaxed sacroiliac connection. This helps us move with outstanding beauty and grace. If we are seeking a *Fountain of Youth*, this is a good place in which to begin!

Many of us live in a sort of "veiled over" state. We often don't really know, or feel, what is going on inside of our bodies. When this happens, we may act in very strange ways.

A good example of this is when we confuse our need for nurturance and love with a food craving. When we get stressed, we reach for our "comfort foods." The problem is that we start to eat without really being present in our experience of eating. When we just stuff down food without taking the time to enjoy the taste, then we're depriving ourselves two ways. First, we're confusing our need for love and strokes with a hunger for food, and thus wind up satisfying the "wrong hunger." Second, we don't even enjoy the food that we eat! Then we get fat, our bodies don't feel as good, and we get even more disconnected.

When we are this disconnected, then we are truly very vulnerable, and vulnerable in a very negative sense of the word. This is not the vulnerability that comes from dropping our barriers and letting ourselves *feel*. That is an open, and good, vulnerability. Even more, the "open" kind of vulnerability becomes a most effective survival skill. The value comes from constantly, although perhaps subliminally, asking the question, "How do I feel?" Recognizing how we feel lets us acknowledge whether or not a situation is good for us – a party, a parking place, a job, even a marriage. In contrast, a perverse or negative vulnerability comes about when we are so closed off that we are not tuned in to our surroundings, be they social, physical, or emotional. When we close ourselves off, then our intuition, our sensitivity, and even our awareness have all been shut down. Given how challenging life can be – in relationships, on the job, or in other areas of our lives – this can be a very dangerous situation.

Developing full body and psyche (emotional) awareness is something that takes time, attention, and diligent practice. The physical movements that we learn in dance class can provide a basis for our awareness. However, they do not, in and of themselves, guarantee such awareness. (This is obvious when we watch many dance performances, especially those done by those women who practice dance as an avocation, not as a profession. Too often, their training has not included deep levels of body awareness and integration. This becomes evident in their dance. However, they could indeed learn greater *integration* strategies, and be much more effective within a very short timeframe – if they accessed and used certain body-alignment and awareness *Principles*.)

In order for any of us to go beyond the simple physical movements, and learn to release emotional and physical tension, we need to specifically practice the dance movements as tension release patterns.

I learned the physical movements from dance teachers. I learned the emotional release by working with Diane Richardson, a *body/mind/psyche/energy integration* facilitator, who coached me for two years on breathing and body connection. "You're making great progress in releasing your spine," Diane said. "But you must learn to breathe, and to feel, even in situations that are stressful or scary for you. You need to do this in order to handle whatever comes up." This is something that we all need to do. The benefits are both effective and powerful.

Diane provided essential insight and guidance, at the perfect time. I was just beginning to realize that Oriental dance had the potential to be more than just a body art and an artistic and creative expression. I was just learning that there could be an energetic, or *ch'i*, component. I was also just starting to connect emotional release with greater release and freedom in dance. However, I needed someone who could help me grow to the next level of understanding. Diane was the right person, at the right time, and in the right place. In this role, she was as important as any of my earlier teachers in martial arts, or my long-term and much-revered master teachers in dance.

PERSONAL PATHWORKING:

1. Get a massage. And if you feel that chiropractic, or other treatments, are right for you, get them going in your life on as regular a basis as you can afford. When you are receiving a massage or other treatment, don't just space out! Practice breathing and consciously releasing tension. (Note: For this **Pathworking Step**, and for all recommendations in this and other chapters, the medical disclaimer, printed in full at the beginning of this book, applies. Use your own common sense, and if appropriate, medical guidance, in determining which of these recommendations is right for you.)

2. As feelings come up (and they will!), connect the feeling with where the "stuckness" is stored in your body. This can take time; even many years. Continue with this process; it may be a life-long journey.

CHAPTER 15:
SOFTENING: BEGINNING TO BREAK THROUGH

"I WOULDN'T STUDY WITH YOU, Alay'nya, if you were the last dancer in the world!" With that, Priscilla, Sally's sister, ended a particularly vicious tirade. I was more than shocked, I was amazed. I had never experienced such hostility!

The cause was simple. I had sent a "marketing letter" to one of my former students, Clarissa. Clarissa had been in my assistant instructor Sally's class for about a year. I was anticipating that Clarissa would join my intermediate class in the next term. I expected this, of course, until Sally broke off to start her own school! Naturally, I thought that the letter I'd sent out was a good one. I wasn't too sure of what Clarissa thought. She had just shared it, though, with Priscilla at one of our local area dance events. What Priscilla thought was evident.

I stood there, letting Priscilla rave on, and practiced what I had learned from Diane, my *body/mind/psyche/energy integration* coach, about "being present in my body." I practiced breathing. I practiced releasing tension in my spine. I practiced staying soft and open. At the end of Priscilla's initial tirade, I turned to Clarissa and said, "You're welcome to study with me, at any time." I looked at Priscilla and said, "And of course, you also." That what was prompted her vitriolic parting shot about how she wouldn't study with me "if [I] were the last dancer in the world."

By this time, I was "getting it." I "got it" that Priscilla not very happy with my marketing efforts. I was also "getting it" that, in the midst of a very emotionally charged, and even hostile situation, I could stay relaxed and soft. This was an interesting exercise. In fact, the only other person who had given me such an exercise was my boss, and I was actually getting used to him. This was a surprise attack; a new source, and a new opportunity to practice.

So I smiled at Priscilla, and said "Thanks for sharing your feelings with me. And you know that I wish you the very best, always." I turned to Clarissa, and to

Sally's husband, who was also sitting at the table (enjoying the whole show, I'm sure), and said, "And the same to you, also." Then I calmly walked away.

That night I received email from Clarissa, followed up by a phone call from her the next evening. She didn't appreciate, or resonate with, Priscilla's point of view at all. At the end of our conversation, I asked her, "Would you like to continue receiving information about our school, just to be included in what's going on?" Her answer surprised me: She planned to start studying with me the next quarter.

It wasn't just my dance qualifications that drew her to me, or the exciting curriculum, or the new style of *Rom* (gypsy) dancing that I was about to offer. What drew her to me was seeing that I had been gracious under fire. This was the real thing. I had just "walked the walk." I was able to do this only because I had learned to release and to "connect in" with my body, and for that I give all the credit to my teachers, and to some fabulous *integration* specialists. In this case, credit went particularly to Diane Richardson.

Diane, formerly a neuromuscular specialist and massage therapist, had evolved into a coach and facilitator. She was not a traditional therapist; she'd become something very different. Therapists usually work via dialogue. When I worked with her, I found that she began by noticing how a person held his or her body, and observing where they were "stuck." Diane had become expert at noticing subtle distinctions. She hadn't come by this easily; she'd had to address her own issues during this process. For her, as for me, training had been time-consuming, expensive, and often frustrating as well as challenging.

In one of my sessions, I went there, as usual, totally in my head. After a bit, she pointed that out to me. "Alay'nya, you want to dance with passion. If you're going to dance with passion, you have to get into your pelvis. Right now, you're not connected there at all. You're stuck up in your head; you've blocked off really being into your body from the neck and shoulders on down."

Then she came and sat next to me. She put her hand gently on one side of my sacrum, and I began to relax and bring my attention towards that area. After a while, she moved her hand to the other side. Then, she slowly moved her fingers up my spine, stopping at each of the vertebrae. As she did this, I continued to bring my attention to my body; to my spine and to my breathing. After a while, as I breathed, a rhythm began to show as my spine naturally moved with my breath, much like a long strand of seaweed moving with the ebb and flow of waves.

I asked her how she did it. Was it her, or me, or both? "A little of both, I think," she said. "It's part my touching you, part my intention, part breathing with you. But it's also you."

When she moved away, she said, "Your favorite defense is to block off feeling, to block off your body. You typically get stuck from the neck on down. You need to feel your emotions, and feel them in your body. This is important for you in your life, as well as your dance."

I felt discouraged, because I realized that not only was she right, but that after more than a year of working with her, this was still a big issue for me. Although I'd made progress – lots of progress – this basic pattern was still right there. Yet there was a new pattern emerging at the same time. And on top of that, I began to *expect* to make breakthroughs. Starting from these new expectations, I, and my dancers, realized that we were going to make significant and enduring changes.

This is where we began to learn about being "empowered." My work with Diane became the pivoting point where I began to take the idea of a possible women's *integration pathway* into my daily practice. She helped me link what I was learning about dance (in the sense of techniques, choreographies, etc.) to body awareness. In turn, I started teaching this to my students. Over time, my dance school began to morph and change. We were no longer the traditional "belly dance studio." Rather, we collectively began to embody what might have once been the ages-old practice of women's sacred knowledge; connecting body wisdom and awareness to our physical expression, which included dance. Because I began teaching this, and sharing with my students what I was doing, we all began connecting with our bodies in a deeper way. We began "listening" to our bodies; a process that I called *feeling-in*.

This becomes the starting point for cultivating our *Hathor* essence. As described in *Chapter 7*, *Hathor* is the ancient Egyptian goddess of love, beauty, sensuality, and all things pleasurable. However, tapping into *Hathor* as a core archetype doesn't mean that we start by becoming party girls. Rather, we begin by becoming much more attuned to both our physical and emotional selves. Often, this means that we start working through layers of stored pain and the emotional "crud" that we have locked into various little tension spots throughout our bodies.

What I have learned, and what I have begun teaching, is that when we start creating *real* power, our egos are not going to be gratified. The pathway to power, at least for us as women, is less about achievements and ego gratification, and more about connecting in to how we really are. When we do this, we often have to feel things that we would just rather not feel; not now, not at any time soon, and preferably not at all, ever. But we have to feel them anyway.

When I was just beginning this process, every time that I went into my body and felt an area where I was "stuck," I would start to cry. Some sort of painful feeling would emerge; it would be a feeling of loss, or hurt, or shame. It was always something that I didn't want to feel. I felt scared about this process. It took a whole lot of time. (Also, I am not yet "done." I still have to do this kind of processing; all of us do. This really is a life-long journey.) Yet, of all the things that I've been doing over the past many years, this is what has made me an exceptional dancer.

I call this process *softening*; where we bring awareness to our bodies, and release our emotional tension and stuck points. *Softening* is primarily a matter of bringing attention into those parts of our bodies that we have blocked off; those areas in which we've congealed a tight little knot of tension. Many things can help us as we begin *softening*; one simple first step is to *feel-in* to our bodies when we do stretches. Rather than imposing a stretch on a body part, we can allow our bodies to tell us where and how certain areas need to move. *Softening* becomes a two-way communication between our cognitive minds and our bodies themselves.

After a major surgery that I had several years ago, I should have lost significant ground. Up until the surgery, I was weak – actually debilitated. I often didn't have enough energy to walk up a small incline, much less do all-out dance. Recovery was simply long. Not hard, not painful in any way, just very long. Yet as I came out of recovery, and began to dance again, I not only regained all my former ability, but was actually better.

I could command my audience's attention in a way that I never could before. I could play with a greater emotional range. Within a relatively short time, my dance was more expressive; more free, more flowing, and with a richer emotional content. I can't chalk this up to practice, private studies, and classes. Almost all of the effect came from learning to release tension, and breathe fully into my body. In short, my gains all came from *softening*.

By *softening*, I have become (in the literal sense of the word) "extra-ordinary" at dance. This is not due to having more or different or fancier techniques than the next dancer. Nor do I necessarily have better choreographies. I practice a fair bit, but there are many who practice more – and sometimes they don't look nearly as good! It isn't a boast or brag on my part to say this; it is just a calm recognition of what is so. (Allow me a caveat: I am a good dancer; I move well, and am very expressive. However, there are women who have combined their personal *integration* work with years of dedicated dance practice, and who are much better than I am. Many of these are highly respected teachers as well as performers, and they offer workshops and regular classes. In some cases, their instructional and performance material is available on the web, as well as in other formats. I link to many fine performers and teachers through this book's website.)

For all of us, whether or not we are dancers, one of the most important realizations is: *How we move is how we are.* (Those of us who are dancers can replace these words with: *How we dance is how we are.*) If we are stuck emotionally, then we are going to be stuck in our physical expression. This will show up whether we are walking down a grocery store aisle or dancing before an audience of hundreds. And definitely, absolutely, it will show up in our love-making.

Beyond a certain basic technique level, the most important thing we can do to improve our physical expression is our emotional release work. We need to learn how to connect into our bodies, find where we are stuck, and practice releasing. We need to learn how to breathe into all parts of our bodies. This is true for each of us, because whether or not we have taken a single dance lesson, or danced for ourselves or for others, we are all involved in the dance of life.

In later chapters, we'll discuss energy work. This is the kind of "real-world" practice that we mystify as learning to use the *Force* in *Star Wars*. This is also taught in some martial arts schools, as well as in *tantra* and *kundalini yoga*. There are some real capabilities that we can learn to use, and they are not all that "mystical." One of the first exercises involves energy circulation. Before we start circulating energy, though, we need to clear out the blockages; physical (tension-based) as well as energetic.

Within the last century, various people have developed body-centered therapeutic approaches that can be very helpful. One of the first persons to make such breakthroughs was early twentieth-century psychoanalyst Wilhelm Reich. His work, although still disputed today, dealt with finding and releasing this "stuck" energy.

Because his work focused on the role of orgasm as a means to regulate emotional energy, and not just as the means for procreation, Reich's work was highly controversial. He introduced the notion of "body armoring" – the process by which a person experiences "chronic muscular spasms representing the somatic anchoring of the characterological rigidities."[1]

Translated into layperson's terms, this means that a person will become stuck in his or her body (the "somatic anchoring") if they are stuck in their minds ("characterological rigidities"). His approach to releasing these "rigidities" focused on increasing orgasmic potency; he developed a theory of *orgone* as a universal life-energy. Reich's work was so challenging to the concepts of his times that he came under attack by the Food and Drug Administration: his works were burned, and he later died in prison. Although he was persecuted in his life, first by the Nazi regime (causing him to move to the United States), and then by authorities within the U.S. government, his work is now receiving greater attention.

Courageous pioneers in *body/mind/psyche/energy integration* have continued to advance the notion that various "stuck points" are common to both our bodies and our psyches. In the last century, Ida P. Rolf, who received her Ph.D. in biological chemistry, developed what she came to call *Structural Integration;* a means for helping people to realign and balance their bodies.[2] *Structural Integration*, which later became known as Rolfing®, is a means by which a practitioner works on a person's fascia (the tissue that overlies and connects the muscles), rather than with the muscles themselves.[3] Rolfing®, in particular, helps people to align themselves with gravity.

Both Drs. Rolf and Reich had something in common when they noted the correspondence between how a person "is" within their psyche and how a person "is" within his or her body. As expressed by Dr. Rolf, "Physical personality is not something separate, strange, or different from psychological personality, but part of an internally covarying psychophysical entity."[4] In layman's terms: our bodies and emotions are linked; if we change one, then we change the other.

Essentially, T'ai Chi Ch'uan offers the same advantage, via a personal body art practice, as does a body therapy. Rolfing® is a means by which a therapist helps a client release tension. Similarly, as expressed by renowned martial artist Peter Ralston, in *Cheng Hsin: Principles of Effortless Power*, T'ai Chi helps a person to re-align his or her body, use gravity effectively, and relax.[5] This means that a person can teach himself or herself a new, "aligned" body pattern, similar to what can be obtained through Rolfing® or other deep tension-release bodywork. For this reason, many dancers, athletes, and martial artists will use a combined approach; they will both practice their art (or area of athletic expertise), and also seek out therapeutic body treatments. The two modalities – practice and therapeutic treatments – work well together. They can not only help us re-align our bodies and feel better physically, but also help us release emotional patterns that may have previously limited our overall happiness and well-being.

Those of us who are studying Oriental dance can use the dance art as the physical substrate for emotional and energetic release. The basic physical practices, particularly those for body alignment, are the first step. We can call this a *Level 1* practice. Almost any dance studio, or any dance teacher, or even studies alone with a set of teaching resources (DVDs, online videos, etc.) can provide adequate instruction on the basic mechanics of the dance: the fundamental techniques, together with some pointers on body alignment, etc. However, many dancers will have learned a great range of techniques without really addressing their body alignment as a first step. To help my students do the core *Level 1* "structural re-alignment" more rapidly, and with greater clarity and attention, I have developed a set of *Basic Principles* that I now teach as part of *Level 1* instruction. In selecting these first seven *Basic Principles*, I have drawn from T'ai Chi Ch'uan, from both Oriental as well as modern dance, and from my own experiments. These *Basic Principles* are all "static"; they have to do with alignment and what I call "body organization." A person can do them at any place, at any time; standing in a grocery store check-out lane is a good time to "check out" how we are holding our bodies!

Once we have mastered the first seven *Basic Principles*, we can start working with *Dynamic Principles*. These *Dynamic Principles* deal with breathing, contraction/expansion, and movement, as well as the connection between all three. This is our entry into our *Level 2* practice, where our true focus is on tension release. We seek to use our bodies as effectively as possible. For many of us, this means finding and releasing stuck tension patterns.

Many years ago, I took a private lesson with Elena Lentini. She noted that my body was very tense. "I'm trying to dance with intensity," I replied. She pointed out that there is a difference between tension and intensity of emotional expression. How very true!

Once we get a sense of what our *Level 1* and *Level 2* practices are like, we need to do them on a life-long basis. It is not as though we can ever say, "Oh, I'm beyond this; I did *Level 1* years ago." I am very often working at *Level 1*; checking and re-aligning my physical posture. I especially need to do this when I take a break from a task where I've been too tight-focused, for too long. For example, I'll do a *Level 1* check as soon as I get up from editing this chapter! In addition, unless we are perfectly evolved, we will probably all need to constantly replenish our *Level 2* training, by noting how we need to soften our physical tensions and release related emotional tightness.

However, getting therapeutic help can make a big difference! We can encourage and accelerate our process by finding the best chiropractors, natural healers (Rolfing® practitioners, acupuncturists, reflexologists, neuromuscular therapists, etc.), and massage therapists within reach. By combining therapeutic support with our own practice, we can achieve personal breakthroughs; not only in movement and dance, but in life as well.

"Sarah," said the mother, "make yourself soft!"

It was one of my gentlemen friends who told me this story. It had occurred just after a church service; he and others were conversing before heading home for the evening. A mother was talking with some friends, and her six-year old daughter Sarah was getting fretful. The mother could see that the girl was about to have a temper tantrum. As my friend recounted it, the directive to "make [herself] soft" was the most effective "maternal commandment" that he had ever heard! Sarah heeded her mother; she *softened* her body, and the looming emotional crisis was averted.

Sometimes, we need to do the same thing with ourselves.

Softening is something that we need to do when we're in a situation that pushes our buttons. When we are stressed, our fears or anxieties are invoked, and we start to tense up. We start to generate "emotional spasms." These "emotional spasms" come from our *pain-body*, which Eckhart Tolle describes as a "semiautonomous energy-form that lives within most human beings."[6] Tolle further characterizes our *pain-body* as having a primitive form of intelligence, somewhat like that of a cunning animal, that is focused on survival.

Since our *pain-bodies* want to survive at all costs, they need to feed. They feed on emotional drama; on pain, chaos, and despair. Thus, to feed, and to survive, they will generate situations (external, or even just internally-felt ones), that produce these negative emotions.

One of my mentors compared the way in which our *pain-body* "spews" emotional mayhem to an octopus which, when startled, will spew ink all around itself! In counseling terms, this is the classic "King Baby" or "Queen Baby" temper tantrum.[7] It can also be more contained, expressed with tightness and withdrawal and judging. The overall effect is the same: emotional havoc and damage all around. These emotional dramas happen when our *pain-body* takes over and generates the situation with its attendant drama, and then "feeds" off the negativity that it has produced.

Every time that we let our *pain-body* take over and indulge in an emotional hissy-fit, we have to clean up. We have to clean up both physically (if we let things get that far) and emotionally. (The disastrous and embarrassing story from the beginning of *Chapter 11* comes to mind.)

We do far better to keep observing that our *pain-body* is trying to come out, and to "make ourselves soft." The way that we deal with our *pain-body* is not to attempt to control it. It will simply find another outlet. Instead, we need to embrace the feelings that are coming up, and bring them back inside of ourselves. The way that we do this is precisely why our practice is a <u>*body*</u>/*mind*/*psyche*/*energy pathway*; we must physically "make ourselves soft." Our bodies get into the act as much as our emotional aspects and our minds!

When we are being tense, stressed, and irritable, then we are not *soft*. If we are aggressive, in any form, then we are not *soft*. If we have "edges" in our personality – things that cause us to be emotionally reactive – then we are not *soft*. It is precisely this quality of *softening* that makes us warm and receptive, and it makes us attractive. In fact, to exert the real power of attraction, we need to *soften* our emotional barriers and resistances.

When we have emotional "edges," of any sort, they will show up in our dance. On the other hand, if we can release these "edges" and *soften*, then we don't need extraordinary technique. We will get a good feeling of emotional release and expression as we move, and whoever watches us will also feel emotionally satisfied. They will feel drawn to us, and enjoy whatever we do.

When we *soften*, we begin the *art of allowing*. When we *allow* something, we *release our resistance* to a manifestation. Instead of taking a karate chop to the universe, we try something that works *with*, rather than against, the ongoing energies. We begin practicing T'ai Chi with the universe itself.

I had an email from one of my dancers a while ago. Priscilla had died the day before, from a lingering illness. She was about our age; an age where we acknowledge the inevitability of death, but feel that it is safely some years away.

Priscilla was a valiant woman, and she had lived a very hard life. I'm sure that she showed courage, even at the end. But I don't know if she ever learned about *softening*.

We can't always make our lives go the way that we want. We don't always achieve every dream, and sometimes we go through times that are very, very hard. Many of us have challenges that seem inappropriately hard. Like many other women, I had some challenges in my younger years. I responded, as many of us do, by developing a certain brittleness and rigidity in my personality. (Of course, this also showed up as chronic back and neck tension!)

What I learned, in working with Diane, was not only to *soften* my body, but also to "put some space" around an issue that was particularly troublesome or challenging for me. This helped me to ease my feeling of identifying with the problem, and instead let me see it as something separate and distinct.

Many of us, by the time that we are adults, have developed a hard shell around ourselves. This shows up in both a physical and an emotional sense. I had certainly developed a rigid and unyielding shell by the time I was a teenager, and it took me many years, using the *Principles* of *softening, releasing resistance,* and *connecting* with my entire body, to begin working through that shell.

Many of us have done what I have done, and have developed our own brittle and impermeable cocoons. These are our hard-wrapped veils – spun out of fragile silk, but shaped into a hard chrysalis.

It is from this place of being scared, of veiling ourselves off from the world – either through disassociation or through brittleness, rigidity, and plain and simple bitchiness – that we sometimes decide that we want power. Power, we think, will shield us more, protect us more, and give us more of what we want. Particularly, our reasoning sometimes goes, we can get what we want if we have power over men.

And thus it is that we go about playing the seduction game, or the manipulation game, or the corporate positioning game. We do so either not knowing that this is just another way of distancing ourselves, or knowing this and simply not caring about the ultimate impact – on ourselves and others. What we often don't know is that our decision to achieve power, of any sort, has come from fear.

If we think that we want power, especially of the good old-fashioned "power over" sort, we have to take on masculine ways of being and thinking in order to get that power. (Credit for the "power over" term goes to Starhawk, a global activist, writer, and early proponent of Wicca.[8]) When we seek this sort of "power over," we go fully in to our *Amazon* mode. As Rick, a former co-worker, once said, "You are not given power. You have to seize it." This is typical masculine thinking. When we think this way, we are coming straight from our egos. Our only real concern in terms of relationships is who is up, and who is down.

All too often, we have adopted an "either/or" strategy. We have either become fully *Amazon*, and lost connection with our other core feminine archetypes, or we have rejected the *Amazon* mode as being too masculine; too disconnected. We know that this kind of distancing – this kind of "power-over" game – simply feels awful, and we feel isolated and lonely when we try to do this.

If we decide that our *Amazon* role does not feel right, then we often retreat into pure *Isis*; the typical feminine path of "relating." We want to connect. We want to feel good, and we hope to get that feeling by helping those around us to feel good. It would upset others if we were more powerful, in any real and significant way, than they are. Thus, in this way of being, we are all egalitarian. We eschew power and its trappings. We relinquish our *Amazon*, we embrace the nurturing aspect of our *Isis/Mother* mode, and we disconnect from power dynamics.

And in the end, we not only don't have power, we don't have survival skills. We have invested ourselves in relationships and in being "Dr. Mom," but we lack strategies for survival and negotiation in a world where power dominance is still the big play. Having become great nurturers, we lack fat portfolios, bank accounts, and (all too often) even competitive job skills. We also find that without some degree of external or overt power, we are too often ineffective in achieving goals that involve influencing others.

Back in the '60's and '70's, Starhawk made a lot of sense when she talked about cultivating "power from within."[9] This is what we are seeking to cultivate as we *soften*, and allow ourselves to be fully aware of how we feel, both physically and emotionally. This full awareness of ourselves allows us to access our innate power. To do this, we must first be very present in our bodies. This means lowering the defenses, taking off the armor, and making ourselves "be here right now." This is where we practice *softening*. From this place of being present in the moment, the next step or process must be to *release our resistance*, which is the subject of the next chapter.

⊗⊘

Recently, I was at my favorite hair salon. Nader had just finished making me as gorgeous as possible. I was ready to head out and tackle the rest of the day. And then, I couldn't find my car key! I emptied my purse and coat, and shook everything out. I went through all the draft chapters that I'd brought in with me, to work on while his "magic" took effect. I searched through the entire salon. No key.

I went out to the car. Surprisingly, I'd left it unlocked. I went through the car, front and back, looking in nooks and crannies and under the seats. No key.

I was about to get a little hissy. You know that feeling; a good, cathartic hissy-fit. Nader suggested that I sit quietly, compose myself, and allow myself to "remember" where I had put the key. I did this. No memories, and no key.

I repeated the entire empty-everything-and-search process. No key. By this time, I had a sneaking feeling that "something was up." I had in the back of my mind that "inner knowing" that we all have, that "there are no coincidences."

At the same time, I was also scared. I had put off all other income-producing activities to get this book done. I had made plans to cover the hair appointment (some things are as essential as heat and food), but other than that, was down to emergency reserves. And yet, there was no key. The friend with whom I had entrusted the spare had left town, taking the key with him.

At this point, I had to *soften*. I needed to stop fighting the fact that this key was simply not showing itself. The only thing that I could imagine was that some other customer had inadvertently mixed it in with her things, and left with the key. Just to be certain, I repeated the entire empty-everything-and-search process *one more time*. Still no key. Accepting this, I borrowed Nadar's *Yellow Pages*, and went to work. Several minutes later, a locksmith promised to be on his way.

The "sneaking feeling" that I had was that this was something necessary as a part of *Unveiling*. I needed a simple, practical example of both *softening* and *releasing resistance* to share with you, because (as I'm finding now, during this final rewrite-and-edit) this chapter and the one following were still abstract; not sufficiently practical. One immediate, compelling, in-my-face example of both *softening* and *releasing resistance* could become an experience with which we all could relate.

With my key lost, and funds tight, so that bringing in the locksmith would be a cost-challenge as well as a simple inconvenience, I was in great danger of having a great big *pain-body* outing.

Instead, I was able to concentrate on breathing. I reminded myself that Source would provide; somehow the funds to cover the locksmith would manifest. The thing to do right then was to simply *be right there.* Just be in the situation without reacting; not generating emotional spasms, but not emotionally backing out either. My job was simply to breathe, to unlock my body, and to *soften.*

This I did, with no hissy-fitting. Though still, there was no key.

PERSONAL PATHWORKING:

1. There is only one exercise for this chapter; you know what it has to be.
   Start noticing your reactions to different people and situations. Start paying
   attention to your response patterns. When things come up that begin to
   trigger your emotional responses, soften your body, and *breathe.*

CHAPTER 16:
UNSTICKING: RELEASING RESISTANCE

ONE OF MY FAVORITE DANCERS is Zandra, who was my teacher many years ago. Over the years, I've seen and studied with many dancers, and yet Zandra stays in my mind. "Why do I have such an emotional response to Zandra," I've wondered, "when I've seen such extraordinary dancers elsewhere?" It's true that Zandra is by no means among "the great ones" of Oriental dance. While she is undeniably a good dancer, there are many dancers who have more complex techniques and more interesting choreography. Zandra stays in my mind, though, and as I think about her, a few other dancers come to mind who have qualities like hers – as well as some that don't! Many of us have similar responses, when we watch women practice the *Art of Venus*, or Oriental dance.

Zandra's dance has an emotional quality that is warm, pleasant, and receptive. It is as though she is putting herself – her very sweet, real, vulnerable self – out there for us to watch. She lets us experience who she really is. Because she is such a receptive person, we each feel as though she is inviting us to get close to her on an emotional level when she dances. We feel "drawn in."

In contrast to Zandra, some dancers actually "push us away" with their dance. This again is not a matter of learned technique; we can appreciate unpolished beginners doing their dance just as we can appreciate beginners presenting a musical recital. We don't expect novice musicians to be at the same level as a concert pianist; we adjust the scope of our expectations and are fully capable of enjoying the enthusiasm and vigor that novices put into their first performances.

The dance-contrasts to Zandra have nothing to do with technique, and everything to do with intention. Instead of being warm and inviting, some dancers assault us with their sexuality. The old-fashioned word to describe this is "brazen." They may be technically very good; they may even be technically excellent. However, when they get up to dance, many of us want to run out the door.

We all know that Oriental dance can be, depending on how it is interpreted, at least a sensual and sometimes even an erotic art. However, there is such a thing as being a bully in dance, just as there is such a thing as being a bully in the martial arts. We've all seen martial arts movies in which the "bad guys" swagger around and show off. They provoke people, just to show off their prowess. Of course, the "good guy hero" is either mild-mannered and unassuming, or (if he is a young fellow eager to show what he can do) he is taught by a "master" who is mild-mannered and unassuming.

The same holds true for those of us who take on the *Art of Venus*, as opposed to a martial art. There are masters in our area, as there are masters in every field. Women who are regarded as "grand masters" in this art are internationally recognized as both performers and teachers. These women are also mature. Over time, they have evolved their abilities so that they are more, rather than less, compelling when they dance. However, when they are not dancing (in the formal sense of giving a performance), they are "normal people." They don't need to attract attention, or prove that they can turn men on with their flirting. *They are mild-mannered and unassuming.* This is one of the hallmarks of their mastery; they don't need to push themselves in people's faces.

When we are young, in any area of our lives – when we are seeking to gain some degree of competence and capability, and maybe even some level of personal growth and breakthrough – we are often insecure. When in this state, we constantly need affirmation from outside sources. The more insecure that we are, the more that we are constantly "on." We are always performing, and always looking for feedback and validation. When we come from a position of insecurity, or of "not having," we are always trying to "have." We then seek to prove to ourselves and to others that we "have" enough. How we feel, especially *how we feel about ourselves*, shows up as we dance! Our audiences immediately respond to our overall feeling; they are either drawn towards us or are repelled.

Even beginners, or people who are relatively inexperienced in watching dance, will respond in a similar manner. I have found this to be true time and again when sharing dance performance DVDs or online clips with students. When I show them performances by dancers at festivals or in special shows, I always ask, "What did you think? How did you feel?" They usually report similar reactions to how I've felt. If the dancer is physically or emotionally tight, we all feel pushed away; we don't resonate with her. On the other hand, if she is centered inside herself and is open and warm, we feel drawn in. We are responding to the person, not to her style, technique, or choreography. If she is emotionally connected inside herself, and if she translates this into her movement, then we simply want to experience her state of being. If is a good state, we want to continue the experience.

One of the most powerful lessons that we learn in martial arts (and in life) is to *release resistance*. This is much like the physical practice of *softening*, which we discussed in the previous chapter. However, now we take this approach into our lives overall. This does not mean giving up when things don't go our way, and it also doesn't mean being a wimp, or letting life events (or difficult people) push us around. The notion of *releasing resistance* is not some obscure, saintly practice. Instead, this is a very practical approach that has been used by the most advanced martial artists in the world. (And if anyone knows about power, it would be this group of people!)

If we offer resistance to something, whether it is a person or a situation, then we get rigid. We also put our focus – our energy – into resisting. As a result, we then lose our connection with our bodies, and with the earth. When we are rigid and disconnected, then we are easily manipulated or pushed aside. (Those of us who have practiced T'ai Chi, particularly the "push-hands" exercises, will have practical experience with this realization.)

Smart and experienced martial artists know that when someone pushes against them, they need to yield to the push, and sink their body-energy into the ground. Then, of course, they come up around or inside their opponent's push, and dislodge their opponent. They have learned to relax their resistance, and to respond strategically instead of instinctively. (Actually, they have created a new level of "instinctual" or deeply patterned responses.) The truly advanced martial artists have adopted a more yielding, or *yin*, approach to attacks. Martial artists who take this approach are very effective. They can also, typically, transform this strategy into real-world applications.

There's a reason why T'ai Chi Ch'uan translates as "Grand Ultimate Fist." It truly is the way of certain very accomplished martial arts masters. When I was studying martial arts over the years, I moved from hard styles, such as the austerely beautiful Shotokan karate, to progressively softer styles. I finally found my way to T'ai Chi as taught by Ron Sieh, and then later studied with Ron's master teacher, Peter Ralston. Each of these martial arts teachers was fully aware of and able to use the "martial" aspect of their art. None were doing it as an "exercise." They had simply realized that the softer styles were very effective.

There is probably a good reason why the novices in the Shaolin temples first had to undergo years of training with hard-style techniques (blocks, kicks, and punches) before they were allowed to train in the softer styles. It probably took years for the young men to get their adrenaline and testosterone sufficiently under control to go beyond ego-dominance and aggression. At least for the smarter ones, there would finally come a time when they would be sufficiently bruised, sufficiently injured, and sufficiently worn out that they would consider an alternative.[1] Older and wiser, they would come into the true potential of their art. Similarly, I have seen the older, softer, and gentler dancer be far more attractive than her young and energetic counterpart.

One evening, I arrived at a dance workshop in New England. Anahid was going to teach, and the evening before the workshop was devoted to an "open floor" of various soloists. Anahid arrived late, after a hard work week and a grueling journey, and was clearly exhausted. Her hostesses and students whisked her off to a back room and got her a cup of tea.

"Do you want to just not dance tonight, Anahid?" They were more desirous of caring for her than seeing her perform, although we all longed to see her dance. "No, just give me a few minutes, and I'll be fine," she said.

I rejoined the audience. The dancer on stage was, as many of us were, young, beautiful, and an excellent dancer. She whirled and twirled. She threw her heart, her soul, and her passion into it. She finished with a flourish and a grand finale.

Then Anahid came out. It was immediately clear why she was the master teacher. Her movements were so limpid, so gracious and gentle, that watching her was a balm for our souls. "This," I realized, "is what the art is about."

☙❧

At an odd interval in my life, I had an experience that taught me a big lesson about both softening (in a physical sense) and releasing resistance (at the emotional, or psyche, level). On a certain Friday, I'd woken with the immediate knowledge that I did not want to see two business associates who were in my life at that time. I'll call these two people Dilby and Dougie. Dilby, high on the corporate ladder, was due back in town that day. Borrowing a term from Julia Cameron's *The Artist's Way*, Dilby was a first-class Crazymaker.[2] I also didn't want to see Dougie, who was also due back. As I thought of typical interactions with these two people, my stomach churned with acid and my back tightened up in knots. With dread and anxiety, I contemplated the coming work day.

I felt a great deal of anger and resentment about that particular situation. At the same time, I was daunted by the effort involved in making a large change. I felt trapped as well as resentful and angry.

I also knew that both Dilby and Dougie were *mirrors* to me of things that I didn't like in myself. This *Principle of Mirroring* was emerging as a "great life truth." Some authors refer to the concept of mirroring in terms of how we often physically mirror someone else's body posture, gestures, and even breathing patterns when we wish to establish rapport. In this context, though, I'm using the *Principle of Mirroring* as a corollary to the well-known *Law of Attraction*, as stated by Esther and Jerry Hicks, communicating the teachings of Abraham. The *Law of Attraction* states: "That which is like unto itself is drawn."[3]

When we understand how the *Law of Attraction* operates in our lives, we perceive that we have already attracted to ourselves those things (people, events, and situations) that already are in "vibrational harmony" with our habitual thoughts. In short, that which we already have in our lives mirrors back to us the "vibration" from which we have been creating. The essence of *mirroring* is that we create our external reality as a reflection of our beliefs. With regard to people, the *mirroring* is not just that people treat us according to our beliefs about how we will be treated, it is more. The people we draw into our lives *reflect back to us qualities within ourselves.*[4] This reminds me of the old proverb that I learned as a child, "If you meet someone that you dislike, examine your inner self."

As I applied the *Principle of Mirroring* to these two people in my life, I thought of characteristics in Dilby that bothered me the most. And with these thoughts, I realized that he reflected those qualities in me! He had other qualities that I also didn't like, and embarrassment alone (since they are in me as well) keeps me from listing them here. Dougie, however, was worse. Much worse. It would do neither you nor me any good to go into detail. It suffices that his behaviors illustrated issues with which I'm still working, and the more I reflect on that time of working with him, the more that I realize that I had – and still continue to have – much inner work to do. This time was a challenge not just because he himself was unpleasant, but because he was reflecting back qualities that I didn't want to acknowledge were in me!

I knew that in order for the situation to change, I had to *soften* my body, and *release* my emotional *resistance* to both Dilby and Dougie. If I was resistant or reactive (this included a direct attempt to create change), I'd be leaving behind an incomplete learning. I might get out of that environment, but then I'd find a new Dilby and a new Dougie with whom to complete the lessons. As Dr. Phil has stated, "You know you're ready for a divorce when you can walk out the door with no anger, frustration, or hurt. Otherwise, you've got unfinished business."[5]

Since I knew there was no real way "out" of the situation, I resolved to find a way "through" it. I knew that when I had learned what I needed, and had accepted what these two people were reflecting back to me, the situation would change of its own accord. I trusted that some opportunity would come up, or the dynamics would change. So, I concentrated on practicing what Diane Richardson, my *body/mind/psyche/energy integration* coach, was teaching me. I consciously attempted to *soften* and *release* my resistance and judgments about them.

Enroute, I stopped by my friend's chiropractic/holistic wellness center. As I was getting treated, and participating in the energy blockage release, I put my attention on Dilby and Dougie, and consciously tried to *soften* my "edges" about them, and to *release* my *resistance* to being in this situation with them.

Something happened for me right then; I suddenly had the answer. I realized that I would have to love them. It wasn't enough to "soften my edges." The core issue was that they each reflected back to me some things that I didn't like about myself. By loving them, I would have to accept and love things about myself that were just as ugly and distasteful in me as they were in them. This was something that I *really* did not want to do! However, I had an internal sense of truth to that realization, and I knew that I had to go with it. So I lay there, doing my best to love them.

Then something else happened. I connected in spontaneously with the feeling that I get when I "release" during dance. Even more, I felt that I was dancing or moving in the way that I'd seen one of my master teachers move. This had been one of my goals since I first saw her perform many years ago. Even though I'd studied with her, I had never been able to internalize her style. I could mimic what she did, but I couldn't generate her kind of movement from within. Suddenly, I found myself generating a feeling inside. I *felt* a kinesthetic sense that *felt* like her dance expression. It was as though I was feeling the movement, and looking at myself from the outside simultaneously.

I realized that I was able to do this because I'd released the tension – the "edges" – that I used to separate myself from myself. As my chiropractor friend released both energy blockages and physical tension, I released my feelings of separation and judgment, and actually tried to love. There was an immediate shift in how my body felt. I could sense a new ability to express myself emotionally through dance.

Over time, as I learned more about physical and energetic anatomy, the reason became clear. We have nerve bundles that start in our backs and connect to areas in the front of our bodies. (These front connection points are also, not coincidently, where our front *chakras* are located.)[6] When we release tension from our mid-backs, and open our hearts to love (from the heart *chakra*), then we open up our entire torso, and are able to move and express ourselves much more freely.

Some of the most fundamental movements in Oriental dance are actually "expanded" versions of intrinsic natural movements. These specifically include our combined upper/lower body undulations and our pelvic figure-eight's. The upper/lower undulations capture and magnify our intrinsic cranio-sacral connection. The figure-eights magnify a very subtle, almost indiscernible movement pattern inherent within our sacroiliac area.

When our bodies are soft and free of tension, these undulation and figure-eight patterns happen naturally. When we dance, we make these intrinsic motions much more obvious, and they become part of our technique repertoire and choreography. If, as we dance, we are soft, connected throughout our bodies, and very grounded (connecting with the earth), then we feel a great sense of release. When our audiences see us doing these movements and sense that we are connected throughout our bodies, they map themselves onto us. That is, they connect with us emotionally and energetically; they seek to feel the way that we feel. The result is that our audiences also get a sense of release.

This is why Anahid's dance, even though she was tired, and it was very simple, had the power to move our souls. We were healed by watching her, because we mapped ourselves into the way that she was so connected in her body.

We have the power to help others heal themselves through dance if we can be soft, connected, and grounded. Alternatively, if we are tight, or if we don't take our movements through our entire bodies, then our audiences feel fidgety and bored. They don't know what to say or how to describe their feelings; they just know that they desire something that is not happening for them. We have the power, as healers and dancers, to heal those who watch us when we perform. This is a great gift and an opportunity.

I sat in Nader's salon, waiting for the locksmith to arrive. My car was unlocked. I had the key when I walked into the salon. But now, it was nowhere to be found. Three in-depth searches had failed to produce a key.

I had already *softened*. I had stopped fighting. I accepted that I was going to pay a lot of money (from a very tight budget) for a new key to be made. But as I sat there, waiting (sort of patiently, and sort of not-so-patiently) for the locksmith to arrive, a new round of thoughts started in my head. These were not so much a direct reaction to the situation. They were thoughts about myself; judgments of all sorts, ranging from how I could have been so "unaware" as to misplace the key, to how I had messed up so much of my life! I was about to enter a negative tailspin of self-judgments and unhappiness.

Once again, I caught myself. This was different from the initial pass of *softening*, which was very situation-oriented. Here, I had to *release resistance* both about how I was responding to life overall and to the set of negative thoughts and judgments that were stored at a deeper level.

Eckhart Tolle describes how this happens.[7] He notes that when we allow emotions from our *pain-body* to gain control of our thinking, then our thinking becomes negative. We tell ourselves negative stories about ourselves and about our lives. We make up stories, or create interpretations, of not only ourselves, but also about other people and life events. We even start imagining unhappy future scenarios.

Our *pain-body* is where we store the shamed, unloved, pained part of ourselves. We feel awful when these feelings emerge, and are also often angry and scared in response! Therefore, we try to keep these aspects hidden from others. In fact, we try to keep our *pain-bodies* hidden from ourselves. However, our *pain-body* craves these negative feelings as food, because it is created from negative energy. Thus, our *pain-body* seeks to bring up stored places of pain; places where we are sensitive.

Sitting in Nader's salon, I could sense my *pain-body* coming up again. While I knew intellectually about my *pain-body*, and (as we all do) have had numerous experiences in dealing with it, I had not had a major *pain-body* outing in some time. As these feelings came up, though, I was not so much in danger of having an all-out *pain-body* hissy-fit, and spewing negative emotions all around the room. Rather, I was in danger of a major decline, and of succumbing to long-term and more pervasive unhappy thought patterns. This was a different form of *pain-body* outing; perhaps not as overtly dramatic, but potentially much more damaging.

My approach here was the same as *softening*; just a bit more comprehensive. As the thoughts emerged, I kept relaxing and breathing, and *releasing resistance* throughout my body. The negative thoughts continued to emerge, and I "embraced" them. I kept reminding myself that I did indeed love myself, very much, that I was happy to be here, and that I had called this specific incident into my life for good reason.

Sometimes, when something triggers our negative thought-patterns, we create a tight, defensive inner wall, and do a "byoing!" of that thought off this internal, tight shell. Internally, we tighten up and "bounce" away the thought that makes us feel bad.

Our *integration* work is that we *soften* our bodies (if you know how to undulate, do this, *softly*), and breathe deeply into our bellies. We stay soft, and allow the thought-feeling to come into us. Instead of pushing it away, we take it inside. This is where we *release resistance*.

It is also good, when we are dealing with our *pain-bodies*, to use some of the *processes* described by Esther and Jerry Hicks.[8] In particular, we can try *pivoting*; finding a thought that will turn us around emotionally. This can be thinking about something pleasant or finding the most positive aspect possible. In the story of losing my key in Nader's salon, the positive thought was that this whole situation was both useful and necessary; it was providing a concrete example to share with you.

As I was putting the final editing touches on this book, I began to get scared. I knew that *Unveiling* was going to come out soon, and that many people would read this. I was putting into *Unveiling* things that I'd previously shared only in the intimacy of my dance studio, or with close teachers and friends.

I called up my friend Kathy Carroll, who has coached me through many steps of personal growth and integration. "It's *Unveiling*," I told her, my voice trembling with a touch of panic. "It's bringing up all kinds of stuff; all kinds of fear."

"Know that this is a false fear," she said. "This is just your *pain-body* reacting."

"Yes, you're right; I can feel the fear, and at the same time, I know it's not what is *really* real. It's as though I can feel both the fear and the what-is-really-so, that I'm okay, at the same time."

"That's it, Alay'nya," Kathy said. "Feeling both, at the same time! And then you can *integrate* the fear-feeling back into yourself. That's what we call *processing*!"

"Oh."

And we both laughed.

This *processing* – allowing our fears, the shamings and judgments and reactive side-turns of our pain-body, to come up, and then being present with them, loving ourselves through them – is what enables us to *soften*. A crucial step is to *release* our *resistance* to experiencing these painful thoughts and feelings, so that we allow them to emerge, and can begin our processing. As we do this over time, our *pain-bodies* have less and less influence.

In Nader's salon, I distracted myself with the latest fashion magazines while waiting for the locksmith to arrive. I practiced a little baby-level *pranayama*. The locksmith came. I focused, not on how late it was or how much this would cost, but simply on being present. I put my attention on the locksmith's process of making the new keys. He tested the new keys, and I tested the new keys. I paid him, thanked him, said goodbye to Nader, and drove home.

Two days later, I found the missing key; it was in the bottom of the snow boot that I'd put back on while in Nader's salon. I had been standing on the key all this time! I'd learned a lesson, revised this chapter, and (thanks to Nader) my hair looked great. No matter what the cost, this was a good ending.

PERSONAL PATHWORKING:

1. When you are lying on a soft surface – for example, in your bed as you doze off to sleep, or if you have some moments before you have to get up – allow your entire spine to "undulate" up and down. Feel the base of your skull (your cranial area) connecting all the way down to your sacrum. Get a sense of what this connection feels like. It should feel very gentle and nurturing.

2. Again, lying on a soft surface – one that will not impede your motions – alternately move your hips downward (in the direction of your feet). Right hip, then left, then right ... This is towards your feet, not down into the bed! (If you know how to do a basic shimmy, a simple alternating downward stretch of your pelvic bones, this is the same thing.) If you have a chance to do some yoga movements or stretches before you begin, then this exercise will work even better. Begin to sense an "opening up" around your sacrum (the big, flat diamond-shaped bone at the base of your spine). Combine this with pelvic stretches when you can. You will feel much better! Over time, you may be able to create a "figure-eight" pattern with your hips; bring one of your hips down (away from your rib cage), then out to the side a bit, then up (towards your rib cage). Alternate hips. "Sense inside" your sacroiliac joint. You should start getting more release in this area. These are especially good things to do after you have had chiropractic treatment or a good massage.

3. As you lie in bed at night, and thoughts or memories come up, note when and how you are responding emotionally. Notice where you have a physical tension that corresponds to an emotional tension or "holding." As you seek to release the emotional pain (be present with it, and love yourself), see if you can also release the physical tension. Imagine that you are hugging or holding yourself; comforting yourself through the remembered trauma.

At the same time, seek to release the physically "held" areas into either the undulation or the figure-eight pattern. Again, if you have a chance to combine this with any kind of body-therapy (chiropractic, massage, Rolfing®, Reiki, etc. – any therapy where you can be passive and quiet and receive healing), seek to bring your emotional awareness and physical awareness together. You may be able to connect your release experience in both your physical and emotional/energetic dimensions. Remember to do this with as much love as possible for all parties involved, especially and including yourself!

4. Now comes the challenge. The next time your *pain-body* tries to take over, put this into practice. Relax, *soften*, breathe. Notice your thoughts, and *release resistance* to the ones that cause you to tighten. Instead of "bouncing" these thoughts away from you, let them in, and continue loving yourself and *breathing*.

5. When your *pain-body* is getting active, treat yourself as you would a much-loved child, and offer a distraction. You can take a walk around the building, call for a bio-break in the meeting, or look at the flowers on your desk. If possible, take a nap! While distractions are good, seek to avoid distractions that you know are unhealthy; the physical and mental "junk food." You really *do* know what to do, and how to care for yourself. And once again, reading the various Abraham-Hicks works is useful, as is listening to their CDs. These steps can help you regain a positive mental frame, and remind you to deal lovingly with yourself during challenging situations.

PART V: THE RITUAL: PREPARING TO DANCE

꘎

CHAPTER 17:
WE'RE WORTH THE EFFORT!

"THINK OF YOURSELF AS THE beautiful jewel within a Fabergé egg," I tell my new dancers. "Everything about you frames how beautiful you are. The way that you hold your veil frames your face, your hair, and your body. Your long earrings frame the beauty of your face. Your bracelets and rings show off your exquisite wrist and hand motions. Your hip sashes, heavy with beads and coins, draw attention to your pelvis and hips. And your costume bra, when you wear full costume, has beaded fringe and designs that accentuate your breasts, along with the delicious motions of your upper torso." As I'm speaking, my students look at me with wide-eyed wonder. They've never thought about themselves this way before.

I try to dress up for dance class. I do this for a regular class, and I even do it when I'm practicing by myself. It helps me to *shift state*. This practice also encourages my students to do the same.

During the first few months of a Beginner's class, I will often see students wear baggy T-shirts over equally baggy running pants. When a new student shows up like this, I give her a couple of months to acclimate. If she hasn't started to build her wardrobe of "dance-play" clothes and accessories by then, I talk with her. "We're worth the effort," I say. "We need to honor ourselves. This may take a shift in our priorities, but it is important to our overall healing."

Some of the most ancient spiritual practices of the world have taught us to revere, and even to worship, feminine nature and feminine sexuality. We need to bring this awareness into our daily lives. We examine the meaning of one of the most famous Tibetan mantras of all time, *Om Mani Padme Hum*! This is often interpreted as "Hail to the Jewel in the Lotus!" In the tradition of Indian Buddhism, the "jewel" is often interpreted as a metaphor for enlightenment, and "lotus" as one's heart.[1] When interpreted from a Tantric perspective, the interpretation has hitherto been based on a metaphor for love-making. The "jewel" has been interpreted as the phallus, and the "lotus" as the vagina, as explained by Trijang Rinpoche, the tutor of the Dalai Lama.

> First, in terms of signification, *mani* indicates the vajra jewel of the father, *padme* the lotus of the *mudrā* [consort], and the letter *hum* [*hung*] [indicates] that by joining these two together, at the time of the basis, a child is born and at the time of the path, the deities emanate.[2]

In short, the most common Tantric interpretation is one that honors male/female union. There is nothing intrinsically wrong with this. However, this inter-pretation – no matter how well-accepted in many circles – may not be the most complete or useful one!

June Campbell, in *Traveller in Space: Gender, Identity, and Tibetan Buddhism*, challenges the male/female union interpretation. She shows how detailed etymol-ogy helps us to significantly re-interpret this passage, in contrast to the esoteric "dogma" that has been accepted for many years. As Ms. Campbell points out, not all Tibetan scholars agree with the phallus/vagina interpretation.

> In the first place, while *padma* clearly refers to the vagina, it is not quite as convincing that *mani* should be interpreted as phallus. In some Sanskrit dictionaries, *mani ... also carries the meaning of clitoris.* However, in almost all instances of what Bhatari calls Tantric 'intentional language', where a metaphor for phallus is used, it is written as *vajra* in Sanskrit, in Tibetan *dorje. Mani,* however, literally means 'pearl', 'jewel' or 'gem' in Sanskrit.[3]

Ms. Campbell goes on to cite the work of A.H. Francke, a scholar of Tibetan history, whose etymological and linguistic studies further support her claim. According to Ms. Campbell, Francke's analysis supports the notion that the mantra is addressed to *Manipadma* – 'the deity *of* the jewel-lotus' [italics hers] or the Goddess Pearl-Lotus. Ms. Campbell's investigations show that this most time-honored mantra could thus be interpreted as an invocation to the "essential sexuality of the female, i.e., the deity of the clitoris-vagina."[4]

In sum, let's all say and hum together: *Om mani padme hum!* All hail [our] clitoral-vaginal deity!

Let us envision the focus of this mantra as a beautiful jewel, brilliantly shining within an unfolding lotus flower, that is (since this is a deity-representation) the center of the universe. This "jeweled center of the universe" represents not only a goddess, but the core sensuality, sexuality, and spirituality of who we are as women.

However we interpret this mantra, there is an important message for all women: We are indeed the *lotus*. We are also the *jewel*. The beautiful flower of Tantric tradition corresponds to our sexuality, and the jewel within it corresponds to our ability to experience ecstatic pleasure.

Taking this to heart, we need to treat our *core essence* as the sacred *jewel*, and consider that everything around us should be designed to showcase our beauty. In short, we need to *become* the "jeweled center of the universe," nestled within our own Fabergé egg. We do this by honoring ourselves.

For many of us, taking the time to "be gorgeous" isn't as easy as it sounds. We might intellectually agree that this is worth our effort, but find that actually *doing* this seems difficult. All of us, whether we are young adults or more mature, have many responsibilities. If we are young, then we are often combining one or more jobs with school. When more mature, our careers not only require more time, they also require more mental attention – even when we are "off the job." In addition, we have partner relationships and family commitments; parents and children both take time. On top of this, there are household chores, spiritual practices, and the myriad things we identify as "life-support tasks."

Often, there just doesn't seem to be the time or the space to be the "jeweled center of the universe." It's true; being glamorous and gorgeous takes time. Mostly, it's inconvenient! Ultimately, though, it's not so much the time involved, or even our sense of priorities, that is the greatest challenge. Usually, the single greatest challenge to our being the "jeweled center" of our own universe is the *belief* that we have about ourselves. We still, by and large, believe that our worth lies in our performance, not in our *beingness*. We still measure ourselves by a masculine, or *yang*, yardstick.

Whether we are young, or simply "young at heart," we are often hard-working, with many commitments and responsibilities. But there is a big difference between those of us who are just entering our careers and those of us who are more established. In our earlier years, even as we took on professional roles, we did not lose sight of our earliest visions of ourselves. We were still connected to a sense that was both playful and erotic. We were still close to our "dress-up" days of childhood.

As we have become more mature, though, we may have found that our successful careers have come at a great cost. After years of struggling to be accepted as "one of the men" at work, we've often become greatly stressed. It seems that we have two different kinds of stress. The first is "performance stress." This comes just from handling a difficult job with many responsibilities; this is the kind of job stress that stays with us all the time. The second, a kind of "disassociation stress," is more pervasive. This happens when we lose our connection with our bodies, and lose ownership of our intrinsically feminine identity. All too often, we have sacrificed our inner *Hathor* and *High Priestess* aspects in order to be *Amazons* and *Mothers*.

Now, we begin our *integration* journey – our real *pathway*. We are seeking to bring our *Hathor* and *High Priestess* essences into our daily lives. Up until now, everything has been preparation. We've discovered the multiple layers of our core desires. We've learned that a *pathway* – a *body/mind/psyche/energy integration pathway* – may truly be ours. We've taken the first steps, those of *relaxing* and *releasing* the tension in our bodies (and our minds). This is all preparation for our journeying.

Now, the moment has come.

In various esoteric traditions, ranging from yogic to shamanic, the initiates experience an "inner journey," during which they encounter all sorts of challenges. These internally visualized challenges range from being physically daunting, such as crossing a chasm or ascending a cliff, to emotionally daunting, such as facing various demons.

The same holds true for us, right now. As we take on the *inner journey of unveiling*, we are doing something that is equally challenging. Even though we will be talking about things that seem to be part of our everyday life, and are using familiar analogies such as closet-cleaning, we know that we are up to something much bigger. We are seeking to cultivate those inner aspects of ourselves that we have most likely shut down, or at least marginalized, for many years.

There is a reason that we have done so. In our earlier years, as we tried this journey in all innocence, we did indeed come upon huge "demons and dragons." These were the voices of massive societal conditioning, and they were speaking against doing *exactly* what we are going to do right now. And what we are going to do, dear sister, is to regard ourselves as sacred and holy.

Not only are we going to *regard* ourselves as sacred and holy, we are going to put some *weight* behind this decision. We will be allocating resources. We will be placing "safeguards" around our experiences; lines of safety, security, and demarcation. We will be doing this *precisely* because we are moving towards something that, for all that it seems softer, less tangible, and possibly not-so-important (like playing with our veil), is indeed *very* important, and worth our utmost protection.

And protect ourselves we must, because our social conditioning provides huge resistance. This social conditioning may come from without; perhaps from other people and subtle cultural lessons. It may also come from within; as with our internalized beliefs about what we should, and *shouldn't*, do.

We have been taught, all of our lives, the overwhelming importance of the masculine way-of-being. This has been such an overarching social premise that masculinity and godliness are co-identified. (How often do we go to a church, synagogue, or mosque, and hear prayers to "God our Mother"?)

Everything about our status and survival relates to the masculine mindset, focused on wealth and achievements. Consequently, the "ways of being" that generate wealth and achievements are highly prized, honored, and taught. In the elite schools, in leadership training, and in military and corporate mentoring, we all learn how to do goal-setting and time-management. This goal-oriented, tangibly-focused approach has much to offer. At the same time, our culture emphasizes and approves of this approach to such an overwhelming extent that feminine approaches, such as using intuition and rapport-building, are typically given short shrift. In comparison to the more masculine modes, the feminine ways of being are marginalized. Feminine understanding – honoring that something very important may be also diffuse, difficult to quantify, and simply impossible to fit into a linear "project management" approach, with well-demarcated milestones – is so contrary to this achievement-oriented mindset that it simply does not fit in.

Over the past two centuries, our work in North America and in Northern Europe to struggle for equal rights has been so successful that we now regard the battle as largely complete. We have finally won the right to freely cultivate our *Amazon* natures. Yet as we take stock, we realize that we've achieved the right to cultivate that aspect of ourselves that is most like men. We can be *Amazon* warriors in business and even in the military. However, we have not yet begun to explore, develop, and integrate the fullness of who we are.

Those of us who begin this inner journey while still young – those of us who are not yet married, and who are certainly not yet mothers – can make extraordinary strides. At this early life-stage, we can cultivate both our sensuality *and* our spirituality while still developing careers, or completing our education. However, as soon as we marry and have babies, our time is necessarily taken up with our new mode: being a *Mother.* It is when we have completed the major portion of our *Isis/Mother* role, and have also fully developed our inner *Amazon,* that we are often aching and crying out inside for the two modes that we have most likely neglected up to this point: our *Hathor* and our *High Priestess.* By the time that we are ready for these modes, we really need them!

One of the most effective steps that we can take, as we begin our *inner journey,* is to *repurpose our inner Amazon.* David Deida, in *The Way of the Superior Man,* teaches men how their own core weakness causes women to overdevelop their *Amazon* natures:

> Your word is a demonstration of your purpose, of your masculine core. When you don't follow through with what you say you are going to do, she feels that your masculine core is weak... And so she feels a great loss.

> Over time, she will begin to build up her own masculine protection against your lack of integrity.[5]

There we go. You know, and I know, that we have developed our *Amazon* natures as fully as we have, not just for the thrill of achievement and for the solid good-feeling sense of competency, and not even for the simple pragmatics of survival, but also because we have not been able to trust certain men in our lives. We have not been able to trust them individually, nor, to a great extent, as a culture. By and large, many men are so self-absorbed with their own glorification that they do not see, and certainly do not honor, the feminine. This is reflected within the masculine culture surrounding us.

Conditioned as we are by society, we have often similarly denigrated the feminine ourselves, unless it has been in the service of men. We must therefore claim time, space, and substance for the most neglected parts of ourselves: our *High Priestess*, and our true, uncompromised *Hathor*.

Lest we think this is trivial or easy, let's recall a cultural icon in the form of a much-loved song from the *Fiddler on the Roof.* Tevye sings "Tradition!" as the chorus of women espouse their time-honored role, which should be to make a "proper," "quiet," and "kosher" home; freeing Papa to "read the holy books."[6] When the weight of "tradition" says that it is equally important that the family make time for *Mama* to "read the holy books," we'll know that we've made some headway!

Until that time comes, we rely, not on men, but on our own inner warrior. We call upon our inner *Amazon*. The challenge now is to bring her to the task of protecting and defending our other inner selves. Thus, our *Amazon*, far from being something that we should relinquish, is an aspect that we must first cultivate and empower. The difference is that we now put time and effort into growing our inner *Amazon* so that she can support our other feminine archetypes. This might be in contrast to what we may have previously done: making her (and her competitive activities) the focus of our lives. Now, our goal is to teach and train our inner *Amazon* to serve and support our *Isis, Hathor,* and *High Priestess* essences, much as we would desire this from and teach it to an external man.

As we make this shift, the purpose of our inner *Amazon* becomes not so much to compete in the workforce, for all the acclaim that such work can bring, but rather to do well enough so that she can provide security for our warm, nourishing *Isis*-essence (*Mother*) mode. Our *Amazon* can provide the safe haven for our *Hathor*-essence, so that she can shed clothes and inhibitions, light the candles, take a hot sudsy bubble bath, and listen to her favorite music, knowing that the bills are paid and she has a little something set by for the rainy day. Our *Amazon's* role is also to provide sanctuary for our *High Priestess*, so that she has a safe place in which to retreat and meditate.

It is lovely when a man can be the *Protector* for us. However, we cannot always count on the presence of a man – or, even if he is present, that he will fully respect and honor our inner selves. Also, even when a man *does* take on this role in our lives, a husband or lover can die, or become ill, or (regrettably) even leave for a "newer model." A wise woman takes care of herself.

Now, knowing how we want to rebalance our inner selves, we are setting ourselves a mission. This is easier said than done, of course. Simply put, we have spent too many hours sitting in meetings or in front of the computer. We have lost our body awareness. We simply do not know how we are holding, or *being in*, our bodies.

Of course we can recapture this awareness. We can reconnect with our inner *Hathor* and *High Priestess*. But if we have been cut off for too long, as many of us have been, then we need a *pathway* to guide us back. Connecting back in, following the *pathway*, starts with recognizing that each of us *already is* the *jewel in the heart of the lotus*.

One of the first things that we learn in Oriental dance classes is the art of *framing* ourselves, especially as we play with our veils. We begin this study early, because much of the basic framing is "static," that is, we learn to hold a certain position. This gives beginners enough time to take note and make subtle corrections. We can then apply poses and framing to our dance, to our photo sessions, and even into our lives! We learn how to present ourselves beautifully in all situations.

Even more, we learn that we are *worth the framing*. We are worth drawing attention to ourselves. And we are worth creating – and re-creating – our entire lives so that they show us off beautifully!

Our "goddesses of the silver screen" have known this, and used this art to perfection. Laren Stover, in *The Bombshell Manual of Style*, describes how Elizabeth Taylor plays this out in *A Place in the Sun*. As a leading "goddess of the silver screen," she starts by walking past the open door to the billiard room, where Montgomery Clift, her love interest, is alone.

> She returns, curls her fingers around the door and presses half her body against it with provocative hesitancy. After she has engaged his attention, she runs her hand down the door edge to heighten the tension. Will she come in? Or slip away? Once she's in, she takes the long route around the table to his side, running her hand along the polished wooden edge of the billiard table before touching a piece of candy, popping it in her mouth, rounding the final edge and posing between two paintings. Bombshells love a little framing around them.[7]

In our dance studio, we love to have "photo sessions," which we usually do at least once a year. In part, these are instructive; we can see how we are presenting ourselves. The camera gives very objective feedback! In larger part, this is more than just instruction, and more than ego, and more than just plain fun. Getting the feedback from an external source (such as a camera) is integral to developing our feminine core. Each of us has a unique style, a unique way of being. We are cultivating ourselves not just as dancers, but as human beings. Specifically, we are cultivating the *feminine* aspect of our beings. For many of us, this is a voyage of self-discovery. Pictures help us connect the dots; they complete our understanding of where we are at a certain moment.

Before we began doing "photo sessions" in our studio, we relied on friends and family to take pictures of us during performances. We found that the value of these photos was hit-or-miss; during a show, we were performing for the audience, not for the camera. After a few years, we began scheduling separate photo shoots, and hiring photographers (usually dedicated amateurs who were building portfolios) specifically for the occasion.

During these semi-professional photo shoots, we found that some of the photographers, and some dancers with modeling experience, had real gifts for "staging." This "staging" was both in terms of finding and creating the right settings, and in positioning us within these settings. As a result, we each acquired a great set of photos, showing us individually at our most glorious, captivating best! Our personalities came out in those photos. We learned a great deal about our sensual *Hathor* – and even our contemplative *High Priestess* – when we saw the objective evidence. These photos have become valuable tools for self-discovery.

As we evolve as dancers, our unique, distinctive "essences" become clearer and more refined. We each get a stronger sense of who we are. This is most useful in discovering our *Hathor* aspects, in which our most playful and sensual natures reside. These discoveries carry over into our regular, or "day," lives as well. In fact, our *Hathor* essence begins to permeate our lives!

Many people will call this "personal style." However, we're after something just a little bit deeper than style alone, although this "something" is very much intermixed with, and often expressed as, part of our personal style. This is the ability that we each have to develop our entire life – every single aspect and expression of it – so that it uniquely reflects and enhances who we are.

Tall order? Perhaps. Certainly, this is more than a weekend project. (Although we may as well get started this weekend; why not?) We can think of this as a gigantic, life-sized closet cleaning, where *all* of who we are is the "closet!"

At one point, I realized that I was enormously unhappy with my life "as it was." I had made some huge mistakes in selecting certain boyfriends and professional associates. At the end, I had to cleanse all these people out of my life, and I lost much of what I "had" in the process.

While this was tough enough, there was an even more challenging issue at hand. I realized that if I couldn't get to the root of why I'd made these selections,

I'd repeat them. What a horrifying prospect! As a former beau used to say, "There's nothing I hate worse than learning a lesson, except learning the same lesson the third, fourth, or fifth time!"

As much to avoid repeating previous experiences as to move on to something much more delicious and fun, I did a total "life-cleansing." This entailed more than two years of rigorous and grueling work with a mentor. Simultaneously, I cleaned house and organized. During this time, much of my life was in constant flux. People moved out from my household; others moved in. There were sweeping, huge changes within a company that I'd helped to create. My dance school also metamorphosed; not just once, but several times. Then, I left one company to start a new one. At the same time, I was getting a clearer sense of what I *did* want to create!

Big changes such as these are life-closet-cleanings taken to a grand scale. What is perhaps most interesting, and most *useful* to us, is to recognize that this isn't a one-time process. It happens in *layers*.

We may shed light on our behaviors, and gain some insight, and develop a new set of relationships and friends. We may take courage and look for a new job, or even change professions altogether. All the while, it is as though we are trying on all the clothes that we've stored in the back of the closet. "Does this really fit?" we ask about a new relationship, job, or activity. As we accelerate the process of refining who we are, everything that we believe, do, and bring into our lives becomes a subject of investigation.

When we take on this process with vigor, we may morph very fast. Rapid changes, in many areas of our life, do not necessarily mean that we're doing anything wrong or bad. Nor does a sequence of rapid life-changes suggest that we've lost our balance. Instead, they may mean that we're getting closer to our core; to our real essence.

The best way to discern if our life changes are good is to assess whether they are getting us into a more balanced, sane, healthy, and loving place. We can apply the biblical adage, "You will know them by their fruits."[8] This means that we need to pay attention to people and situations *over time*. We need to attend less to words; to what people say. We are much better off putting our powers of discernment to how people express themselves over time, and how their lives are out-picturing. We observe how they act, with us and with others, when things are going well – and when they are *not* going so well. We look at how people's values are exposed under crisis and stress. Naturally, we need to apply the same criteria to ourselves as well – especially when life stresses expose how we *really* think and feel! Sometimes, when our lives morph without our planning or intending for a change to happen, we need to give things a little time and a little space to see what unfolds.

We use this process to create inquiry into our lives. We observe what we're creating, and use it as a *mirror* to discern how we truly are. Deeper and more pervasive inquiry may take longer periods of time. As we deepen our inquiry, it is likely that we will have multiple "transition stages." Our goal is to get through these times as gracefully and gently as possible, often while deconstructing and reconstructing our lives.

Remember, when we are painting – whether we are creating art on a canvas, or painting the walls of a room – the most time-consuming step is the preparation. Once the "prep work" is done, the actual painting – the final transformation into the glorious, desired result – can happen very rapidly. People could walk into a room several hours after we first put brush to the wall and say, "Oh, this is completely different! What a wonderful new look! And you did it so fast!"

What they didn't know is that before we opened the first can of paint, we spent *hours* spackling, sanding, and taping off the trim. The "prep work" is vital. It is often grungy, and even boring. We need to persevere through these stages. We do this by staying focused on our vision of the new situation/life/relationship/job that was the inspiration to lead us into the initial tedious and sometimes messy "pre-painting" stage. We can ensure our transition through the challenging parts by staying positively focused. By analogy, this would be like envisioning how much fun it would be to put on our pretty clothes, invite people into our newly-done-up room, and entertain. Such will be our life, *if* we persist through our "internal makeover."

Our "inner housecleaning and painting" job may take several forms. It may range from the psychological to the physical, from relationships to jobs to where we live, and even with whom and how we spend our leisure time. We may have to identify patterns that have held us back. Simultaneously, we may also have to take concrete, specific actions; take risks and make changes.

One woman whom I know has stayed for years in a job that by no means honors all of who she is. She has a vision for what she'd like to be. Ever since she was very young, she's wanted to be a healer. In her twenties, she enrolled in a pre-nursing program in college. Life events came up and were enormously disruptive. She backed into a job that, at the time, was supposed to be temporary. Now, it is over twenty years later, and she's still there. The difference is that her job situation is getting rougher by the day. Her manager is shrill and unappreciative, and she knows that the whole corporation is seeking to eliminate its senior, and thus more highly-paid, workers. While her job situation was never ideal, it is now becoming unbearable.

This is actually a positive situation. It is making her look at change. It is forcing her to ask herself who she really wants to be, while she is still young enough and energetic enough to go back to school and to prepare for the career that she has always wanted.

The stress of a life transition can be enormous. Because we often stay in difficult situations well beyond the time that would serve us to leave, we often "pull" very tough transition-incentives (such as difficult or unreasonable bosses) into our lives to help "force" the transition that we really desire, but will not make until our comfort zone disappears. We thus act in cooperation with our Higher Self (our Higher Power) to bring these transitions into our lives.

It is most difficult at these times, but like Esther and Scheherazade, we need to cultivate our inner wisdom – our core of stillness. It is during these times that our inner *High Priestess* becomes our most significant mode. We need the wisdom and discernment, as well as the spiritual stability, that our *High Priestess* provides for us at such times. When we go through these times, it is useful to ramp up whatever spiritual discipline has been underpinning our lives. Even if we don't subscribe to a particular religious dogma or doctrine, our *High Priestess* will draw strength and solace from the intention of connecting with God, or Source.

As we go through these transitions, we have the opportunity to focus on what it is that we truly desire to create. We can get a much more powerful, coherent, and consistent vision of our desired selves and our desired lives. This deeper and richer vision is one that integrates *all* of who we are, not just a portion. This is the time to re-develop an appreciation for who we are as a special, lovely *jewel*.

These transition times, with their great flux, are also often powerful opportunities during which we can recreate some of the physical aspects of our lives. It is important for us, during these transitions, to pay exceptional attention to surrounding ourselves with colors that we find to be calming, soothing, and energizing. This is one of the easiest and most straightforward ways in which we can each design our lives as a "setting" for who we are as the *jewel*.

There is more, much more, to our personal use of color than the simple *Color Me Beautiful* four-seasons approach. However, *Color Me Beautiful*, or some similar guide, is the easiest way to get started. As a somewhat more advanced approach, we can go to the work of Suzanne Caygill, who pioneered the notion of color analysis in the United States. She applied an artist's understanding of "seasonal" color themes to individual color analysis and personal style. Caygill was an image consultant to the stars, and wrote *Color: The Essence of You*.[10] She offered up not just four, and not even just sixteen, but sixty-four different personality types distributed across the four seasons!

Caygill went so far as to make a bold assertion: the color palettes that suit us the most are related to our personal characteristics.[11] This is worth our attention, as we progress in developing our understanding of color, form, arrangement, and other aspects of personal style.

We can begin by starting with a simple color system, such as given in *Color Me Beautiful* or in a similar book or online resource. After we get a basic understanding, we can progress to more complex and subtle variations. For example, we can learn to distinguish, within one "seasonal" color group, the depth, intensity, and complexity of colors *within* that season that are most flattering for each of us.

For example, I'm an *Autumn*. But I'm sort of a mid-range *Autumn*; I wear colors that have a certain richness, but are neither too bright nor too muted. In contrast, I've seen *Autumns* who can carry much more intense color (and they are still *Autumns*, not *Springs*). These people have a stronger, more forceful personality. Similarly, I've seen women who are very muted *Autumns*; they have tended to a more gentle personality. The same observation seems to carry through with other "seasonal" types. Thus, I've seen anecdotal evidence that supports Caygill's insight: that there really *is* a personality correlation with the colors that work best for each person. This means that we can potentially learn more about ourselves by finding our best colors!

As we re-create our lives, working with our colors helps us to gain clarity. This can be an important step as we continue to "clean out our lives." As an example, many years ago, I and a colleague self-trained in color analysis. We worked together as color and wardrobe consultants. As part of our self-education and life-cleansing, we cleaned out not only our wardrobes, but also everything that we owned, using our new color insights. My colleague was a *Winter*, in contrast to my *Autumnal* coloring. She gave me her wooden jewelry and copper earrings. I gave her a beautiful velvety caftan-robe. The maroon robe had a blue-red base, and I needed warmer red colors. It was the only robe that I had at the time, but I made a decision. Better to do without, better to wrap myself in a towel (of the right color, of course) than to have something so intimately in my life that did *not* work for me.

Each of us can develop and heighten our color sense, and also do a color-based life cleansing. Sometimes, it is more fun to do this with a friend, or with a small group of friends. We can readily buy fabric to use for draping at a fabric store, or assemble enough fabric choices from things that are available at home. This process works very well within a small group of three to six people. Each of us gets a much more heightened sense of our own color palette when we can compare our color-responses to those of others!

Over time, we continue refining other aspects of our lives. We begin to look at everything, from our jobs to our dishes, with new eyes. We examine everything, from with *whom* we connect, to *how* we connect. As we do this, we may note that when in different modes, we have slightly different styles. For example, how we do correspondence may shift; we might use e-texting and emails when in our *Amazon* mode, but shift to a phone when we move into our *Isis* mode. We may, in our *Hathor* mode, prefer carefully selected cards; something unique for each person and occasion. In this mode, we may focus on special touches that add playfulness and sensuality to our experience. For example, in our *Hathor* mode, we may keep cotton balls, spritzed with a favorite perfume, in the stationery and notecard boxes. We may even keep little collections of iridescent "confetti," or silk rose petals, that we add on occasional whim!

Each style is good. Each is permissible. Each is a matter of *personal style*, which we are now cultivating as a means of knowing the various aspects of our inner modes. What is more, our personal style may shift as we transition between these different modalities or archetypes.

This may lead us to noting that our style preferences go even deeper. We may find, for example, that in one mode (*Amazon*, or even *Isis*), we are primarily a linguistic person. In this mode, we may like to talk or write. However, we may note that in our *High Priestess* mode, we prefer to refrain from too much cognitive thought, and to be very quiet inside.

By noting our basic preferences, and correlating them with our different modes, we build a basis for transitioning from one mode to another. With practice and attention, we can start invoking certain modes as our needs and desires indicate. The next four chapters give us specific tools for this purpose.

PERSONAL PATHWORKING:

Create a specific, physical place – an altar – which honors your intention to experience both "stillness" (your inner High Priestess) and "playfulness" (your inner Hathor):

1. Select a place for your altar. The top of a bookcase or a dresser will work, or a shelf that you can make and attach to a wall. Find some pretty fabric, and use it to drape your altar. (You may want to change the fabric with the seasons.) A wonderful book, *Altars*, by Denise Linn, has imagery and ideas that may inspire you.[12]

2. What sort of things do you have that speak to you as belonging on your altar? Do you have a vase that you can use for flowers, a beautiful statuette, an incense burner? How about the bowl or basket of jewelry that you've culled from your collection? Does that belong on your altar as well?

3. Do you need a background image for your altar? Try making a collage from beautiful notecards (another vision quest; what is it that speaks to you?), pictures from magazines, photographs of you and your friends. Mount your collage on posterboard, or artist's backing board, or even pin them to a corkboard, and set it up above your altar. My friend Kirene (the one who is on a *Heroine's Quest* to reclaim the family estate) has used family pictures, framed and mounted on the wall, as a backdrop for her sacred altar. Since her focus is on reconnecting with her family's lineage and carrying it forward, these photos are especially suitable for her right now. Something of a similarly personal nature may be right for you.

4. Consider making a scrapbook of images and clippings that appeal to your *inner self.* Notice that your cognitive, rational mind may have comments, such as, "That's crazy! Who would ever want a thing like that?" Notice, but don't let the judging, harsh thoughts dominate you. Allow your

newly-emerging inner modes – your *Hathor* or your *High Priestess* – to come forth. *She* will select those things that let *her* communicate *herself* to you. These can provide inspiration for later play. Right now, you are seeking to develop communication between your non-verbal self (selves) and your cognitive, rational-mind sense of self.

5. Go on a mini "vision-quest," and let your *inner self* guide you to finding the things that belong on your altar. Go on a long walk, and be open to miraculous "finds."

6. What is something you would like to do in, or something that is characteristic of, each of your modes? Do you have activities or ways-of-being that are specific to your *Hathor*, or to your *High Priestess*? Can you set up little mini-environments conducive to each? Even Donald Trump regularly schedules three hours daily of "quiet time" – he allocates a couple of hours each morning together with evening time for reading newspapers, periodicals, and books, and for reflecting on their content. He notes that this practice is essential for his well-being.[13] If "The Donald," with his busy schedule, can do this, then is this perhaps also useful for you?

CHAPTER 18:
THE RITUAL – AND WHY WE NEED IT

THIS CHAPTER IS PERHAPS THE most challenging one of this book. That is not to say that this chapter is hard to read. We'll have no problem with the reading itself, and we'll understand it perfectly well. Possibly, we'll even agree! Intellectually, this is easy.

The challenge comes, as it always does, from the practical application.

We're not going to let the chapter title, *The Ritual – And Why We Need It*, scare us off. Of *course* we're not going start doing strange and arcane things. In fact, anything that we do, based on this chapter, will be something that each of us designs and initiates.

However, up until now, we've been largely in our heads.

Of course, there have been a number of things "to do." They've ranged from paying attention to our bodies (*softening* and *releasing*), to building an altar. They've included buying and playing with a veil, starting a life-cleansing, and learning (or refining) our colors.

All of this will have been child's play: the easy stuff. Previous chapters have given us the warm-up exercises.

From this point forward, we're getting deeper into *life transformation*. We will be experimenting, in a much more focused and intentional manner, with how we can each get from one mode to another. In particular, we will start cultivating the ways and means for accessing our *Hathor/Love-Goddess* and our *High Priestess/ Madonna*.

Of course, *each of this does this already!* In fact, one of the first things that we'll attend to will be the ways and means by which each of us *already* does the exact thing that we desire to do!

The difference is that now we will combine being a scientist and a sleuth. We're going to conduct experiments; we're going to do investigations. We're going to track down clues. We're going to try different things, and different combinations; we'll be like master chefs coming up with new recipes.

Like all good scientists (and all good sleuths, and all good chefs), it will help us enormously if we take notes. The **Personal Pathworking** steps have been guides for this note-taking. They've also given us suggestions for noticing what is *worth* our note-taking: everything from dreams to daydreams, from planned experiments to unexpected events. These are all ours for the investigating. Since we want to draw upon more than our observations – since we want some "experimental inputs" – we can benefit by returning to our earlier **Personal Pathworkings**. This is a time to find our *image* collections. These collections will be part of our subject matter. Or rather, they will be initiating points; triggering our inward journeys.

In the next three chapters, we will develop some very straightforward and pragmatic steps and tools that will help us shift into our *Hathor* and *High Priestess* modes. Right now, we'll start with one of the most powerful means at our disposal – *ritual*. We are going to use the full powers of our inventiveness and creativity, and all of our insight and wisdom, in designing ways to nurture ourselves into shifting into our desired states – *at will*.

Very specifically, we will use ritual to shift from our *Amazon* mode, which is often overly dominant, into any of our other modes; nurturing and caring *Isis*, sensual and succulent *Hathor*, or contemplative *High Priestess*.

This is just a little tricky, because we need to invoke our *Amazon* to set aside the time and place for these rituals. We also need to do this before any of our other modes become so deprived and needy that they pull a major "interrupt" (health crisis, temper tantrum, etc.) on our goal-focused *Amazon*! This is where the dialogues that we've begun in the earlier part of this book become useful. When we were collecting pictures and building collages or image-collections, we were operating in any of our *Isis, Hathor,* or *High Priestess* modes. We gathered these images so that we could show them to our *Amazon*.

Our *Amazon* is direct and cognitive; "talking" with her is really like talking with a man. Give him (or her) a task, and it will get done. Our *Isis* is a little less talkative, although sometimes she needs to talk, in order to communicate with others. Our *Hathor* and *High Priestess* selves, however, are not "talkative" in the same way as are our *Amazon* and *Isis* modes. In fact, the deeper that we get into these states, particularly into our *High Priestess*, the less verbal we get. (Yes, for all that we are women, and masters of verbal fluency, there are aspects of our being that are *not verbal* at all!)

Thus, we collect pictures, and show them to our *Amazon*. We collect statues and symbols; we make altars, and bring our *Amazon* to them. "This," we say to her, "is what we want. Now your job is to help us get there!" We invoke her help; we make her our ally.

We get our *Amazon* to schedule some time for our *other* "inner selves" in her day-planner. This might be honoring our *High Priestess* with a commitment to get to a church/synagogue/mosque service, or to have special devotional time, or to take a weekend (or even a week's) silent retreat. This might be pleasuring our *Hathor* by setting aside one evening a week for self-pampering and beauty rituals. This may mean nurturing our *Isis* by setting aside daily time (or a weekend brunch out) to write letters, birthday cards, and thank-you notes to special people. We might even combine modes. For example, we may take our *Isis* and *Hathor* together to shop for birthday cards. Our *Isis* is pleased to be nurturing, and our *Hathor* relishes the decoration of "special" cards, which can come with glitter, feathers, and jewels!

If any of these time-commitments also require a certain space, or certain things, we let our *Amazon* lead the way in getting these organization and preparation stages accomplished. But once we are gathered together, in the time and space that we've set aside, we need to make the transition. This is where our *ritual* comes in.

Let's imagine, for a moment, that you're going to try this transition without ritual of any sort. Suppose, just for the sake of example, that you've decided to study Oriental dance. Suppose that you've signed up for lessons, and have gone to class diligently for a month or so. Now, suppose that you want to take what you've learned, and see if you can *be* what you *desired to be* when you first envisioned yourself dancing.

The moment has come. You are cultivating your *Hathor* essence, and you've decided that you're going to do this for yourself, for all the right reasons.

There you are, in your leotard and tights, or even in a cute little outfit that you've pulled together, standing in front of the mirror. You've got your music queued up and ready to go. This is music that sounds great (your teacher plays it all the time), and you've invested in building up your personal collection. Maybe you're even wearing a hip scarf or a hip sash loaded down with fake coins. (They jingle so nicely when you move!)

So the big question is: What do you do next? Practice the techniques you learned in class this week? (OK, where are my notes?) Review your choreography? (Ohmigod, how did that thing start off again?) By this time, you're feeling maybe just a bit anxious. Your internal critic is about to kick in with negative messages: "Do you really think you can do this?" Your critic may even go for the jugular: "You, *sensual? Erotic?* Come on, don't make me laugh! OK for somebody else maybe, but for you? Get real!"

Before you know it, Oriental dance, or whatever you've chosen as your own personal art form, starts to feel less like empowerment and more like penance. You are one-on-one with those nasty, negative little voices that we all have.

But suppose that you *know* that you want those qualities that you saw in the dancer on stage last night, or in your teacher, or in the dancer you just watched on a DVD or on the web. You want to *be* that gorgeous, sensual creature that you saw; the one that was all your childhood Cinderella and circus-performer fantasies grown up into a real adult woman who was just so incredibly fabulous and sensual! And you know, realist that you are, that you're going to have to practice some to get there. You know that this won't happen just by going to class once a week. So you're game, you're willing. The question is: How to get from *here* to *there*? *There* being this totally gorgeous erotic creature that you want to become, and *here* being, well — *you* know.

By now you've tried (at least I hope you've tried) this whole concept of *shifting state* in your own life, and maybe you've gotten it to work for you — at least a time or two. And by now, you're familiar with the theory. Theory is good. But this is practice. So the big, compelling, question is: How do you make the theory work?

⸎

We know what we want out of this. We know that we want more than just physical practice. What we want is that intangible essence, that *feeling*, of being erotic and alluring, and being able to attain that state *at will*.

So here's the secret. This *shift* (for most of us, on most days) doesn't "just happen." Just like romantic evenings don't "just happen." When we want something to happen – when we want a feeling-state to emerge – there are all sorts of things we can do to trigger the feelings. In fact, we can trigger the *state* itself. As we do this more and more often, and get more proficient with triggering what we want, we get better at doing this. We can sometimes do the *shift* without external cues. But as beginners, especially when our negative conditioning gets in the way, we need to give ourselves every advantage possible.

In our *Hathor* state, we think differently (*when* we think; it's not a particularly "thinking" sort of state). Very definitely, we *feel* differently than we do, say, when we're balancing our checkbook or making out a grocery shopping list. The approach that we use – the thing that makes this work – is to make the transition into dancing (or entering our *Hathor* state) a *ritual*.

Let's give ourselves a definition: *A ritual is any behavior, usually physical but often including mental components, which we use repeatedly ("ritualistically") to induce a state.* We all have rituals, and being the comfort and security-loving creatures that we are, we tend to develop them early in life. Babies have rituals. Even animals have rituals. Families, churches, big organizations (and small ones), and even couples have rituals. Rituals are necessary to our lives.

We take great comfort in repetition. That, in itself, is part of the reason that rituals are so nourishing: we expect them to follow a known script. Most of us are familiar with the fiercely demanding bed-time rituals of babies and toddlers. The favorite blanket or stuffed animal *must* be there; no substitutes are accepted. There is a predetermined order of events. A story is often essential, and it may even be the *same* story, read again and again from a well-thumbed book. As every parent knows, the "lay me down and go to sleep" ritual is *not* the place in which to introduce novelty into a child's life.

Rituals do not always have to address major experiences such as death, birth, or marriage. According to Rabbi Harold White, a chaplain at Georgetown University, the orthodox Jewish tradition offers women many rituals. Some of them are designed to help women overcome a sense of loss; these range from dealing with postpartum depression, to menopause, to weaning a baby. Each of these instances is a time when our hormonal balances change. Rabbi White went on to describe the role of rituals in our lives as "help[ing] us overcome our fear of transition. There are two aspects to any ritual; the verbal and the nonverbal. For example, in the Roman Catholic tradition, the Holy Mass consists of a verbal component (preaching the Word), and [a] non-verbal one (Holy Communion)."[1]

If couples and families, babies and animals, and entire religions can each create rituals, can't we do the same for ourselves? All it takes is figuring out what we want, and what will get us there.

The first step in getting ready for any ritual is to create the *intention*. We need to get a distinct feeling for what it is that we want to experience. This might include thoughts about what we want, which we can express to ourselves using both images and words. Sometimes there is a body-feeling that we want to evoke. Sometimes a piece of music comes up from our memories, demands to be played in our heads, and then finally insists that we build on the feeling that it evokes in us; this segues to ritual experience through movement or dance.

Sometimes, we create impromptu rituals; moments so charged that they will forever resonate in our minds, and be touchstones for the kind of experience evoked. For example, we may spontaneously create a special moment with a lover or a child. However, most of our human rituals are embedded within environments that we've designed specifically for this experience.

Throughout history, we humans have devoted our highest and noblest efforts in each and every art to evoking a "state of consciousness" that is a little distinct and removed from our everyday state of being. This includes architecture (ranging from cathedrals to temples), music (ranging from the simplest to the most sublime), and the visual arts (encompassing everything from decorative surfaces to sumptuous statuary). This use of art – often in conjunction with ritual – is one of the things that most characterizes us as a race of "intelligent beings."

When we take note how we humans have used such a wide range of arts to support our ritual experience, it comes as a bit of a jolt to realize how little we have – especially in North America and Northern Europe – used movement as part of these same rituals.

Throughout history, people of most cultures have typically used purposeful movement as part of ritual. Sometimes, they've even allowed for spontaneous, free movement – including the resulting ecstatic moments! As Iris J. Stewart notes in *Sacred Woman, Sacred Dance*, movement and dance are one of the most time-honored (and reliable) means of accessing a different state.[2] However, many of us now live in a society that highly constrains movement. As a result, not many religious rituals currently incorporate sacred movement or liturgical dance.

We are now seeking to use dance, and in fact any kind of movement, as part of our own personal ritual experience. While this may intellectually seem easy, this can – for some of us, at some times – be a bit more daunting than it would seem. This is because we have so much cultural pressure against using our bodies, and movements within our bodies, to connect to a different state. Because of this, we may need to give ourselves a little more time, and use a little more gentleness, as we feel our way into our own *pathway*. We may need a little less in the way of "performance expectations" and a lot more in the way of self-nurturance and approval as we take even tiny, halting baby steps.

As we build our own personal vocabulary of ritual movements, we are once again taking on huge cultural shibboleths. We may need extra time to work through our culturally-instilled prohibitions about dance, and movement in general. Because we may be working through internal resistance as well as figuring something out for the first time, it can take us more time than we would initially expect to find ways to use movement, and even dance, in creating rituals or desired experiences.

Noting that our culture largely represses movement, especially in a ritual context, we can heighten our awareness to those few ways in which we *do* have culturally-sanctioned movements. What we are doing now is turning our *sleuth-ing* skills onto our culture; we are searching for *psychological* clues. The value of these clues to us is that – since we already know that ritual movement is largely repressed – that which has endured has to carry great significance. The value of what is still used has to be strong enough to have overcome our overall social prejudice against movement.

We begin our sleuthing within a realm that has cultivated the art of ritual for two thousand years, and at the same time, has largely minimized free body movement: the Roman Catholic Church. The High Holy Mass, one of the most well-cultivated and formal of rituals, uses three well-ensconced movement patterns, all part of the elaborate Mass choreography. These three are *processionals, presenta-tions,* and *salutations.* Because we're being smart sleuths, and want to discover what kinds of movements likely carry the greatest value, we'll look at each of these.

The Catholic church, along with many other religions, uses *processionals* as a means of identifying the significance of a special occasion. When I lived in New York City, I made a point of attending weekly Mass at St. Patrick's Cathedral. In particular, I went to the 10:15 AM Mass, presided over by Edward Cardinal Egan, which was the most splendid of the Sunday Masses offered. Cardinal Egan had (and presumably still has) a knack for the theatrical. He used all the means offered by both the cathedral's grandeur and the ritual service itself to create an experience that was "set apart" from the workday world.

During this high, "sung" Mass, Cardinal Egan made a point of both the entry and exit *processionals,* for which he assembled numerous altar boys, deacons, lay persons (who would later read Bible selections), and any visiting priests. Each person (except the lay-people) wore appropriate religious garb. Various people carried large lit candles, mounted on ornate candlesticks. One person carried the incense in a special incense-burner. Another person was assigned to carry the Bible up to the altar. Cardinal Egan, in full regalia, took the place of honor as last person in the procession.

This kind of *processional* makes use of many cues, both subtle and blatant. The attention put on gathering and organizing so many people, and taking so much time for the entry and exit, demarks the occasion as being important. The special attire and the formality add to the significance.

We use the same idea of a *processional* in our weddings, where the "supporting cast" of flower girls and bridesmaids come in first, and the bride comes in last. We see the same approach when we have the rare occasion to watch a significant royal or political event, such as a crowning or inauguration. When we have a special Thanksgiving meal, we may make a point of carrying the roast turkey into the dining room. Even if this wasn't the tradition in our home, we can each imagine one of the many Norman Rockwell-esque movie versions of the traditional holiday meal. Carrying the turkey from the kitchen into the dining room is a *processional* act, even if the total distance covered is less than ten feet! We humans have an innate need for drama, and using a *processional* to open and close an event meets this need.

We may note that a *processional* does not always need to be linear; those who practice many forms of "magical arts," ranging from Wicca to High Magic, will often use the ritual opening of "casting a circle." (For this, the leader moves in a circle around a prescribed area, stopping at each of the four cardinal directions.) Similarly, we may open a dance by walking, to the pulse of the music, in a large circle around the stage. In both esoteric ritual and in dance, this purposeful "walking in a circle" is a means of both claiming and circumscribing the space for that which is about to take place.

Often, we use the body language of *presentations* both in *processionals* and within the ritual event itself. For example, in the High Holy Mass just described, the Bible that was brought up to the altar was both massive and massively decorated with gold and jewels; it demanded to be the focus of attention. Also, the person carrying the Bible didn't simply tuck it under his arm; he held it high above his head. The body language said, "Look at this – this is important!"

By carrying the Bible high, and having it be both so large and elaborately decorated, the church is putting a great deal of psychological "weight" behind it. We are seeing now that within the *processional*, as well as within the Mass itself, *presentation* is a means for invoking attention.

The impact is clear. We are to regard the church-sanctioned texts as important. Other texts, whatever their provenance or message, are not as significant. (Is it any wonder, then, that we may think that works such as the *Pistis Sophia*, or other recently-discovered works, are not as important?[3] We note that they were deemed important at one time; important enough to be the focus of a widespread search-and-destroy campaign.[4])

Although our holiday feasts at home are entirely different from a ritual event within our church, synagogue, mosque, or temple, there are still psychological similarities. When we bring out the Thanksgiving turkey, we make a point of having it arranged beautifully on a large platter. We are making a *presentation* statement. The object is for everyone to "ooh" and "ah" at such a fine roast bird. There is drama involved! In medieval times, a great feast would involve having the servers make a *processional* of carrying the boar's head, in full *presentation* mode, around the room – while people sang, "The boar's head do we carry, bedeck'd with bays and rosemary!" We recall that in those times, having fresh meat was not a simple matter of going to the supermarket or corner deli. A great feast of roast pork, especially if the hunters had to put their lives at risk to gain the meal, was probably worth breaking out in song!

My dear friend Joe Williams is probably the world's greatest proponent of the Delsarte method, a means of identifying and using the innate emotive quality of various movements and postures. He has spent most of his career researching and piecing together the insights first elucidated by François Delsarte in the late 1800's.[5] During workshops with Joe, I learned that when we want to show something as being important, we lift it up and actually lean back from it a little. This is almost a feeling of "stepping back," so that we can appreciate this important object more clearly. Thus, when we "lift something up" in a processional or in a ritual, we are saying, "This is important!"

I've used this idea strategically in my candle dances. In the opening, I don't just walk onto the stage carrying a candle in each hand. Instead, I use a very slow, stately, and stylized step – my movement towards the audience is a form of *processional*. I enter holding the candles behind my back. Then, I make a point of *presenting* each of the candle flames ritualistically, by lifting first one, and then the other, of the candles up for the audience to view. I drop my body weight a bit and lean back as I do so, so that my "candle-lifting" appears both more emotive and natural. My body languages is saying, "This is not just a candle – this is light! This is about the *meaning* of light when everything around us is darkness!"

There is one other aspect of opening and closing an event that is common to many rituals, across many different cultures. In addition to *processionals* and *presentations*, we also use *salutations*. These are formal greetings, and we use them to both open and close our ritual events. In a Mass, the priest begins by saying, "In the name of the Father, and the Son, and the Holy Spirit." He closes by blessing the congregation and then saying, "The Mass is ended, go in peace." Similarly, in a wedding, the minister opens by saying, "Dearly beloved, ..." In a formal, sit-down meal, the "host" for the event will make a few "opening remarks." Even if the food is served before the speaking begins, there will come a time at which someone will rise and, at the very least, welcome everyone in and perhaps propose a toast.

In the martial arts, the notions of *processionals* and *presentations* are minimized, but every martial arts class begins and ends with a formal *salutation*. When karatekas and judokas enter the dojo (or before they step onto the mat), they bow. When the teacher comes into the room, they bow. Before they start a *kumite* (sparring) or *randori* (grappling) session, each person bows to his or her opponent. This is a ritual act; it denotes respect for the place and the person. Also, in martial arts studios, the teacher and the students will take a moment for meditation at the beginning of class. This may be short; sometimes no more than thirty seconds. However, the act of centering themselves mentally before they begin practice is again a part of the ritual. It denotes setting the time apart from daily concerns.

We've noted that every formal, ritual experience usually includes the elements of *processional*, *presentation*, and *salutation*. Now, let's take this closer to home, and much closer to daily life. We certainly do not expect to make the grand, theatrical entrance every time we want to evoke a certain mood or state. However, we do note that we humans have an innate awareness and appreciation of not only ritual, but also staging. We respond well to things that create mood, and this includes both the surroundings and the way an event is introduced.

By taking just a little time to evoke the kind of atmosphere and ambience that we desire, we can create a different mini-environment when we intend to be in our *Hathor* or *High Priestess* states. Combined with movement, our attention to environment gives us cues that we intend to *shift state*. The easiest way to do this is to play with the lighting. We can introduce scent, by using incense or other options, and we can also select mood-inducing music.

Careful control of lighting is one of the easiest and most reliable means for inducing a special ambiance. Recently, I saw *The Sorcerer's Apprentice*, and almost laughed at the scene in which the teacher (Nicholas Cage) sat down with his apprentice (Jay Baruchel) to study an ancient book. The lighting for their study was provided by a grouping of candles on the desk. Now, there were substantial overhead lights available in the laboratory where the two "sorcerers" worked. When it came to doing a detailed study of an ancient manuscript that had faded ink, delicate line drawings, and nearly-illegible handwritten text, however, they used "mood lighting!" None of us would do this in real life, for real work. We'd bring over every strong light that we could find, and set up a magnifying lens – the kind that we would use for quilting or cross-stitch embroidery. But if we wanted to set the mood, then of course we'd use the candles!

Along with selecting the lighting, we can also use scent. Incense sticks are an easy option. Lately, I have preferred putting a few drops of scented oil into a little oil diffuser, lit by a tea light. The aroma is a bit softer, and I can not only scent the room, but put a drop of scent on my "pulse points" after I add a few drops to the oil.

In addition to lighting and scent, we can use music to help "set the mood." Our choices need not be limited to dance music; we can select from New Age, nature sounds, aboriginal or drum music, or any number of choices. If we have ever used a certain piece of music to "psych ourselves up" for a demanding day at the office or for going out to a party at night, or used other forms of music to help ourselves relax when we come home, we are already attuned to our preferences in this area.

One additional method for creating an effective ritual is to *reserve some special things* just for this purpose. When we use certain objects over and over again, for a special purpose, they acquire a psychological *charge* for us.

We all have things that carry psychological *charge* in our lives, such as a dress that we know always makes the evening special. Taking this into ritual preparation for dance play, we might select and reserve some things that we already own (but don't often use) for our private dance time. Maybe we have an incense burner, or a scented candle that we love but haven't used the way we'd like. Maybe we have a little bud vase or a bowl in which we can float a flower. Maybe there's a special lipstick or pair of earrings or something that we love to wear, but it's just not right for the office. It could be that this item is right for our special ritual "private time" – the time that we reserve for ourselves.

Pulling all these ideas together into a simple example, we may choose to start our ritual of dance experience by setting a room's lighting so that it flatters us the most. We may take a shower or a bath, and change into special clothes. We will certainly freshen up our cosmetics and put on some perfume! Then, as part of a *mini-processional*, we may light a candle and carry it to a table or shelf that denotes our "special space." Placing the lit candle into a selected spot is a form of *presentation*. We may light a stick of incense or use an oil diffuser to add scent.

We may choose to open our dance practice, or any time that we deliberately invoke our *Hathor* or *High Priestess states*, with the *Namaste* gesture as a *salutation*. (This is a simple bow with hands folded in a prayer-like manner and held at heart level.) As we do this, we can mentally invoke the presence of our Higher Power, and any other entities whose blessings and support we desire, such as our Guardian Angels. Very simple little thoughts and actions such as these can help guide our inner selves to *shifting state*, because they are body movements, and our psyches are already deeply programmed to connect movement with intentional states.

All these actions denote that what we are doing is special; we are opening up a ritual occasion. When we close, we blow out the candles, and perform the *Namaste* gesture once again. As we do so, we thank our Higher Power for this time. Gratitude is a means of acknowledging that we've just experienced something significant! These combined thoughts and actions now tell our psyche that we are leaving the ritual; we are going back to "daily life."

We have seen that if we go into a dance session thinking, "Oh, I'm going to practice dance now," it soon begins to seem like work. And work, in most of our lives, is what we already have. What we need is joy, spontaneity, and play. Approaching our dance time through a ritual of *preparing for pleasure* helps us to experience just that; pleasure!

If, every time we dance, we repeat the same preparation, then if we have a good experience, we will learn to associate the good experience with the preparation. We learn to *expect pleasure* when we prepare for it in a well-chosen, repeatable way. These preparation steps become a *trigger sequence*. As we build up our experiences with our personally-designed *trigger sequence* and create our mental association to a pleasurable state, then the *learned expectation* will help us in the future. Once we've learned to expect pleasure after we go through the preparation, we will tend to get that feeling, even if we're feeling out-of-sorts or "so-so" when we start. Just the preparation alone will begin carrying us into our desired *state*!

As we learn what works for us, we can start using some of these movement patterns and special actions as *triggers* on a regular basis. If we are careful to build the right associations – between trigger experiences and desired states – then frequent practice (at least initially) will make it easier to move our felt-sense into our desired *state*. We will teach ourselves some internal shortcuts.

When I dance, even just practicing at home, my ritual preparation is very important. This is something that I share and encourage in my students. "Even if you have only half an hour to practice," I tell them, "it's better to spend fifteen minutes of that time getting ready – getting into *state* – because it will change how you *feel* about yourself as you do this." This is particularly important because no one likes to practice. Who really wants to do drills and exercises?

We can do things from a sense of discipline. But why not do things out of pleasure? And why not make our dance practice (or whatever we do for our own *pathworking*) one of the greatest pleasures in our lives?

PERSONAL PATHWORKING:

1. Identify rituals that are used by the people and organizations around you, where you either participate or observe. Start with easy things, such as Thanksgiving dinner at Aunt Suzy's large house, or Christmas stockings early on Christmas morning. These rituals can be annual corporate retreats, or annual family vacations – especially if taken at the same place each year. These can be anniversary dinners, or drinks with friends at a favored spot at the end of the work-week. Simply start by identifying these rituals, and begin to take note. Begin to be a "sleuth" about yourself!

2. Now, pay attention to those rituals (personal or social) that you find *most effective*. For example, the Roman Catholic High Mass, especially in a larger church (and most especially in a gothic-style older church, such as New York's St. Patrick's Cathedral) is a highly structured, elaborate, and often effective ritual. This chapter discussed some of the "cues" and "triggers" that it uses to help congregation members *shift state*. Even the organ music contributes substantially, with its wonderfully deep, resonant tones! This is an extreme example. Think of other rituals that you know, or in which you have participated, that have been *most effective*. Start *sleuthing*! What *states* are the "ritual designers" trying to induce? What triggers do they use? In which combinations and sequences do they use the various triggers? (If you know something about neuro-linguistic programming, you might apply it here.) Which of these "cues" and "triggers" are most effective for *you*?

3. Now, bring your attention to some social rituals that *you've* designed. An example might be announcing promotions or team awards at work, or hosting a special birthday party for a family member or friend. Your "social rituals" can be deceptively simple and informal, but still have very strong psychological structures and triggers. For example, you may have a

big "family ritual" about summer barbeques, or trips to the beach. When do certain *triggers* kick in?

4. Look at some very personal, private rituals that you use. Your *sleuthing-skills* are sharpened by now; you'll detect subtle things with more ease and have greater insights, now that you've practiced on situations and people around you. Do you use an aromatherapy candle at your desk if you have a project requiring extra-special focus and concentration? Do you use a scented hand or body lotion to soothe yourself or to "get in the mood" for a special event? I have a mini-ritual in simply making a cup of tea. The actions, the tea-aroma, and the first few sips help me to get calm, centered, and focused. (In fact, the *ritual* of making tea has been used as a meditative experience within the Japanese Zen culture for years.) What do *you* use?

5. Now, reviewing what you've observed and noticed so far (observe that the simple act of *noticing* things informs you that something is important to you), what *triggers* work best for you? Are some things supremely important? For example, do you need a clean desk before starting a new project? With your enhanced sensitivity and awareness, can you take note of things that truly *are* important, but to which you haven't consciously paid much attention up until now? For example, smell and physical movement patterns are important to me. Smell is a very emotional *trigger*, and I will devote a full chapter to it shortly. Also, my dance and martial-arts training makes me very responsive to movement patterns; they can be as simple as a walk along a known path, or as complex as a detailed choreography. Once again, what works for *you*?

CHAPTER 19:
A SACRED TIME, A SACRED SPACE

ONE SUMMER, A FEW YEARS back, my friend Annabelle wrote and produced a musical "passion play" for Easter Sunday. Creating an ambience that evoked village life, she had the child-actors running to and fro, shouting and waving toys. Their actress-mothers, in the center of the melee, were at wit's end with all the noise and confusion. Off to the side, the "disciples of Jesus" observed in song, "They need a sacred space." The entire audience broke out in laughter.

"But I didn't *mean* for it to be funny," said Annabelle later on. "I know, Annie," I replied, "but what was funny about it was that we all resonated with that kind of need. It was just really humorous to have it shown so fully. This is something that goes on in all of our lives, whether we have children or not."

So it is. We all need a *sacred space* from time to time: a space that is carved out from our phones, various digital distractions, the kids, and our husbands (no matter how much we love them). We need, every so often, time to be just alone with ourselves. Perhaps because this need is one that is so often denied, we need it all the more.

There are certain times that are profound chrysalis-stages in our lives. These are those infrequent times when we are cut off from our mainstream activities or relationships, because of illness, loss of a job, or loss of a mate through death or divorce. We can, and often do, emerge from such passages as a different person. In fact, at some level we may even call these losses into our lives so that we are forced to spend time with our "inner self." In our society, where work and productivity and achievement are sanctioned, and spending time with ourselves is denigrated, it sometimes takes extreme measures to get what we need for inner work.

Several years ago (just prior to drafting this chapter), I had ample opportunity to learn this lesson. During my slow recovery from surgery, there was a time where I was so tired that I didn't have the mental or physical energy to focus on any task, much less carry it out. For several weeks I lived in a sort of "space-time bubble," cut off from the usual concerns of work and commitments. I knew that I would return as soon as possible, but since it wasn't possible just then, I didn't place expectations on myself. It was one of the very few times in my life where I deliberately gave myself permission to "let go" of my normal, dominant, get-things-done *Amazon* mode. I emerged deeply changed. I not only had a new direction in life, but a new ability to communicate and share. I also had a much deeper sense of purpose.

Loss of relationships, health, or a job are all extreme. We hope that they are also rare. But on a daily and weekly basis, we do need some way to nurture ourselves by having true *sacred time* as well as a *sacred space*. We need a time not dedicated to productive work, but rather set aside for reconnecting with our inner selves. The ratio of what we need seems to be one out of seven. Consider the old scriptural injunction about "keeping holy the Sabbath" – this was probably less to satisfy God than to force us to take the rest that we need!

Making the transition from our combined *Amazon* and *Isis/Mother* modes into our *High Priestess* and *Hathor* modes is often more difficult than it would seem, for many reasons. Most of us live with a very dominant inner *Amazon*. When "she" takes over our brain, she likes to keep control. Day-to-day life supports our being in this mode. Many things, from professional needs to home maintenance, often require our *Amazon* abilities. Further, every last thing in society seems to support our *Amazon* mode more than any other. We organize our lives by clocks and calendars, rather than by "feeling" what seems to be best for a given moment. Punctuality is prized, in everything from people to trains. While this gives order and structure to our lives, it has become dominant to an extreme that often does not allow for other ways of being.

When we are in *Amazon* mode, we operate largely in a cognitive, task-oriented, and goal-driven manner. No matter how grueling the pursuit, no matter how many hours spent or miles travelled, and no matter how much sleep, family, or "me" time we sacrifice, all of our *Amazon* goals at least give us concrete, tangible endpoints. More importantly, they give us timelines. We know exactly where we are in pursuit of our goal.

In some ways, our *Isis/Mother*-mode is similar to our *Amazon* natures. Our *Mother*-mode can include any form of care-giving; this could be caring for an elderly parent, taking in rescued animals, or volunteering at a hospice. In this mode, we focus our attention on the well-being of others. Our lives are governed, at least to some extent, by *their* needs and by *their* time-tables. At a recent Mass celebrating the Holy Family, Father Richard Curry, SJ (Chaplain-in-Residence at Georgetown University), spoke about the "asceticism of being a parent."[1] How very true! Being a parent, or a constant care-giver for anyone, is a spiritual discipline as demanding as being in a cloister. You get up when the *other person* needs you, not when *you* want. This becomes a spiritual practice. And even though there is some oxytocin-neurohormonal "reward" for being a parent (otherwise, no care-needing species would *ever* survive), the practice is sometimes grueling.

Each of us, especially those of us who are care-givers, need some time off. We particularly need to be released from "mommy-duties" when others are pulling on us from both convenience and habit, even though they may have grown enough to take care of themselves. Fortunately, as our children mature, the oxytocin wash diminishes from our brains, and we start attending to our own needs. Dr. Louann Brizendine, in *The Female Brain*, describes one client saying "'Make your own damn dinner'" to her husband. He was startled to find that his wife was more interested in finishing a painting than in caring for him![2]

Our *Amazon* mode, even in cases where it involves caring for others, is a task-oriented state of mind. In this mode, we produce (typically) measurable results. In contrast, the challenge in developing our *Hathor/Love-Goddess* and *High Priestess/Madonna* modes (and even our *Isis/Mother* mode, to the extent that it is feeling- and nurturance-oriented, more than task-oriented) is that all these other states are much more open-ended than our *Amazon* mode; they are not designed to give us concrete and tangible results.

This is precisely *why* it is a challenge to develop our feminine-specific *body/mind/psyche/energy integration path*. We desire to learn how to access these other states-of-being. We also desire some sort of structure, some guidance or feedback to let us know how we are doing in cultivating this ability. However, our usual ways-of-being and ways-of-working do not work very well in our *Hathor* and *High Priestess* realms of being!

This leads us to the heart of our dilemma. No matter how difficult or challenging a particular *Hero's Quest* may be, men typically have a fairly direct and straightforward experience. The much simpler masculine psychology is oriented towards tangible, measurable goals, with clear and obvious indicators of achievements and progress. Even their "inner traditions" or mystical paths – the various occult brotherhoods and societies – are full of rituals that at least supposedly connote evolutions of their abilities.

David Deida puts the ultimate challenge of the masculine quest very nicely: "The most potent forms of masculine realignment involve both austerity and challenge."[3] He recommends that a man take on practices such as going alone into the woods, with minimal food and comfort, to focus his attention until he encounters his vision.

Society romanticizes this process. In fact, we almost revere it! In contrast, the feminine path may almost be seen as mushy and self-indulgent. It certainly is less tangible than the masculine mode.

It is simply *because* our path is more "diffuse," and less tangibly goal-oriented, that it is more difficult. From a Myers-Briggs (or Jungian-based) Type perspective, what we are dealing with is a deliberate and intentional shift from a Judging (J) mode to more open-ended Perceiving (P) state. We desire first to be able to *shift* into this state, and then to become very aware of things we can do (and ways that that we can feel and be) within this state. One example of how we can translate this into our daily practice is to ask questions such as: "How can I access more of an interpretive, feeling-based state when I dance, instead of always being technical and cognitive? How can I release the hold that my day-to-day mind has on me, so that I am flowing and expressive in the moment?"

Some dancers excel in finding their "expression in the moment." We can study with them – in person when possible, and via online or other resources as well. Eva Cernik, a gifted dancer and a protégé of Anahid Sofian, has also studied with a master teacher in the Sufi tradition. She says, "My focus in this dance has always been to embody the beauty of the Natural World ... to be a channel for Divine energy. And just to be clear, I have no image whatsoever of a separate God or Goddess from myself that I worship in any way ... I only believe in 'Truth and the Logic of Nature.'"[4] Eva's dances have inspired me tremendously over the years, and I have also benefited through studying with her in various workshops. Videos of her performances are available through online sources.[5]

Artemis Mourat, internationally acclaimed and on a peerage level with my master teachers Anahid Sofian and Elena Lentini, also does exceptional improvisational dance. In various workshops and in her regular classes, she teaches women to develop their listening skills and to feel the music so that they can use their bodies as their instruments.[6] She has also produced a collection of instructional DVDs and CDs, with a new release focusing on Oriental dance rhythms and patterns for zills (finger cymbals).

Dalia Carella similarly has a wonderful improvisational style, and I've found it helpful to watch her videos again and again.[7] Through watching dancers who excel in improvisational dance, and by using the teaching materials that they provide, we can all be inspired to do something similar. Each of these master dancers illustrates a unique style. However, each also shows us what it can be like to express our *Hathor* essence through dance!

Once we work through our resistance, even a little tiny bit, then we can make it easier for ourselves to access different *states*. The previous chapter described how we can do this by creating rituals for ourselves. The purpose of these rituals is to help us disassociate from work-day concerns, and enter into our own private world.

Expressive movement is an important part of our *pathworking*. We are unfolding a *body/mind/psyche/energy pathway*. No matter how entranced we become with the mental aspects, we must cultivate our bodies. It is through moving our bodies that we truly gain access to our emotional (psyche) realms, and then are able to do energetic release. Thus, we need to create (or create access to) some sort of dance-space. This means setting apart both the *time* and the *space* for our dance.

Having a place for dance, even if it is just a shelf, a mirror, and a few square feet, is a good beginning. This area, no matter what its size, becomes our temple; our *sacred space*. Women who take on the dance art as an integral component of their *pathworking* understand this intuitively. Almost all students, once they get serious about dance, will take on *creating their sacred space*. This is a way that they communicate to themselves about the depth of their desire and commitment. They know that they need to *create sanctuary* for this emerging new sense of themselves.

Literally, we need both a *sacred time* and a *sacred space*. The word "sacred" should not scare us off. Yes, it does have strong religious connotations, but the root word for "sacred" is *sacre*, ultimately from the Latin word *sacer*, meaning "sacred" or "holy." The origin of this word, and of the idea of "sacred," literally refers to that which is "set apart." Not coincidently, this is also the root word for "sacrum," the roughly diamond-shaped bone at the base of the spine. Our sacral bone is "set apart" from the rest of the spinal vertebrae. In ancient Judaic rituals, the priests offered a sacrifice (see that root word again?) to God, with meat placed on the sacrum of the slaughtered animal.

Thus, when we speak of creating *sacred time* and *sacred space*, what we refer to is making time and space that is *set apart* from our regular day-to-day activities. The purpose of making this arrangement is that we set out to *honor ourselves in a special way*. Words such as "consecrating" our space (and our time) are not too extreme. In fact, it takes extreme measures, such as consecrating (literally, to *set-ourselves-apart-with*) to create the brief intervals out of our achievement-oriented days.

So, then, the practical question becomes: How do we do this? How do we go about setting space, or time, apart? How do we make it *sacred*?

The physical aspect is the most straightforward (although it can still be a challenge). We need to find a space, cleanse it, set it up, and consecrate it. Thereafter, we need to keep it *sacred* (set apart), as much as possible; from the kids, from our partners, and from our own other, enervating activities. This probably means negotiation, even with ourselves, if not with others. The point is, we must dedicate something (if even just a shelf) to the "dancer" aspect of ourselves.

After we find and designate our *sacred space*, we cleanse. We cleanse *thoroughly*. This is important. What woman among us doesn't start some new experience without a good, thorough cleansing? When we move into a new house or apartment, don't we always clean out the shelves before we set down our dishes? A woman with whom I once worked was as pragmatic as she could be: none of this "ritual stuff" or "inner work" for her! Nevertheless, when she and her husband and child moved into their new home – the one they had dreamed of, the one they had designed, the one they had watched grow from the ground up – she let go of her housekeeper. Why? Her mind didn't think in terms of such "practical abstractions" as consecration. However, she intuitively knew what she was doing. She was claiming her space for herself. Historically, the way that we claim is to clean.

When I started writing this book in earnest (as opposed to just general meandering), my first step was to clean my space. I moved everything, absolutely everything, out of my home office. I swept and mopped. I cleaned out and dusted every item that I moved back in, and asked myself, "Does this really belong in this space?" If yes, it went in. If not, down to the basement. I even burnished the brass table lamp to a soft glow. When I was done, the room had taken on a soft, almost magical glow. Everything was purposeful. Everything was clean. Everything was in functioning order.

Then, once everything was calm and clear, I *consecrated*. I brought in flowers. I meditated on the purpose of this space, and envisioned the work that I was about to create.

I always know when a student is starting to get serious about her art. She starts looking at her home with a new eye (much to the alarm of her family). "Where," she wonders, "can I best squeeze in some dance space?" Then, she starts moving things around. (The family members groan, even if they are not brought in as available labor.) Even if it is just a shelf, or the corner of a table or desk, the student sets up things that will help her connect to her sense of purpose. Usually, she places a pretty scarf (or two or three) on the new "altar." Often, she uses pictures of dancers, or a statue of some sort. Many of us love keeping fresh flowers in this area, and often keep our incense burners there as well.

When I first started teaching, I rented studio space. The room was an ordinary dance studio: wood floor, ballet barre, and lots of mirrors. This was too austere for our purposes. My students and I began bringing in a little table (yes, for each class) that we could drape with fabric, and on which we could create a mini-altar. We each brought in items, the nature of which changed with the seasons of both our gardens and our lives. This became a communal way of creating a *sacred space*, and was a lovely practice that we shared!

Martial artists have a time-honored tradition of creating their dojos, or practice halls, as *sacred spaces*. A Japanese martial arts dojo typically has a small alcove holding a beautiful pen-and-ink drawing with inspiring calligraphy; a beautifully written poem. These dojos also often have flowers in the alcoves. (This just goes to show: very masculine men can appreciate the softer things as much as we do!) The purpose, in both the dojo and our own, private *sacred space*, is the same. Whether we are martial artists or dancers, we seek a distinction between space that we use for usual, daily activities, and space that we reserve for our art.

Claiming, cleaning, and consecration, the three acts that tell us that we are creating a *sacred space*, are universal. Now, how do we go about creating *sacred time*? No matter how much space is at premium, our time is even more so.

To some extent, the same principles hold. We have to find the time (the same as identifying space), claim it, and consecrate it. The difference is: Once we identify a space for dance or movement expression, we can usually claim it on an ongoing basis. However, it is often more difficult to find and claim those little patches of time. It is even more challenging to use them in a sense that brings about real emotional satisfaction.

For a little while there, I was thinking, "What more is there to creating the time for dance then scheduling it in my day-planner, and then doing it?" I had forgotten what I had gone through in order to make dance (or any other creative expression) a central part of my life. I had trivialized my own struggles, and my own breakthroughs, when they were actually one of the most important things I could share with you.

My mother once told me, "Budget money for fun, and budget time for fun!" It took me years to embrace her advice, and (even though I'm writing a book on this subject) it is *still* a challenge for me! (As the saying goes, "We teach that which we need to learn.")

I have learned the value of vacations. My mother, drawing on her knowledge of Latin, told me that the purpose of a "vacation" was (literally, from the Latin source word *vacare*) to *vacate* our lives from our usual habits and concerns. We periodically need to leave our work and responsibilities behind.

In my *Amazon* mode, and conditioned by the rigors of the various start-up companies with which I've been involved, I'd spent far too many holiday weekends (and normal, everyday weekends) on work-related tasks. When I was in graduate school, I pushed myself to extremes, working hard through the weekend after a very demanding workweek. I wound up getting sick, simply from exhaustion. I finally figured out that the days lost to illness were the same number of Sundays that I'd put in at the study cubicle. I realized that the biblical adage to "keep holy the Sabbath" had some merit.

Since then, I've found that, while I don't normally get my insights while in my *High Priestess* mode, when I "return" to "normal" (*Amazon*-dominant) activities, I am usually not only refreshed, but much more creative. I can tie each of my major inventions to a time in which I was "set apart" from regular, mundane activities. Even being snowed in has become a fruitful, creative time! Similarly, we can each benefit by getting cooperation from our *Amazon* in scheduling both *Hathor* and *High Priestess* time.

As we go about creating both *sacred time* and *sacred space*, we use both our intuition (coming from our *High Priestess* mode), and our desires for what would feel best for us (coming from our *Hathor* mode), to connect with our *Amazon*, and get agreement on this "claiming" of both space and time. Sometimes, we need to negotiate amongst our different modes. If we are going through a period of very intense work – whether it is a significant career project or objective, or simply the ongoing challenge of balancing career with care-giving – then we must promise ourselves some time off when the opportunity does arise, and then we must *keep our promise*. In the interim, we need to give ourselves little "retreat and play" breaks. As we refine our abilities to tap into our inner knowing, we will cultivate an awareness of that which we need the most. Then, the truly important step is to honor that knowing, instead of constantly "overriding" our own needs.

We wouldn't constantly deprive a child or a lover, would we? If we loved someone, we would never make promises, only to casually break them! We thus need to treat our inner modes – *High Priestess* and *Hathor* – with the same love and nurturance that we would give to an external person whom we loved. This is where our opportunities for *integration* begin.

PERSONAL PATHWORKING:

1. To the best of your ability, eliminate (or at least minimize) digital distractions. From excessive emails (and all the other social media that simply eat your time), to TV, get as much of this out of your life as possible. Much of this is simply cognitive "noise," and makes it impossible to tune into either your *Hathor* or *High Priestess* modes.

2. One of the best opportunities, for those of us who are dancers, is to take one of the extended workshops; a long (holiday) weekend, or even a week-long music and dance camp.[8] This is a superb time for both your *Hathor* and *High Priestess* selves!

CHAPTER 20:
EVOKING A STATE: THE POWER OF SCENT

YEARS AGO, WHEN I WAS in graduate school in the Southwest and living far from home, I went back to see my family for Christmas. This is a journey that many of us make at this time of the year. What was different here was that "home" was in the upper Midwest, and at Christmas-time, the temperatures often plummeted to –20 degrees Fahrenheit. This was more than a "brrr." It was a shock to the system!

As I crossed the threshold of my parent's home, wonderful warm smells banished the assault of the frigid outdoor cold. The aroma of oranges and cinnamon filled my nostrils. As Mom placed a cup of spiced tea in my hands, I knew that I was home. Accidental timing? Not at all! "I wanted you to feel loved and nurtured, and to know that you had really come back home," said Mom. "So I made this for you. I wanted you to smell this as soon as you walked in." Her strategy worked beautifully.

Almost all of us, at different times, have used scent to trigger associations. Every time that we've planned a dinner with the wonderful smells in mind, we have deliberately used our knowledge of how smell ties into our feelings. We can go back in our minds to some of our favorite holiday feast memories. Yes, the food on the table was wonderful, but don't we remember, even more, the joy of anticipation? The hours ahead of the meal were filled with aromas such as those of roasting herb-stuffed turkeys and sweet-flavored hams, and of densely rich pies baking in the ovens. We remember when other people have created these sensual extravaganzas for us, and we remember when we have done so for others. If lavishing these aromas on our psyches was not so important, we'd all buy pre-cooked turkeys, or go out to eat! When we choose to create the holiday meal at home, aren't we thinking of nourishing our families with not just the actual meal itself, but also with the aromas of cooking?

I wrote the first draft of this chapter on December 21ˢᵗ, many years ago, knowing that late on Christmas Eve, I would be flying from Manhattan back to my home in the Southeast. I hadn't been home in three months, and finances were tight. "How important is a Christmas tree to you?" my beau had asked on the phone the previous day. He was looking through his wallet, which was as thin as could be. "After all," he continued, "it'll only be up for a short time, and then we have to take it down. And I priced them today; oooh-my-Lordy, they are expensive!"

"Well," I answered, "we could do without. It's just that I like waking up in the early morning, coming downstairs, and smelling the pine scent," and my voice broke.

"Hold it right there," he said. "I've got a visual just now. Sweetie, this place will stink like a pine forest when you come home!"

My beau maintained that Christmas was not that important to him. To me, it was filled with emotional associations, all of them important, and all revolving around smell. On the streets of Manhattan, my senses were filled with "Christmas cues" as soon as I stepped outside the apartment building. Church bells played carols throughout the day. The cold wind nipped at my face as I leaned into the sharp wind. The Lord & Taylor windows showed scenes from a Christmas-themed circus. The windows at Macy's were rich with decorated Christmas trees and mantelpieces covered with dried fruits, nuts, and trinkets. Piles of gifts and toys were stacked nearby these window-dressing fireplaces. But the one thing that said "Christmas" to me, more than anything else, was walking by the street stalls of freshly cut pines, with boxes of juniper, fir, and holly on the side. During Christmas season, until I smell this particular combination of scents, Christmas is a mirage; it is as real as a movie or TV show. But once the scents kick in, Christmas "happens," and I feel just wonderfully alive.

Smells can take us back to childhood memories, and even induce recollections of specific events. As Edwin Morris points out in *Fragrance: The Story of Perfume*, "there is almost no short-term memory with odors."[1] Instead, our sense of smell is very connected with our long-term memory – and particularly with the emotional aspects of memory. Those of us who have read Marcel Proust's *Remembrance of Things Past* may recall that the protagonist is suddenly brought back to his earlier years by the smell of freshly-baked madeleines.

Smell is the most basic of our senses. Senses such as vision and hearing are very complex. Our sense of smell, in terms of our brain structure, is much more straightforward. Our "smell-sense" connects directly to our limbic system – the part of our brain that is pure mammal. Our limbic system generates our emotions and our feeling-responses to our environment. Emotional feelings of comfort or anxiety, and of affection or fear, all come from our limbic system. This means that they are all tied directly to our sense of smell.

Since our sense of smell is tied into not just "cognitive" things like memories of places and events, but directly into our limbic emotional response center, it makes sense that we can make a conscious decision about using scent to deliberately induce distinct emotional states in ourselves. Essentially, we can learn to program our own brains.

We use the cognitive, thinking part of ourselves (our *Amazon* mode) to decide how we want to feel, or what *state* we want to induce. Next, we figure out what sort of scent gives us a good association with that *state*. Then, we deliberately increase the association between the scent and the *state*, until finally, the scent itself acts as a "shortcut." We put on the scent, and easily find ourselves in the desired *state*.

This is not a new concept. Any time that we have bought an aromatherapy candle and lit it for an evening meditation is a time that we've deliberately used the strategy of "scent to induce *state*." If we've cooked our sweetheart's favorite meal – the one that his Mama cooked for him years ago – we have deliberately played with *his* emotional state. If we've ever rubbed a "balancing blend" of essential oils onto our third eye or on pulse points during the middle of a stressful day, we were using our self-programming knowledge to help ourselves to calm down; to *shift state*.

The suggestion that we are exploring in this chapter is that we take something that we already know, and that has worked well for us before, and simply enhance it a little. We will blend this approach in with our overall strategy for creating a transition to our *Hathor* sensuality or our *High Priestess* quiet time.

When I was sixteen, I read in fashion magazines about having a "personal signature" with scent. Wanting to have my own signature, I made a foray into the department stores, deliberately looking for the one that was "me." No stranger to quality, even then, I selected Chanel No. 5. A while ago, I repeated the experiment in one of New York's 5th Avenue department stores. And again, despite the plethora of new scents that arrive every season, I still selected Chanel No. 5.

This scent says something to me *about* me. It suggests an image that I would like to have of myself; poised, confident, worldly yet serene at the same time. I love wearing this scent to business meetings, for going out for dinner, and for innumerable professional and social occasions. But I would never, ever wear this scent for Oriental dance. *Never.* I would rather go without perfume completely than to wear my favorite "day scent" when doing Oriental dance.

Why?

It's simple. For me, Chanel No. 5 conjures an old-world sense of sophistication, elegance, and refinement. While suitably erotic in its own unique way, it has an entirely different feeling than what I desire to evoke during dance. (However, there are times that I have something in common with our beloved silver-screen icon, Marilyn Monroe. On being asked what she wore to bed, she is reputed to have said, "Chanel No. 5.")

Early in my years of Oriental dance training, I learned to use a different scent for dance, and for anything associated with my more feeling-oriented sensual state, than what I would use in the boardroom. After a while, I began to use the dance-scent to condition myself; to help myself "get in the mood" to dance, even if I was nowhere near the mood in the beginning.

Before I started teaching Saturday morning dance classes, and well before I moved to Manhattan where my teachers held Saturday classes, I used Saturday morning as a personal "dance time." This sounds easy, but actually, it was hard. After a week at work, all that I wanted to do on Saturdays was to relax and putter. It was so easy to find one little thing to do, and then another, and then before I knew it, the entire day was gone!

Thus, I started a strategy of doing dance choreography first thing on Saturday mornings. To do this, I had to get myself into the right *state*. I would wake up early on Saturday, shower, dress (in dance warm-up clothes, of course), and put on cosmetics. (Yes, this meant full makeup; the kind that I would wear if I was going out in the evening. Even if I wasn't going to see anyone for the next 24 hours, I would have to see myself; I would be practicing in front of the mirror.) Finally, I would put on my "Oriental dance scent." Once I applied perfume, that was it! I'd given myself the *trigger*, and it was time to go practice. The perfume helped. It really did.

Sometimes, my students set better examples than I do. Such is the case with the power of scent. Samira, who studied with me for almost four years, made a point of dressing beautifully and grooming herself elegantly, even for a weeknight dance class. She unfailing arrived with her cosmetics freshly done, her fingernails polished a beautiful dark red, and wearing a lovely practice costume. Moreover, she smelled fantastic!

"I mix my own perfume from scented oils," she said. She has a full collection, ranging from sandalwood and rose scents to special "mixes" that she buys, and to which she often adds her own private perfumes. Samira not only uses scent on herself (and has generously shared her own oils with the rest of us); she has gifted us with incense and oil diffusers. The fragrance collection that she brought to us includes ancient fragrances such as myrrh and frankincense, as well as the more floral and contemporary scents. We can use the same scents to perfume both our rooms (via oil diffusers) and our bodies!

Over the years, we've made our studio into a wonderfully exotic (nearly erotic) environment, with multiple sources of soft lighting, cushions, decorations, and mirrors. When we focus on creating a lovely studio atmosphere, we light candles, and sometimes even have a fire in winter. Even the music helps us get into the mood. More than anything, though, it is scent that helps us transition rapidly into our *Hathor*-selves! When we perfume both our surroundings and our bodies, we *trigger* scent-based associations. This is perhaps the fastest means available for us to communicate with the nonverbal, feeling-based part of ourselves.

If we take this one step further and combine scent with a movement pattern, especially one set to music that we use for this specific purpose, we increase our ability to "program ourselves." We can more easily *shift state* into a zone where we let down our daily cares, and allow ourselves more feeling-based expression and freedom.

My cats go around the rooms, rubbing their cheeks (and their tail ends) against furniture, especially everything soft; those things that will hold their scent. Animals know how to "mark territory" with their own personal scent-signature. Can't we learn from animals? Using scent becomes our most powerful boundary-marking tool; it helps us to identify both our *sacred times* and our *sacred spaces*.

We can draw on a rich set of scent (and sensual) resources to help ourselves not only create, but also demark, our *sacred spaces* and *times*. When we enter a church, synagogue, or temple in which incense has been used consistently over time, and if we have made a habit of entering such a place in order to direct our minds to God, then we draw on the association that we've built up. Each time that we enter our well-known *sacred space*, we draw on our "internal programming" that helps us move our attention towards the Divine. Similarly, if we use a special scent in our bath, or to give someone (or to receive) a massage, then every time that we encounter that scent, we can tap into our already-formed "neural connection" between the special scent and a relaxed state. Now, knowing how readily we can "program ourselves" (not literally, but through inducing a felt-sense association), our task is to apply what we've learned to honoring both our *Hathor* and *High Priestess* states. We can do this by intelligently, creatively, and even strategically selecting and using scents within our environment and as personal perfumes.

PERSONAL PATHWORKING:

1. If you've never found a signature scent, now's the time! Treat this as a mini-vision quest, much as you did in *Chapter 4*, when you went out to find your first veil.

2. Fairly often, different magazines will run articles describing the "personalities" of various scents. Collect the articles, and take them with you when you try on various scents in department stores. (Collect as many samples as you can!) Learn to correlate what your "nose" tells you with the concepts (floral, spicy, Oriental, citrus, woodsy, etc.) behind each scent.

3. Spend a little time (you might add this to your dance journal) noting the various ways in which you already use scent to *trigger* awareness, or even different *states*, in your day-to-day life. Do you use the smell of coffee in the morning, as much as the actual coffee itself, to send a "wake-up" signal to your brain? Do you use a scented candle on your desk, or put a few drops of scent onto a blotter for a light bulb? Identify the various scents (and associations) that you already use. You may realize that you are much more consciously using scent than you had thought!

4. Notice when you already use scent to *shift state*. Do you have a particular perfume that you wear on special nights out? What scent do you use to tell *yourself*, even more than your partner, that you are ready to make love?

5. Once you've identified your basic "signature scent," explore how you may have different scents for different moods or "feeling-spaces." This may be a good time to experiment with how you match scent with dress/ornament, activity, and even the "persona" that you inhabit for a period of time. Do you have a scent that gives you an upbeat, powerful note; one that you use for a special presentation at work? Do you have a scent wardrobe, including

scents for sports and just being-around-the-house? Do different scents correlate with different moods for you? Do they evoke different aspects of your personality? Try integrating scent into your rituals; you may find that different scents correspond with different desires and feelings.

6. Various sources cite a "legend" that Chinese concubines were fed a diet that, while otherwise bland, was flavored with civet and musk. When aroused during love-making, their bodies would exude the musky aroma, providing a little aphrodisiac-extra to their partners.[2] While I've not quite gone so far as to add musk to my food (yet!), we might consider forgoing the garlic a day or so before the hottest of our "hot dates."

CHAPTER 21:
DRESSING THE PART

I COULDN'T HELP BUT LOOK at her. In fact, I was actually studying her, and committing the details to memory. Of all the students that I had seen in this class, she was the first one to do something interesting with her clothing. And she was the first one to make it really fun! Add to it, she had not spent much money on the effect. Time and attention, and a willingness to be creative, is what she'd invested in her outfit that day.

The scene, once again, was downtown Manhattan. The setting was a class with a leading dance teacher; one of several with whom I studied. This teacher, and others like her, taught class wearing the simplest of clothing; a thin, long-sleeved black sweater, loose black pants. A little black hip scarf was the only indication that we were doing Oriental dance, as opposed to jazz, tap, modern, or ballet. She wore no jewelry; no adornment of any kind. The severity of the teacher's garb was often taken one step further by some of the students, who usually wore the darkest and dullest colors possible. They were good dancers, but their clothing denied the beauty of this art.

In the midst of all this black and gray severity, the new student stood out like a hummingbird against crows. She wore a simple little printed skirt in a bright, vivid batik of pink, orange, purple, and yellow. Over this, she had layered a sheer pink veil, tied in sarong manner. The effect was wonderful! The sheer embroidered pink sarong fabric, embellished with a few sequins, softened the impact of the vibrant batik, and pulled all the colors together. On top, she wore a simple little maroon sports bra; nothing expensive, nothing extraordinary, but it went well with her skirt.

The rest of her outfit was in the details — and how lovingly she had put them together! She wore finger-rings and toe-rings, and had little ornaments braided into her long, black hair. She wore a few other pieces of jewelry – the most wonderful of which was a long beaded necklace that circled her waist. Made of multiple strands of tiny iridescent yellow beads joined at intervals with deep carnelian-hued beads, I know that it could not have cost more than a few dollars, and could have been made as an easy evening's project. This simple little piece added a lovely sense of fun and lightheartedness. For such a small piece of jewelry, it did wonders in taking the entire outfit into a realm of playful fantasy!

Many women come into Oriental dance because they want to express a side of themselves that they can't express during their normal, workday lives. They (and many of the rest of us) have a part of their being that cries out for expression, and pines away when hidden under our daily uniforms of suits, jeans, or any of our culture's staid dressing. Our alter-egos crave more intensity, sensuality, exuberance, and passion. Our *Hathor* essence is a real and vital part of who we are. It's just that in the normal course of our lives, we don't have a way to recognize this "inner self," much less to invite her out to play!

For many of us, creating a special wardrobe that helps us express our "alternate" personas – our sensual and playful *Hathor* and even our quiet, internal *High Priestess* – is an important part of giving ourselves permission to enter these states. My own transition into developing such a wardrobe is one that many of us take over time.

For years, I did my Oriental dance practice in my then-standard "dance gear" – leotards, tights, and leg warmers, with a hip sash to give that all-so-important sense of "pelvic awareness." Like all dancers, I used a large mirror to check out my posture and form while practicing. Thus, it was useful to wear something that showed my "body line." A while back, though, I morphed just a tiny bit in attitude – with a big change in results!

In the previous years, I'd made some real breakthroughs in terms of *anchoring* my sense of body awareness into my pelvic area. Thus, I was surprised when my master teacher Anahid Sofian told me that I was still carrying my sense of body awareness too high; more up in the solar plexus than in the pelvis. She suggested that I get a heavier hip scarf – one with lots of coins sewn to it, so that it would bring my awareness at the hips, and *anchor* it there. I thought I had been doing so well!

Shortly thereafter, I traveled to Virginia to study with my friend Pilar, who has a wonderful dance style. Pilar never dances in leotards and tights. She always wears a skirt, dropped to the hip line, and a little top that leaves her whole abdomen bare. Even if she has to take her blouse and tie it up and tuck it into her bra, she opens up her whole abdominal region. This is just for practice! As she puts it, though, "It's belly dance. How can you do belly dance without using the belly? And if it's all covered up, you don't see it, you're not as aware of it."

This is not to say that leotards are no longer "socially acceptable" for Oriental dance, but this is a new way to think about things. There is also something about wearing a long skirt – one that starts at the hips instead of the waist – that seems so much more fluid and romantic.

Over the past several years, I've applied the inspiration from Pilar and that singular, lone New York hummingbird to my dance wardrobe. I've even extended the feeling behind their approach to my professional and play wardrobes as well!

Now, I try to make at-home practice a bit more special. Wearing a long elastic-waist skirt, yoga pants, or the similar (but much more flared-leg) belly dance pants gives a great base layer. All sorts of basic tops work. Some dance suppliers provide fabulous little tops, ranging from stretch velvet in many sizes and shapes to little tie-under-the-bust numbers that have all sorts of interesting sleeves, and which come in different fabric types and weights. These, combined with what we probably already have in our drawers and closets, will get us started with a basic set of practice clothes.

The "Oriental dancer" look comes about as we start layering on hip scarves and fanny wraps. Hip scarves are usually triangular pieces of fabric, or large fabric squares folded into triangles. We can make these ourselves, and all sorts of interesting fabrics will work. The most popular are metallic, lurex, and even heavy-weight chiffon. We can also buy them pre-made; they usually have long fringe, or are decorated with sequins or a crocheted edging of shiny little beads. To wear these, we simply wrap the hip scarf around the widest part of our hips, and tie the ends of the triangle either in front or to one side. Fancy ones with fringe, coins, or beads may be a little pricey. However, dancers often find lovely scarves available for only a few dollars from a major discount chain. With the right colors and patterns, even an inexpensive scarf, or simple piece of fabric, will do wonderfully. (We can also find great options via online catalogs and bazaars!)

Fanny wraps are exactly what the name suggests: long rectangular pieces of fabric, wrapped from behind and tied in front. Many dancers favor the fanny wraps festooned with rows of crochet in the back, hung with little fake silver or gold coins. The coins jingle together when we move, and add a nice sound.

The purpose of wearing a fanny wrap or hip scarf is to *anchor* our attention and awareness into the pelvic area. Martial artists do this with their belts; a kara-teka or judoka wears his or her belt at the hips, not at the waist. The idea, with both the *Art of Venus* as well as the martial arts, is to focus our awareness into our geographic body-centers. This helps us tune in to our vital energy, or *ch'i*, which is used in both art forms.

In addition to wearing basic dance gear and hip or fanny scarves, we also (optionally) wear jewelry. Oriental dance is different from commonly-seen dance forms, such as ballet or modern dance. Our art has a note of lushness and opulence to what we wear, even just for practice!

Of course, in any movement-based art, it makes sense that we don't want to wear something that will be caught and pulled. But for Oriental dance, which is an earthy, grounded, and sensual art, we can allow ourselves to dress up a little, even for everyday practice. There is no need in this dance form to be spartan and spare. Instead, the feeling is more like, "Come out and play."

I have earrings, bracelets, and other bits of adornment that I keep exclusively for Oriental dance. As I was sharing this with some of my students, they also began to find clothes that said, "Let's play!" Samantha, not much of a one for jewelry or cosmetics, showed up for class one day wearing beautiful gold-toned sandals, inset with "jewels." "I'll have you all know," she said, "that these are my belly dance sandals. I've bought them just to wear to class, and to places where there might be dancing."

One of the most wonderful aspects of putting together this kind of costuming is that it doesn't have to cost a great deal. It can, and of course we often love to buy costumes and jewelry and other adornments, but spending lots of money doesn't have to be part of the game. Some of the most delightful "mood" pieces come from different import shops, where jewelry and clothing with an exotic flair are easily found.

Better yet, I've seen a number of instances where no money is involved at all; just opening up consciousness to receiving. My friend Annabelle, a beautiful woman and an extraordinary dancer, studied with me for over two years. After a year of Oriental dance studies, she started to "invite" dance adornments into her life. This was a big shift for her, because in her previous ballet and modern dance training, she had cultivated a sparse approach to dance attire. As she opened up, and told people about her new love for Oriental dance, people started to "find" things for her. She received gifts, for no reason other than that people wanted to give her lovely things. Beautiful jewelry, gorgeous bits of fabric, lovely skirts – all these found their way into her life. By practicing gratitude, she drew in even more!

Thus, on a tight budget, or even on no budget, each of us can still "draw" beautiful and useful items into our lives; these things will enhance our new-found sense of play and sensuality in "dressing up." It helps us to take note of these items. We can observe how the universe continues to support us in our new passion and love!

"You folks get to wear all the neat costumes," sighed one young jazz dancer as she watched us prepare for a gala performance. As she spoke, I was pinning a little triangle of golden coins just beneath the clasp of my golden hip belt, which overlaid two layers of sheer fiery-orange and gold hip wraps, layered over my russet-orange and gold full-length circular skirt, which I wore over sheer, iridescent orange harem pants. I had already put on the ornately jeweled bra, the golden, tiered necklace with the little tinkly bells, the snake arm bands and bracelets, the earrings, and the gold and silver mesh head wrap. She was right. We *did* get to have all the fun!

Costumes for actual dance performances *are* different from practice-wear. It's not so much that they're scantier; it's that they're more elaborate. "I had no idea," a friend once remarked as she watched me get ready for a show, "that there was so much!"

The basic elements for a cabaret-style costume are a bra with lots of decoration, and a low, hip-slung girdle or hip belt, also with lots of decoration. The hip belt is worn over either a very narrow or very full skirt. Harem pants can also be worn; either sheer ones under a skirt, or more opaque ones without a skirt. This is the costume most familiar to people who haven't seen much Oriental dance. Another style of costume, usually worn for folkloric dance, is much more covered. It is a dress, usually long-sleeved and with a modest neckline. It might have deep slashes up at the side seams, and if this is so, then harem pants are worn underneath. This is also worn with a large, heavily-decorated hip belt, or set of hip sashes with an overlying hip belt. Because this costume is more covered, it is usually the costume of choice for more mature women, or for anyone who feels that she doesn't want to put too much of her body on display.

It is possible that the bra-and-skirt "cabaret-style" costume is of Indian ancestry rather than Middle Eastern. In several forms of Indian dress, there is a bodice cut short at the midriff, typically worn with a full-skirted sari. Coming from this context, the short blouse has been less a matter of sexual titillation and more a matter of much-needed ventilation. Gradually, as this costume began to be adopted and adapted for Oriental dance, the blouse-top became smaller, until it was simply a very ornate bra, and the skirt became fuller and wider, to accommodate the dance movements.

Historically, dancers wore vests and hip girdles on top of their regular clothes. Both the vests and hip girdles were decorated with pierced coins. Young Berber girls built up their dowry by dancing for friends and family at gatherings.[1] They would take the coins given or thrown to them during performances, and sew them onto their costume. The coin-decorations were not just wealth, they were status! Not only that, when little brass bells were added to the ensemble as well, the costume gave a satisfying accompaniment as the dancer moved; a soft susurration to go with her shimmies, and nice crisp cascades of sound to accompany hip drops and thrusts.

It is one thing to develop and wear costumes for special occasions. Now, though, let's see what we can do to bring some of this joyous, exuberant, and playful sensuality into a broader aspect of our lives. Let's pick up, once again, the idea of being our own *jewel in the heart of the lotus*. We discussed earlier how important it is to design our entire lives so that, for each of us, our individual beauty is shown as exquisitely and as uniquely as possible. This means that we pay great and attentive care towards discovering and cultivating our personal style.

It helps us if we keep in mind that not only physical objects, but also our activities and relationships, are aspects of our personal style. These are all ways in which we can honor ourselves, in which we can cultivate being the jeweled elegance of the gorgeous Fabergé egg, in which we are the central *jewel*! As we start cultivating greater body awareness, we can also consider how our clothes interact with how we feel. This is a separate area of study and investigation; again, it is something that we evolve over time.

In our culture, we often wear clothes that cut us off at the waist. Of course, our waists are a natural point for bringing in our clothing when we want to keep our pants on, or our skirts from falling off. However, the side effect of having tight, pinched waists is that we lose the connection between our heads and our pelvis. By occasionally wearing a dropped-waist skirt, with a low-slung belt (simply as a more decorated "daytime" look), we can move our feeling-sense beyond our waistline, and from there, to the rest of our bodies. This is a choice for us, which we can implement by selecting one or two such outfits for our wardrobe.

The combination that I most love, and have found to be the most beautiful, most sensual, and most romantic, is a mid-length sarong-style wrap worn over a floor-length circle skirt. The sarong over-layer should be just long enough so that it is tight around our hips and upper thighs; it should cover the hips completely in the back. At the same time, it should be short enough so that the circle skirt has plenty of room to billow out as we move. Having seen many costumes, on many dancers over the years, I've realized that this particular combination yields the most alluring look possible. The bias cut of the underlying circle skirt gives that wonderfully feminine sense of fluidity. The volume of the circle skirt gives mystery and opulence, while the tight sarong over-layer shows our figure to perfection. The next time you look at red-carpet gowns, see how many of the most attractive silhouettes follow this design pattern!

As we start opening up to our *Hathor* essence, we pay attention to how a particular style of dress offers sensual and erotic possibilities. We find that there are rich opportunities offered by some clothing styles that may be very different from flagrant skin exposure, or from an ultra-tight fit! For example, the kimono, for all its apparent modesty, offers a subdued and elegant eroticism. The way the collar/front band is attached (a simple result of its design) beautifully showcases the back of the wearer's neck. Since this was the exposed area, in an otherwise completely covered look, it began to carry with it an erotic *charge* for the (typically male) viewers. By studying such classic garments and cultural styles, we learn that the sensual and erotic subtexts in our clothing can be very underplayed, and yet become both interesting and exciting. We notice how subtly our clothing can enhance our personas.

We have learned from the kimono how selective, and perhaps surprising, revelation – of even a small portion of our figures – can pack a much stronger emotional punch than showing too much skin! We can gain similar insights by studying classical dress from other cultures, such as Indian saris. The important thing is to notice how the costume's line works with the wearer's figure, and how the two come together to give an interesting silhouette. Another time-honored style tradition comes to us from Grecian clothing; this was re-interpreted by Mariano Fortuny with his elegant, pleated silk and velvet garments in the early 1900's.[2] The Grecian/Fortuny styles continue to inspire us with our "goddess dresses" today. The natural flow of fabric over our bodies in these styles provides its own supple grace; this is well worth our consideration.

We can similarly study recent and modern designers to learn how their clothing structures work with different bodies. Each of us will find certain overall styles, or "lines," to be most flattering. Over time, we can rework our wardrobes to emphasize the looks that not only flatter us the most, but also most express our unique natures!

As we come into greater appreciation of our bodies, and grow an increased understanding of our own body proportions, we can be more adroit in how we use proportion in our clothing combinations. The ancient Greeks were the first to discover the "golden ratio" – a ratio which works out to be about 1.62 – which shows up in many natural structures. These range from the size ratio between increasing chambers of the nautilus shell to the proportions between various parts of our bodies. This "golden ratio" became a fundamental tenet underlying Grecian design of temples and other artifacts. Even today, astute designers will build this ratio into their works, as it aesthetically pleasing. You may want to consider working this ratio into the proportions of your clothes. You may consider the ratio, for example, of the length of your suit jacket to the length of your skirt, when worn with the jacket. The point is that for good design balance, these two lengths will not be equal. The length from shoulder to skirt hem (your total ensemble length) should ideally work out to be 1.62 times *either* the total length of the jacket, or the length of the skirt that is visible when you wear the jacket (measured from the bottom of the jacket to the hem of your skirt.) This is a slightly more advanced and analytic approach to your wardrobe design, but can be of great value to you. Once you have mastered this in your wardrobe, you might also think about using this in laying out furniture in a room, or selecting objects which you will put next to each other.

My very first dance costume was based on the gorgeous russet-orange and gold circle skirt that I described earlier; it was absolutely spectacular, and I couldn't wait to wear it. New to the art, I had never owned such a wonderful piece of fantasy clothing. It also, like almost all circle skirts, was made of two separate pieces; a half-circle in front, and a full circle's worth of fabric in the back. It opened up to "there" on both sides!

It takes about seven yards of fabric to make one of these full circle-and-a-half skirts. In contrast, most of the skirts in our "daytime" wardrobes require between one and three yards of fabric. How is it that a skirt with two to three times more fabric than usual can be more entrancing and exciting than something that has less fabric? Once again, the secret lies in selective revelation. The added interest is that even when we *do* reveal an aspect of ourselves, we do *not* reveal it all at the same time! Intermittent and occasional flashes of a typically covered area (such as part of the leg) are much more interesting than putting all of what we have on display.

The first time that I wore my gorgeous new skirt, I made the mistake of showing too much leg. My teacher at that time, DeShara, took me to the side. She tucked the back edges up into my hip belt to cover me up a bit more. "You don't want to show too much," she said, and she was right. As a former New York showgirl and model, she knew how to make a dramatic effect. "Most girls wear harem pants under a skirt that has high slits," she told me, and I made a pair of sheer orange pantaloons the very next day. It was not so much that the sheer pantaloons provided more coverage – instead, they provided the illusion of coverage! That made the entire ensemble more interesting.

DeShara was right, as I've realized over the years. A good part of our being interesting, both as performers and as women, lies in how we are subtle, complex, and multi-layered. Innately, we have mystery. Yet how can we keep the quality of mystery if we're showing everything that we have in the first few moments?

DeShara also told me about the time that she and a friend, also a model, were doing a swimsuit shoot on the beach. One wore a white swimsuit with black trim, black high-heeled sandals, and a large black straw hat. The other wore a black swimsuit with white trim, white sandals, and a large white hat. As they strolled down the boardwalk to get refreshments, people got up and applauded! There is nothing like having costume, and style, and the panache with which to carry off your look! Not only do we feel great, but others appreciate us as well.

As you form a mental picture of these two lovely ladies, dressed in such wonderful costumes just for the beach (or so was the photo-shoot suggestion), imagine them first with, then without, those wide straw hats. The effect is lost without the hats, isn't it? Hats literally "top us off." They provide dramatic impact, and they add an element of mystery. They balance the rest of our ensemble, and give a sense of finish or completeness.

Over the past few decades, we have – culture-wide, for men as well as for women – moved progressively towards more casual styles of dress. The extra accoutrements such as hats require greater effort. They demand that more attention be given to creating a "polished" look. Adding in just one new ingredient, such as a hat, can require a shift and a rebalancing in other areas. We may feel that "upgrading our look" by adding a hat then requires a bit more attention to our cosmetics and to other accessories. We may feel the need to complete our "look" with gloves or an interesting brooch. Thus, making the decision to wear a hat actually involves a much more thoughtful and pervasive commitment to "dressing up," which is really a form of pleasuring our inner *Hathor.* As an alternative, certain hats can take us into a more playful realm, giving us a more fun and light-hearted total "look." Although more apparently carefree, they also require thought – and a certain level of commitment to playful self-expression!

Hats give us opportunities to have more "polish" – or more "playfulness" – in how we present ourselves. They also have something in common with veils; especially if they hide or shadow a portion of our face. Thus, thinking about hats brings us back to the topic of veils, previously addressed in *Chapter 4.* Sometimes, even when we have the most delightful, wonderful, or even sinfully outrageous costume, we need to keep the best to ourselves, and to control how much we reveal. Hats, veils, or clothing options that present a little, intermittent extra view (such as a skirt with a slit, or a jacket over a camisole top) help keep this sense of mystery!

Whenever swimsuit season rolls around, notice that in fashion magazines (and on the beach), the most interesting ensembles (and the most intriguing women) invoke something besides a simple swimsuit or bikini. The women may wear a sheer embroidered tunic over the swimsuit, or overlayer with a long sheer sarong skirt. They add jewelry. They wear a large hat, or tuck some silk flowered hair-combs into their hair. The less that is on blatant display, the more alluring is the woman. So, even if we are wearing the briefest of "looks," we should consider adding embellishment and layers. The extra effort makes us much more fascinating.

Anahid once told her students, "When a dancer starts taking off her veil, all the men are interested; of course! The women, though, are just as interested as are the men. They want to see her costume!" We are fascinated with the dancer's ensemble – with how she has put herself together. The mind-play of slow revelation is indeed as fascinating to us women as it is to men. (This is perhaps because we all, at some level, want to learn this art, however we employ it – whether in conversation or with physical action!)

Whatever our motivation, and for whomever we dress, when it comes to adding an element of *eros* — less is definitely less. With the right selection, more is definitely more!

⊱⊰

Personal style is exactly that, personal style! Although this chapter has dealt largely with an approach that many of us would typify as "basic glamour," this is not the only look that makes a woman glow with self-confidence and vitality. The most important thing is that we find, and cultivate, what is most appropriate to each of us, *individually.*

My dear friend Julie Rahm is an extraordinarily effective personal coach and life-trainer. Her presentations are not only inspiring; they are jam-packed with useful "tools" so that people can consciously create the lives that they most desire. Julie has evolved a distinctive personal style that is almost the antithesis of what I've described here. However, it is uniquely "her," and it perfectly showcases her vibrant, warm, and enthusiastic personality! When she gives a talk, her "presentation outfit" is no longer the standard business suit, but a blue work shirt, jeans, and a tool belt, complete with tools. She wears comfortable, black leather sneakers that let her cover distance easily and confidently. The tools on her tool belt are metaphors for the "life tools" that she imparts to her audience. When audience members later recall Julie's talk, their memories of how the different tools are used in carpentry helps them to recall how they can be applied to their mental states and to their overall lives. Using their memory of the physical tools as *triggers,* audience members are much more likely to recall and use Julie's "working tools" in building and rebuilding their lives.[3]

Julie's "presentation outfit" is in complete alignment with both her personality and her message. Because it is a bit unexpected, it carries (along with her words) an extra emotional "punch." Her personal style is different from what most of us may select, but in a way that is healthy and effective, and truly in keeping with *who* she is.

As each of us fulfills our own "vision-quest" in self-discovery, we will each similarly find that which is truly enhancing to our vibrancy, zest, and passion. Whatever style it is that we discover for ourselves, if it is personally right, then it is worth the effort to keep developing it. It is very much right and appropriate to lavish this much care and attention on developing this aspect of ourselves. This is a core part of our *Hathor* essence, and is ours to claim!

PERSONAL PATHWORKING:

1. As you continue with your "life-closet-cleaning" (and perhaps a literal one), start collecting your adornment "pretties" and bringing them to one place. These are the things that you bought on impulse, but they never fit in with your "day job" or even your "weekend play." However, they spoke to you, and you bought them. Now, bring them all together. What do they say to you? What can you do with them? Is there a "look" that you can create; something that is very special, just for you, and just for fun?

2. As your time (and budget) will allow, start shopping some very inexpensive places, and looking for things that will enrich your fantasy-sense without depleting your wallet. Check out thrift stores, if that's your style. There are all sorts of things waiting to come into your life, if you will allow them!

3. Make yourself a dressing table. Yes, this means a real "movie-star" dressing table. Dress it up! Over time, get the fancy lights above the table, as well as a little lit mirror that has both "regular" and "magnifying" sides. Get trays and boxes in which you can organize and store your cosmetics.

4. When is the last time that you bought yourself flowers? Find the place nearest you that has the cheapest flowers, and find out when they get the fresh ones delivered (often on Monday afternoon). Make it a habit to buy a small bouquet every week. You'll be surprised at how far you can stretch a single bouquet!

5. What can you do that expands your "emotional range" – your *Hathor* essence – for day and evening dressing? Can you add a bit more jewelry? Can you put a little hat with the suit, or wear a pair of gorgeously-colored gloves? Can you add a brooch, or some sparkly earrings? Can you ramp things up just a little bit? Try it, and see how much fun you have!

6. Just for fun, see if you can't wear something to the office that has a hip-centered belt, rather than one at your waist. Look for a longish dress in your wardrobe; perhaps a sweater-dress. Find something that does not have a pre-defined waist. Then, try wearing it with a wide belt or sash that you tie at your hips, instead of at waist-level. Check out how you hold yourself during the day; how you move. Do you discern a difference?

PART VI:
PLAYTIME FOR YOUR EROTIC SELF

CHAPTER 22:
LOOKING LIKE A DANCER (EVEN IF YOU'RE NOT)

THEY WERE SENSUAL, EROTIC, AND down-right gorgeous. Also, every single one of them had that "little something extra" – maybe 20 or 30 pounds of it! But did that get in their way? Not in the slightest. My attention was caught by this troupe of mature women, with the figures that many of us mature women have. Even today, these women have had a more lasting impression on me than the official "star" of the show; a beautiful young woman who did a long, demanding, and technically-difficult concluding solo dance.

The women in the troupe were no longer young. Their costumes, while beautiful, were very modest. They wore long-sleeved, long dresses that covered them from the neck down to below their knees. The side seams of the dresses were slit open, showing the full harem pants that they wore underneath. However, they were far from plain. They wore elaborate headdresses formed of short, colorful, full-bodied veils held in place with wrappings of gold and satin. They wore heavy Turkish belts of gold and multicolored cords, festooned with tassels and hung with coins. They wore heavy, authentic jewelry, elaborately constructed from emblazoned and enameled metals. Each woman presented a powerful and striking image.

What made these women so very memorable was not their costuming, but rather their stage presence. Though their dance was simple, their impact was great. As they moved their hips in circles and figure-eights, and anchored into hip thrusts and shimmies, they projected a clear sensuality. As we watched, we *knew* that each of those women was seeing herself as being warm and sensual; as someone who was both comfortable with and clearly enjoying her own erotic vitality. What is most important is that they didn't have to lose weight in order to both feel, and *look*, absolutely wonderful!

Since then, I've wondered many times why I was more attracted to this group of mature women than to the star of the show. These women were good dancers, but they were not nearly as good as the young star dancer. They looked "exotic," and they carried the full sense of fantasy, but underneath their beautiful costumes, they were normal, ordinary women. These were women who had day jobs, families, and responsibilities. In that sense, they were no different from any of us.

I believe that what that attracted me the most about them was not just their dance skills, although they were very good as an amateur troop. More than skill, they had sensuality, and also something just a little bit more. The closest that I can come to it is *that they knew that they were beating the game.*

The "rules of the game," as most of us know them, say that when you're older, you're not as attractive. When you've got a little something extra on your belly (or hips, or thighs), you're not as attractive. Well, these women *were* older. They were also a substantially fuller – in the belly, hips, *and* thighs – than most swimsuit models. They were also much, *much* more sensual and erotic than most women will ever be. (This includes the swimsuit models!)

They had learned the secrets. Since watching them, many years ago, I've learned the secrets as well. The secrets start off with three basic things that we need to master. To make it easy on my memory, I call them the "three P's": *posture, poise,* and *presence.* (There is actually a fourth "P"; *passion*; but we'll keep that for a later chapter.)

Good posture is a basic. Even at that, few of us have it. If we were lucky, our mothers told us, "Stand up straight!" Some of us had mothers who sent us off to ballet class – more in the hopes that we would acquire good posture and grace, than that we would someday become a *prima ballerina.* The reason for our early training is that good posture must be learned and consciously practiced; it does not come naturally. If this seems odd or difficult, there is a reason for it. The reason is that we need to *retrain* our bodies to walk upright, after we have originally learned to do this when very young. Yes, we learned to stand upright and to walk as young toddlers; but that just gave us bipedal locomotion!

Learning to move with beauty, power, and grace is another matter altogether. It is something that we need to learn all over, after we have been walking for some time. This means that we will have to unlearn some body habits, and learn new ones. This can be challenging. However, those of us who want to be beautiful will need to learn this. Think about it. If we have beautiful faces, and gorgeously tanned and toned bodies, but move like cows, how beautiful are we, really? So long as we don't move, we're fine. However, life involves movement. Moving with natural grace and beauty is something that we can all learn to do.

We may have seen, on talk-show makeovers or on reality programming, stories of full-body transformations of different women. In some cases, these transformations would have been extensive, covering all aspects of their physical appearance. At the end, each woman was, in her own right, as gorgeous as she could possibly be – until she started to walk! The one area that such shows typically have not addressed has been how each woman *walked*; how she *moved*. They have not addressed how she *was* in her body, or how she connected her body movements to her center.

Typically, these women didn't learn how to move in a beautiful and graceful manner. As a result, although each woman became more beautiful in a simple physical sense, and probably felt much better about her new appearance, there was still an element of awkwardness. It takes time to learn a new way of being in our bodies!

When babies first learn to stand up, they do so by locking their knees and their pelvis. This gives them a certain balance, although a precarious one. It also gives them the "cute" posture that we associate with toddlers and very young children. This is the "belly out in front, butt out in back" posture. However appealing it is on a youngster, it doesn't do us any good as an adult. We need to relearn.

We begin by taking off our shoes and by paying attention to how our feet feel on the floor. We "soften" our feet; and let our toes get all "squishy" with the floor. Next, we bend our knees just a little bit, and drop our weight. At this point, we can start to check out our body. We discover where we are "holding" ourselves in. Then, we let ourselves go – we simply drop the "holding." (We'll put ourselves back together soon, but the first step is to let go of unnecessary and unnatural tension.)

To create the posture that will give us greatest beauty – whether standing still or moving – we begin by putting our hands on our hip bones. Our thumbs point to our backs, and fingers wrap around in front. Now, we notice whatever angle or tilt that we have in our pelvis. Many of us will have tilted our pelvis forward; our fingers will be slanting down towards the ground. We desire to have our pelvic girdle aligned level to the ground. We can see this as we adjust the tilt of our hip bones, and we do this by using our fingers and thumbs to gently guide our repositioning. This often means that we need to stretch out and lengthen our lower backs. We gently move our pelvic girdle so that it is level to the ground. When level, we will feel ourselves pushing down with our thumbs and up and in with our fingers. Once we get "level," we will probably feel it; we will have a "felt sense" of being "right" or "good" within our body. (Using a mirror to check our alignment here is a good step, and it will reinforce what we're doing.)

Once we have leveled our pelvic girdles, we check again to make sure that our knees are ever-so-slightly bent. When we lock our knees (bad habit!), then we also tend to lock up our pelvis (a worse habit; the one that we're trying to break). Knees are essential. We keep ours "soft" – just a little flexed. We "check in" with our knees from time to time, to make sure that they are slightly flexed.

With our pelvic girdle lined up even with the ground, our next step is to stretch out our sacral area and lower back. To do this, we reverse the way we've been placing our hands. Instead of pointing our thumbs to our back, we place our thumbs on the front of our hip bones. Then we place our fingers on the sides of our hips, pointing back. Finally, we slide our hands further towards our lower back; towards our sacrum. (This is the big, diamond-shaped flat bone which is just above our tailbone.) We take a moment to massage that area, and begin to consciously ease out the tightness. This is preparation for the first *Principle*, outlined in the following paragraphs. It is also, in itself, valuable for releasing lower back tension. This is the first step towards "reorganizing" how we hold our bodies. Aligning our pelvic girdles, and releasing lower back tension, is a necessary precursor for all the other kinds of physical, emotional, and energetic release that will be part of our personal *unveiling*.

One of the reasons that the dancers in my school look better than their peers is that we teach them a set of *Principles* that help them align and move their bodies in a beautiful and graceful way. Many of these *Principles* come from martial arts masters, and I've translated them into a dance context. For each *Principle*, I've devised a visual/kinesthetic "image" – something for the dancers to experience in their imagination. As soon as they imagine each *Principle* happening in their body, they get the results that they want – without having to remember all sorts of cumbersome details!

Our first *Principle* is that of *Anchoring*. (I credit my understanding of this one and certain others to martial arts master teacher Peter Ralston.) This is one of the most important body alignment *Principles* that anyone could learn. It is the first step, and the benefits will include increased health through releasing lower back strain. We'll also gain other benefits for the whole spinal column! As a natural consequence of using this *Principle*, we will develop stronger abdominal muscles; a "torso wall" that contains and supports our internal organs. This also contributes to increased and lifelong health and vigor. As a side advantage, we will look much more gorgeous. We will immediately look as though we've each dropped five pounds!

To use this *Principle*, we begin by finding the center of our bodies. Generally, this is just a couple of inches below the navel. (Of course, it is *inside* our body, not on the front!) From this point, we can imagine that we are dropping a great big ship's anchor; at least forty or fifty pounds, preferably more. It is on a big chain, connected right to our body's center. We notice what happens as we begin imagining our personal "anchor." One of the first things that we observe is that our pelvis aligns level with the ground (if it hasn't already). Also, our lower back lengthens beautifully.

After we've *anchored*, we also need to *reach upwards*. This second *Principle*, the *Lotus Flower*, is just as important as the first. However, it should only be done *after* we are *anchored*. To *reach up*, we each imagine that there is a lotus flower that is growing up out of our spine, and that it is reaching towards the sun for light and nourishment. Lotus flowers grow out of the bottom of a shallow pool of water; they have very long stems that allow them to float on the water's surface. We imagine that the roots of the flower are at the base of our spine, coming up through our tailbone and sacrum. We imagine that the stem is going all the way up through our spines, and up through the backs of our heads. We visualize the lotus flower blooming right on the crown of our heads; a beautiful, pale, glowing lavender color. It is so luminous that it is almost like a little sun in itself. (Yes, of course this is our *crown chakra*.) For each of us, this lovely, luminous lotus is rising up, up towards the real sun, and pulling and lengthening our spines along with it. As we do this visualization exercise, we begin to feel ourselves "flowing upwards." Then we note that our backs and necks really *are* lengthened! (Some of us may feel as though we've gained inches of height in just seconds!) And as we do this exercise, it is important to remember that *we are still anchored!*

These are the first two of the seven *Static Principles* that I teach my beginning dancers. (We also practice additional *Dynamic* and *Energetic Principles*; they are studied by advanced beginners, and by intermediate and advanced students.) These *Principles* are part of the reason that those in my dance school look so good – even when compared with other dancers. The *Principles* are not hard; we simply have to do them until they become second nature. Each of us, if we begin practicing just these two *Principles* alone, will soon not only be looking better, but feeling better as well!

Along with *posture*, we can also develop *poise* and *presence*. Again, just like good posture, these are learned skills; they don't come naturally to anyone. The basics for *poise* are simply the energy and emotional equivalents of *posture*. Our first step in gaining *poise* is to *anchor*, and get *emotionally grounded*. Through becoming both physically and emotionally *grounded*, we lessen the extent to which surrounding events can impact us. By continually practicing *anchoring* down into the earth, we will feel less of a need to be impulsive, and more able to respond appropriately.

If we let our memory go back to any time when we did not feel *poised*, and access our body memory around that time, we will probably identify a sense of disconnection. In particular, at those times when we were not poised, we were disconnected from our centers. It is a near certainty that we were also disconnected from the earth; we were not *anchored* or *grounded*. Then, things that were really not important had an ability to throw us into an emotional reaction. If we can revisit these scenes in our imaginations, and replay them as though we were *anchored*, we can create a new memory of how we can handle such situations differently.

As we practice *physical anchoring*, following the steps just outlined, we begin to feel different in how we are inside our bodies. We gain an increased overall awareness of our bodies. Through this increased body-awareness, and by consistently checking on our *anchoring*, we begin to increase our overall feeling of being connected; both throughout our bodies, and with the earth. This is the basis for *emotional anchoring*.

If we ever start feeling a bit "spacey" when stressed, we will benefit by remembering to *anchor*. Similarly, if any of us starts to feel "fractured" – a sense of coming apart inside (and a good case of PMS can do that to almost anyone) – then the first step is to *anchor*. *Anchoring* helps us to "pull together" inside.

While *anchoring*, at both the physical and emotional levels, is essential, complete *poise* includes other things as well. The ability to *reach up* through our spines, at an emotional level as well as the physical, is also important. If all that we do is *anchor*, we get too dense; too heavy. We're not fun anymore. The beauty and the joy, and the gift to others, is in the balance. That is why *reaching up* is essential; it is a way of "rising above" the little irritations of daily life.

Just like good posture, this is something we have to practice. After years of study and practice, getting numerous corrections from my teachers, and even becoming a teacher myself, I still have to practice even these most basic *Principles* on a daily basis. However, this is much like how a concert pianist still plays the scales as a warm-up exercise, every single day. No matter how advanced we are, we all need to keep a regular practice that supports our more advanced and challenging aspirations.

The last of the three "P's" is *presence*. *Presence*, more than anything else, is what distinguishes a first-tier dancer, a master, from someone who is second-tier – even a very good second-tier.

Too many of us "lock in" our *presence*. This shows when dancers perform. Many of us practice in a relatively small room, in front of a mirror that is rarely more than ten feet away. As we practice, we get used to projecting our "energy persona" – our *presence* (or *ch'i*) – only as far as the mirror. Then the mirror reflects our energy back! Thus, when we do a live performance, where the audience is sometimes a hundred feet away, our energy doesn't "reach" out to them. From the audience perspective, our performance – even if we're smiling, even if we're bouncy and energetic – seems "contained." Then, as an audience, we get bored. Technical skill and fine choreography notwithstanding, we as an audience are bored if we cannot connect with our dancer both emotionally and energetically.

A few years ago, at *Rakkasah East* (a major East Coast dance festival), I was able to catch glimpses of round-the-clock performances. Almost anyone who wanted to could get "stage time." On the auditorium floor furthest away from the big stage, a large number of vendors sold everything from hip scarves and veils to full, gorgeous costumes imported from Egypt and Turkey. During most of the performances, the vendors did a brisk business. Occasionally, though, all activity would cease. That would be the signal for the rest of us, vendors and purchasers alike, to slip towards the seating area. One of the "great ones" was about to perform.

In the midst of the swarms of back-to-back performances, the "great ones" indeed stood out. Not by virtue of technique, choreography, or even pure stamina. Rather, they projected their *presence* to us. They reached us, grabbed our attention, and brought us in. They did this without tension, without straining. What was particularly notable was that when less-than-wonderful dancers performed, they were overwhelmed by the poor conditions. The large stage, flat with harsh lighting, was much too stark for most of them.

Oriental dance is essentially an intimate art form. It relies much on the communication between the dancer and the audience. Unlike many of our Western dance styles, in Oriental dance, both eye contact and a sense of one-to-one relationship are important. In this *Rakkasah East* performance, the large stage made the usual intimacy impossible. Yet even under these conditions, the "great ones" prevailed. In fact, the conditions faded into the background, as their *presence* surged forward.

One of the dancers who kept our attention was Suhaila Salimpour, daughter of the renowned Jamila Salimpour. Suhaila has built on the excellent tradition of performance and teaching that her mother established on the West Coast. Another outstanding performer at that event was the famed New York dancer Dalia Carella. Both Suhaila and Dalia are extraordinary. There is no way that words can communicate how their *presence* illuminated the space and captured our attention. We can, however, visit their websites, and watch their performance DVDs. (They also each have good instructional DVDs.[1])

The "great ones" – Dalia, Suhaila, and others – were using their intrinsic energy, or *ch'i*.

Many years prior to this, I had participated in a Shotokan karate workshop hosted by Robert Fusaro Sensei. His guest of honor for the weekend was his teacher from Japan: at that time a sixth-degree black belt (6th Dan) to Fusaro Sensei's then-5th Dan. When the master teacher arrived, accompanied by Fusaro Sensei and surrounded by a swarm of devoted junior black belts, he did not seem particularly prepossessing. He was an ordinary-looking Japanese man, rather slight of build.

The many students were busy with their own interests, and conversations swirled around the auditorium. Then, without saying a word, Fusaro Sensei's teacher did something. He didn't raise his voice. In fact, I didn't even hear him speak. As best I can describe it, he simply "bounced" his *ch'i* off the far wall. It was like sending out a nonverbal thunderclap. *Everyone* paid attention. Within moments, the large room was quiet; we were ready to begin.

We don't have to be sixth-degree black belts, or world-famous dancers, to learn how to create presence using our personal energy. All of us can learn to access, build, and direct our *ch'i*. Simply by being aware of this possibility, and experimenting, we can make progress. (Imagine how this can help with our corporate presentations!)

This kind of "energy projection," along with other techniques, is something with which we're experimenting in my dance studio. Each of us can find her own practice opportunities right within daily life. Go ahead, experiment and enjoy!

PERSONAL PATHWORKING:

1. For now, practice the first two *Principles*: *Anchoring* and reaching up with your *Lotus Flower*. Remember them during all the odd times that you are out and about; while shopping for groceries, walking down the hall at work, standing in line to get movie tickets. Practice them as both an "energy feeling" as well as a physical practice, and you will cultivate *poise* along with fabulous *posture*. This will give you the foundation for being extraordinarily attractive!

2. If you are a dancer, or if you do any kind of stage presentations, do some of your practices in front of a window with a large, expansive view. As you "present," direct your energy far out away from you; some tens of yards away, or even more. When you are performing, direct your personal energy, or *ch'i*, to the audience furthest away from you.

3. Consider adding some *chi kung, kundalini yoga* or *pranayama* (energy-breathing methods), or even T'ai Chi Ch'uan to your daily practice. (Within reason, of course; see the medical disclaimer at the front of this book.)

CHAPTER 23:
IN PRAISE OF A FEW GOOD MEN

"THE GOOD ONES ARE ALL taken." How often have we heard that? Or, the corollary: "They're either married or gay." When we want to be in a relationship, and we're not, it seems as though there's a scarcity of really good men. Alternatively, if we're already in a relationship, we're often frustrated with our men. Of course, there is no lack of "relationship advice" in this world!

There are lots of wonderful "relationships" books, and most of us have both read and applied much of what they offer! These books often provide us with good tools, techniques, and insights – both into the nature of men, and into ourselves. Only more recently, though, and in relatively few of these books, do we find discussions of how we *mirror* ourselves in creating our relationships. This includes relationships with men, with family, with co-workers; with the world around us.

As is often expressed in the Abraham-Hicks books,[1] "That which is like unto itself is drawn." This phrase seems a little awkward, and a bit archaic in style, but it gives us the *first law of relationship dynamics*. We will draw to ourselves men who reflect how we think and feel about ourselves. In fact, the men (and family, and co-workers, etc.) in our life will be *mirrors* to us about ourselves.

Sometimes, we don't notice this *Principle of Mirroring*. That's usually when things are going well. It's not that we take things for granted; we're simply acknowledging that the universe is working as it should. We're in a good space, we're vibrating all kinds of passion, zest, and enthusiasm about life, and of course, our relationships *mirror* how we feel. Having our relationships feel this good seems as natural as the law of gravity. That's because our relationships *are* following a natural law: the law of *like-attracts-like*.

We opened this book acknowledging that, for many of us, we at least *start* with desiring "power over men." These next few chapters will deal with men and our relationships with them. (This can also address same-sex relationships, when one person is more "masculine" and the other is more traditionally "feminine.")

Our overall experiences with men tend to be consistent, because *like* does indeed *attract like*. Thus, whatever we experience in one relationship will probably have overtones and undertones that are expressed in many other relationships. These can include men in different professional roles (our bosses, coworkers, and employees), and also within our family and circle of friends.

As we start changing our inner dynamics, and how we perceive men, we will change the nature of our relationships. We will also start inviting new kinds of relationships into our lives, and seeing some of the old ones disappear. If we are consciously changing our dynamics, one of the first "success-indicators" is that we start getting different kinds of people in our lives. We can actually use these new people, and new relationships, as a means of gauging how much we have shifted!

Years ago, I realized that I needed to start changing my relationships with men. I'd had an early experience with someone who was mean-spirited, and who took pleasure in hurting me and in playing little "power-over" games. I left this person, but deeper change seemed too daunting, so I immersed myself in work and in dance. However, trying to hide from my own dynamics did not mean that I could escape. The same pattern repeated itself in work, with a variety of men.

I knew that I wasn't ready for an intimate relationship, so I decided to draw good men into my professional world. (My thanks go to the gentlemen who responded; they showed chivalry at its highest level!)

One of the men to show up was Scorpion. (This had been his call-sign, not his real name. His mother would *never* have done that to him!) As a former Navy fighter pilot, Scorpion had flown everything that the Navy offered. In many of his Navy roles, he held positions of great responsibility; coordinating people, logistics, and complex operations. He did this with graciousness and ease, while still getting optimal performance from his team. His people both respected and loved him.

We've all heard the phrase, "an officer and a gentleman." Scorpion exemplified both. After retiring from the Navy, he accepted a job offer at the company where

I was working. For the next year and a half, I had an opportunity to work with the best "Executive Officer" with whom I've been privileged to work in my life! During this time, I not only got some good scientific work done, I revamped my entire perspective on men.

Scorpion's coming into my life was a breakthrough. It didn't matter that he was married. What mattered was that for the first time, in a long, long time, there was a man in my life who treated me both as a lady and as a scientific professional. He was balanced, sane, and together in his own life. Add to it that he was courteous, competent, and a joy to have around. This doesn't mean that I'd never met such a man before; I had. The difference was that Scorpion's presence changed my day-to-day dynamic. This was the first "reflection" that told me that I was starting to change.

Scorpion was making life much better for me, but he wanted to fly. Over time, he arranged for a new situation that gave him this opportunity. At a different time, and in a different situation, I manifested Rocky, another great man. Having Rocky join the firm at first seemed like both good news and bad. Good news, because I absolutely loved him, and bad news, because I absolutely loved him. Rocky also was married. Initially, I was a bit conflicted about working with him. Within a few months after having him come on board, though, I realized that I was much better off having him as my immediate boss than in any other possible role. I settled happily into a work-and-friendship relationship with him.

Rocky also moved on, to a position that gave him greater autonomy. In yet another situation, another man who came in to take in a leadership role was Gary, who was retiring from military service after having commanded an important test and training installation. Once again, I met a great man. Earlier in his career, Gary had led a team of scientists, engineers, and military personnel who envisioned, and then actually built, a critical system. We take this system for granted today, but it had been an uphill battle to sell the idea to military leaders. It had taken all of Gary's vision, tenacity, and great ability to work with and lead people to bring that project to fruition.

Over several years, I had a chance to work closely with each of these three men. We took business trips together, and each time – *consistently* – they acted like gentlemen. We worked hard at whatever tasks we had. We could be up late at night, and up early again the next morning, and throughout, they were consistently even-tempered, focused, and positive. When we traveled together, after the work was done, we'd work out at the hotel gym, each of us would shower and change, and then we'd go out for dinner. Dinner with these gentlemen was like being on a date, except that they never crossed the lines of being professionally appropriate! We'd have a good meal, tell interesting stories, and laugh. Then we would say goodnight at the elevator.

In such a pleasant and non-threatening way, I began to realize how much I could enjoy my time with men. We went through enough difficult and stressful situations together so that if they were going to crack, they would have. They didn't. As human beings — not romantically, but very much appreciating their masculinity — I loved each of them.

These three in particular, Scorpion, Rocky, and Gary, gave me insight into how real leaders worked and lived. They were people who looked out for their entire team, not just for themselves. When crises hit (and they would), these men stayed focused and calm. Collectively, they formed my new "template" for what men could be. I decided that when I was ready to have a man in my life on a personal, rather than a professional, basis, he would be someone of the same character.

The best way to explain what happened next relies on the adage, "What we focus on expands." I had been focusing on bringing high-quality men into my life, just to experience the best of masculinity. I'd seen three great examples, and was ready to meet a larger group. So, I manifested the U.S. Marine Corps.

Not the entire Corps, naturally. That would have been a little exhausting. Rather, I won a new contract that brought a group of technology-oriented Marines into my life.

I was a little dubious at first. My impression of the Marines (knowing nothing about them at the time) was that they were a bit on the knuckle-dragging side of things. Shortly after getting the contract, my opinion changed. These men were high-energy, high-testosterone, and very alpha. Exactly my kind of people.

Over the following year, I had ample opportunity to be with them. I watched Marines from desert dunes as they practiced landings and assaults on their favorite patch of California coastline. I stood on a flat-topped building in their mock-up town while they practiced dusk-time urban warfare. I watched them tics operations and test out new technologies that would help them ge things to the right people at just the right time.

In addition to seeing them as close to action as possible (outside of an act war zone), I had a chance to do technology development and planning with them in various working groups. I was able to brief them on our projects and get their inputs as we developed next-generation technologies.

Naturally, I had a great time. As I jokingly told my woman friends, "The next time I marry, it will be to an active duty or retired military officer. They're pre-selected, well-trained, and know how to follow orders!"

Of course, when time came to pick the next man in my life, I didn't follow the plan. (This is probably obvious from the previous statement; I wasn't yet willing to let go, and to trust a man's leadership. I still felt that *I* had to be the one "in charge." This had a huge, and rather disastrous, effect on what I created next!)

Instead of selecting someone who was calm, centered, and focused, I manifested (and selected) a new beau who was as high-energy as the Marines and the other leaders with whom I'd worked. (However, he didn't share their sense of self-discipline and focus.)

After a few dates, my new gentleman friend visited with one of his old friends and gave him a progress report. "I'm seeing this woman," he announced, "and I think this is getting pretty serious."

"What can you tell me about her?" asked his friend.

"Not much, I'm still being interviewed," my beau said. "I don't have the right to ask questions yet."

He knew that the man's role is to do the pursuing. Ours is to do the selection, and "interviews" were part of the process.

Pro-offered loyalty was one of the deciding factors in his favor. "I live to serve the queen," was one of his favorite proclamations. However, his actual service was not up to his promises. Within a few years (and yes, it should have been *much* sooner), I had to show him to the door.

...ut of my life, I recognized that he had been a great
... Kathy Carroll said, he broke up a great deal of my
... that he helped to shake up some of my rigid attitudes
... reactions to provocations were like a hugely distorted
... great accelerator.

Of course, not all "lessons" come from times of dating and relationship-building. As it turns out, people in the professional realm have also given great opportunities for learning. Professional relationships, as well as intimate ones, can both provide opportunities for *Mirroring*.

In one instance, I and others founded a new company, focusing on a new and emerging technology. In short order, I had insights that led to substantial breakthroughs, and we were convinced that a new product would meet a crucial marketplace need. In order to get the company focused on building a product based on that core invention, we had to bring in a new management team with skills focused on product development.

At this painful juncture, another wonderful man came into my life, and I thank those who found him and convinced him to guide our course. Jeremiah was a seasoned CEO, and wore the scars from many a boardroom battle. He was principled, and cared both about people and the bottom line. He coached me and other Board members through the grueling process of a necessary executive-level transition.

Jeremiah, and a dear friend, Andy, helped me transition to a new level of professionalism. They helped me move from a stage where I looked for strong men to protect me and provide leadership, to taking on necessary leadership roles directly. This was the first time that I had to create a significant change for an entire organization within a challenging situation. I am deeply grateful for their coaching and mentorship during this time.

The company reformed. At the same time, I realized that certain core dynamics had their roots in my own initial attitudes and intentions, back when the company was first formed. I wanted to move beyond my earlier patterns. While continuing to work with this company, I reflected on how I needed to make a change – inside myself – in order to have the next creation in line with a more complete and satisfying vision. To do this, I had to re-envision myself. Also, I had to envision my inventions being transformed into products that were being eagerly purchased and used by happy, satisfied clients – clients who were eager to purchase our next product releases as well! This meant confronting some deeply-held beliefs. A deep round of internal healing was in order.

I started a new company, and asked three men, each of whom was an experienced leader and a strategic genius, to be on my Board. Two were neck-deep in their own new venture, and were willing to advise, but not be Board members. The third, Theo, was the one whom I most wanted to be on the Board, and in my personal life as well.

Like Scorpion, Rocky, and Gary, Theo was former career military, which he followed with a successful corporate career. Theo was not only a great leader, consistently urging his people towards excellence, but he also challenged himself in ways that inspired me. He recognized genius in others, and used it to call forth similar efforts within himself. A brief, sweet time ensued. However, instead of moving into a deeper relationship, when things got tough, Theo disappeared. I was very sad, and extremely disappointed.

Just as Theo faded away, though, wonderful new people came into my life again. From within a Bible study group that I joined, there were several who helped me through the worst of the transition, with a range of both practical and emotional support. Just as had happened years ago, various men in this group were colleagues and friends. Each of them had strong established careers, and each was highly successful. Each man also had a quality spiritual life, was married, and they and their wives had often adopted children from different foreign countries. Many of them gave hugely of their time and personal resources to help others. One created a ministry with the purpose of visiting people in prisons. Others traveled during their two-week annual vacation to a Latin American country, so they could physically create buildings that would serve people in remote areas. Without making a "big deal" about their spiritual convictions, they led lives that were both successful and of great benefit to others.

As I looked at the new collection of men in my life, I saw a repeat of the best of my "old" patterns. Here were men whom I admired, in all ways. They respected me both as a woman and as an inventor/entrepreneur. They honored my decision to start a new business, when the easy thing – the "fall-back" position – would have been to simply get a job. One of them, in particular, willingly shared connections with friends and business contacts. The people whom he introduced to me were ready to become strategic partners and investors. I held back only to first get my new business on more stable footing.

It would be lovely, at this juncture, to write about a new romance. But as I pulled together the new company, I recognized that time spent with Theo reinforced my awareness of my own intimacy fears. This has given me more practice with *softening*.

Yet, my life is full of men; men who are absolutely wonderful. Without the pressure of a romantic agenda (as they are all married or engaged), I get to interact with their masculine fabulousness, and appreciate their courage, nobility of purpose, and (to take a phrase from one of Peter Ralston's books[2]) their "integrity of being." Working with these men on both corporate and non-profit endeavors gives me a deep appreciation of what I can best describe as *masculine virtue*.

Fortunately, for all of us, what emerges predominantly in relationships between men and women is that men desire to serve us. They want to make us happy. Napoleon Hill said, as he analyzed the lives of great leaders in *Think and Grow Rich*, that in each case the man's great achievements were "…largely inspired by a woman."[3] My former beau was right when he said, "I live to serve the queen." Most men do! The kind of man who became a knight chevalier in olden times is now seeking a new way to honor the women in his life, and through them, to honor *Shekhinah*, or the *feminine face of God*.[4]

David Deida, in *The Way of the Superior Man*, tells men to honor the *Sacred Feminine*. He writes to other men, "Relax your body and feel the ocean of feminine energy around you … Do the same in the company of human women. Feel them not merely as friends, coworkers, and sisters, but as walking blessings of energy."[5]

More and more, we can see that the men in our lives really *are* "knights in shining armor." These men may not realize this, but they are part of an emerging trend. My friend and colleague Ron, a partner in one of the global consulting firms, noted (as did his colleagues) that the best of the new people coming into their firm were the young women, not the young men. As recent college graduates, the young women had more focus, more ambition, and more social skills than their masculine peers. They formed better client relations, and worked harder to make sure that their clients were satisfied.

Ron and his partner-level colleagues noted that these young women did not have as clear-cut a path to corporate leadership as did their male counterparts. To meet this need, they created such a path. They devised a mentorship program for these young women, designed to fast-track them to higher positions.

The program started with initial great success, but hit a rough spot when each of the young women left to become a full-time mom! This is precisely the complex dialectic that we observed earlier, in *Chapter 2*.

This is one of those areas where aspects of our culture collide, like tectonic plates pushing against each other and causing earthquakes. We know that the young women's early-career focus (their *Amazon* stage) was because they needed to establish professional stature before they shifted their attention (for their *Isis/ Mother* stage). This dynamic will work out over time. They will return to their professional world when their children are in school, and they will make their mark. When they left the work-world, or even just stepped down the pace, they were young. Their lives and careers are still ahead of them. They'll be back, and their experiences of having been mentored in their youth will give them the confidence to more readily pursue their ambitions and dreams.

We are seeing a case of how men, particularly those men at the highest levels of corporate leadership, are actively acknowledging and supporting women who are in their *Amazon* roles. Ron and his partners were by no means trying to hold women back. Instead, they were using their positions of leadership and authority to create opportunities for these women. Yes, we still need to negotiate the next step, which is to create re-entry tracks for these women so that they can rejoin after their children are a bit older. However, it is very important that we acknowledge the positive steps that men have taken to support women.

Ron and his colleagues were by no means unique in their support of women's professional growth. In *How Remarkable Women Lead*, authors Joanna Barsh and Susie Cranston present the life stories of numerous women who have achieved top levels of corporate leadership, and have sometimes moved into political or other realms.[6] Frequently, these women credit male mentors and bosses who have coached them to the next level of success.

Back when I was in the most extreme of my *Amazon* phase, I studied Shotokan karate. My first teacher in this art was a young black belt who taught at a college campus. A career move brought me to the city where his teacher, Robert Fusaro Sensei, had his school or "dojo." At the time, Fusaro Sensei was 5th Dan (a fifth-degree black belt), and the first Caucasian to reach that level within the Shotokan style. (Fusaro Sensei is, as of this writing, 7th Dan, and is a world-recognized leader.)

One winter morning, with the temperature about 15 degrees below zero (Fahrenheit), I showed up with other students for the 6:30 AM class. The furnace had gone out over night, and they were awaiting repairs. The top floor dojo was icy cold. Harsh, northwest winds buffeted the exterior walls, stripping away the meager warmth provided by kerosene heaters. Our feet cringed against the frigid floor as we donned our karate gi's. Leading us slowly and carefully through warm-up stretches, Fusaro Sensei gazed at us firmly. "This is *Bushido* ["way of the warrior"] training," he said. Fusaro Sensei taught us to take all of our life experiences as part of our training and overall development – including an early-morning cold dojo!

Fusaro Sensei was as much an advocate for his leading female students as for his male ones. In his dojo, I studied with and observed Anita Bendickson Sensei and Mary Brandl Sensei (who as I write this are now 5th and 4th Dans, respectively), and occasionally met Nina Chenault Sensei, another of Fusaro Sensei's senior students. Chenault Sensei was the first woman in the United States to receive 5th Dan in the Shotokan karate system. All these women were 1st and 2nd Dans when I first met them.

Fusaro Sensei created new opportunities for women karatekas. He was the first in this style to propose that women should be allowed to compete in tournament *kumite* (sparring). By hosting regional tournaments, he actively gave women a chance to compete. Bendickson Sensei and Brandl Sensei both have taught in his dojo, and have developed self-defense courses that they've taught at the University of Minnesota as well as in regional businesses. Fusaro Sensei's wave of influence has spread around him, and he has encouraged and helped women as much as (perhaps even more than) he has helped men.

We have all very likely heard the phrase that we need to "be the change that we wish to make." In addition to this, we also need to notice and give honor to others who are making changes. In particular, if we want men to change in their attitudes towards us, we need to take note of those men who *are* leading the way. We need to put our attention on them, and talk them up. As we all know, "that which we focus on expands." If we want quality men in our lives, our first step is to put our attention on the men of quality.

We can seek to find a balance in our thoughts here — in how we frame our viewpoint about men. This is important, and helpful to us, in two ways. First, we already know that our viewpoint — our belief system or set of "filters" through which we perceive the world — is really much more than that. We not only "filter" our observations so that what we observe fits in with our existing beliefs, we do *much* more. We actively *create* a reality that is in accordance with our beliefs!

Our power over our reality-creation lies in how we place our attention. As we look at the people in our life, particularly at our men, and focus on their kind and noble behaviors, and their *Protector/Provider* instincts, we invoke more of that experience into our lives. If we focus on their ignoble behaviors, we get experiences to corroborate that.

We are getting close to the core of our journey; one of finding and defining a particular kind of women's *path*. It is in being on this *pathway* that we create our true power. However, we acknowledge that this can be frightening to many people. In particular, it is often scary to men. We are moving them from being central in our lives (to whatever extent they may have been), to somewhat off-from-center. We are becoming much more open to a feminine consciousness, and orienting ourselves, and those around us, towards *Shekhinah* — the *feminine face of God*. This challenges male beliefs about God (as fashioned in the image and likeness of man), and about the supremacy of the masculine way of *being* and *doing*.

Our history is replete with violence done by men towards women; particularly done to wise women, and to women who have held the roles of priestess and healer. This violence, propagated over millennia, is precisely why we do not have a flourishing *body/mind/psyche/energy integration pathway* for women right now. While the masculine path went "underground," in the sense of being hidden in various societies, and secreted behind the doors of initiation, ours was completely destroyed. Now, we seek to recreate our *pathway* for ourselves. We further seek to call on men as allies.

This is possible; there are sufficient men with kindness and goodness in their hearts who will authentically honor and support us in our journey. As Sherry Anderson recounts her initiation-dream, in *The Feminine Face of God*:

> "Will you help us?" I ask the assembled patriarchs.
>
> "We are your brothers," they answer, and with that the entire room is flooded with an energy of indescribable kindness. I am absolutely confident in this moment that they *are* our brothers. I feel their love without any question. They say then, "We have initiated you and we give you our wholehearted blessing. But we no longer know the way. Our ways do not work anymore. You women must find a new way."[7]

Finding, and creating, such a new-way path is our task. Let's acknowledge the many wonderful men who can and do support us in this venture!

As we refocus our awareness of men, we create different kinds of relations with them. We not only enlist (and gain) their support in our highest callings, but also our intimate relations change as well. This comes as we not only honor the best in men around us, but also give our own inner *Amazon* the right kind of honor. We don't have her "controlling" our lives all the time; we no longer live oriented towards the "masculine pole" as contrasted with the feminine. However, we do recognize that our inner *Amazon* plays, for each of us, multiple roles. She is, in her own right, encapsulating and carrying out for us our own dreams and visions (as *Magician*). She is building our safety and security (as *Emperor*). Finally, she is teaching, mentoring, and guiding others (as *Hierophant*); these "others" may very well be our own children and grandchildren!

At the same time, while our *Amazon* projects our desires and visions in the world, she also assumes the role of being our own *Protector*. In addition to whatever actual men we have in our lives, our *Amazon* functions similarly to a man. She protects, provides for, and takes care of us.

For many of us, our lives require that we be much more in our *Amazon* modes than we would like, while our inner *High Priestess* longs for contemplation, our *Isis* wants to immerse herself in relationships, and our *Hathor* simply wants to play! When we do not have the time-balance that we desire, we start feeling conflicts inside ourselves. We are torn between that which we feel we *must* do, and that which we feel that we'd *like* to do. The end result, oddly enough, is that we get a little "bitchy" with ourselves. Truly, we take more of our frustration and unhappiness out on ourselves than we do on others. (Of course, the people around us are by no means spared.)

If we can change the relationships within ourselves, appreciating what our own *Amazon* does for us, then we can also become softer, gentler, and even more appreciative of what the various men in our lives do on our behalf. This allows new kinds of relationships to emerge. The easiest way to do this is to start with the external: simply note and acknowledge the many acts of kindness and support, of consideration and encouragement, which the men in our lives already give to us and to other women.

There is one more subtlety here. When we have a well-developed inner *Amazon*, and know that she is caring for us (in a kindly manner), then we can bring about that kind of relationship with our external men. Having just made this realization during the final editing of this book, I'm ready to change my earlier statement about why I especially prefer men who have gone through "martial" discipline, either with the military or the martial arts. Now, I tell my women friends, "They're pre-selected, they're well-trained, and they know how to *lead*!"

When we see excellent men in our lives, and purposefully put our attention on honoring and appreciating them, we are giving respect to the *Sacred Masculine*. This helps them honor us in our femininity, and paves the way for them to honor the *Sacred Feminine* – often through tangible acts of service and support for us! Further, when we acknowledge and appreciate men, we do so from the feminine aspect of our being. Doing this lets us honor our inner *Amazon* as being distinctly different from our other feminine archetypes. As we honor our *Amazon's* strengths and gifts, we then pave the way for greater appreciation of our other feminine modalities.

I've applied the realizations from this chapter to my own life, with increasingly positive results. Even though I have a strong internal *Amazon*, I have become more comfortable and confident with the prospect of releasing the "leadership" role to a man, especially an intimate relationship. Although this may sound contradictory, it actually makes very good sense. I know that I can take care of myself. With this knowledge, I can "let go," and let someone else be in the *Protector* mode. If I have made a wrong decision, I know that I can recover.

At the same time, because I have an equally strong *High Priestess*, I know that when I pay attention to my intuition, I make good decisions. The likelihood that I will get far into an intimate – or corporate – relationship with someone who will turn out to be a bad choice is much, much less than it was in the past. My *High Priestess* is my source of inner knowing. This aspect guides me in big areas, such as deciding whether a person is a good choice for a professional or personal relationship, and in small areas as well.

In a like vein, I've discovered that I have an innately very strong *Isis*, or nurturing, component. Earlier, I felt that being an *Amazon* was necessary for survival. I had latched onto the masculine model as the only "safe" way of being; I had felt that the feminine *path* did not offer enough strength or support. As a result, I was largely out of touch with my own desires to both nurture and be nurtured. Over the past two years of rewriting, editing, and refining this book, I've had ample opportunities to see how I've put my desire to nurture others into practice. I can now recognize that this nurturing aspect is one of my greatest strengths. I can use this gift on behalf of a friend, a non-profit organization, a corporation or client, or even a lover. The extent to which I call upon my *Isis* mode (being caring, and putting other's interests high on my own priority list) is one of my "distinguishing gifts." In short, the richness of my *Isis* aspect fully supports my *Amazon*. I am finally mastering a skill that Mdm. Clinton has already mastered, that of *Isis/Amazon* integration, which we saw in *Chapter 11*.

By opening up to my inner *Hathor*, I lighten up the "heaviness" that my inner *Amazon* sometimes feels, as she works through responsibilities and commitments. Using my *Hathor* essence, I also draw much more support from men, and really, the entire universe. The laughter and lightness of my *Hathor* essence draws positive and joyous events into my life!

What I am finding most valuable, though, is the interaction between my inner *Amazon* and my inner *High Priestess*. Now, I not only trust my inner *Amazon* to protect me, I also trust my inner *High Priestess* to guide me in making the right selections. I, and many other women who are gaining some life-experience and perspective, are learning to find the balance. We are, when necessary, using our *Amazon* to be our own *Protector*. At the same time, rather than pushing our other aspects into the background and identifying wholly with our *Amazon* persona (something which we may have done when younger), we now know how to nurture and give attention to all of our core feminine aspects. Especially important is the greater confidence and comfort in our decisions that we gain by tapping into our now well-developed *High Priestess*.

PERSONAL PATHWORKING:

1. Take note of the excellent men in your life, not only from your job, but also those who are in your church, family, and social circle. Write about them in your journal. Tell your girlfriends about the men who are extra-special wonderful. Talk them up! Keep working with the metaphysical principle, "That which we focus on expands." The more that you focus on the wonderfulness in the men around you, the more you'll draw men (and people overall) with wonderful qualities into your life.

2. Begin to pay more attention to your thoughts. One of the ancient yogic teachings is that our minds are "like monkeys." They are constantly chattering away at trivia. In particular, our minds like to find negative thoughts and pursue them. Monitor your thoughts, and consistently, graciously, and gently keep bringing your attention to positive things.

CHAPTER 24:
MEN: A SHORT OWNER'S MANUAL

"HOW DO I ATTRACT MEN?" That was one of my friends, several years ago. "It's easy," I replied. "Yes, but then, how do you keep him once you've got him?" she demanded. "Again, that's easy. Men are easy to own and operate; they only require a three page *Owner's Manual*." She looked at me in shocked bemusement, and then burst out laughing.

Much though our "inner journey" of *unveiling* is about ourselves, and our own processes, a big part of our lives has to do with our relationships – particularly our relationships with men. That is the reason for this chapter, which serves a dual purpose. First, this chapter goes over *basic male* psychology. Basic males are different from the less developed males, or the "King Babies" of the world.[1] We also discuss the more developed men – those men to whom we award the accolade of being a *superior man*. Far more importantly, though, this chapter outlines our own dilemmas as we decide on the extent to which we will take on the care and feeding of a man.

A *basic male*, as I am defining him for this work, is a simple, straightforward ego machine. What a *basic male* is *not* is a man who is still working out psychological issues that keep him from being an ego machine. In short, he is not caught up in replicating unhealthy family dynamics. He has done some emotional work (as needed), and has at least some adult maturity. He does not have any crippling addictive tendencies, and he has his temper more-or-less under control. In short, he is free to focus on the core issues of his masculine self-development. As a *basic male*, he lives to gratify his ego. The more Type T he is, the more he is ego-driven.

As men progress on their journey, their *Hero's Quest*, they transform their raw ego-drive into a more noble one. As described by author John Eldredge, in *Wild at Heart*, men can transform their innate need for "wildness" – for danger and adventure, and for experiences that push them to their utmost – into a personal calling.[2] A *superior man*, as described by author David Deida, aligns his ego with a higher cause. His purpose in life is to find and fulfill his calling: "Your mission is your priority."[3] Men affirm that their purpose in life is their *mission*, however it is defined by each man. No matter how much they want a relationship with one of us, for the *superior man*, the *mission* is upper-most. A good example of this is the series of "trials" endured by Tamino, the emerging hero in Mozart's opera, *The Magic Flute*. We examined this plot in *Chapter 6*, and noted that a crucial test of Tamino's fitness for initiation was that he could ignore pleas for recognition by his true love, Pamina.

One of the things that excites us about masculine energy is its focus, its intensity – the whole mission-directed nature of masculinity. We really don't want this to change. At the same time, we need to know that we are sufficiently loved in order to trust ourselves to a man.

Much of the tension and difficulty that we've had over the past decades (and centuries, and millennia) is that as men focus on their mission, we can be left both emotionally untended, and actually bereft of real support. In the course of our supporting men in their feats of derring-do, we often leave ourselves exposed. Sometimes our very physical and practical needs go unmet. Sometimes we defer taking care of ourselves in order to care for others, and then are left with the proverbial "short end of the stick" later in our lives.

We don't really want to change men, in terms of their core nature. And the truth is, we can't. At the same time, we must take care of ourselves. This is one of the reasons that we've so strongly developed our *Amazon* natures. Now that we have secured the privileges, as well as the demands, that we've claimed as *Amazons*, we need to re-examine our overall relations with men.

This puts us firmly on the horns of not just one, but three dilemmas. We can transform each dilemma into a challenge. Thus, this chapter has two lines of thought. First, we look at men, and understand their core dynamics. We identify what works in a relationship with them, to the extent that we choose to apply these methods. Then, we consider whether or not – and why – we would choose to do so.

We broach once again the subject of male psychology. Note that it takes most of this book for us to address our *own* natures. By contrast, we're covering the male psyche (complete with their higher reaches and aspirations) in three chapters; *Chapter 6* (*The Hero's Quest*), the preceding *Chapter 23* (*In Praise of a Few Good Men*), and this one. This is an approximate 10:1 ratio for female complexity versus male. Many of us would agree that the proportions are about right.

Men's basic needs are typically covered with just three areas: sex, steaks, and strokes, listed in increasing order of importance.

Sex is number one – in our man's mind. Yes, he needs sex, preferably as often and with as many variations as possible. (Without turning this book into a sex manual, the next chapter shares some benefits gained by applying what we learn from Oriental dance – strong control over our abdominal muscles is definitely a plus!) It goes without saying that *basic males* are strongly driven (as in, obsessively consumed) by sex. A *basic male's* primary fantasy in life is to have sex with as many different, beautiful women as possible. Further, since he is an ego machine, such a man wants to be a hero to each and every one. He is willing to accept a toned-down version of this fantasy as his reality, by having sex with just one woman. In this case, he still wants her to be beautiful, and he still wants to be a hero to her – sexually and otherwise.

But while sex is his primary fantasy, it is not the primary emotional driver for a *basic male*. His primary driver is, and always will be, his ego. That is what pushes him onward. A man's pathway takes him on his *Hero's Quest*. Ultimately, for those who become a *superior man*, a *basic male's* ego aligns with a "noble cause." Even at this level, though, a man is still largely ego-driven.

However, there are those men – a still smaller group, to be sure – who go even beyond their desire to align themselves with their "noble cause," or their *mission*. In *Chapter 7* of this book, we introduced the Tarot's Major Arcana as a guide to the six core archetypes of the human personality. There were three masculine and three feminine archetypes, and the goal of the first sequence of adult personal growth was to *integrate* each of these. This *integration* step was represented by the seventh Major Arcana, *Winged Victory*.

In the next Major Arcana sequence, an integrated person faces his or her next major life-challenge – that of going beyond the "ego-self." The central god-figure of ancient Norse myths was Odin, the god of both war and wisdom. The myths record that he hung himself upside down from a tree, for nine days and nine nights, until he achieved transcendence. This gave rise to the imagery behind the *Hanged Man* (Major Arcana Card XII).[4] This card similarly depicts a man hanging upside down, suspended by one of his feet, from what can be interpreted as the *Tree of Life*. This *Hanged Man*, near the center of the Major Arcana, speaks to a pivotal point in an adult person's life-journey. It lets us know, also, that the *Hero's Quest* is not the only quest taken by an adult male. We saw earlier that both young men and young women have their *Heroic Quests*. Then, we noted that both men and women must, as their first major adult life-challenge, come to know and *integrate* each of their core archetypes. Now, we are realizing that *integration* is not the last step. Rather, it is a prelude to a more demanding challenge: releasing the ego. This is one of the core adult growth tasks identified by Daniel Levinson, in *The Seasons of a Man's Life*.[5]

We women face similar challenges. However, our basic psychological organization is different from men; we do not start off as simple "ego-machines." We begin with a combination of ego-drives (our inner *Amazon*) together with our needs to connect with and care for others, as well as our desire to experience pleasure-in-the-moment and also our yearning for spiritual awareness. Because our *High Priestess* is such an integral part of our psychological core, we do not have to go as far as men do to access and *integrate* this aspect. Our life journey may involve strengthening our ego, more than transcending it. However, as we take on our growth challenges, we gain greater appreciation of men who have similarly had the courage to take on their own growth and development. Also, as we go through our own journey, we become oriented towards ego transcendence, in both ourselves and others. As a natural consequence, our interest in not only the "King Babies" of the world, but even in *basic males*, is lessened.

Not surprisingly, the impact of our own growth is that our criteria for selecting men become more discriminating. This is not as simple as saying, "I've developed my masculine, *Amazon* persona – have you developed your caring and spiritual aspects?" Rather, our questions are a bit more complex. They are more along the lines of, "I've developed all of who I am, and I have been finding my life's direction. I am reasonably complete within myself. Now, what is the purpose of your life? Why should I devote my resources and attention to nurturing and caring for you? How would this serve a higher purpose?"

The fact that we have developed our *Amazon* natures over the past few decades has propelled the dialectic between men and women into a new realm. We know that we are nurturing and caring; this will not change. We know that men – no matter what sort of transcendent experiences they may have – will continue to be "mission-driven." We know that in relationships, we will continue to support them in their missions, as we always have. What may be different now is that we ask whether not just the mission, but the whole person, is worth our caring and support.

This translates into very practical and real-world considerations. Earlier, we were – very appropriately – interested in whether a man could support us as we took time to bear and rear children. We were also very interested in whether he not only *could* support us, but *would* support us. Would he be devoted and caring, or would he be distant, profligate, or – worse yet – controlling, mean-spirited, and abusive during the times in which we were most vulnerable? In our younger years, we have tended (as we often do) to undervalue the extent to which our support of our man was essential to his career success, as well as to his comfort.

Now, we are more aware of the value of our time and energy. Years of negotiating for pay raises – and seeing the better positions go to less qualified (but male) persons – have taught us to put a dollar value on our hours. We are also more attuned to our need to have time for ourselves.

Thus, as we consider any specific man, we have to ask ourselves: Is this man so worthwhile that it serves my life purpose to be supportive of his career and his family? Is it the "right thing" to make sure that his life is as well-ordered and comfortable as is mine? Should I place his needs and desires on a par with my own? Although we are still as likely to succumb to "falling in love" as we were when younger, we now know ourselves much more. We can – in advance of giving ourselves over to a man – make a decision as to whether he is worth the most valuable resources that we possess: our attention and our time.

With a view to how we will make our decisions regarding men, we can examine how men develop over time. Further, we may gain more compassion, as well as insight, into their nature by observing their core drives. When a man is ego-driven, he has to "keep up appearances" at all times. The more that a man is Type T, the more he must present to the world (and to himself; he has to actually believe that this is true) the belief that he can do anything. He can solve any problem and manage any situation. In the ongoing "whose is biggest" competition between men (to see who is "top dog"), no one can back down. Men simply cannot, *with each other*. And this is where we come in – if we choose to provide this attention.

The one person with whom a man can let down his guard is with "his woman." Wife, lover, mate, close girlfriend – however we define the role, when a man thinks of someone as "his woman," he begins to let down the "I can do anything" demands of his ego. This will be just a little bit at first, to see if it's safe, and then more and more, as the situation demands, and his comfort level increases.

Several years ago, when I was going through my (*de rigueur*) "feminist stage," I read a book that made some fairly accurate (although unkind) comments about male/female dynamics. The author noted that one common dynamic between a man and a woman is that the man needs to be nurtured, but his ego demands that he appear "strong" and "in charge" at all times. So the woman meets the man's need for nurturance, and does so in a way that he does not have to ask for support or help. In a sense, she "reads his mind" about what he needs, and makes it available to him – whether "it" is sex, steaks, or strokes. She does this without his having to ask, because if he asks, then that's a weakness on his part, and he can not afford to be seen as weak or needy.

The author described the whole dynamic in an undertone of barely suppressed rage, as in: "Why should we have to cater to their needs all the time? Why should we let them continue ("enable" them) in their posturing? If they want something from us, let them come and ask for it, *dammit!*"

It's not that a good family systems therapist can't have a field day with the above dynamic. Most of us, with fairly simple knowledge, have learned to spell "codependency." So let me be clear. I am not talking about codependency. I am talking about compassion.

Several years ago, when I first started writing this chapter, I had a breakthrough in how I both thought of, and worked with, men. What happened was that somehow, in my dealings with men, I had *released resistance* and *softened* enough so that I could perceive men in a different light. In doing business with men, watching them do business with each other, and simply watching them interact with each other, I got an intensified sense of how much they are "locked in" to the alpha-male dynamic. I found that the smarter ones – the real alphas – will use their shared experience of being under the "alpha-male pressure" as a means of bonding with other alphas.

I saw this in action once when I traveled with Rocky to a technology working group for the Marines. There was someone there that we wanted to get to know. He was a former Naval officer; so was Rocky. That gave them something in common. They both had nearly adult sons. That gave them something else in common, because each of them had gone through the experience of "having it out," in a good old, man-to-man fistfight, with a son who had decided that "I can whip my Paw." Of course, each of them had won. (They were alpha males, right? They *had* to win.) Not only that (this is what was most interesting), each of them had "seen it coming." Each of them had responded appropriately; they had hit the gym for months in advance, doing weight lifting, cardio-vascular training, and the like. They knew what was coming up, and they were determined to win.

The alpha male bonding between them was the shared commiseration that it never gets easier. In fact, it gets tougher all the time. Since they were not in direct competition with each other, they could afford to let the other know, in a pretty comprehensive way, that each was an alpha, and each was paying the ongoing price to stay that way.

No alpha male can afford to really let down his guard with another alpha. He certainly can't do it with a male of lesser stature. He also can't do it with a female who, in her *Amazon* mode, is playing the alpha male game; if she's doing her best to qualify as an alpha in the workplace, then she counts as one. He can let it down some with his mother, but the whole male individuation process is to separate himself from his mother, so that isn't really safe either. He can't really do it with his children; he's their provider, and feels (in his mind, at least) that he needs to be strong for their sake. That leaves just one person: the woman in his life.

When we are the primary woman in a man's life, then we are the one person in the world with whom he can let down his guard. So why not be gracious? Why not be generous and kind? When a man approaches one of us in this "letting down his guard" state, we are the only one who can meet his needs. We are the only one with whom he feels safe enough to be either vulnerable or, as is the case for most Type T men, just plain grumpy.

When a man is in this state, he doesn't need sex (although he might not object, simply as tension relief). What he really needs are the two real keys to man management: steaks (nurturance) and strokes (for his ego).

I remember reading an article many years ago in which the author was figuratively rolling her eyes as she described her mate. She could see it coming, she noted, and described what her husband needed as "Mommy time." Her friend, of course, agreed with her. Yes, men were needy and demanding. Yes, it felt as though we were always "mothering" our men. Yes, it seemed as though even our real physical children were less needy, less demanding, then our men.

This is all probably very true. At the same time, our children are not the same kind of "ego machines" that our men are. (Or rather, when they are in their "terrible twos," at least they grow through the stage!)

If any of us, as *Amazon*-dominant women, have chosen a man who meets our demanding criteria, then we probably have selected an alpha. We were possibly drawn to a man who was more Type T than we were. In fact, we may have relished the prospect of easing more towards one of our "feminine" archetypes, and letting go of our *Amazon* – at least when with this particular man.

The more Type T the man is, the more he will be under severe performance pressure. (Note that this also applies to us, especially if we are *Amazon*-dominant at a given time in our lives.) This is part and parcel of being an ego-driven performance machine. No human can live under this pressure at all times. But if we try to make such a man be less ego-driven – to make him be "more open" or insist that he "share his feelings" – then we are undercutting the very ego structure that holds him together.

When a man gets comfortable in a relationship with one of us, he will continue to be ego-driven. There will be times when he will get ego gratification out of pleasing us, whether by performing in bed, building a garage, or doing anything else that makes him seem wonderful in our eyes. But often enough (we might say, too often), he will come home at his grumpiest. He will have been in "alpha-ego" mode all day, slugging it out with other ego players. When he comes home, he is tired, hungry, and usually somewhere between ego-bruised and ego-bashed. (Unless he is ego-victorious, in which case he will be buying and grilling the steaks, and talking about his victory all night.)

We can respond to our man, when he is in such a state, by accessing any (or all) of our intrinsically feminine modes, as our wisdom and guidance indicate. We may offer nurturance or solace, coming from our *Isis* mode. From our *High Priestess* essence, we become a muse; the proverbial "wise woman" who helps a man tap into his own inner wisdom. Finally, in our *Hathor* mode, we can lighten his somber feeling, by re-introducing laughter and play. All of these choices and options are available to us, and give us opportunities to be great blessings to our intimate partners.

A friend of mine said to me, "Men are high-maintenance items." I disagreed with her immediately. (Her statement was understandable: she had not yet recovered from a relationship with a very controlling and undermining man. Her former lover was thus *not* a *basic male*.) "We're high maintenance," I claimed. "Men are easy."

I still hold to that claim. Men are easy. But what they want and need, they do want and need. If we want a man in our lives, he will need to be nurtured, and to have his ego stroked. And this, dear ladies, is the essence of erotic power. It is not just sex. We can be an absolute siren, and even though we can turn a man on tremendously, we will not have real erotic power in the relationship with him *unless he gives it to us.*

Men are smart about this, especially after they've been through a life experience or two. They will not give us power unless it is safe for them to do so. "Safe" means that they can let down their guard with us and, at the very least, not be further damaged. Preferably, we hug them, kiss them, and bind up their wounds. We give them dinner at the table, and something else in bed, or reverse the order and change the locales; they don't care much about how and when.

The decision that we each need to make is whether or not each of us is willing to do this. When we are willing to be loving and caring and kind, and to truly have a sense of compassion for who and what they are, we have our choice of men. We also have the option of having men in either intimate or non-intimate relationships. We do not need to offer sex, and we do not need to select them as life-partners. If we simply acknowledge their egos with loving-kindness, rather than with judgment, we gain their respect and appreciation. More and more good men – ones who are truly seeking to be of noble character – will infuse our lives.

With all this said, we take on the first dilemma in dealing with men. We know what they need, and we know how to give it. We've been trained throughout our life (perhaps throughout all of our lifetimes) to care for others. We are even making progress in caring for ourselves.

The thing that holds us back, in many cases, is not so much lack of knowledge on our part, or even time (we are willing, typically, to make nurturing-time). It is that we look at the nature of certain men, and simply decide that they're not yet worthy of our whole-hearted attention. They are not yet, to use Deida's phrase, *superior men.*

Our very wonderful, patriarchal society has, over the past several millennia, indulged men in their ego-driven ambitions. The basic covenant between men and women was that men would provide safety, security, and protection, and women would "take care of" men, even as they cared for their own children. Much though we can offer up specific cases to the contrary, the balance of power has been in favor of men. They owned the property, and they had the money and power. We were limited by the needs of our children. We had to play by their rules.

With the balance of power decidedly in favor of males, men all too often did not have to grow up emotionally. They could go through life as "King Baby." Their needs and whims would receive attention. If they were denied, they had sufficient power to make everyone's life difficult. In particular, highly-driven alphas (those who had the greatest power and financial resources) often traded their status and security for not just female attention, but also for female compliance. The women that they kept would be those who catered.

This behavior was not limited to the alpha males, of course. In any family with children, the woman usually had no other option. She needed her husband's resources to raise her children. Yes, we all know that the woman wielded great power on the home front. ("When mama's happy, everyone's happy.") Still, the scales were heavily weighted in favor of the masculine.

This is *precisely* why we've had to cultivate our *Amazon* natures over the past decades. As soon as we had the option to make changes, through lower mortality rates in childbearing and greater control over our reproduction, we've focused worldwide on gaining greater equity in the male/female power dynamic.

The indulgence with which society has favored men over the past several millennia is beginning to unravel. Men are now finding that the compliance that they once could elicit is no longer as readily available. They are being forced to some level of self-examination, and from this, they are beginning to make changes in their own attitudes and actions.

As an example, one of my dear friends has work that takes her into contact with a wide range of people. As she has observed her various colleagues and friends over time, she's noted that the divorces come most often when children reach their teenage years. During early career-building stages, men would trust their wives to take on the full spectrum of child-raising duties. This would include being the disciplinarian, which was all well and good when the children were small. Over the years, the men continued to defer child-disciplining to their wives. The strategy that worked sufficiently well when children were young did not work nearly as well when the children became more mature. The teenage children, with their combined greater independence and emotional volatility, were more difficult to manage and control. The women needed their husband's active participation. The men didn't want to take time from their careers. They wanted to come home and be catered-to, not to take on additional responsibilities on the home front. This all too often led to divorce, when the women decided that they could manage the needs of their children, but not the needs both teenage children and a self-centered husband. Even on a smaller budget, and with the logistical constraints of custody, they were better off managing the family solo. "King Baby" was left to fend for himself.

Situations like this have been an emotional turning point for many men. When we pull back the resources of devotion and attention that we have given so freely, men reconsider their priorities.

Not all men grow up, of course. Many continue to parley their financial and social position to jockey for continued immaturity. I once attended a small church where one of the men had divorced a woman whom he'd married several years earlier. She had been his second wife; he had divorced the first one and "traded in" for this one who was similar, but younger. (Same make and model, newer year.) When he divorced her and "traded in" for his third wife, he showed up with the new wife at church. She was at the height of lusciousness, with a firm, full figure, and demure, downcast eyes. During the service, his hand rested possessively on her shapely thigh.

Wife Number Three divorced the man a few years later. She decided that she didn't want to play the combined roles of nurse/housekeeper and courtesan during his declining years. He finally had a chance for some deep self-examination. As the song that I learned in Girl Scouts says, "The growing-up tree lives inside of us all." It just matures a little later in some.

And yet, to return to the theme of the previous chapter, *In Praise of a Few Good Men*, there are a great number of men who are excellent fathers and husbands; who devote their time to both work *and* to family. They have fully embraced the challenges of parenting, and are active in child-raising from the time the baby is born until well after he or she graduates from college. While this section has addressed the character deficiencies of some men, we very likely all know many men who are stellar examples of kindness, devotion, and caring – in addition to being excellent business leaders!

With this as background, we confront **Dilemma Number One:** Is the man that we're considering mature enough to have largely, or even somewhat, grown out of his "King Baby" stage? This is a little hard to determine, but it's essential. This dilemma is really not with men, but with us. To what extent have we conditioned and programmed ourselves to serve men, no matter what? To what extent have we foregone developing ourselves professionally? Have we taken prudent and practical steps to first ensure our own survival, regardless of the presence or absence of someone else in our lives?

Many of us (this includes some of the most intelligent, sensual, and desirable women) have opted out of intimate relations with men, not so much because men have not grown up, but because we know that *we* haven't shifted sufficiently within ourselves. We are still susceptible to indulging men. We haven't yet fully developed our *High Priestess*, so we have not yet built the deep connection to our inner wisdom. We also have not yet, by and large, fully integrated our *Amazon*, so she is still brittle. We have not always treated her with gentleness and compassion, yet made clear the priorities of our other, gentler, inner archetypes. Until we have a good relationship with our inner *Amazon*, we cannot have a good relationship with an external male. Thus, until we accomplish our own inner healing and *integration*, we erect the artificial barricade of staying out of intimate relationships.

Dilemma Number Two is closely related. We've acknowledged that we need to take care of ourselves, and not rely overly on men. We've made enormous strides in this area. But in so doing, we may have overly-cultivated and overly-emphasized our *Amazon* natures; we may have built up that aspect of ourselves that is most masculine. This means that we ourselves now need exactly what it is that men desire. We may not have the same sexual drive (although perhaps we may), but we crave nurturance and having our egos built up. We, like men, come home tired and cranky after a long day. All too often, we (and sometimes our husbands) go into "second shift," caring for children and home responsibilities.

There is no way that we can reasonably give to someone else that which we desire, and are not getting in our own lives. Even if we are single with no children, when we "push" in our *Amazon* natures, we desire more support and nurturance.

"You need a wife," said my friend Diane, many years ago. I took her advice. Not that I "got a wife," but I started bringing in the "wifely services" that a man would get from a spouse who devoted her life to making his life easier. Men think nothing of co-opting as many services as possible. We're starting to learn this lesson.

Even so, if we are largely in *Amazon* mode, it is difficult for us to offer someone else the level of attention and devotion that would come if we were able to be in our *Isis* and *Hathor* modes more often. Simple pragmatics and logistics dictate our actions, not to mention time and energy.

What then, if we seek to release our *Amazon* nature, even if just a little? What if we seek to enter into our *Isis* mode, not so much for the sake of a man, but to nurture ourselves? What if we set aside time to renew our inner self, to listen to our inner wise woman, or *High Priestess?* What if we seek to bring ourselves pleasure, in our *Hathor* mode? (Regena Thomashauer's books, particularly *Mama Gena's School of Womanly Arts*, are helpful to many of us in this area.[6] "Mama" emphasizes getting to know our core desires, and designing a life that serves us bountiful, nourishing courses of pleasure. This is excellent *Hathor*-training.)

Attending to our own pleasure, and identifying our core desires, is an important means of getting clear on who we are. This is useful, because *Dilemma Number Three* is coming up.

We have, by and large, given ourselves permission to fulfill our *Amazon* natures. This is healthy and good. Cultivating our *Amazon* essence gives us the ability to take care of ourselves, and frees us from relying on a man to do the job. That gives us great security. However, this is a secondary form of security compared to what we *really* desire; relationship and intimacy.

Dilemma Number Three is perhaps the most subtle and complex. It is a question of using our own *Amazon* mode, with self-love, care, and skill. When we decide to love a man, we release our *Amazon* defenses.

As David Deida writes:

> One of the deepest feminine desires in intimacy (though not in business or simple friendship) is to be able to relax and surrender, knowing that her man is taking care of everything. Then, she can ... be pure energy, pure motion, pure love...[7]

Regrettably, not all men are

when we have released into pur[e]

an idealized situation, and a ma

an intimate relationship, we are

allow ourselves to yield, and tr[u]

this gentler state.

Deida points to the way of

like many women, have had e[

find that the man either used [

This means that we have t[

mode. We may have to use this more oñen, ~

face of having given too much, and having lost our boundaries, we need to pull

back, and reclaim our *Amazonian* strengths. These kinds of experiences can lead

us to be sad and disappointed in men, and in ourselves, for having made a decision

that led us into a weakened position.

During this time, we must also examine ourselves, to learn why we gave

ourselves to someone who was truly not worthy of the gift. Often, we need to go

back several steps, and practice our basic lessons, learning them deeper. We need

to re-learn how to be the *jewel in the heart of the lotus*. Only when we love, honor,

and cherish ourselves, will others be able to treat us in that same manner. We

need to provide the example that the rest of the universe can follow.

Thus, our inner *Amazon* is important. She gives us safety and security, within

ourselves. Her "armor" provides the chrysalis within which we can take ourselves

apart, do our inner work, and come back together again, with new insights and

behaviors guiding our next steps.

Yet for all that being an *Amazon* lets us gain or recapture control in our lives,

we cannot stay rigidly in this mode. We have the inner flexibility to be more than

ego-driven. We have an extraordinary range in our ways-of-being – far more so

than men. We can go beyond being *Amazons*, no matter how ego-gratifying that

may be, or how we may need that role to care for ourselves and our families. Even

if we have gone back to our *Amazon* mode in order to recover from having "loved

pend all of our lives. We also need to be more
selves for others.

e need to be careful, as moving into our *Hathor* mode
opens us up in a way that may not be honored. Thus, let's
e dilemmas into three challenges. Let's get our minds and
, and onto ourselves. (This is always a more intelligent course of
hree new challenges are as follows:

nge *Number One:* How do we not just reprogram ourselves, but change
ire *operating system*, so that we function differently in our relations with men?
t as many men still keep a "King Baby" component, we (at some level) have
supported them, *no matter what*. How do we pull ourselves out of the conditioning
that says that the masculine mode is more important? How do we honor our own
Hathor and *High Priestess* modes, as well as our *Amazon* and *Isis*? How do we put
our focus on ourselves, and our own completeness, first?

Challenge Number Two: How do we support our own inner *Amazon*, so that
she is not brought to the extremes that render her tired, angry at life, and simply
bitchy? How do we provide for ourselves the same support that we would normally
reserve for a man in his ego-glory? Let us take into account that over-emphasizing
our inner *Amazon* has much greater consequences for us than it does for men. Men
are ego-creatures, so everything that they do to create achievements feeds their
core. We are more complex. We desire relationship as well as achievement. When
we over-emphasize our *Amazon*, our inner *Hathor* and *High Priestess* pay the price,
and we become deeply unhappy. We may not even have time to nurture ourselves
and others in our *Isis* mode. Yet at times, we must be *Amazon*-dominant. How
then do we care for ourselves?

Challenge Number Three: How do we give ourselves our own support and
structure, so that we can indeed be "pure energy, pure motion, pure love ..."
without necessarily relying on a man to provide this structure? (We note that this
"structure" may be financial; it may be a home and a steady income. It may, and
likely even should be, of a very practical, down-to-earth, supportive nature.) How
do we take care of ourselves in the all-too-frequent cases where we've misjudged,
and the man is *not* present when we overflow the boundaries of our own lake? How
do we use our own *Amazon* modes to provide us with a "safe zone"?

૭⸰૭

One day, still heart-sore and slowly recovering from Theo's departure, I called my sister Annie for emotional support. She listened to me patiently enough, and provided her own summary. "Men are highly over-rated," she said. We both laughed, and I got a much-needed shift in perspective.

Our solution is to focus less on men, and more on ourselves. As a first step, we need to refocus our *Isis/Empress/Mother* mode into caring for ourselves. As a small example: Even if we're living alone, we can put together a crockpot of stew before leaving for work in the morning. Then, when we come home tired, we are not simply choosing between a microwave meal or ordering in a pizza. It's the *little things* – the things that we would do for a man, or a child – that we need to give to ourselves. We begin by giving ourselves some basic nurturance. Over time, the message will seep through. No matter what our other commitments may be, our *Isis* is there to take care of ourselves, too.

Then, if we develop our *Hathor* role, again focusing on ourselves, we open ourselves to pleasure and play. In our *High Priestess* mode, we access our spiritual side. As we do this for ourselves, and not for someone else, we truly do find a path for healing and *integration*.

As I came to greater awareness on this (which was coincident with the last rewrites and edits for this book), I realized that the key lies not so much in strengthening our inner *Amazon*, but in cultivating and listening more to our inner *High Priestess*. As we get more and more in touch with ourselves, and work through layers of "stuff," she will guide us in the right decisions. We learn how to connect with her by attending to how we *feel*. This involves strengthening our awareness; our ability to listen-inside, together with our discernment. If we make decisions that ultimately are not in our best interests, it is often our inner *High Priestess* who forces a situation that shows us, very clearly, something that we have been willfully trying to ignore. It is ultimately our *High Priestess* guiding our *Amazon* that gives us our greatest strength. At the same time, it is our *Hathor* essence that gives us the juiciness, the raison d'être. We *need* our *Hathor* energy to make life worth living! Thus, our *Hathor* and *High Priestess* roles are the subjects of the next two chapters.

PERSONAL PATHWORKING:

1. You may have a most wonderful, excellent man in your life as a partner. However, if you sense that you are experiencing any of the three dilemmas posed earlier, review them to see which is most appropriate to your situation. Can you transform your "dilemma" into a "challenge"?

2. As you continue journaling, take note of how your inner *High Priestess* has guided you – especially as you've selected the various men in your life. What do you know now that you didn't know when you were younger? What can you take from your "lessons learned" that you can apply to future experiences?

3. What core values are most important to you? If you are in the process of evaluating someone as a potential partner, what is most important to you in terms of purpose for the rest of your life? Now, would giving time and attention to this prospective (or current) partner be in alignment with your highest purpose?

4. To what extent are you being nurturing and kind to your own inner *Amazon*? Remember, kindness to yourself will enable you to be kind to others.

5. Similarly, are you giving the time that is needed to your *High Priestess* and *Hathor* modes? If not – and if life circumstances dictate that you simply cannot create more time at this moment – then please "covenant" with yourself to give yourself a certain kind of time, and certain kinds of experiences. Write these commitments down, as formal promises! And then, try to incorporate "micro-slices" of what you intend for the future into your life today. This will keep your *Hathor* and *High Priestess* from expiring on a "starvation diet." (Remember, both your *Hathor* and your *High Priestess*

are very powerful and real inner aspects of your inner landscape. If denied too long, without any real prospect for attention, either or both are all too capable of pulling a major life-interrupt. Planning and prudence now, even if you are horribly time-constrained, will allow you to complete your current life-mission, and keep your *Hathor* and *High Priestess* "on your side" as you accomplish that which must be done in order to clear the way for them to emerge.

6. The dear friend who told me about the divorces that most often occur when the children reach teenage years also had wise insight to offer. She noted that those marriages that *did* survive were those in which the couples took time to be with each other. They did not let their marriage denigrate into simple "life maintenance" roles. They would take weekend trips with each other, and simply date each other from time to time. We can take her observation to heart, and – once we've brought out our *Hathor* sufficiently well to nurture ourselves – start creating playtime with our life-partners once again!

7. Lastly, let us never overlook the value of prayer. Relationships with a "significant other" are as much a spiritual discipline as any form of spiritual asceticism, including that of being a parent (as described by Father Curry in *Chapter 19*). Pray for yourself, to be loving, kind and humble (that is, willing to relinquish your own ego from time to time) within your relationship. Pray for your partner's well-being. Pray for wisdom and guidance. One aspect of God is known as the *Comforter*, and if we are going through hard times – which are part and parcel of human life – ask for the presence and blessings of the *Comforter* in your and your partner's life. Ask for an indwelling spirit of graciousness, gentleness, and loving-kindness, which will make it possible to overlook little things, and appreciate both the little and big ones. And if you are really feeling bold about this, ask your partner to pray with you! (This is not such a bad idea, even in a strong,

healthy and happy relationship. You will both build a solid base which will weather the hard times, and you will also – at the same time – build the strength with which to share your combined sense of loving-kindness with others.) If you are not in a relationship, prayer is *still* a good idea. As my mother once told me, she sought to "*See* Christ in everyone, and *be* Christ [that is, the expression of God's love] to everyone." Not a bad precept for living.

CHAPTER 25:
SEX "SECRETS" OF BELLY DANCERS

"ARE BELLY DANCERS BETTER LOVERS?" asked Chrissy, my then-beau's former girlfriend. She wanted to know how she was faring against the competition. "Much better," he replied; both in honesty, and because he had to! Now, what's the truth of the matter?

Many of us find that our practice of Oriental dance helps us in our intimate relations at three distinct levels. Of course, by practicing a demanding body art we gain both greater awareness and mastery of our bodies; this is in addition to the obvious benefits of being more physically toned, limber, and having greater muscle control. However, we bring our increased mastery at the mental and emotional realms ("mind" and "psyche") into play as well. Further, some of us – those of us who have accessed the energy-realms of this art – can bring yet another dimension into our love-play. The emotional aspects have been interwoven throughout this book. Upcoming chapters will address the combined realms of mind and psyche, together with the energetic aspects. This chapter focuses on the physical.

The physical realm is the easiest of the love-making realms to learn and explain. When we learn to do Oriental dance correctly (and some, although not all of us, do), we gain superlative control of the muscles covering our abdominal area, together with control of our three diaphragms. (Yes, we really do have *three* diaphragms; the one with which most of us are familiar is the one that separates our lungs and heart from our abdominal organs. In addition, we have two others: one at our pelvic floor, and a much smaller diaphragm at the very base of our torso – the "uro-genital" diaphragm.[1])

In addition to being better able to use our physical bodies, we also learn to use our breathing. We increase our overall contraction/expansion awareness. All of these are important precursors for skilled love-making. In fact, many magazine articles to the contrary, it is far more important that both partners have good body awareness and control than it is to have a variety of sexual "positions." This is what we gain, both directly and indirectly, as we develop proficiency in Oriental dance.

When many of us think about "muscle control" in relation to love-making, we often think of the Kegel exercises. These exercises strengthen the pubococcygeus muscle, which is close to the lowest diaphragm – our uro-genital diaphragm.[2] Many of us have learned to practice these Kegel exercises; they help not only to minimize urinary incontinence, but also to increase sexual pleasure. However, these exercises address only a very small aspect of our lower torso musculature and diaphragms. Using Oriental dance (and, for those dancers who are well-trained, some other forms of dance would also work well), we gain more precise awareness and control over a much greater range of muscles. Our ability to use these muscles and the associated diaphragms, coupled with our ability to selectively release tension in other areas, is exactly what would make additional sexual positions not only possible, but also satisfying.

The techniques learned by my students as part of our *Level 2* training are somewhat advanced. We focus on anatomical understanding and precise muscular training. This gives us a basis for other realms of mastery. As we gain precise control, we learn to release emotional and energetic tensions, or blockages. This not only allows us to express ourselves more beautifully as we move, but paves the way for advanced work in energy circulation as well.

Our *Level 2* work begins when we shift our attention from simple, in-place movements such as hip drops and hip circles, to the more rounded and circular movements; these include lower and upper body undulations along with the pelvic figure-eights. In fact, a dancer is noticeably doing *Level 2* work when she begins to generate *all* of her movements from a lower-body undulation. (Prior to that, in *Level 1*, she is focused on proper alignment and freeing up her body enough to execute basic techniques.)

By way of comparison, Martha Graham based her entire dance form on expansion and contraction. In Oriental dance, we not only use expansion and contraction, but make the core expansion/contraction cycle come from a lower body undulation. Even when done very subliminally, we connect every other movement that we do to an internal pattern that circulates vertically around our lower core muscles. This movement encompasses pelvic and lumbar flexibility together with abdominal muscle control. This is a connection point to advanced energy circulation work, as taught by Mantak Chia and others, in the tradition of Taoist energy practices.[3]

The correct technique for a lower body undulation involves using our lower abdominal muscles. Specifically, we use the lower central portions of our internal and external oblique abdominal muscles. There is a "surprise factor" that comes into play here. Anatomical studies[4] show that our clitoris is much larger than we often think it to be. It is more than just the single little bulb of pleasure that we know so well. Instead, it is a fairly large organ that bisects and lies, under our labia and fatty tissue, to each side of our vaginal opening.[5] When we use our lower abdominal muscles to "roll downwards" in the classic undulation movement, we actually massage the lower internal portion of our torso. We can also, optionally, contract the lowest portions of our musculature. The combination of these moves means that we can give a little rolling pressure to our clitoral "wings." This is indirect stimulation, and applied to the not-most-sensitive portion of the whole clitoral organ. Including this level of internal pressure is optional; it is not necessary in order to execute a correct, and beautiful, technique. However, some of us find that increasing the muscular intensity of certain "internal" movements actually does make our dance more powerful, even if the extent of the muscular control cannot be directly observed. This has the indirect effect of making the dance more stimulating for ourselves, as well. Again, this is strictly optional, and depends on how the dancer chooses to use internal muscular pressure.

We can also apply the ability to exert more internal pressure (gained via increased muscle control) to benefit our partners during lovemaking. Though this is a matter of personal preference, experiments in this area can leave a dancer with her own arsenal of "private techniques."

Those of us who have not yet developed dance proficiency, and those of us who are new to the art, can benefit tremendously by developing core muscles. Simple "crunches," by themselves, are not adequate. Leg raises (and leg lowerings – very slow, controlled, and deliberate) are of more help.

It takes time to develop complete mastery of our core musculature; it is a matter of both strengthening some muscles, and releasing tension in certain others. Because we often store emotional stress in our lower backs and pelvic areas, we can expect to gain mastery in "layers," and this will take time. It will encompass emotional release work as well as physical mastery. One very excellent resource is *Core Training for Belly Dancers*[6], a DVD produced by Gerson Kuhr, the "Fitness Pharaoh." Though designed to meet the needs of dancers, almost all women can benefit by following either of the two routines demonstrated on this DVD.

Even with this as a general guide, there is a specific set of exercises that is most useful for working with our external and internal oblique muscles. These exercises help us create both awareness (being able to isolate certain muscles and feel them as distinguished from others) and control (being able to selectively use these muscles in contrast to others).

To start with, we need to identify just which set of muscles it is that we are trying to isolate, strengthen, and control. To feel our oblique abdominal muscles, we begin by standing comfortably, and extend our hands out in front, palms facing outward. We make a leaf shape with our hands, by touching our forefingers together at the top, and our thumbs together at the bottom. The "leaf" is the space between our two outward-facing palms, which now connect to form a roughly triangular space between them. Our two thumbs, touching each other, make the pointed stem end of the leaf. Our two index fingers, touching each other, make the tip. We place the "stem end" of our leaf (our two thumbs) into our navel. We place the "tip end" of our leaf on our pubic bone. Then, we lay our palms flat against our lower abdomens while keeping our index fingers and thumbs in place. Now, we roll our hands out to the sides, keeping the outer edges of our hands in place. From here, we feel into our abdomens with the outer edges of our hands. We should be able to feel our way into two muscle layers that will be underneath the big longitudinal muscle group that runs from sternum to pubic bone. The muscles that we now feel will be the external and internal oblique muscles. We particularly want to work with the internal oblique muscles, which control our deepest-level abdominal movements.

Many of us may initially find it difficult to identify our internal oblique muscles. Even if we work out, we have probably concentrated more on the first two muscle layers (longitudinal muscles and external obliques). It takes a lot more work and attention to get underneath these two layers and work with the lower, internal oblique muscles. As we try the following exercise, we need to be diligent and faithful. After a while, we too will begin to differentiate and sense a distinct new muscle group: our internal obliques.

This exercise is probably the toughest abdominal exercise in the world. However, it works. To do this, we lie on our backs, and then shift to one side or another so that our weight is mostly on one side of our derrieres. Then, we do the "scissors" contraction. Arms are off the floor (we support ourselves solely on that one side, using our overall abdominal strength). Our legs are out in front, toes pointed. We contract our torsos towards our thighs, so that we are raising our body and our legs simultaneously. We do this on one side; then switch and do the other. We can vary the number that we do per side; it can be a whole set, or just a few, switching back and forth.

As we first begin this exercise, we dominantly use our external oblique muscles. As we gain proficiency, and increased muscle awareness and control, we can shift the work to our internal oblique muscles. This gives us the much greater overall control that we desire. As we do this, we also gain the ability to discern, and selectively strengthen and use, our two distinct lower torso diaphragms.

In our studio, we often use Brian Keane and Omar Faruk Tekbilek's *Beyond the Sky* as warm-up music. The fifth cut, *Chargah Sirto*, is for a sprightly 2 ½ minutes. This is plenty for an abdominal workout; emphasizing these "dancer crunches," with enough time for some leg lifts and regular crunches as well. These exercises are hard, and 2 ½ minutes is a long time to be doing them. Persistence helps. If we stay with them over time, both we (and our partners) will feel the difference.

In addition to having abdominal muscle control, we also need to release tension throughout our bodies, and particularly gain greater flexibility in our lower backs and sacral areas. All of the *softening* and *releasing resistance* aspects of our *pathworking*, described in earlier chapters, are very helpful. But also, for simply achieving greater lower back, sacroiliac and hip girdle flexibility, we can gain great advantage by practicing a combination of Oriental dance movements and yoga. Of course, we also benefit by adding in the other basics; a little cardio-workout and some resistance training, some Pilates, and whatever other practices we find useful for getting healthy, oxygenated, and vigorous!

All of this involves the mechanics of how Oriental dance relates to the physical aspects of love-making. These mechanics are wonderful; they open a new door beyond Kegel exercises for all of us. Our interests, though, are much more in the realms of *eros* and energy than simple mechanics. It is our minds that seduce; we use our minds to build interest and capture attention. In this realm of mystery and enchantment, Oriental dance is the greatest vehicle for mastery, should we wish to use it as such. That is the subject of the next chapter.

PERSONAL PATHWORKING:

1. Go work out! (What else were you expecting, darling?) Leg-raising and lowering. Try the oblique abdominal exercises described in this chapter. Make them part of your daily routine.

2. Order the Fitness Pharaoh's DVD, *Core Training for Belly Dancers*. Work with the DVD. What more can I say?

3. Make sure that your regular fitness routine includes some yoga/stretch/ Pilates movements, some cardio (may I recommend Oriental dance?), and some resistance training. (And if you haven't played with your veil lately, it is amazing how much of an upper-arm workout that even simple veil play can give you – and so much more fun than lifting weights and doing gym exercises!)

4. Practice the results with a partner, if you have one. No partner? We'll be talking about one of Napoleon Hill's favorite subjects, *transmuting the emotion of sex energy*,[7] in *Chapter 29: Pragmatic Esoterics*. You'll have a head-start on building up some energy worth transmuting.

CHAPTER 26:
UNVEILING: SELECTIVE REVELATION

THERE I WAS, FEELING THOROUGHLY humbled. I'd been developing a new dance choreography, and had flown to New York for a weekend intensive of dance lessons, including a private session with Anahid. I had just finished showing her my new dance. It was a veil dance, and was set to one of Anahid's favorite pieces of music.

In my opening movements, I was coming on full force, swirling my veil all over the stage, and overly dramatizing the role. Now, Anahid had just shown me something quieter, more reserved, and much more elegant. It was a very simple opening. However, hers had the true drama and intensity that my opening, for all my running about, had lacked.

I should have known, of course. I had been studying with Anahid for years, albeit via long distance. What she had just shown me was not something new. I had not only known it; I had taught it to my students. And here I was, taking my new creation in to my master teacher, and realizing that I'd forgotten the basic lessons.

What was it that Anahid had, and that I had totally forgotten?

Simply, it was the power of *holding something back*.

In my dance, I had started the way that many dancers start these days; holding my veil behind me, and using it to frame myself as I moved across the floor. There is nothing wrong with this. In fact, if the music is very active and dynamic, this can be a great dance opening! However (and this is important), this approach lacks the power of mystery and suggestion.

In the dance that Anahid showed me, she started by staying in one place, with the veil wrapped around herself. She held the veil edges in such a way that her hands were covered. She held her hands high enough so that, with the veil wrapped around her from behind, it covered her face as well.

Slowly, hypnotically, she moved her hands in an alternating, graceful up and down pattern. She managed this is such a way that I couldn't get a glimpse of her face, or any part of her body. She was a mystery. Later, as she "unveiled" herself, she had total control over the timing, the pacing, the very selective revelation that she offered.

The dance art of *unveiling* is too beautiful and subtle to put into words. The website for this book contains links to some of the best online resources available to illustrate this art. Nominations for "best dances" in different areas come from many sources, including those from my students, teachers, and colleagues. Our intention with this site is to share with the community that which we regard as the "best of the best!"

Any of us, especially if we are not currently a dancer, might wonder how watching a performance by a fabulous dancer can be of assistance. Any one of us, unless we are already at a mastery level, could be saying something like, "If I don't have the dance technique and training, how could I practically apply what I've seen to my life?"

What then can we learn by watching a skilled dancer? Simply put, we can capture and incorporate the *psychology of the dance* into our own lives.

Not every business tycoon has to be a martial arts expert in order to use the winning strategies of Sun Tzu's *The Art of War*.[1] There are excellent business executives who literally have had prior training as warriors; they were military officers and very fine ones. There are also equally effective business leaders who have never donned a uniform or fired a weapon. Often, though, these leaders who do not have a military background will study and glean what they can from military campaigns and strategies, and even the whole zeitgeist of military and martial disciplines. Then, they will then apply what they've learned to their corporate world.

Similarly, we can add the *art of allure* to our arsenal, without ever taking a class in Oriental dance, or performing before an audience. In this case, our strategy is to study the "great ones": we learn the essence of what they have done, and apply it to our own lives.

⒜⒝

My two foremost master teachers, Anahid Sofian and Elena Lentini, are from the "old school." They came of age in an era where there was an active New York Mid-East nightclub scene. In the late sixties and early seventies, there was a strong Mid-Eastern immigrant community in New York, and a thriving entertainment business grew to serve them. Anahid tells me that while she was learning to dance, she worked during the day, and went to a different nightclub every night. There were no classes in Oriental dance, or "belly dance," back then. If a woman wasn't taught by her mother and her aunties, or by a dancer whom she befriended, then she would have to do what Anahid did; go to the nightclubs and watch.

After watching the dancers late into each night, Anahid would go home and practice what she had seen. After spending a goodly long while on the sidelines, she made friends with a very fine dancer who eventually gave her some pointers, and told her to "go out and get a job!" So, she finally got the courage to start dancing in public.

Once again, night after night, she was out in the clubs. This time, however, she was not sitting with the audience. She was onstage, both as a soloist as well as being part of the "on-stage sidelines." Junior dancers hired by the clubs were expected to stay on stage all night long, both before and after they did their individual solo dances. They played rhythms with their dumbeks (Mid-Eastern drums) or tambourines for the other soloists, adding to the overall ambience.

Over the years, Anahid developed her skill and proficiency. Over time, she progressed to teaching, developing a dance company, and choreographing major events. At the peak of the New York nightclub scene, she was sought after for performances at weddings, major parties, and even traditional American nightclubs.

In a rare video tape of Anahid doing a twenty-minute performance, I saw what her full-length dances were like at this time.

Anahid entered the room, her beautiful costume fully covered by a veil wrapped around her body. The veil was centered on her back, and was brought to the front under each arm. It was then crossed over in front, with the edges firmly tucked under her costume bra straps. This left her arms free, but kept her costume and body from being revealed. For the entire dance opening, she kept her veil fully wrapped around her. Her movements were buoyant and enthusiastic; she was getting the crowd into a happy and upbeat mood, but she wasn't giving away a thing!

After several minutes, the music shifted both tempo and mood. Anahid slowly did an *unveiling*; showing a little here, a little more there, until – finally – she floated her veil free. She completed that dance section with a series of lyrical movements, creating beautiful patterns as she swirled her veil about her.

Dalia Carella is another of my favorite dancers, whose vision has led her to create new fusion works as well as historical retrospectives. In one of her performances, she was initially covered with a long, nearly opaque black veil. Coming over her head, it covered her both back and front. In this dance, Dalia held the two edges of the front part lightly, keeping the veil horizontally taut. Slowly, ever so slowly, she lifted the veil up and over her head. We were mesmerized. Her power of creating dramatic tension kept *our* attention rapt.

In contrast, I recently saw a lovely young woman perform a dance at an "open stage" event. (This is much like a singer's "open mike" night.) She was beautiful, and clearly skilled. Her dance was mostly floorwork – an art form which has been largely forsaken by today's Oriental dance community. Kneeling on the floor, with her back to the audience, she did a full backbend. She rolled her abdominal muscles, using them to lift herself up of the floor and then release back again. Her dance continued like this; very technical, very advanced, and very demanding.

Her dance was supposed to portray the height of *eros*. Yet, I was not attracted to her performance. I felt her dance was too much like picking up a novel and jumping right into a sex scene, without any buildup. There was no drama; there was no erotic tension. There was no *anticipation*.

Anticipation, as we know, is the foreplay of the mind. We are far less interested in the final result (in many cases, the end is known). We are much more interested in the journey. We want the *story*. We want to be enthralled with the process of *getting there*.

A wise, earthy, and very sexy woman once said, "Only show a man half your ass." This is very much the same thing as *unveiling*. We learn to hold something in reserve. We don't give it all away. Particularly, we don't give it away in the early stages.

⚚

A couple of years ago, I realized the role of *unveiling* during the dance. I suddenly understood that it had less to do with controlling the drama, and still less to do with sexual titillation, and much more to do with allowing vulnerability. Lowering our veil is a gesture of intimacy, not necessarily a sexual invitation.

(Women understand this intuitively. Men sometimes have problems with this concept. That is another good reason to lower our veils slowly. We need to take a measure of the situation.)

Elena Lentini confirmed this insight for me in a summer workshop, during which she taught an exquisite veil dance. The dance was set to Turkish music, using a *chifti telli* rhythm. *Chifti tellis* often underlie the most erotic and seductive music in the world. This dance was no exception.

With Elena's unique interpretation, she spent the first two minutes of the dance, during a long musical preamble, simply waiting. She had wrapped her veil loosely around herself. It was neither hiding her, nor particularly framing her. It was simply – *there*. Her pose was also, simply – *there*. If she suggested anything, with her downcast eyes and open-handed gesture, it was the image of one of the classic *Madonna* poses. She opened her dance from a meditative state.

This meant so much to me. In this art, and in our lives, many of us have our self-image tied up in some aspect of our ego; our achievements, our performance, or even our ability to be sexually attractive. Too often, this means that we come across as being brazen. This is not an attractive quality or essence.

My friend Kathy Carroll, whom I've mentioned in *Chapter 16* and in other parts of this book, helped me make this distinction. She taught a course on the Abraham-Hicks teachings[2] for *conscious co-creation*. One of the most important things that she taught us was the difference between *asserting* and *allowing*.

When we *assert* something, we have a sense of "push" behind it. Our ego-self is in full force. Metaphorically speaking, we are entering the room with our zills clanging non-stop, and we don't let up on the frontal assault. As another example, we jump immediately into the most provocative, intimate portion of a dance. We know what we want, and we are *making* it – *causing* it – to happen. We are using the full force of our will and intention.

In contrast, when we enter a dance (or a relationship or life-situation) wrapped in a veil, we can *allow* the veil to drop. We can reveal ourselves slowly. We can *allow* the other person to delight in discovering who we are. We can build the intimacy gracefully, over time.

Imagine meeting two different women. One pours out her entire life story, all at once. She gives us all the painful, gory details. She lets it all, so to speak, "hang out."

Suppose the other woman is more demure. She is present, and is in rapport with us, but she doesn't just dump everything that is going on in our laps right away.

With whom would we rather share a long train journey?

When we do a physical *unveiling* during a dance, we are not simply making an erotic or intimate statement. We are using our veil as a symbol, or metaphor, for separation between ourselves and others. It even represents the layers of "personality" within ourselves, so that our "veiling" separates us from ourselves as much as from an external person. The act of *unveiling* – the process – is one of becoming more intimate with ourselves; more knowing and accepting and becoming all of who we are. *Unveiling* becomes a spiritual process, and an inner journey, as much as an erotic element.

For women, our body-self and our spiritual-self are closely united. Our *pathway* is an *integration journey*. To know ourselves fully, and to express the fullness of who we are, we need both the sensuality and erotic vitality of our *Hathor*, combined with the spiritual awareness of our *High Priestess*. For women, erotic expression and spiritual transcendence are linked, and both are *pathways* to knowing our inner selves. The *unveiling* process, especially during dance, is a means of integrating both essences into a single experience.

Integrating both our *eros* and our spiritual aspects, through the art of *unveiling*, would be enough for many of us. However, there is something much more. This final realm is much deeper, much more vital, and much more exciting. If anything, we could compare it to discovering, within ourselves, our very own *Fountain of Youth*. This is something we address in the last section of this book.

PERSONAL PATHWORKING:

1. Go get your veil. Play with it. This time, recognizing that *you* are the *jewel in the heart of the lotus*, treat revealing yourself as something very special; almost sacred.

2. Begin to practice *selective revelation*. You don't always need to tell everyone everything. Start to keep a quiet core and center. Observe what happens as you do this.

3. If you are a dancer, think about bringing this *unveiling* process into your dance, as well as your life.

PART VII:
DANCE MAGIC: THE SACRED AND THE PROFANE

CHAPTER 27:
LETTING GO: THE INANNA STORY

"INANNA WAS A VERY HEALTHY goddess," stated my friend and colleague Joshua many years ago. I could understand why. Rarely have I encountered someone, even in myth and legend, who could so completely expect and enjoy self-fulfillment. As a picture of this ancient goddess came to life through translations of ancient Sumerian myths[1], it became clear that Inanna could readily serve as a model of today's "totally integrated person."

"Oh, no," exclaimed my friend Diane several years later, when I mentioned that I was going to use Inanna as a key figure in this book. "She was horrible! She was a real bitch!" Her comment on Inanna led us into Diane's extensive collection of books on history, archeology, and cultural mythology. As I found out, there was support for both points of view. Inanna is renowned for being one of the most complex goddesses ever known. She was both a warrior and a lover, both an innocent young bride (albeit a lusty one) and a harlot, and both nurturing and destructive.[2]

Fascinated by Inanna's story, Jungian analyst Betty De Shong Meador spent years learning – with the help of Sumerian scholars – to translate and poetically interpret certain hymns to Inanna. These were written about four thousand years ago by Enheduanna, daughter of the great Sumerian king Sargon. He was the first ruler to build a widespread empire, a feat that involved developing and then aggressively deploying large-scale military forces (perhaps for the first time in human history). Sargon appointed his daughter to the position of High Priestess to the moon god Nanna in his temple at Ur. At the same time, Inanna was Enheduanna's personal deity.

Enheduanna's love for and devotion to Inanna inspired her to write great epic hymns. De Shong Meador described Enheduanna's role as being the High Priestess of the god Nanna. In this role, she served a male deity loyally and with great devotion. Further, as High Priestess in the land, she upheld the Sumerian tradition of worshipping all the male as well as female deities."[3] Nevertheless, Enheduanna's epic Inanna stories, when read today, carry a sense of vibrancy and passion that resonate over millennia.

From a clay tablet containing one of Enheduanna's poems, Meador translated (with the help of her scholar friends) a hymn in which Inanna exults:

> peg my vulva
> my star-sketched horn of the dipper
> moor my slender boat of heaven
> my new moon crescent cunt beauty[4]

The Inanna singing this hymn to herself is still a virgin. She has come into her sexual ripeness, but has not yet selected her first lover.

Diane Wolkstein, who has skillfully interpreted and retold some of humanity's greatest stories,[5] investigated the Inanna legends with the help of famed Sumerian scholar Noah Kramer. Together, they wrote a book presenting much of Inanna's story and many of her hymns. In *Inanna, Queen of Heaven and Earth*, Wolkstein and Kramer were the first to make the Inanna legends accessible outside of the scholarly community. Pulling together all the story fragments, taken from multiple baked clay tablets and carefully translated by scholars, into a single, cohesive grand saga was a complex task. Wolkstein's vivid prose captures both the richness and detail of Inanna's story, which we take up as Inanna revels in her youthful energy and delights in her role as queen.

Flush with her own erotic vitality, Inanna decides to "honor" Father God Enki, the "God of Wisdom," by visiting him in his holy city Eridu.[6] Enki was delighted to see the child of his lineage, and set out to play the grand host. They drank beer together and got thoroughly drunk. Enki, in a burst of enthusiastic generosity, offered Inanna all of his great gifts; his *me*, which were the things that made him such a powerful god. (These *me* were a complex and varied lot. They ranged from rights, roles, and privileges, such as "godship" and the "high priesthood," to knowledge protocols, such as the "craft of the reed worker." Other important skills were included in the *me*; these ranged from the "art of song" to the "art of the elder" to the "kissing of the phallus"![7])

Unabashed (and not nearly as drunk as Father Enki), Inanna accepted each *me*. As quickly as possible, she closed out the feasting, and took off with her newly acquired *me* in her "Boat of Heaven." When Enki sobered and realized what he had done, he tried to reclaim his *me*. First, he ordered her to return them. Inanna replied that he had sworn "'in the name of [his] power, in the name of [his] holy shrine'"[8] that he was giving her those gifts, and she wasn't about to return them. Six different times, Enki sent his various magical servants to reclaim his *me*. Six times, Inanna's warrior-companion, Ninshubur, fought them off. On the seventh occasion, Inanna landed safely with her *me*, and more *me* magically appeared with those that she had brought back. Her city broke out in rejoicing.

So far, we have seen a journey, and a heroine returning home with great prizes. However, this story is utterly lacking the trials of not only strength but of character that form the basis for the young man's *Hero's Quest*. From a mythological (and human archetypal) perspective, Inanna's initial journey has been all too easy.

Inanna continued from this point the way any successful young person would. Endowed with the blessings and prosperity that came with her *me*, she selected her husband, raised two sons, and governed her kingdom with what seemed to be wisdom until she reached her middle years. Then, a change came over her. Without much apparent forewarning, Inanna decided to make a journey to see her sister Ereshkigal, the "Queen of the Underworld." They had not previously been close, and Inanna had never visited her sister. Yet, her sister's husband had just died. This gave Inanna a rationale – although not necessarily a reason – for her visit.

Inanna prepared carefully for her "descent into the Underworld." Even at the outset, she knew that this would be a dangerous venture. She spoke to her trusted companion, Ninshubur, telling her that, if she did not return, Ninshubur was to lament for her in the ruins. Ninshubur was then to approach the Father Gods; Father Enlil and Father Nanna. If these two refused to help her, she should approach Father Enki. Ninshubur was to weep and plead for help with each one, until one of them agreed to save her.

Inanna dressed in ceremonial splendor. She carefully arranged her hair and anointed her eyes with an ointment called "Let him come, let him come."[9] She took with her seven of her precious *me*, and entered the Underworld; the domain of her sister, Ereshkigal.

Inanna was in her prime. She brought with her certain *me*; accoutrements of her success. Yet as she passed through each of the seven gates separating the Underworld from the world of the living, she had to relinquish one of her *me*.[10] The first gatekeeper demanded that she give up the *shugurra* (the crown of the steppes). Successively, she yielded her earrings and her heavy, six-pointed necklace. At the fourth gate, she gave up her starry cloak. Cold, and without adornment, she arrived at the fifth gate, only to be told that she needed to give over her jeweled shoes. At the sixth and seventh gates, respectively, her diamond-encrusted belt and her skirt were demanded of her. Naked and bowed low, she entered her sister's throne room.

Ereshkigal was another matter entirely. Where Inanna had been arrayed in a royal robe and costly jewelry, Ereshkigal was without even simple clothing: "No linen is spread over her body. Her breasts are uncovered." Where Inanna had carefully arranged her hair before her descent, Ereshkigal's hair "swirls about her head like leeks."[11]

Inanna was at the height of her power, beauty, and glory – and her sister Ereshkigal suffered from numerous ailments. Just as Inanna was "Queen of Heaven," Ereshkigal was "Queen of the Underworld." Author Debbie Ford, in *The Dark Side of the Light-Chasers*, describes how even those of us most devoted to bringing "light" into the world still must confront a "shadow self."[12] This notion is not unique to her, of course. As described in her book, Carl Jung is famous for acknowledging our need to first know, and then integrate, our "shadow selves." However, we see in the Inanna story that this recognition of a polar opposite is as old as human mythology. Carrying the notion of a "shadow self" to our interpretation of the Inanna story, we see that Ereshkigal was Inanna's dark side.[13] This was the first time that Inanna had ever gone to see her sister in the Underworld. It was the first time that Inanna had confronted this aspect of herself.

Once Inanna came into her sister's presence, Ereshkigal fastened on Inanna the "eye of death." Inanna's body became a rotting corpse, and was hung on a hook on the wall.

After three days and nights of waiting, Ninshubur realized that Inanna was not going to return. She publicly mourned Inanna, setting up lament for her by the ruins. Dressing in beggar's clothes, she approached each of the Father Gods in turn. Father Enlil and Father Nanna were both angry at Inanna's decision to enter the Underworld. "She who goes to the Dark City stays there," they each told her.[14]

Ninshubur then approached Father Enki – the same Father God who had generously given Inanna all of his *me*, and then sent his magical servants to retrieve them again! Father Enki grieved that Inanna was lost to the Underworld. From underneath his fingernails, one from each hand, he took dirt. From this dirt, he created two creatures, neither male nor female, the *kurgarra* and the *galatur*. He sent these creatures down to the Underworld, and told them to slip in like flies. When Ereshkigal cried and moaned, they were to cry and moan with her. When she noticed them, and offered them a gift for their empathy, they were to request Inanna's body.[15]

They did as they were told. When they received her body, the *kurgarra* sprinkled the *food of life* on it. The *galatur* sprinkled the *water of life* on it. Inanna arose, and made her way back to her domain.[16]

Inanna's story is about loss. It is about *integration*, and about rebirth. These are not things that we take on casually, or lightly. In fact, we generally would prefer not to take them on at all. This "descent" happens either because real-life events occur that shake our foundations, or some sort of inner compulsion drives us (as it drove Inanna) to leave our comfortable, secure homes. Note that this home-leaving need not be physical; it can be our experience-allegory for leaving any form of physical, emotional, or even spiritual security.

At every station of her journey, Inanna gave up not just a physical object, but a part of her identity; a part that let her feel secure and strong and confident. All this was just while she was enroute! Once she met her sister, Ereshkigal, things immediately got worse. Instead of being greeted and hugged, she was killed. She was powerless to save herself. She was in her sister's domain, and had yielded up every prop and tool of power. Once she was slain (because the story was not over), she was completely reliant on others to save her.

Inanna was indeed saved, but not by her cavalry storming in to her rescue or by heroic exploits from her husband. She was saved by the empathy of little sprite-spirits that were so insignificant that they seemed like flies. They were made of dirt from underneath Father Enki's fingernails. Doesn't this just add to the sense of how Inanna's ego was humbled?

Myth-stories such as the descent of Inanna (and all "grand opera" types of stories) operate by taking our human experience and exaggerating the contrast. That's why these myths help us. When life events hit home – when it's personal – we feel as though we're going through our own private Inanna-legend, Romeo-and-Juliet drama, or Tosca-style grand opera.

I've had my own *Inanna-descents* – each of us has. In fact, I've had several just during the course of writing this book. One such *Inanna-descent* came several years ago, when I realized that I would have to leave the life I'd known. I would have to close my dance school, close my new consulting business, leave my home, my boyfriend, my friends and students and cats, and travel to another city in search of a job. I pushed this decision back to the absolute final hour; when the time came to leave, the mortgage was late, and the bank was threatening to repossess my car.

Dora, a New York friend-of-a-friend, invited me to stay with her while job-hunting in the "Big Apple," and offered the possibility of moving in once I found work. She sent me a one-way plane ticket to New York. I cancelled classes, placed hurried voice-mails, hugged my boyfriend and cats, and left town. That night I moved in with Dora and her two other roommates in a two-room apartment in downtown Manhattan. I got a sleeping area on the floor, an air mattress, and use of the "secretary's computer." This was my new home. I felt lonely, isolated, and scared.

When I looked at my friends, though, I realized that I was not alone. It seemed as though everyone was going through some sort of crisis. For some, these were job-related. They felt stifled in jobs that sucked up too much of their time, and were a poor match for their souls. Another dear friend had a wonderful job in which she felt challenged, secure, and appreciated. But in terms of her relationships, she was having an *Inanna-descent*. Her father had passed away two years prior, and the anniversary of his death brought back a renewed sense of loss. Her daughter, a young adult, was involved with her natural father's (my friend's ex-husband's) world, and had little time for "mom." My friend was breaking up with a boyfriend of several years, both of her cats had recently died, and her best friend at work was acting jealous, spiteful, and strange.

Meditating on this, I realized that we all go through Inanna-crises many times in our lives. When we do, we go through events that touch our core. These "Inanna-times" involve things that are very central to our lives – to our sense of comfort and security, and to our self-concepts. At the same time, they often seem to come when we, like Inanna, are emotionally mature and have the inner resources to handle intensified challenge. This doesn't mean that we're not stressed, unhappy, or downright despairing and depressed as we go through these "descents." (Generally, in the midst of these *Inanna-descents*, we are all of these.) But often, these events form the framework within which we do our deepest soul-work. This work often involves *letting go*. Like Inanna, sometimes we have to ask for help, or be willing to receive it when we are too crushed to even ask.

How does this relate to the desires that we identified in the first five chapters: our desires for power over men (or over our own lives), for attractive allure, for status, for play-time, and even for a certain "stardust" in our lives? At first glance, it seems that an *Inanna-descent* time doesn't relate at all. At such times, it may seem that being empowered, erotic, or any other fun, luscious, and wonderful life-aspect seems laughable, if not downright ludicrous. It may seem, from where we are – so very, very far down in our personal descent – that we will never be lighthearted, carefree, or playful again. This is all part of the process.

As my friend Kathy Carroll reminds me at these times, "You're in the fire. It doesn't feel as though you're powerful right now, but this is where you're most powerful. Just relax and breathe. And keep reminding yourself, 'This is temporary.'"

"Even if it lasts for the rest of your life," she adds, "it's temporary." And at that, we both laugh – but not for much or for long. At times like these, it seems as though what we're dealing with *will* last for the rest of our lives.

When we go through an *Inanna-descent*, we are doing our *pathworking* at its deepest level. As Kathy has said, "This is mastery work." As we go through these times (and despite how it seems at that moment, we *do* go through them, *and beyond*) we gain something that we would never otherwise have. We do our own, private-unto-ourselves *unveiling*.

The veils that we have inside ourselves are those that separate our "head-sense" of who we are, our "egos," from our shadow-self. This is the part of our being that not just feels fear, but crawls up into a little ball to hide. This part not just feels rage, but is willing to be totally destructive; a fire-breathing dragon. This part not just feels unloved, but feels totally unwanted, unworthy, and shamed.

Each time we go through an *Inanna-descent*, and encounter our "inner Ereshkigal," we do a small bit of taking down a veil, and a small bit of bringing that lonely, shamed, and desolate side of who we are back inside. Over time, we may even be able to give that aspect of ourselves a warm hug and an embrace. Minimally, we bring her inside and allow her to be accepted. This is where a new level of power begins. When we tap into our newly-claimed "inner Ereshkigal," we access a very primal part of ourselves.

If we want power – real power, not just power as a concept in our heads – we need all of who we are. As our "inner Ereshkigal" gets embraced and freed up inside, we access a potent source of life-energy. The rage that can come out from feeling shamed and neglected and unloved can be a powerful force as we transform our lives. Most of all, the "inner Ereshkigal" part of ourselves is where we lock up the animal side of who we are, including our sexuality. The more that we can *unveil* and accept our "inner Ereshkigal," the more that we can draw on our vital sexual energy. Ultimately, we become more erotic, more powerful, and more at peace within ourselves.

The keys, as always, are to *soften* and *release*. These are the same lessons that we have been learning all along, we're just applying them to more challenging circumstances. This is the only way that works for us, and (please believe me, especially if you are going through your own "Inanna descends into hell" experience) things will work out.

※

Like Inanna, I had lost many of the things that were ego-props. In New York, my Ph.D. gave me little advantage in my new and revised job-hunt. In fact, it was sometimes a detriment. My previous technical expertise was also to no advantage; that area had been superseded by new technologies. My credit was trashed, my dance school was gone, I had given up living in my wonderful home, and was gratefully accepting the charity of an air mattress in Dora's office/living room. During job-hunting, I amassed a good number of interviews, only to be declined again and again. I was depressed, demoralized, and thoroughly discouraged.

I figured that I was at the end of my *Inanna-descent*, and that things would have to get better.

I was wrong.

Though I had given up many props that supported my ego, I had yet to be killed and hung up on a hook. That part was yet to come. And come it did.

In the course of developing a new approach to teaching dance, both to my former students in the Southeast, and to new ones who responded to my email postings for a new interest group, I began to send out notes about what I was learning in New York. However, I hadn't cleared the material in advance with my teachers. They both took offense. I was promptly disinvited from their studios.

This is where the real ego-death came about for me. Between the drudgery of a forever-fruitless job hunt, and being cast out by both my teachers, I hit the bottom. I still got through each day, but was emotionally bereft.

This time was not without its benefits. I realized how much I had been coming from ego. I had been thoroughly humbled, and had accepted that with as much good grace and willingness as possible. Just my willingness to accept this was like strapping on booster rockets to my growth; had I resisted in the slightest, I knew that major spiritual lessons would remain to be learned, and I would be locked into a negative situation until I resolved these issues.

Once again, I remembered Kathy's words to me. "You're in the fire, Alay'nya," she had said. "When you feel the weakest, that is when you are the strongest. Besides," she continued (ever one for practical support), "think about how this will be a wonderful chapter in your book!"

Each of us, at different times, goes through our own personal descent into the Underworld. Each time, we have something to learn from the experience. Our descent can be short-term; as in when we have a severe and lengthy cold or a bout of pneumonia. Our descent can also be longer-term. My entire descent (in this instance) took over two years, and was really and truly hellacious for about the last two months of that time.

Like Inanna, I came out of that stage with a new lease on life.

I got a new round of advice from my friend Diane. "In New York, they do 'deals,'" she said. "In D.C., they work with proposals. You can write good proposals. Go to D.C.!" I did, and within two weeks, had a new job. I began to rebuild, but was physically and emotionally exhausted. My energy level was low, my concentration was poor, and my credit was in shambles.

My ego was crushed, my life-situation greatly weakened, and I didn't have the strength or wherewithal to "assert" myself anymore. Since I had no other choice, I had to become an *allower*, instead of always being an *asserter*.

I had learned a powerful lesson in *releasing resistance*. During the job hunt, I had resisted doing work for military interests, where I had previously found much success. I had resisted moving to northern Virginia, the area most tied to military and Federal contracting. Over the preceding years, I had resisted picking up certain new technical skills that would have made me more versatile. I wanted to go in a different direction, and I was *asserting* my desires.

I learned from all of this that *releasing resistance* was essential.

There is a fine line between finding our vision and staying with it through a time of unfolding, versus *asserting* our will into our lives. One of my mentors had often chided me on being "stubborn." Sometimes, we don't really know if such stubbornness is good or bad – if our vision is really the right thing and we should stay with it at all costs, or if we are attempting to "force" things in a way that is just not right for us at the moment. The ability to stick tenaciously to a vision is a quality common to all great leaders; it characterizes every person who has created "something" from "nothing." Yet life circumstances have a way of indicating what we need to do, regardless of momentary (or even long-term) preferences!

Sometimes we can't push our way towards a goal. Instead, we have to "ooze." When we can't take direct action – when life circumstances truly do force us to a "Plan B" – we can still keep feeling our desire for that which we intend to create. Then we use feedback from the "external world" to give us course-correction on how to reach towards our goal.

For example, even in my weakened and reduced state with the new job, I was attracting new miracles and wonderful people. Within the first week in the new environment, I found a wonderful chiropractor/natural healer, Dr. Dennis Sievers; he helped me rebuild strength and energy. I met Linda Heflin, who counseled me on nutrition and supplements, and who started me on the path of raw foods and raw food juicing. Between these two wonderful people, and others, I began to heal.

Within nine months of being in the new environment, the job that had brought me there closed out. Yes, I was scared. Yes, I was angry and unhappy – more at the loss of security than anything else! That afternoon, though, I started a new company – the one that I had desired to create two years prior. This time, I was in an area where I could meet and work with the people who were the best possible clients, partners, and team-members for the new venture. *Releasing resistance* to being in this place, at this time, put me exactly where I needed to be to start building out the next vision.

Over time, I was able to heal relationships with my master teachers. Also, I realized that while being with them, for a short time, was lovely, I needed to evolve my own understanding, and that required living in a different place. The initial "shattering" led to a rebuilding, and to new growth, that was far more than what I had originally envisioned.

PERSONAL PATHWORKING:

1. Dearest, how can I possibly ask something specific from you about something as big as this? Search your own heart; you will know what to do.

CHAPTER 28:
GOING DEEPER

WE ARE MYSTIFIED. INANNA RETURNS from her visit to the Underworld, where she had been put to death by her sister Ereshkigal. She has been rescued by her warrior-companion and advisor, Ninshubur, who enlisted help from Father God Enki.

What we still don't know is *why* Inanna made this journey in the first place. Didn't she know that her sister was out to get her? Didn't she know that there would be no warm welcome; no heart-to-heart chat?

Of *course* she knew. As one wise woman has said, "We *always* know. We are *never* surprised. We may choose not to take note, or not to take action, but we *always know.*" So Inanna, at some level, *knew* what was going to happen. Why did she make this journey? This is an important consideration, since she knew that she would not be able to leave easily. Even though Inanna returned to the world of the living, there was still a debt that she had to pay to the world of the dead.

Inanna was not able to return alone. *Galla,* demons of the Underworld, accompanied Inanna's return, demanding that someone be given to take her place. Once Inanna reached the surface, the *galla* variously tried to make off with Ninshubur, then Inanna's son Shara, and then her son Lulal. Each time, the person whom they tried to take was grieving for Inanna, dressed in "soiled sackcloth," and mourning for her at a holy shrine. When each of them – Ninshubur, Shara, and Lulal – saw Inanna, they "threw [themselves] in the dust at her feet."[1] Each time, Inanna defended them against the *galla.*

Finally, the group came upon Dumuzi, Inanna's husband. He was not wearing sackcloth, nor was he mourning:

In Uruk, by the big apple tree,

Dumuzi, the husband of Inanna, was dressed in his shining *me* garments.

He sat on his magnificent throne; (he did not move)...

Inanna fastened on Dumuzi the eye of death.

She spoke against him the word of wrath.

She uttered against him the cry of guilt:

"Take him! Take Dumuzi away!"[2]

Inanna had loved Dumuzi. At their wedding, she had praised him and proclaimed him worthy of sharing her domain.[3] Yet something had changed during their marriage. Previously, their hymns had resounded with joy and passion. Now, with his wife and queen missing for three days, Dumuzi could not be bothered. He was free to enjoy himself; he was ruling alone in her absence.

When Inanna took her journey, she was alone. When she was put to death by her sister, she was alone. When she was rescued, the rescue came from her devoted, trusted companion, and from Father God Enki and his creatures – not from her husband!

Now it makes sense. Inanna made her journey in order to provoke the situation with her husband. She wanted to make clear what she already knew, so that she and everyone else would have the truth staring in their faces.

When Inanna and Dumuzi first met, they were a perfect match for each other, each dwelling both on their own and their mate's splendor. They were full of excitement and passion for their lovemaking. Yes, at that time, they were *both* shallow and self-centered. In short, they were full of themselves, and young. However, two children and a kingdom later, they had grown in different ways.

Dumuzi was an accurate reflection of the youthful Inanna. The young queen was unabashedly in love with herself. Yet, her love for Dumuzi was also real. She honored him, and she shared rulership with him. In keeping with the largesse of her personality, she held nothing back from him.

Dumuzi came from an ancient and noble family. However, he received his kingship through his marriage with Inanna, when he became a co-ruler with her of the city of Uruk. Thus, Dumuzi courted Inanna to obtain this role. He made a point of asserting that his lineage – and his immediate family – was as good as hers. He courted her with romance and sweetness, saying, "My sister, I would go with you to my garden."[4]

Over time, though, his real interests became clear. Dumuzi was more interested in his role as ruler than he was in her. Inanna recounts how he spoke to her:

> "Now, my sweet love is sated.
> Now he says:
> 'Set me free, my sister, set me free...'"[5]

Inanna grieves the loss of his love, of what they once shared, saying "How sweet was your allure..."[6]

Inanna was a strong woman. She had exceptional self-esteem. Yet even with her immense ego, she had given Dumuzi both respect and honor, describing herself as his "armor-bearer" and his "advocate."[7] Inanna was extraordinary, by any standards. Yet, when whatever love Dumuzi may have had for her died, she was ready to die herself. That, of course, is precisely what happened. She *did* die, although (since this is an allegorical story) she came back to life. Her death and resurrection brought great clarity.

There are times that each of us must do our own journey to the Underworld. We must embrace our "dark side." In fact, the more that we aspire to be of value in this world, the more essential it is that we take on this journey.

Each of us has an "inner Ereshkigal," as described by authors Wolkstein and Kramer in their analysis of the Inanna story.[8] She is an activation of our *pain-body*. Our "inner Ereshkigal" is where we store the shamed, unloved, and pained part of ourselves. Like Ereshkigal, this aspect of us appears to be very *unlovely*. Therefore, we try to keep this aspect hidden from others. In fact, we try to keep this hidden from ourselves. However, like the Ereshkigal of the Inanna legend, our "inner Ereshkigal" has *enormous* powers of destruction – a destruction wrought from feelings of pain.

Relatively few of us will completely eliminate our *pain-body*, or "inner Ereshkigal." All of us, though, can learn to discern when it is active. As my friend Kathy says, "We need to embrace and love that part of ourselves that is so unloving. That brings down the wall of separation." Kathy would describe this as discovering our *core wounds*.

⁘

Each of us has one or more painful yet powerful experiences (*core wounds*) which influence how we believe our world – and ourselves – to "be." Based on our interpretation of these experiences, we create beliefs. These beliefs act as filters on how we experience the world around us. These belief-filters shape and distort our perception of the world.

While this is difficult and challenging enough, we add yet another layer. We not only interpret our life events in light of our *core wounds*, but we actively draw into our lives – we *create* – experiences that will replay our *core wound*s for us, with all the associated pathos and drama.

This means that in every relationship that we undertake, we will not only draw into our lives someone who is a "mirror" for how we are, we also (often with the same person) cause, or set up events, to re-enact our *core wound* experiences.

Each of us, no matter how spiritual we are – no matter how evolved, and no matter how much "inner work" we have done – will have (or have had) *core wounds*. We can speculate that even Jesus had a *core wound*; as he was growing up, other children (in a village where everyone counted the number of months between Mary's marriage and his birth) knew that he was conceived before his mother was married. The children would have taunted him with being a bastard, saying, "Who is your *real* father?" Jesus found peace with this through knowledge of God as his Heavenly Father. This addressed his *core wound*. Yet as he died on the cross, he felt abandoned. The Bible attests to this, calling him in prophecy, "A man of sorrows, and acquainted with grief."[9] The emotional devastation was as great as the physical pain.

If even Jesus can possibly have had a *core wound*, then it is a given that each of us does as well. Our *core wounds* surface throughout our lives. They especially come up in our intimate relationships.

Inanna appeared to be healthy and happy. She had an immensely strong ego. Yet by the time she traveled to the Underworld, she had been carrying, for many years, a deep wound. She had accepted Dumuzi as her husband, had honored him, and had held nothing back from him. Then, she realized that his interest was not in her, but in the position that he was able to get *through* her.

Despite her inner knowing, Inanna was still locked into marriage with Dumuzi. What was she going to do: divorce him because he no longer loved her? That was, if he had *ever* loved her? Remember, this situation had been going on for *years*, and superficially, everything seemed just fine. Her two sons adored her, her country was peaceful and prosperous, and Dumuzi (we can bet on this) *always* treated her with courtesy and respect — especially in public! Dumuzi relished his role as king, and was probably very good at it.

When Inanna reached the point where she could no longer "live the lie" — when the difference between the stately image of her marriage and the lack of love from her husband was no longer tolerable — she had to make a change. She needed a *trigger incident*. She needed one that was big enough, loud enough, and resounding enough so that even the most complacent, the most status quo-loving member of her domain would have to admit, "It was enough."

Thus, she made the trip to the Underworld.

She did this not because she wanted to see her sister-goddess. Most certainly, she did not think the visit might heal old wounds, create a little bonding, and get her away from the palace for a few days.

Let's visualize the scene as Inanna returns to Uruk, her seat of power. She had already told Ninshubur what to do if she didn't return. ("If?" we might ask. "What 'if'? She knew very well what was going to happen.") She had left with head held high, looking gorgeous. She returns looking, very literally, like "death warmed over." (Wouldn't any of us, if we'd been hung on a hook to rot for three days?)

Ninshubur is tear-streaked and exhausted, having gone head-to-head with each of the three Father Gods. Someone has thrown Inanna a cloak, or pulled a shift down from someone's wash-line, so Inanna's not exactly naked, but certainly she's not in her high-court finery. Each of her sons, as she meets them on her return, is dressed in dirty, stained "sackcloth." Their faces are tear-stained, they haven't shaved in three days, and they are simultaneously exhausted with grief and jubilant that their mother is back. And then, of course, there's the *galla* – nasty stick-like things, "hated and feared by men"[10] – that accompany her.

Not to mention that by this time everyone, Inanna included, probably *stinks*. (Hanging on a hook for three days … not a part of our beauty and pampering ritual, is it?)

This is the fine assembly that approaches Dumuzi, who is handsomely groomed, because he has to keep things going while his wife has outlandishly abandoned her responsibilities. Dumuzi is dressed in his beautiful, luminous *me* garments, and is sitting on his throne. He sees them approach: his wife, his wife's most faithful and trusted companion (one who has loyally served his wife at least since their teenage years), and his two sons. And *he doesn't move.*

He doesn't want to get associated with their dirt, their muss, their drama. He doesn't want to look bad. And he certainly doesn't want their stink to rub off on him.

If his wife wanted to foolishly go off and put herself in danger, and upset everything that they had worked for over the past few decades, then *someone* had to keep the country going, right? Yes, the loving husband.

Inanna's descent is well-known, and because it is so dramatic, we tend to focus on it. However, the point of the story is not so much the descent, nor is it the return. The real point is the *reason* why she did this, and the *change* she wrought via this terrible passage. *Galla* haul Dumuzi off to the Underworld, in a fate that he alternates with his sister, Geshtinanna. (Geshtinanna loves her brother; things get a little interesting there – she volunteers to share his fate, on an alternating half-year basis.) Henceforth, Dumuzi spends half the year in the Underworld, and during that time, Inanna is effectively a widow.

Whatever happens after this, in both their joint rulership and their marriage, things are by no means the same as what they were before.

Inanna's story can be seen as a metaphor for creating change in a stuck situation that has become truly untenable at a deep level, but is still so superficially comfortable that no one really wants to "rock the boat." It is about creating a pivot point; about forcing a transition. It is about great courage, and willingness to not only seem, but actually be, "out of one's head." Certainly Inanna's approach was outside of any logical, rational, cognitive way of dealing with things. Her story is about dealing with situations where company reorganizations, team-building exercises, and therapy simply will not work. It is about going radical, and destroying a suffocating old order, in order to make the underlying truth known, and starting a from-scratch rebuild.

People go through *Inanna-descents*; so do churches and companies, and so do countries. The global financial crisis of 2008-2009 was an *Inanna-descent* for all of us. Yet, it was a breakdown that *had* to happen. What seemed lovely on the outside (the market was up, prosperity abounded) was hiding a mass of exaggerated expectations, layers of leveraged financial instruments, numerous deceits, and a completely unstable underpinning. Despite the pain and the trauma, we needed this in order to have a *chance* at some new level of sanity. (This is not to say that we have or haven't gotten sane, just that we've needed a *chance* at it.) The financial and ecological shocks that we have had lately are *Inanna-descents* on a global scale; to some extent, we've all participated in them.

Let's bring this home.

We not only go through *Inanna-descents* from time to time, we *need* them. Sometimes, the only way to clear out a stuck and stagnant situation is to take dramatic action. This is much like when an earthquake releases the tectonic plate pressure that has built up over time.

When we do an Inanna-style cleansing (and keep in mind, the point of the story is not the descent and return, but the resultant shockwave and cleansing of the status quo), we look as though we have just plain gone crackers. We've abnegated our responsibility. We've gone completely cuckoo. We're out of our heads.

Literally, we are. We are most certainly outside of our familiar and safe rational selves by this time.

Keep in mind: an event with the force, the drama, and the huge repercussions of an Inanna-style descent and return has tremendous tension leading up to it. This kind of experience doesn't just happen out of the blue, even if it seems to be coming up "all at once." Rather, this is a last resort. By the time that we "go Inanna," we have tried everything else, and it has failed.

Don't we think that Inanna tried, with Dumuzi, to regain the love and passion (and even the affection) that she *thought* enlivened their earlier relationship? It is more than likely that each of us has gone through a lost relationship (or two or three); we *know* what we do when we try to "save the relationship" (or marriage).

I've had multiple *Inanna-descents*, and many of us can probably say the same. As I look back on them, they *each presaged a needed change.* In my life, two of the biggest descents or losses, each going on for a lengthy period of time, initially seemed to be about money. They were really about relationships.

At one crucial point, I was putting all my energies into starting a new business, despite awareness that I was running out (and in fact had run out) of money. Business opportunities that I had lined up fell through. At the same time, I was making new inventions that were not only major breakthroughs, they were likely to be very lucrative – if deployed correctly. If I kept on with my new business, I would not only create, but I and my investors would own, substantial new intellectual property. There was a good chance that we would all make enormous amounts of money. However, if I got a "regular job," the first thing I'd be asked to do would be to sign over all inventions I would make during my employment.

I had a choice between going for the comfort and seeming-security of a job, or walking the thin financial tightrope of starting a new business. Should I give over my next round of inventions to a new employer, or chance changing the world and becoming wealthy in the process? This was the choice described by Milton, in *Paradise Lost*, as between "reign[ing] in Hell" versus "serv[ing] in Heaven."[11] I tucked my head down, kept going, ran out of funds, and ran off the cliff.

At the same time, of course, I was not in my very best (and comfortable and familiar) *Amazon* state. I had succumbed to the dopey-making effects of dopamine, and was running with an "over-the-limit" level of oxytocin. (Over-the-limit for practical and sane decision-making, that is.)

Theo, of course, knew all of this. I asked for his help, seeking his active support and business acumen more than anything else. I had romanticized and idealized Theo, believing (at the time) that he was a "superior being" compared to most men that I had known. I had lost perspective!

My then-mentor was appalled at my lack of "awareness," at my "expectation" that Theo would take care of me. Theo, of course, "sat on his magnificent throne; (he did not move)..." Rather, he moved ever so discretely out of my life.

Was this my letting go of responsibility, or was it an Inanna-action?

David Deida, in *The Way of the Superior Man*, says:

> ... if a man abnegates his responsibility to provide his woman with the
> gift of masculine clarity and decisiveness, then she will ... become her
> own man.[12]

Like Inanna, we tend to give, we tend to honor. Once we've decided that a man is the "right one," we hold nothing back. Our nurturing *Isis* combines with our succulent *Hathor*, and the lovely wash of intimacy-inducing neurochemicals blot out conscious awareness of everything else. But a deep, knowing aspect inside us pushes us to see if the man truly is worthy of the honor that we have given by selecting him, and are willing to continue to give.

It is at times like these that our inner *High Priestess* comes to our rescue. She does so not with the direct take-charge actions of our *Amazon*, but by bringing us to greater awareness. Sometimes, she works by bringing us into a life-situation where the harsh dose of reality washes out the blurry good-feelings of our emotionally-connected *Isis* and *Hathor*. We need to switch, in Myers-Briggs or Jungian terms, from Feeling to Thinking. Our inner *High Priestess* does this for us. She does not "think" in the traditional, linear, cognitive sense that most of us are used to. Rather, she thinks in a very non-linear, holistic, and intuitive (iNtuition, or N) manner. What our feeling-oriented *Isis* and *Hathor*-aspects, enmeshed in personal relations, are not willing to confront, our *High Priestess* already knows. She brings this to our attention.

We test our men, to see if they are willing to exert their masculinity on our behalf. We note that the "man" in this situation need not be an intimate partner. He is not necessarily a husband or lover. He can be a boss, a respected person in the family, or a trusted mentor. "He" can be the actual job situation or company in which we work, or even our church, expressed as either our local or global religious structure. "He" can even be a woman, who is coming more from her *Amazon* essence than from awareness of being an integrated person.

So what if the man holds back? What if he is willing to use his *Emperor* protective and sustaining mode in building his career, but not to give us the benefit of his analysis and strategic thinking? What if he exerts his *Magician's* creativity brilliantly on the job, but not at all to help us? What if he shares his *Hierophant* wisdom with masculine colleagues or fellow Masons, but not with us?

We have to know. And sometimes, we really do know; we simply need it to be made very, *very* clear. Thus, we create the "Inanna moment." At the end, when we acknowledge that one particular man (not all, we are not blaming the species) has cared only for himself, we call on our inner *Amazon*.

Our *High Priestess* brings awareness. Our *Amazon* rebuilds.

It is grueling. It is exhausting. (Do we think that Inanna had fun, putting her domain back in order, with her husband down in the Underworld? We think of all the committee meetings she had to attend, the advisors with whom she had to meet, and the decisions she had to make. She was picking up her workload, and his, and handling everyone's crisis along with her own sorrow.) Inanna, who could be very loving and generous (*Isis*), and very, *very* much in favor of pleasure in all its forms (*Hathor*), called on her own *Amazon* nature.

Like Inanna, we need our inner *Amazon*. It is she who not only provides us with bounds and sanctuary, but also with protection and provenance. Our *Amazon* makes it safe for us to enter into our *Isis*, our *Hathor*, and our *High Priestess* modes. Even those of us who have external protection require an *Amazon* aspect, at least sometimes. Our *Amazon* helps us create and hold our boundaries, which are needed even in the best of jobs, and the best of relations.

❧❧

With Theo, I knew (or my *High Priestess* knew) that he wanted only the "show" of a relationship. What I wanted most from him was not so much direct support (that would have been lovely, but not necessary). I wanted to have the benefit of his advice, his input; the sense that in a crisis, he was on my side.

Sadly enough, he wasn't.

My *Amazon* came to my own rescue. With the help of family, friends, and church members, I rebuilt my life, profoundly grateful for those who saw me through. I moved into new technology areas, and created new ventures.

At the same time, what came very much to the front was a re-opening of one of my own *core wounds*, a feeling of being abandoned by the important man in my life. I had to stay soft and experience this fully, while still focusing on survival-activities. This was probably the greatest experience that I have ever had in practicing *releasing resistance* and *softening*.

As we do this inner work, we start dissolving the barriers that prevent us from experiencing our *core wounds*. This does not mean that we eliminate the *core wound* experiences. In fact, it means that (especially at first) we re-experience these emotions as poignantly and as painfully as we did the first time. This happens because we stop walling off our awareness.

By the time that we've done this level of work, we are probably far less interested in power (erotic or any other form) than we were when we began. By now, we have realized that yearnings for power are part of our ego-self. We know that; we've called ourselves on that, and we are on to our own game. (This doesn't mean that we've given up our game-playing; it's just that we have more insight into and awareness of what we're doing.)

As we go through all of this training – this learning to be both honest with ourselves and present with others – something remarkable occurs. Actually, two very remarkable things happen.

First, our ability to be with someone else – totally being with them in that moment, truly hearing what they have to say, and appreciating them fully for who they are – increases dramatically. We have learned to lessen the amount of "mental noise" that distorts our attention and awareness. We can perceive what is being said to us – in many different ways – much more clearly. Our increased ability to "listen" to another is possibly the most powerful and erotically charged thing that we bring to our time with another person. We are now much more able to give someone else our full attention. This is a rare gift for anyone to receive.

Second, we have begun to open up to our own energy. By the time that we've learned to identify and release tension patterns, to breathe into our entire bodies, and to lessen the energy-grabbing hold that our "inner-Ereshkigal" has, we begin to have more vital energy. Yes, this literally is the *ch'i* quality that infuses the greatest yogis and martial artists. This is also the subject of the next chapter.

If we are not in the kind of relationship that we desire, as we step back and examine our recent relationships, we may see that we are dramatically shifting our patterns. This is a kind of chrysalis time. This is a time-unto-ourselves. Drawing in a new intimate relationship, before we have shifted our pattern, is much like forcibly opening up the chrysalis before its time. But if we can wait, the butterfly – our refined self – will emerge. This interim, or chrysalis, time is valuable for *processing*.

We do a lot of *processing*. We clear out a great deal of our *pain-body* influences; we learn to detect when our *pain-body* is acting out. We get much more sane and balanced. At the same time, to use an analogy, we are like onions.

Jerry, a friend of mine with great carpentry and handyman skills, recently took a job replacing the flooring on someone's kitchen. He took a look at the new tiling, and decided that the best way to do the job was not to just lay the new tiles on the old linoleum, but to strip off the old flooring and lay the tiles on the original surface.

He didn't realize, at first, how many layers of linoleum were stuck together. Hammer and chisel were not enough. Crowbars were not enough. Finally, a blowtorch and lots of sweaty hard work were enough to remove the old, caked layers.

During the time that I was doing my own *Inanna-descent*, I felt much like the old house that Jerry was describing, only worse! The first stages had been getting the "boxes of junk" in my self-scape out of the way. This was just clearing the path so that work could get done! Peeling back my layers of determined resistance was a blowtorch-level effort. Then, I repeated exactly the mistakes I had warned others against (and knew about) in my relationship with Theo. This time, my then-mentor clearly pointed out the ways in which I was indulging in romanticism, and was failing to take responsibility for my own life. As I later realized, this was just the first layer of linoleum!

If life were easy (and it never is), I could have put down some nice, new tiling and moved blithely on to my next set of goals. But instead, peeling back my "resistance" of romanticizing Theo, and pretending that he would help me through a crisis (or guide me through the time) when things got rough, exposed a whole group of *core wounds* that made my fears of real intimacy painfully clear. This was like finding that the wooden joists under the subflooring were riddled with mold and mildew!

Deeper dives into why I was creating these romantic fantasies – and my ego assertions – were like finding a basement under the moldy timbers full of swampy muck! This *unveiling* process is often not romantically beautiful. That which we *unveil*, however we do it, often shows us areas that need intensive cleansing.

Even if we find ourselves surrounded with layer after layer of debris and the exposed inner-mold of our psyches (our real "inner Ereshkigal"), we do have something beautiful to claim, and that is our journey. We have each had to do an enormous amount of hard work to get to the place of discovering that which is truly ugly. In the process of getting there, and owning that aspect of ourselves, we are creating beauty.

This is again lot like renovating a house. We are each a "work in progress." We are not yet ready for the *House Beautiful* multi-page spread. However, the pathway that we are forging to create beauty is perhaps far more exciting than the finished result.

In our *Isis* and *Hathor* modes, we want to nurture, connect, and create intimacy. Our brain chemistry changes when we move into these modes. Under the influence of our neurohormones, our boundaries soften and sometimes dissolve. We may know that we are giving way, *way* too much (of our heart if nothing else), but can't seem to pull ourselves into a more "rational" frame of mind.

Remember that our *High Priestess*, much more internal, and much more deeply aware, intuits when we have gone too far. It is this aspect of ourselves that communicates our deepest sense of knowing: our wisdom. It is she who tells us, "It's time to leave this job/lover/living situation/friend …" Our *High Priestess* is aware of when she is not being honored, and causes us to pull back.

As we do, and as we re-create our lives, our *Amazon* is our strongest ally. Her no-nonsense, take-charge, get-things-done attitude helps us establish priorities and focus our energies. Most of all, she helps us set and defend our boundaries. This is vitally important as we become more and more able to play with *ch'i*, or personal energy.

Integrating our various core archetypes influences how we assess our relationships. Also, this directly impacts how we evaluate men.

We are able to come full circle, and look back at our first response to the ages-old question, "What do women want?" From *Chapter 1*, we had an early (and superficial) answer; "dominion over men." Now, we realize that this answer came from a time and place where we had little power and few rights. This has been largely remedied over the past two centuries. Now that we can provide for ourselves that which we previously could obtain only indirectly, we are less interested in "mastery" over men. Thanks to our opportunities to exert our inner *Amazon*, we can now develop mastery in our own lives.

As we bridge from being *Amazon*-focused to a more integrated dynamic, we change our criteria for evaluating men and potential relationships. To the extent that we are in our *Amazon* modes, we judge men by *Amazonian* standards. Simply put, we know that if and when we shift *out* of our *Amazon* to any of our "softer, gentler" modes (whether they are *Isis*, *Hathor*, or *High Priestess*), we are less able to provide for ourselves from within the *Amazonian* framework. We are masters of time-slicing and multi-tasking, but there are only so many hours in the day. Further, whenever we submit to the double-dosing of dopamine and oxytocin, we are less interested in metering out time in 15-minute "billable increments." We simply want to experience connectedness and flow.

This means that when we (consciously or subliminally) consider easing towards a state of receptiveness, at least a part of our attention is on the quality of the person (or organization or belief) with whom (or with which) we are joining. If we are releasing our *Amazon* persona in relationship with a man, we traditionally give at least some attention to his apparent ability to care for us in a pragmatic way. Mary Batten, in *Sexual Strategies*, compares a man flashing his credit card to a male firefly flashing his natural bioluminescence. Males of all species know that females do the selection.[13]

What we find, though, is that our personal definition of a "successful" or "desirable" male may change. This is often a function of not just experience, but personal growth and increased awareness. We become less focused on a man who simply makes a lot of money (or has power, status, or other social accoutrements). We become more interested in a man who has taken on true responsibility for himself; one who has become, in Deida's terms, a *superior man*. This is a much more demanding requirement. However, it is a necessary one.

PERSONAL PATHWORKING:

1. Go back to the various timelines that you've constructed. Identify the times where you have undergone your own *Inanna-descents*. There are the obvious times: a divorce, a job loss, a lengthy illness. There are also the not-so-obvious ones: living for a prolonged time in an area, or with people, where you felt isolated or emotionally drained; where the environment was more an "Underworld" than a place where you felt supported, nourished, and happy. You may have been in a job that was simply not the right one for you. Long transition times, such as being in a job that you don't like, while actively looking for the right one, also count. For the moment, simply identify those times as your personal "descents into the Underworld." It doesn't matter how many, or how few, or even that two or more different *descents* may have gone on simultaneously. (An example would be breaking up with a boyfriend while going through chemotherapy for cancer.) What is important now is simply to recognize each distinct *descent* in your life.

2. Who played the "Ereshkigal" role during your personal "Underworld" journeys? This may be obvious; a peevish roommate, an unappreciative or manipulative boss, even a lover who undercut or demeaned you. This may be more subtle: the job environment or corporation itself, or the place in which you lived. Look for what manifested as your "shadow" – that aspect of you that you didn't want to see, but was in yourself as much as it was in the person or situation.

3. In each case, how did you finally break free? There may be both the overt and the more subtle aspects here as well. If your "Underworld" was a job, and your "Ereshkigal" was your boss, you may have started an all-out job search. That would have been the overt action. At the more subtle level, you may have had to give up some sort of dream or ideal in order to become free again. For example, you may have been in a job that had

a lot of prestige, and paid very well, but was a "slow death" for your soul. How did you come to realize that peace of mind, or using other gifts, was worth the price of transition?

4. Similarly, before you broke free, a part of you would have had an "ego-death" of some sort. Can you identify where and what that was? What did you learn from that time?

5. What did you realize, and how were you changed, by each of these *descents*? In some translations of the Inanna legend, Inanna pushes her sister Ereshkigal off Ereshkigal's own throne, thus claiming her sister's *me* (special gifts).[14] (This was, of course, just before she was put to death.) Inanna, being Inanna, liked to get everything that she could; but after she emerged from this encounter with her sister, Inanna became *Queen of Heaven and Earth*. Her sister remained *Queen of the Underworld*. Did you gain any new knowledge, insight, or realm of personal mastery as a consequence of emerging from your descent? Did you ultimately create a much better life-situation?

6. We have to thank those who have helped us. Who was your "Father Enki," and who was your "Ninshubur"? Who were your little "sprite-spirits" that got you free?

7. Finally, of course, there is Dumuzi. Who – or what – was the "Dumuzi" in your life? How did your story resolve? (It may, of course, still be resolving.)

CHAPTER 29:
PRAGMATIC ESOTERICS

IF THERE IS ONE THING that women want these days – more than sex or status, more than playtime, and more even than cultivating a little "stardust" – it is *juice*. *Life force*, *juice*, or *vital energy*, whatever we call it, we simply want – and need – a whole lot more. This is probably our single greatest desire, right after getting a good night's sleep. With *juice*, we can conquer the world. Without it, we are wan, depleted, and constantly "running on fumes," when we would much prefer to have a full tank of fuel and a finely-honed, powerful engine at our disposal. In short, we both want and need our very own, personal *Fountain of Youth*.

Fortunately, the secrets to getting this *juice* into our lives have already been discovered. We simply need to re-discover them, and use them in an intelligent manner. We need to translate the insights and mechanisms for *juice-generation* that have been known for thousands of years into simple, practical everyday terms. Then, we need to figure out how to apply these *juice-generation* techniques to our own lives.

We know that we're ready for this. Over the past decades, in addition to increasing our lifespan, we've also radically re-organized our life principles. We know all about supplements and exercise. Many of us have taken up yoga, Pilates, and other practices resulting in enhanced youthfulness and vitality. We are ready, because we no longer treat the predecessor steps – such as yoga, and even meditation – as being too "far out" or esoteric. Rather, there is now a yoga studio in nearly every other shopping center.

However, the yoga that most of us practice is simply *hatha yoga*; the physical component. We may have teachers who discuss *pranayama* methods with us, or who teach *kundalini yoga* (the art and science of raising "serpent energy" up our spines; a very close cousin to *juice-generation*.) Relatively few of us, though, have had a *kundalini* awakening. This is largely regarded – within yogic circles – as a supercharged experience; one that requires a great deal of both mind and body cleansing before it can be done safely. We may not want to invoke something so extreme. Yet, at the same time, we are definitely ready to have a *lot* more *vital energy* in our lives.

Some of us are already sensitized to how this *juice*, or this extra *vital energy* or *ch'i*, might feel. We may feel a "tingly something" when we practice T'ai Chi or give someone a massage. We may feel the *charge* that we get from certain powerful, energized people – and want to get that quality in our own lives! The question is, then: How can we do this repeatedly and reliably, and *at will*?

There are three overall areas in which we would reasonably ask questions:

1. **Getting Started:** How do we access this *juice*, *vital energy*, or *ch'i* the first time? What does it feel like, and how do we know that we've "gotten it," or "done it," right?

2. **Working It:** Once we've managed to create this *vital energy* "flow" the first time, how can we bring it under our direct control and keep this *juice* going? What promotes or sustains this *vital energy*, and what diminishes it? What can we do *with* this *ch'i*? Are there any downsides?

3. **The "Extra Edge":** Does *ch'i* circulation help our health? Will we live longer? Will it cure warts, arthritis, and cancer? More importantly, will it affect our sex lives? And can it do even more?

This notion of *juice*, or *vital energy* has already been a subject – albeit a bit indirectly – throughout this book. It also may not be too foreign to us. We may have had significant experiences with this in our personal lives. We may already have a sense of what it is that we are after, and are now simply following the breadcrumb path of clues in learning more about our *vital energy*, much like we have been piecing together clues about our overall woman's *integration pathway*. In fact, by now it should be no surprise that this aspect of *vital energy* cultivation would be an intrinsic and essential aspect of such a *path*.

I have been on the trail of *juice* discovery throughout my life. In fact, this has been a major component of my personal *quest*; one that has underlain my study of both martial arts and Oriental dance. Early in life, I discovered a natural affinity for energy work. I could feel things with a greater degree of empathy and awareness than seemed normal. The depictions of *vital energy*, or *ch'i*, within the martial arts were a major reason that I began martial arts study. It was as though I had a set of *juice-tuned* antennae; these kept me oriented to where I could learn the most about this quality. And of course, I later brought both my personal search and practice into my studio.

"You have an esoteric dance school," said Kathy, several years ago. She was helping me to make sense out of something that had just torn the roots out from me. My assistant instructor, Sally, with whom I'd entrusted all my beginning students, had just told me that she was resigning – to form her own competing business! What's more, she was taking all of the beginner students with her. She sent out a letter to all the beginners, telling them that everything would proceed as usual; they were just in her school now! (And as people are wont to do, none of them had thought to check back with me on this new "arrangement.")

I was devastated in a business sense. Clearly, I had trusted too much. But there was more to it than that; this was a tremendous personal loss as well. "The school was your baby," Kathy continued, "but you left it with the sitter. You gave too much to Sally, and this is the result."

"You'll learn something from this, Alay'nya," she continued, "and you'll put it in your book."

I snuffled and sobbed, but felt better after talking with her. Over the next several years, I continued to think about what she had meant. With time, the understanding *did* become clear. I realized that I was not running a standard "belly dance" studio at all. Even though I taught, and we all practiced, the physical forms of Oriental dance, our fundamental orientation towards energy work permeated everything that we did. This gave greater richness, and indeed succulence, to our movements!

In the classes that I taught, we used dance as means for developing greater personal awareness and as a means of tapping into the *Sacred Feminine*. We also used it for healing ourselves emotionally. In fact, those women who came into my studio looking for life-healing were far greater in number than those who simply wanted to study Oriental dance. I was attracting women who had personal *quests* similar mine.

In contrast, those who were drawn to my former assistant instructor were attracted to her approach. In this context, our separation was appropriate and natural. I realized that those students who were aligned with my own purpose and vision would ultimately find their way to me. This gave me a sense of complete-ness and closure, and helped me to focus on finding that "esoteric" or energy-work aspect that was unique to my studio.

My first Oriental dance teacher was a woman named Medea. I didn't know then that I wanted this dance art; what I *did* know was that much though I loved the energy, intensity, and focus of the martial arts, I had realized that these arts were no longer right for me. I had moved progressively from the so-called "hard" styles to "softer" ones; from the elegantly austere forms of Shotokan karate to the more rounded Chinese styles. In these latter arts, "energy work" was part of the main menu. But still, I was restless. Something was missing. I was ready for a more feminine art form.

My chiropractor friend David said, "The most powerful woman that I know is a woman named Medea, and she teaches belly dance." I was in her next class.

Medea, a protégé of the internationally-known Cassandra[1], had begun teaching a more energy-based approach to dance. What I got out of even my first class with Medea carried me through many years and many other dance teachers, not all of whom understood the energy aspects of this dance. Without her unique insights, I would have passed this off as a simple physical art.

Medea had studied yoga. Her lover was also her guru. He had, she explained, taught her to bring up her energy during love-making – and to give it to him! Then they broke up. What, she wondered, was she going to do with her energy, if she wasn't going to give it over to a man? She finally figured it out. As she told us, "Instead of giving it to him, I've learned to bring it up, and then to 'fountain' it back down and take it in again!"

Medea was the first woman I met who knew how to create, direct, and use her personal energy. Since then, I've met many others with the same insights and gifts. Many have been involved with dance or some form of body art, or they focus on *body/mind* healing and integration. Others simply have the basic ability, and have cultivated it through consistent practice and study.

⊗

One of my first teachers in the Chinese martial arts was Danny, a handsome young man who moved beautifully. I was entranced with his energy. He seemed to have a "special something"; an energetic quality that was possessed by very few. I could almost "feel" when he entered the room, and promptly developed a grand, teenage-level "crush" on him.

Finally, I realized that this would be an "unrequited love." I gave myself over to feeling the pain.

Instead of sinking into greater levels of misery, something else happened. The best way I can describe it is by reference to an event in the biblical story of Moses. The Israelites were in the desert, and lacked for water. God spoke to Moses, and said: "Take the rod and assemble the congregation ... and tell the rock before their eyes to yield its water ..."[2] Moses struck the rock with his staff, rather than speaking to it. The rock complied anyway, gushing forth life-giving water.

Something similar happened to me that day. No one said a word, or struck me with a stick, but I felt something open up inside – much like water coming out of a rock. It lasted only for a few seconds, but I recognized it as being the same energetic essence as what Danny had. I told him about this experience. He was clearly not comfortable with my having this ability, and was perhaps even less comfortable with my gaining something that his other devoted acolytes did not possess. (This would have disturbed the social-power structure within his following.) Within two weeks, he politely but firmly invited me to leave.

Devastated, I quickly found another martial arts group, and found that in this class, such energy experiences were the norm, not the exception! My new teacher was Ron Sieh, and he taught a range of Chinese internal martial arts, including T'ai Chi Ch'uan. I studied with him for a year, and then, after I moved from the area, with his teacher, Peter Ralston.[3]

I remember one class, in which Ron was working with an advanced student, and I was doing basic partner-play with another. My back was to Ron and his partner, but I heard Ron describing the technique. "Create an energy vortex that is away from your body to draw your opponent's attention," said Ron. "Like this."

With my back to him, I could feel him creating the "energy-hole" that pulled his partner's strike. It was as though he was turning a light switch on, then off, then on, … "And Alay'nya," Ron added (without looking at me), "Pay attention to what *you're* supposed to be doing!" (Ron was a great teacher, by the way. His book, *T'ai Chi Ch'uan: The Internal Tradition*, does a superb job of explaining what he taught us in class.[4])

Over time, although I was working with the "best of the best" in martial arts, I found myself increasingly drawn to Oriental dance. Once again, I found excellent teachers. Sometimes it took travel to get to them, but they were, in their genre, again the "master teachers." It wasn't until I opened my own studio, though, that I found the teachers who helped me with real breakthroughs. These various teachers and facilitators gave me core insights. I built on what they taught me, and created ways to integrate the physical dance motions with energy cultivation and circulation. This has become the foundation of what, by now, truly has become an "esoteric dance school."

This hearkens back to the first set of questions that we were likely to ask, posed at beginning of this chapter. The first, and most obvious starting question that we can ask is simply: what does this *juice* (*vital energy*, or *ch'i*) feel like? As a close follow-on, we might also ask: how do we know that we are correctly identifying this *vital energy* or *juice factor*? Similarly, we might also ask: how do we know that we are doing the "right" sort of *juice* practice or *vital energy* access?

Simply put, this kind of *ch'i* flow *feels good*. In fact, it feels *very* good. This is really our primary reason for creating this ability.

Imagine creating a drink. We could have just cranberry juice, perhaps with a bit of lime juice thrown in. This is like working with our physical bodies alone. Let's pretend that the cranberry juice is good, ordinary sexual excitement and pleasure. The lime juice is the extra "oomph" that we get if our bodies are well-toned through exercise, with lots of wonderful endorphins circulating.

Now, imagine that we add in a little vodka and triple sec. We've just made a *Cosmopolitan*. Isn't this more interesting? This is like mixing our physical sensory responses with internal energy, or *ch'i*. The sum is much greater than the parts! (Yes, of course, many of us who are doing energy work refrain from alcohol and other substances that can affect our consciousness. Please think of this as an analogy only, and not a recommendation.)

The way in which I spontaneously accessed my *vital energy*, or *ch'i*, for the first time is one instance of how this might happen. Some of my students say that they've had this ability all their lives. Others of us may find that our *ch'i* "opens up" in response to a deep yearning, perhaps coupled with a moment of release.

Suppose that we decide that we do indeed want to experience this. How then do we access our *vital energy*, or *ch'i*, the first time? My primary suggestion would be to study and practice with those who have already accessed their *ch'i*. The idea behind this suggestion is that our bodies and entire internal energy systems are designed to be fully operational. However, we have gotten stagnant with the mental demands, physical stresses, and the various environmental and social "toxins" in our lives. We can potentially re-awaken our innate energy abilities through contact with someone who has already developed his or her *ch'i*. This is a lot like putting one tuning fork in a room with another. If we strike the first tuning fork, the second will begin to resonate also. Similarly, if we use an electrical current to generate a magnetic field, then this field can induce a secondary electric current in a neighboring system. By way of analogy, this method of "induction" has been used by gurus and master teachers over many millennia to bring students to the next level of ability.

The persons that are most useful in this area will very likely *not* be offering to awaken our energy flow directly. They will especially not be willing to do this "on demand." We may need to study with certain teachers over a period of time, and let them ascertain our character and readiness, before they are willing to impart anything of an energetic nature. At the same time, the aspect of "character study" works both ways. We need to carefully assess the nature of someone to whom we would entrust so delicate and potentially charged an experience as a *ch'i* awakening. (Medea's story comes to mind, as does my own.)

In particular, we should be cautious of those teachers or gurus, even if they seem to be very energetically "charged," who seem unduly eager to have us study with them. We might note (with tongue very much in cheek) that a so-called master who wants us to study "under" him might not be considering our own best interests!

The persons most likely to be competently able to help us with our *ch'i* awakening will likely be "internal" martial arts practitioners; this would include teachers of T'ai Chi Ch'uan and related arts. Other potentially useful teachers are those who practice and teach yoga – particularly *kundalini* or *tantra yoga*, as well as practitioners of *pranayama* or *chi kung*. These teachers may or may not be overtly teaching energy work. However, by simply working with them over time, we will grow in our sensitivity and awareness to this kind of *ch'i* cultivation.

In addition, we can learn and practice *ch'i* cultivation and circulation exercises, such as *chi kung* and/or *pranayama*. If we don't have good teachers immediately available, there are many instructional resources that can help us begin simple practices. Even DVDs and online resources can get us started. There are also a number of good books; many of these are included in the endnotes of this work. Of course, it is important to get our bodies into reasonably good physical condition; all the preliminaries discussed prior to this point apply. If we are physically "clogged up" with either poor posture or lots of body tension, we are unlikely to experience an energetic release. There is a reason that most esoteric traditions include lengthy physical training and conditioning as a preliminary!

However it is that we have the initial "*ch'i* awakening," our next set of questions will probably be: how do we cultivate this *ch'i*? What keeps it going, and what diminishes it? Also, what can we do with our *vital energy* or *ch'i*? This is really the next level of skill where we desire, if not mastery, at least some competency. Let's note that even though *ch'i* circulation is a simple step, it is not trivial. We can spend months and even some years mastering the basics.

We keep our *ch'i* circulation going by practicing *ch'i* circulation exercises. Yes, this seems simplistic. However, why else would an art such as *chi kung* exist? The grand art of T'ai Chi Ch'uan is of course devoted to *ch'i* generation and circulation.

In logical contrast, the type of thing that diminishes *ch'i* flow is to be locked into a single posture (such as sitting at a computer desk) for long periods of time, and to be "in our heads," without attending to our bodies. However, by building up our *body/mind/psyche/energy integration pathway*, we should be already incorporating the right kinds of body-art disciplines into our lives, and releasing emotional stress and tension through the *softening* and *releasing resistance* practices described in *Chapters 15* and *16*.

There are numerous energy-circulation methods within our European-based esoteric tradition, which traces its origins back to both Judaic and Egyptian mystical studies. Israel Regardie, one of the most widely respected esoteric scholars and practitioners of the last century, wrote several detailed works. His book, *The Middle Pillar*, carefully explains a time-honored energy cultivation method.[5]

In my personal practice, and in the exercises that I've developed for both myself and my students, I work with a form of *ch'i* circulation based on the *Microcosmic Orbit*, as described by Mantak and Maneewan Chia.[6] In the *Microcosmic Orbit*, we first bring up and store our intrinsic energy, or *ch'i*, in our lower abdomen. (In Chinese martial arts and internal energy practices, this area is called the *tan tien*, and is in the exact geographic center of our bodies.)

We then use our attention and awareness to direct this energy into our sacral area. We compress it there, and the energy changes nature somewhat; it becomes denser. Then, we bring this condensed *ch'i* up our spines and down the front, closing the loop. The condensed energy that we use in this practice feels a bit different from our usual internal energy. The best I can describe it is as "honey-flavored *ch'i*." It's like sexual arousal, only different. We can learn to overlay this on top of sexual experience (mutually sharing our condensed *ch'i* with a partner), or we can learn to play with this energy without having sexual excitement. Either way, this feels very, *very* good.

Perhaps even more important, according to Taoist tradition, this form of energy circulation not only feels good, but has a potent healing and rejuvenating effect.[7] In short, this really is the long-sought and greatly-desired *Fountain of Youth*! For some of us, this may also be the next logical step in our personal evolution.

The energy circulation exercises described by Mantak Chia are technically detailed and anatomically precise. However, even though his book addressing a woman's energy circulation method is co-written with his wife, Maneewan Chia, I personally find the approach that they describe to be a bit dry. Also, we need to take into account how we would interact with this kind of energy experience emotionally. This is an important consideration for us as women, since *ch'i* access and circulation of this nature can be a life-changing experience!

Early in my study of Oriental dance, and drawing on my earliest exposure to T'ai Chi Chuan and related arts, I intuitively felt that it would be possible to bring the *ch'i* circulation aspects of the internal martial arts into dance. Experimenting with the *Microcosmic Orbit* and related exercises, my sense of this possibility grew. I felt it was likely that at one time, this *integration* – of energy cultivation and circulation with dance – was a core part of a woman's *pathway*. However, it took several years of work to create even the first link, and then to embed this discovery into a set of practical exercises. Before I could even begin this, though, I had to first learn many different things – including basic body awareness!

Many years earlier, in my first karate exam, our young Shodan (first-degree black belt, or 1st Dan) teacher had invited his teacher, Fusaro Sensei, to give the exam. In critiquing my performance, Fusaro Sensei looked at me sternly and said, "Weak upper-body/lower-body connection!"

I fumed. What *was* this upper-body/lower-body connection? And why hadn't our local teacher ever mentioned this? How could I develop the connection if no one ever taught it?

As it turns out, most martial arts teachers (at least the very good ones) *do* teach this. (Very likely, I simply wasn't "hearing" it at the time!). Ron Sieh points to a "split," or a "gap," in our upper body/lower body connection. In short, the critique that Fusaro Sensei leveled against me is common to many of us, and one of the primary things that we all need to address, whether we do this using a martial art or dance!

Ron has suggested the practice of *chi kung*, a breathing practice, as a means to "fill and empower the abdomen and solar plexus."[8] Elena Lentini has similarly practiced and advocated *chi kung*, which helps us with increased body awareness and energy cultivation. It is one way in which we can develop the upper body/lower body connection that is so essential.

I personally began to get a sense of upper body/lower body connection when I learned the proper technique for an undulation, which was taught to me by Anahid Sofian. I sought Anahid out on the advice of a mutual friend. "If you're going to be in New York," my friend and fellow dance artist Antonia had said, "You have to give her a call." Antonia knew how to be both insistent and persistent. Finally, more to quiet Antonia than for any other reason, I called up Anahid and requested a private lesson with her. Within due course, I showed up at her studio.

"Show me what you know," she said. I fumbled around, not knowing where to begin. "Well, show me your undulation," she encouraged. I did, and a look of horror passed over her face. "Who taught you that?" she wanted to know. "Well, everyone," I muttered sheepishly. Anahid, a technical purist as well as an artist of high caliber, set about making matters right. What she showed me was not only the technique itself, but also how – when done correctly – it motivates and underlies a range of other dance movements. In short, the simple lower-body undulation is the foundation and basis for many other techniques. When used appropriately, it allows us to do these other movements in a way that is naturally powerful and graceful.

With Anahid's instructions firmly in my head, I revamped my entire approach to dance movement. I began to connect *everything* to an undulation, whether the undulation was visible to observers or very internal. As a result of this study, and through working with my *body/mind integration* coach Diane Richardson, I finally did get my desired "upper body/lower body connection," as first identified for me by Fusaro Sensei. It took about fifteen years to develop this connection. I had to learn how to both release physical tension and bring my body attention or awareness from my head all the way down through my spine to my pelvis, and from there through my hips, thighs, legs, and feet into the floor.

Fifteen years, and training from some of the best martial artists and dance teachers in the world – that's a long time to get a single breakthrough! Now that I've put this together, though, one of my goals is to help students dramatically shorten this timeline. (Visually-based resources can help us learn the undulations and related techniques. Kathryn Ferguson and Suhaila Salimpour offer particularly good resources for Beginners.[9])

Once I had finally created the upper body/lower body connection using the Oriental dance undulation technique, and had further used this as a basis for full body awareness, my next step was to consciously integrate an expansion/contraction dynamic into the movement.

At one point, I was in a modern dance workshop taught by Floyd Flynn, a member of the Martha Graham Dance Company. "Everything in this dance is based on contraction and expansion," said the gorgeous Floyd. Mdm. Graham may have built her dance practice on this "innovative" approach, but expansion/contraction is the intrinsic core of Oriental dance.

Once I had deliberately brought this expansion/contraction dynamic into my dance, I added conscious breathing – a sort of simplified *pranayama*. *Pranayama*, like *chi kung*, is a breathing practice that helps us energize.[10] By integrating conscious breathing into my undulation, together with actively using the expansion/contraction dynamic, I created a "building block" that would serve as a basis for *ch'i* circulation. This is very similar to how energy work is done within T'ai Chi Ch'uan.

Throughout this entire time, my intention was to realize – as deeply and completely as possible – what Diane Richardson had taught me many years prior. She pointed out that Oriental dance is built on a natural undulating and flowing movement that connects our entire spine, from our cranial vertebrae down to our sacrum. In addition, she helped me to sense a very subtle and naturally-embedded "figure-eight" motion at the base of my spine. In short, the two most entrancing movements in the Oriental dance vocabulary – undulations and (pelvic) figure-eights – are based on intrinsic and subtle motions that already exist in our bodies! All that we are doing, as we dance, is to tap into these innate, natural rhythms, and magnify them into a dance.

৯৩

The physical practices based on lower and upper-body undulations, the expansion/contraction dynamic, and conscious breathing are all part of what I refer to as *Level 2* training. *Level 2* deals with all aspects of tension release, and opens up our bodies so that energy has a chance to flow. *Chapters 14 – 16* described the important tension release steps in terms of *softening* and *releasing resistance*. By combining a basic physical "building block" with tension release, we start creating the means by which we can do effective *ch'i* circulation.

To maximize our potential for *ch'i* circulation, we also need to give some attention to our feeling of energy throughout our bodies. In both the martial arts and in Oriental dance, we seek a feeling of "dropping" the energy-sense that we have associated with our bodies, so that it feels as though we are "sinking" into and through the floor.

Peter Ralston, one of the greatest martial artists of our time, makes the point of linking our notion of "power" with "dropping" our body-sense, including our sense of where our *ch'i* is centrally located within our bodies:

> ... Concentrate the idea of power in your lower abdomen, allowing the straight spine to follow it, and the sacrum to press into one foot. ... Stay relaxed but full of energy and unity, and hold the idea of dropping (attention, ch'i, strength, etc.) and pressing down. The lower half is what you should concentrate on, considering the upper half as resting on it, and subject to it! Nurture the breath down into the lower abdomen. Do not be distracted!"

The precursor *Level 1* work deals with *grounding* and *anchoring*, described in *Chapter 21*. At *Level 1*, we re-organize how we align our bodies. We also learn basic in-place movements during our *Level 1* training. However, "life basics" are part of our *Level 1* work as well. Getting our apartment or home cleaned is *Level 1*. Working at our job or getting our education is a *Level 1* practice. So is balancing a checkbook, sweeping out the garage, and shopping for groceries. Everything that gets us "grounded" in our lives is *Level 1*. Most of us spend most of our time at this level. Even when we are advanced, we still do some *Level 1* exercises as part of our daily practice.

Level 2 rests on observing our bodies (and our psyches) more deeply. For example, I can be standing in the checkout line at a grocery store and notice neck tension. I can start releasing this, very softly, without being very obvious or attracting attention. This is a *Level 2* practice as part of daily life. If we get a massage, or have some sort of release work done (such as chiropractic or Rolfing®), we can take note of how an emotional "pain-nexus" corresponds with a tight spot. By simultaneously releasing both the emotional pain and the physical tension, we are doing a *Level 2* practice. In dance, we can focus our attention on the connection between our emotional and physical sensitivities more intimately. However, any of us can add this practice into our daily lives. (I've been doing *Level 2* work for nearly twenty years, and it is still the area requiring the most attention!)

Once we do some basic release, we can start energy circulation. In our *Level 3* training, we add in energetic principles from T'ai Chi Ch'uan, and incorporate the basic *Microcosmic Orbit* and related exercises.[12] We also include energy generation and circulation techniques from other disciplines. Our *Level 3* goal is to incorporate simple energy circulation, and to direct energy patterns within our bodies as part of our dance. At this level, we're not trying to accomplish anything other than accessing and moving energy in certain patterns, and noting how this feels.

This adds a new level of complexity, but not unreasonably so. If we are dancers, we've already mastered doing two or more complex things at once. For example, we've learned how to do things like play zills (metal finger cymbals) when we dance, and overlay veil moves on top of other movement patterns. Thus, adding in an energy circulation component is something else that we can learn to do, with enough patience, practice, and time. However, this is a very personal area for most dancers, which is why I teach it only in small groups or in private sessions.

Most of my *Level 3* exercises are simply that; "exercises." They are simple movements, which we do with some breath control (*pranayama*) together with conscious energy access and direction, again in very simple patterns. We may put the movements, the breath control, and the energy work together (again very simply) into something that looks like a dance but is really an *etude*; a study or practice piece. This gives us a way to build our proficiency over time.

Some dancers, such as Suzanna del Vecchio, have a strong yoga component to their personal practice. Eva Cernik (a protégé of Anahid Sofian) has studied Sufi mystical practices extensively. It is easy to see where master dancers such as these may be adding a form of *Level 3* energy work to their dance. We can also see, from their performance and instructional DVDs, where we can be inspired by their movement sequences and add an energy circulation component to our own work, drawing on the patterns which they offer.

Even this *Level 3* work of energy circulation is still a prelude to yet another capability. In *Level 4*, we seek to combine energy work with intention, and encapsulate this within our dance.

Let's take a moment to ask the obvious question. Why, if *ch'i* cultivation is potentially such a natural experience, do we not have more of this going on in our lives without special exercises and practices? In fact, why is it that so many of us experience the complete reverse — chronic fatigue, myofascial tension, and other symptoms?

We can start by realizing that we, as women, innately and intrinsically *should* be able to "hold" a great deal of energy within our bodies. If we imagine our pelvic girdle as a kind of "energy cauldron," there is certainly room for a lot of energy! Also, Taoists and martial artists identify the location of our "energy centers," or *tan tiens*, as being precisely at the geographic center of our bodies. This is right above our pelvic girdle. So how then do we manage to lose our energy, if we're naturally supposed to have so much of it?

There are predominantly three ways in which we lose our energy. Let's stay with the idea of having an "energy cauldron" situated right within our pelvic girdle. First, we too often "tip" our cauldron and simply "spill out" our energy. This happens when our posture is off, as described in *Chapter 21*. By cultivating the *Anchoring* and *Lotus Flower* exercises, we can mitigate this. (These exercises are starting points for both T'ai Chi Ch'uan and Oriental dance.)

Second, we can have "holes" in our "energy cauldron." In short, our "cauldron" sometimes gets leaky; it becomes a "colander" instead of a "cauldron"! This happens when we start giving our energy more than appropriately, and is often tied in with our *Isis* aspects. The same loving, caring, nurturing aspects that cause us to pour our energetic-natures into caring for our young can often motivate us to the same degree of "pouring out" on behalf of others who will take, but not return, our gifts.

Finally, we may simply have an energy version of corrosion, or tarnish, in our system. This is the accumulated "gunk" that we get from not only external toxins, but also as a residue that we build up over time as we indulge in negative thought patterns. When we do a "life-cleansing," as described in *Chapter 17*, we begin to clean up this "internal tarnish." This allows our inner energy system to start healing and repairing itself. As it does this, we are more able to hold and circulate energy within ourselves.

Let us recall, from *Chapter 13*, that our second primary adult passage was to transform ourselves from the gentle *Strength Maiden* to the *Temperance Angel*. Depending on the symbology used, the *Angel* was either pouring out both water and fire, onto respectively the fire and water aspects of its being, or it was pouring a "magical" fluid from one pitcher to another, where the same fluid would pour itself upward and back into the original vessel. In short, the *Angel* was doing energy replenishment! This is exactly and precisely what we need in our lives. In our *Isis* modes, we tend to "pour out." What we need to do is to ensure that we are also "receiving."

To be even more to the point, we have probably achieved some degree of personal *integration* by the time that we approach menopause. It is around this time that we are often in greatest need of "energy rejuvenation." *Temperance* shows us that, indeed, the most time-honored esoteric pathway of our tradition recognizes this need; this is precisely what our greatest life-challenge is at this point. Thus, the *Level 3* energy circulation work rightfully should be part of our personal adult journey. Let's keep in mind that in the Shaolin monasteries, the *ch'i* cultivation and circulation aspects were not taught until the monks were more mature. Similarly, the Major Arcana dominantly depicts full adults. Thus, it may be appropriate that we seriously begin our energy work in our mature years!

⁦⁦⁦

The previous discussion has focused on the advantages of *ch'i* cultivation and circulation. Naturally, being prudent women, we must ask: what are the possible "downsides"?

One would think, with all of the discussion of positive benefits, that there might not be "downsides." On the whole, I strongly believe that the benefits outweigh any negatives and any potential risks. However, there are three areas in which I strongly urge caution.

First, let's recall the analogy introduced earlier, comparing the combination of energy work with physical movement to creating a mixed drink. To carry this analogy further, let's think of the need to "drink responsibly." When we start circulating energy, we can create energetic jam-ups in our bodies if we bring energy into "uncleared" areas. This is why so much of *kundalini yoga* deals with preparing our bodies (using *hatha yoga*) for the energy surge of an awakened *kundalini*. (Instead of a generic *ch'i* flow, the *kundalini* approach seeks to release a "coiled serpent" energy from the base of the spine, and bring it up the spine to the head, producing a dramatic and powerful altered state of consciousness.) The entire *kundalini* tradition is rife with warnings to neophytes, and strongly advises that this practice be done only under the supervision of a guru who has already (safely) accomplished this task.

Our goal is that of cultivating basic *ch'i*, which is not quite as dramatic as a *kundalini* awakening, and not as likely to have adverse side effects. However, we wouldn't play with an electrical wiring system without taking precautions, would we? A wise woman exercises a certain amount of prudence. (As a side note: This is yet another reason why I am only teaching this privately or with very small groups; each person responds differently and therefore requires personal attention.)

The second potential downside is that as we start to do various forms of energy-play and energy-interactions, we can open ourselves to people who may not ultimately have our best interests at heart. These may be teachers; these may be intimate partners. Those who have accessed their *ch'i*, or *vital energy*, are often enormously charismatic. It is part of our human nature to want to be with such people. We absolutely must take the time to observe the actions of such persons – and the effects of their actions – over time. (I am speaking not only from my own experiences, but also those of students, teachers, and friends with whom I've worked.) Once we begin looking for teachers who are skilled in the area of energy cultivation and play, we will undoubtedly find them.

Some people with whom I've worked have encountered "gurus" who have taken advantage of their student's energies for their own purposes. Not all interactions have required physical proximity. (Medea's story is not the only one that I've heard along these lines.) Such behaviors are very unethical, and far from enlightened. However, they are not that uncommon. Without over-dramatizing, we need to realize that this is a realm in which certain kinds of "predators" exist, just as there are normal, ordinary, garden-variety predators in all other realms of life.

There are three defenses against sexual-energy predators; including those who may start off seeming like very enlightened persons. Our intention is to develop a strong set of "energy boundaries." The challenge for us, as women, is that our "boundary" behavior tends to be part of our *Amazon* persona. As we seek to cultivate our less-guarded states, our "boundaries" become softer, and perhaps even more permeable. We can, however, take certain steps to strengthen our "energy boundaries." As a first defense, we can invoke the protection of our personal Guardian Angels, and any other angels that seem appropriate.[13]

Second, we can learn and practice the well-known rituals, developed within the European esoteric tradition and going back to much earlier practices, which have been devised precisely for the purpose of creating and strengthening the "energy boundaries" around ourselves. One of the most well-known is the *Lesser Banishing Ritual of the Pentagram*.[14] Although this is within the High Magick esoteric tradition, it is fully aligned with honoring the Judeo-Christian perspective. All invocations are to God and the Archangels.

Third, we can add the practice of going to a "sacred place." In times where there is stress to an "energy boundary," we can go to a church, synagogue, mosque, or temple. Such places truly do give "sanctuary," and allow us to regroup. Prayer is a vital aspect of working effectively with strong energy. We may wish to consider a directed retreat at a monastery or abbey, or at a retreat house.

In addition to these options, we can strengthen our inner "energetic core" through practicing some form of daily prayer, or participating in a regular religious or spiritual services. Various devotional practices can exert a powerful effect. One such practice that may be useful would be the spiritual exercises of St. Ignatius of Loyola.[15] A similar Hindu tradition is that of reciting the *Gayatri Mantra*, which is a powerful hymn of praise to the Divine.[16] In almost every religious or spiritual tradition, there will be a comparable devotional practice. We can each find one that works, and make it part of our lives. (This is a worthwhile step, no matter what is happening with our energy boundaries.)

The third potential downside to accessing our *vital energy* is that when we, as women, begin cultivating our *ch'i*, and using it in various forms of energy play with our partners (this may or may not directly involve sexual energy play), we often tend to "pour" our energy towards the other person. This is simply an amplification of our natural tendency to be loving, nurturing, and supportive – especially when in our *Isis* mode! Energetic intimacy greatly strengthens the bonding effect of sexual and emotional intimacy. We often tend to over-give in this realm, even when in a mutually loving relationship.

When a relationship ends, especially one that has included energy-connection and exchange, the effect can be especially devastating. We may continue to "pour out" our energy towards our former partner, even if the real "relationship" (and any form of reciprocal caring or support) no longer exists. This is perhaps the greatest danger for us as women. (It is also a danger for men, if they have been the one who has been more "giving" in the relationship, or if a man has taken the more feminine role. Thus, for a man in this situation, the same precautions should hold.) It may take more time to heal from this kind of exchange than from a "normal" love relationship. Conscious self-nurturing back to good health becomes essential at such times.

One final word of caution: There is a growing interest among our younger generation (and among some of the more mature ones, as well) in various "vampire" and related cult-genre literature, movies, and related media. (I referred to the enormous popularity of the *Twilight* series in *Chapter 5*.) Many young people engage in various forms of fantasy role-playing. There is nothing intrinsically wrong with this. However, they may be (and very likely are) inadvertently finding that they can indeed do various forms of energy work with each other. (As we know, the nature of our young ones is to seek extreme experiences.) Thus, some members of our younger generations are very likely already dealing with the various kinds of "energy challenges" that I have just described.

Those younger ones who are experimenting with sexual energy play may be without anyone of their maternal generation with whom they can discuss these matters, or to whom they can turn for help. It may be part of our duty to our daughters to attend to this possibility, and to counsel them towards "energetic safety." Consider that this may be the energy-equivalent of having the "safe sex" discussions! Should it be necessary to find someone who can serve as a counselor for a young one who has gone too far with energy play, it would be important to find a person who can address the situation without an overload of religious bias or dogma.

Our final realm of questions deals with how the kind of *ch'i* circulation that we've been considering can affect our lives. We may have questions about how increased *ch'i* can influence everything from our health to our sex lives, and perhaps even other areas.

There is a realm that goes far beyond simple "rejuvenation." This is the realm of what some call *sacred sex*. Others will call it *sex magic*. In *The Da Vinci Code*,[17] Dan Brown describes how the ancient *hieros gamos* ritual, using sexual energy for a directed purpose, might have been carried out. However, Brown's envisioning, while probably not too far off the mark, is about as useful a prescription for real sexual energy work as are the Harry Potter books for how to do "real" magic. It's not in the formalisms – the people, the costumes, the chanting, or the masks. It's not about the sex itself. Rather, it's about the energy created and directed as part of the sexual experience. The most skilled lovers know how to direct their sexual energy without physical release; this is part of most yogic and internal martial arts disciplines. This is a time-honored and, in the past, often a closely-guarded secret. However, there are some books that discuss this. One of the most revered of the ancient sources is *The Secret of the Golden Flower*, a Chinese treatise on sexual energy work.[18] This work is a little obscure. Fortunately, Donald Michael Kraig's book, *Modern Sex Magick*, is both authoritative and readable.[19]

The true essence of the *hieros gamos* is to focus and direct the combined sexual energy of the man and woman involved. Since it is that simple and that direct (although there are levels of subtlety and refinement), many of us will have done something of this nature without calling it "ritual." We've simply benefited from the extraordinary results.

However, there are traditions of using sexual energy in many great civilizations. In some of these traditions, the woman is often simply the "cauldron" in which an energetic essence is stored, or she contributes her own energy to a process which is defined by the man. According to Louis Culling in a book titled, simply enough, *Sex Magick*, a woman who has occult expertise becomes "impossible" because she has her own "preconceived ideas." These get in the way of her being a "good, cooperative partner." A woman's role, in this (rather antiquated) mentality is that the woman should become "responsive automatically to the aspiration of the male."[20] This is rather like using a woman as a tool, rather than acknowledging her as a conscious participant in a shared energy experience!

Men continue to view themselves as not only the initiators of sexual energy work, but the ones who are more endowed with purpose and wisdom. In describing how a man would relate to his partner in this kind of energy exchange, Culling states:

> **If one should desire to bring soul transcendence to the woman partner, one cannot imagine anything more potent than to feed some of the transmuted quintessence to her!**[21]

What Culling is stating, in the tradition of this approach, is that the "transmuted quintessence" is a man's semen, charged with the energetic intention that he has created prior to, during, and for this energetically-charged sexual experience. Thus, the man will endeavor to bring "soul transcendence" to his partner by "feed[ing] some" to her.

Mighty godly of the man, we must say.

We have our work cut out for us. We are as capable as men of using our sexual energy for higher purposes. This is true whether we have actual sex or not. We are using the *energy* – and this can be done in different ways.

As we become more and more adept with energy work, we naturally draw greater attention. By this time, our abilities go beyond the realm of physical attraction, and are much more in the realm of (nearly subconscious) energetic attraction. This means that we "stand out from the crowd." Men with even the smallest gift of energy awareness or sensitivity seek us out.

In addition to being literally more attractive, we have more to offer than those who have not cultivated personal energy. Energy work, shared between partners, is particularly refreshing and rejuvenating. This is especially true if we have been practicing *relaxing* and *releasing*, as well as some basic energy circulation exercises; these give us greater access to our own energy sources. If we have become at all adept in the dance art, or any form of expressive movement, and bring our energy play into this art, then we are even more desirable; even our simplest movements help charge a situation.

Most men haven't the foggiest idea of what to do with women who have developed energy proficiency, except to keep suggesting that we should have sex with them. A relatively small number, though, have learned something about energy work themselves. Such men will have mastered the basics. As Deida says, "Breathe down the front, ... Ejaculate up the spine."[22] A smaller, but still significant number, have developed even greater abilities. Such men would prefer a partner who can bring something to the venture. (And so, for that matter, would we.)

It is here where we must, once again, continue to regard ourselves as the *jewel in the heart of the lotus*. We are worth being regarded as incarnations of the Goddess in an energetic exchange. Before we release our energy to someone else, we need to have some confidence that we are not simply becoming sexual energy "batteries," feeding a man's purpose and ego. We are worth being cared for. As we open up to the full realms of energy flow, in both love and love-making, we access the most potent part of our being. The energy flow that we can give to someone else is the most highly treasured and prized gift that we can possibly give.

If we are going to release ourselves, fully and completely, to another, it is most helpful if our lover is steadfast in his presence and caring for us. As Deida says:

> **The best way that you can serve your woman is by helping her to surrender, to trust the force of love, so that she can open her heart, be the love that she is, and give this love which naturally overflows from her happiness... Let her be the ocean ... Be so full in your loving, so strong and stable in your presence, that she can just let go and surrender the limits that she has put on her feelings.**[23]

The power of sexual energy, and its potential emotional (as well as energetic) impact on the participants – especially on the woman – may be one reason that sexual energy cultivation was done in the context of a ritual, such as the *hieros gamos*. One of the values of keeping such a highly-charged experience within the confines of ritual is that the ritual itself has provided a demarcation. It gave the boundaries that contained our emotional, as well as energetic, over-flowing.

When we do sexual energy work outside of a ritual occasion, then we rely on the man's protective nature, love, and caring to establish the "boundaries" against which we can release. Again, these boundaries are important not just during sex, or a short-term encounter, but in a more comprehensive manner. With the boundaries provided by someone operating within a masculine framework, we are free to be as "overflowing" as we can be. Without such boundaries, in our *Isis* and *Hathor* modes, we spill out our energy, and too often lose our sense of self. If needed, we must then rely on our inner *Amazon* to help us put ourselves back together. However, if we are relying on our own inner masculine, then we have clearly not chosen what Deida would describe as a *superior man*.

We need to bring ourselves to the point where we recognize that our purpose may be more than to be "responsive automatically to the aspiration of the male." This is an area in which we may need to re-cultivate ourselves. Bluntly put, the advice that our mothers and grandmothers gave us — to hold ourselves back until we have reasonable confidence in the man's nature and abilities, as well as his intentions — is even more important as we develop our combined *Hathor* and *High Priestess* essences through *internal energy* cultivation.

A factor in our favor lies with the basic orientation of men. As Napoleon Hill states, "Man's greatest motivating force is his desire to please woman!"[24] This is the fulcrum on which our next evolutionary step pivots.

This brings me to full cycle with what Medea taught in the first class that I took with her. Instead of "giving our energy over" to a man, we can fountain it back into ourselves. Dance is a means by which we can do this. As Medea taught, we can find our energy, cultivate it, circulate it, fountain it around ourselves, and bring it back in. We have a total right to use our energy for our own pleasure, healing, and well-being! Dance, as an alternative to love-making with another person, gives us a means by which we can play energetically as well as physically. And once again; this feels very, *very* good!

Using energy play within dance, as an alternative to sexual energy play, gives us a means for cultivating our *internal energy*, or *ch'i*, for our own purposes. We do not always need a sexual focus in order to make good use of our *vital energy*. Napoleon Hill, in his various books, makes a point of noting that all major business leaders have the ability to apply the "emotion of sex energy" to their business creations.[25] We note that he is not speaking of sex, or even of sex energy, itself, but rather the *emotion* of this energy. He is talking about how business leaders (typically men) use not just their sexual energy, but also the *power of their desire* to charge their business situations.

We know that the various fraternal orders have largely lost the power that they may once have had through their rituals. By excluding women, and the potent factor of sexual energy, they have devolved into highly structured "boy's clubs." It is also straightforward to realize that many, if not most, of us, may find that ritual "sexual energy work" would be a bit beyond what we personally wish to experience. However, if there were any "great secrets" to be found in the ancient mystical orders, they would certainly have to include an understanding of sexual energy.

We can use dance as means of not only cultivating our personal energy, but also for providing an energetically-charged ritual experience. This allows us a culturally "comfortable" means of bringing an entire group of people into a different state, and pouring group energy into a desired purpose or intention.

⚚

In *Chapter 17*, we discovered a potentially more correct interpretation of that most time-honored mantra, *Om Mani Padme Hum*! As we reconsider this mantra, in light of what we've just learned about *ch'i* cultivation, it seems that our earlier interpretation may not be complete. The mantra comes from the Tibetan tantric tradition. *Tantra yoga*, like all yoga disciplines, is devoted to the ultimate goal of God-realization. Enroute to God-realization, the tantric practice encourages a great deal of personal energy development.

Doesn't it make sense that such a powerful and revered mantra should refer to more than simple sexual union or the body's pleasure centers?

Now, knowing a little bit about how we can cultivate and circulate our *ch'i*, let's recollect that for each of us, the energy center for our *ch'i* storage (our *tan tien*) is in the geographic center of our bodies. In a woman, this would be about where our cervix is located; the entry from our vaginas to our wombs. Right about in this location – right where we would hold and nourish a baby inside of ourselves – is where we hold our personal energy.

Wouldn't it make much more sense – if we are speaking of a *jewel* in the *heart* of the lotus – that the *heart* would be deep in the interior of the vagina, perhaps just where it touches our wombs? The *jewel* would thus be our condensed and stored internal energy, or *ch'i*. There is one further level of interpretation; it has to do with what partners create during energetically-infused lovemaking. That is, however, a very advanced practice. For now, we simply note that the potential is there.

Let's consider that *Om Mani Padme Hum!* may be interpreted at multiple levels. For many of us, our first immediate and practical application of this mantra may be to cultivate and store our *vital energy*. In fact, this mantra may be a praise of our innate ability to do so!

Personal Pathworking:

1. The topics here are rather advanced. This chapter is designed more to help us create awareness than to take specific actions. We might all, however, benefit from more attention to our breathing; some basic forms of *yoga* and *pranayama* may also be beneficial. The remaining steps will be left to the reader's discretion.

CHAPTER 30:
RELEASING PASSION: PLAYING WITH YOUR EDGE

ELENA WAS LEADING US THROUGH her new choreography. Spanish-Moroccan influenced, with a touch of flamenco, it had, as always, that special Elena-quality of emotional intensity.

"What makes Elena, *Elena*?" I wondered. "How is it that her dancing is so intense, so powerful, so emotionally rich? Why do so few others have it? In fact, what is this 'it' that I'm noticing and wondering about?"

Valid question, because few people have this quality. Elena does, and most top dancers do. But what exactly is this "it" that I was noticing? It was not just sexuality. There was definite sexual energy, but it was not just sex. Nor was it just emotion, although there was a strong emotional quality as well.

"You need to play with your edge," she was saying. My ears perked up. This is exactly what Peter Ralston, my martial arts teacher, had told us years ago. When two extraordinary masters, totally unconnected in terms of lineage and art form, are saying the same thing, that thing is probably worth attention. "Let yourself go," said Elena. "Go to your edge, and if you knock a couple of wine glasses off the table, well, then you have to pull back some."

I visualized Elena doing just that. Over the years, Elena had performed around the world, but her home base had been Fazil's in New York, which was part of the Oriental dance nightclub scene of the 70's and 80's. Elena was still performing there regularly in the mid-1980's, when I could occasionally get to New York for Saturday's dance classes. After teaching during the day, Elena would perform at night. As one friend put it, we would see her "creating the dance," night after night, week after week, in Fazil's. She would evolve it emotionally as well as choreographically. Probably, she knocked over a good many wineglasses during this evolution. I don't think the audience minded.

My mind flashed back to Peter Ralston's workshops, some years earlier. Peter was unique, like Elena, in being highly original and innovative in his art. "It's *your* art," he would say to his students. "Own your art." I knew what he meant. So many students were patiently and passively waiting for the teacher to "give them" the art form. They measured their success by the extent to which they scrupulously followed their teacher. Peter and Elena each had teachers, of course, but they were taking ownership by asking themselves what their art meant to them; by actively discovering principles and synthesizing new expressions.

"Play with your edge," Peter would say. What he meant was: go beyond your safety zone. Get out of your comfort area. Go to where it's not so comfortable, so that you lose your balance, so that you fall down. He made it clear that each person made his or her real advances when at their personal "edge"; not while on safe ground! In his book, *The Book of Not Knowing*, Peter talks about how his willingness to go to his "edge" – and beyond – was critical in giving him the personal breakthroughs that made his martial arts practice so powerful and effective. As he put it, "I was relentless in my pursuit of understanding every facet of being human, including the nature of perception, relationships, and even reality itself. An essential contribution to this effort was a breakthrough in consciousness, which Zen people call an 'enlightenment.'"[1]

Because Peter had made a conscious effort at inquiring into this notion of "edge," and into communicating it to his students, his students were familiar with what their "edge" was. They had permission to go to extremes: to fall down. Not many people do.

I thought about the many, many dance events that I'd gone to – mostly Oriental dance, some others as well – where I'd simply been bored.

I haven't been alone in this. Once, after one particular way-too-long dance concert, a dear gentlemen friend of mine said, "I spent four hours watching scantily dressed women dancing in front of me, and I was bored." So was I. The big question that I took away from the evening was: "How could I *possibly* be this bored?" These were all technically good dancers; they had each put a lot of work into developing their dance. Nevertheless, I was fidgety and squirmy from within the first several minutes of the show. What was going on?

Was it the dance form? Was it the technique? Feeling unsettled, I had let the question recess to the back of my mind.

There, in that workshop with Elena, I began to get the answer. The dances where I was bored were when the dancers were "playing it safe." They not only weren't going to their edge, they probably didn't know where their edge was, or even that they had one!

In contrast, Dalia Carella tells a story about the first time she was invited to perform at *Rakkasah*, a major dance festival. She came out on stage with a great forward kick – and fell flat on her butt! Instead of feeling ashamed or embarrassed, she broke out in laughter, and the audience laughed with her. As she recounts the story, "It was such a joyful moment – the audience laughed with me – and I've never had such applause in my life!" She went on to describe that moment as a "lesson from the Universe," taking her to a new spiritual level. She had been excited about doing that performance, she says. She was wearing a beautiful new costume, with a gorgeous gypsy skirt. She was eager to show it off, and her choreography was designed to make the best use of its layers and tiers. When she fell down, she said that the Universe was saying to her, "It's not about the skirt; it's about spirit! Your dance has been all about your costume. But it's not about being in ego, it's about being fully present in the spirit of the dance!" The experience of – literally – falling down and going "boom" on the stage was a huge and wonderful awakening for her.

Dalia described how her life changed from that moment on. "I started really going inside," she said. She had been wearing beautiful costumes, designed by the famous Alia Michele. When she started wearing plainer costumes, people began to see *her* – not the costume – and her career skyrocketed.

In that one, overly-long dance concert which I attended with my gentleman friend, the star of the show was Dalia, who performed at the end of the evening. She was well worth the wait. As my previously bored friend said, after he saw her dance, "I saw Dalia, and all I could think about was sex!"

Dalia's dances – then, and now – are about far more than sex, of course. Her work is about creating and sharing her personal energy, or *ch'i*. She is soft; she has no tension or resistance impeding her movements. When she dances, she is clearly in-the-present-moment. She projects an extraordinary emotional range: from the depths of passion to simple, exuberant *joie de vivre*. Thus, her dances are not so much about sex. Rather, they contain great energetic and emotional content. She presents pure, *life-force energy*. (And of course men, being men, interpret this immediately as "sex." We love them for what they are, but are not really surprised.)

In her *Rakkasah* performance, Dalia, like Elena Lentini and Peter Ralston, was "playing with her edge." This means that she was willing to take risks – to put herself "out there." She didn't let the possibility of losing her balance keep her from coming on stage with a great big high kick. And when she did fall down, she laughed at the experience – and everyone else joined in with her! Playing with our edge is scary. We don't know in advance that people will laugh *with* us, instead of *at* us. Our egos are very much at stake. Yet at times, this is exactly what we each need to do.

Sometimes, we need the jolt of going out and doing something physical to get to our "edge." Anything from horseback riding to surfing to a karate class can do that for us. But more often, the "edge" that we need to play with is not so overt; it is hidden in the everyday nature of our lives. In this case, we need to check in with our feelings, and once again, acknowledge our fears. Are we staying in a job, relationship, or life situation that provides us with security, at the cost of slowly bleeding away our souls? Are we afraid to contradict or challenge some-one because it would upset the balance of a relationship? Are we "stuffing" our fears? This means, are we overeating, over-indulging in television, online escapes, shopping, or anything that will drown out our awareness of how unhappy – and afraid – we really are? Are we indulging in gossip about others or fault-finding with our life situations, but are too afraid to take action? When we do this, we often find ourselves becoming bored, depressed, or irritable. Sometimes we just have a general sense of listlessness and overall "life malaise." If this is so, perhaps we need to start making changes.

First, we need to acknowledge that which fills us with passion, and that which truly inspires us. Then, we need to build on it, bit by bit. This is not to suggest that we drop all of our responsibilities and commitments, and run off to find fulfillment in our favorite escapist fantasy. However, we can change our lives in increments, working daily to feed ourselves with true "soul food." Little tiny doses of what we truly desire can help us as we recreate our lives to have more and more of what we want. Books such as Julia Cameron's *The Artist's Way*[2] provide valuable encouragement as we take on this process of nurturing our "true selves."

There are times in our lives when we truly *are* following our passion – following our bliss. But the particular patch of road that we're on might be a bit tedious. Sometimes "following our bliss" requires substantial, long-term work. One example of this is getting an advanced degree – especially if we are doing this while working a full or even part-time job, or while caring for children or parents. Making a career commitment that requires long stretches of extra work can similarly be draining. Buying and renovating a house, even if it is the "house of our dreams," can sometimes absorb every spare moment. When we are in such situations, we need to provide ourselves with little moments of pleasure along the way; we need to recharge our *juice* batteries.

During these times, we need to rekindle both our desires and our beliefs in ourselves. At such times, I like to read (and reread) books and listen to books while on travel that will help me maintain good focus and positive mental discipline. Napoleon Hill is one of my favorite authors, and so is Joe Vitale. Whenever we get a little droopy and dragged-out, we need to be especially careful in how we feed our thoughts. This is a means of nurturing both our *Hathor* and our *High Priestess*.

Sometimes, we need to rekindle our passion by bringing out our playful side. At these times, I'll often reread *Mama Gena's Guide to the Womanly Arts*.[3] This last winter, I realized that even though I was writing about our *Hathor*-rich juiciness, I was spending much too much time in my *Amazon* state! Since I was working from a home office, I had begun getting careless about dressing up. Too often, I'd start the day wearing whatever was warmest, and would be deeply immersed in writing well before the sun came up. I was neglecting cosmetics and jewelry, and eating whatever was easiest to prepare. I caught myself in this little downward spiral just in time!

I began a little self-therapy by reclaiming beauty and "pleasure" time. Feeling a need for more "sparkle" to offset the dreariness of late February, I took the time to make some pretty earrings with lots of shimmery Swarovski crystal beads. I began putting more attention on creating fun combinations of things to wear, even if it was just to amuse myself and the cats. (Who were, I might add, largely indifferent to these efforts.) I also started taking the time to make meals more pleasurable to all my senses. I even began taking "play-time" breaks for dance once again! (If we haven't "played with our veil" lately, isn't it time to do so again; or maybe for the first time?)

While we need to give ourselves permission to cultivate our feel-good states, we also need to allow ourselves access to our full range of emotions. This is one of the most important ways in which we can "play with our edge." Sometimes, these emotions may include sadness, or loss, or even grief. Throughout history, dance has been used to mourn the passing of loved ones as much as it has been to celebrate the high points of our lives.[4] One of my most poignant reminders of this came when I mentioned to my dancers that if anyone, at any time, felt that they wanted to share a dance, they were very welcome to do so. My invitation was well timed, because Sue Ellen then said that she needed to do a dance to honor a friend who had died. Her friend, she said, was a woman just a little older than she was, so perhaps in her late forties. She had never married, and never had children, and so she "mothered" all the people around her, including Sue Ellen. She had grown up in a very straight-laced environment, and had never had the chance to express herself through dance the way were doing that night. Sue Ellen asked me to play a certain piece of music that we both loved – one which always induced a deeply "felt" state in us.

Sue Ellen's request reminded me once again of my first dance teacher, Medea. One evening, out of the blue, Medea did a funeral dance for us – one that she had learned from her teacher, Cassandra. The dance was beautiful and stately and stylized. It was the sort that would have been done by a group of women in procession. That first "funeral dance" performance helped me to realize and connect with how deeply personal and appropriate Oriental dance could be. It wasn't always sexy, and it wasn't always light and fun. Sometimes it was the deepest response we could make to a life event.

Sue Ellen's dance, totally improvisational, deepened that realization for me. Her dance was strong and powerful, and yet very open and expressive. Gaia and Maria got up to dance with her, and as they did, I felt that we, as a group, were reconnecting with an ancient feminine heritage of honoring each other through dance. At the end, we were silent for a bit. Then Sue Ellen said, "Well. Now I can go to the funeral tomorrow as a 'straight, proper' (and here she mimed an overly serious expression) person. But at least I've honored her spirit."

Sue Ellen, and earlier Medea, and earlier yet, countless generations of women, have all used dance to honor the passing of friends. They have used it for grief, and for mourning. Others of us have used dance to work through fear. In fact, the big thing about "playing with our edge" is to go into those areas where we are afraid. I have used dance for this, though we can dance, draw, write, sculpt, sing, shout, or do any sort of creative process. Anything that lets us pull from our guts to outside of ourselves will work.

One of the first times that I used dance as this form of powerful "self-therapy" was when I was still healing from a tough emotional wound. Several years ago, I was at a weekend dance workshop. There was more going on for me then than just the workshop. I had been (and still was) very much in love with a man who had recently married someone else. He had handled the interaction with me very poorly; in fact, I had found out about this man's wedding date from someone else! Suffice to say, I was in some real pain. We were going to get together after the workshop was over. I didn't know what I was going to say, or what I would do, but it was necessary to clear the air. We met, and he apologized for leading me on. (I appreciated his gesture, although his timing was a little off.) During the workshop, though, I had heard some music of exquisite and haunting beauty. This music helped me tap into a state that was more sensitized to emotional feelings. I bought a CD containing that music, feeling as though I'd found a "buried treasure."

I went home to lick my wounds. Several months afterwards, I had to see the same man again, at a business meeting. More than that, I knew that I would have to work with him. I was by no means over my feelings. To work through things (enough to face him in a meeting the next day), I played that music from the workshop in dance class, several times. I told all the women there that the music had a lot of emotional significance for me, and that I needed their support in using dance with this music to be emotionally ready to meet the man about whom I'd cared so much.

The first time we danced through it, I felt a lot of vulnerability and pain – a lot of emotional openness and loss. The second time, I felt a bit stronger. By the third time we'd done improvisational dance to the same music, I was feeling strong and powerful. I could still feel the pain, but I was no longer overwhelmed by it. Instead, I felt a real sense of just being me – of being in my own center again. Those three dances were transformative for me. They carried over into the meeting the next day as well; I was powerful, clear, and confident in my presentation.

Whatever it takes for us to let the "inner person" out, we need to begin doing those things. Using dance, or any form of creative, interpretive movement, is one way to reach into our full range of feelings. It lets us access how we feel. In this way, our dance is simply for ourselves, whether or not we ever have an audience.

PERSONAL PATHWORKING:

1. Find one time in life where you gave yourself permission to "release" the inhibitions that kept you into a sort of predefined state; one where you were mechanically going through the "dance of life" – and then found yourself doing a much more *real* kind of dance. When and how did you get your personal "release" moment? (This may have been spectacular, such as Dalia's public fall onto her bottom as she started her performance – which had everyone applauding and laughing with her! It may have been very small and subtle, such as how my "dance feeling" emerged only after I had finished practice, as described in *Chapter 11*. This inspired me to go back and dance very different way!) We all have such times, and – most of the time – we are doing the "dance of life," rather than a physical dance. What did you learn from your "release" moment?

2. Think through to times where you had to find – and *play with* – your "edge." This could have been: proposing the toast at your best friend's wedding or retirement party. Deciding to lead a corporate or community initiative. Going on a vacation trip that was much more physically challenging than your normal, day-to-day activities. What happened for you as you began your personal "edge-play"?

3. Is there an area in your life, now, where you are holding back from your "edge"? Are you willing to go there? Are you willing to go beyond?

CHAPTER 31:
FOR ALL OF US (SPIRAL PATHWORKING)

AFTER A WORKSHOP, ANAHID WAS talking with some of her younger dancers. "When I am dancing," she said, "I am in my pure joy. And when a woman is in her pure joy, she is attractive." There, without my asking, was the answer to a deep question that had initiated my *Unveiling* journey. As I had come to realize the power of attraction as a dynamic that made our lives much richer and happier, I wanted to know what would make this power real in my life — and in the lives of other women as well. I kept wondering, "What makes us attractive?" The answer, for each of us, is to find and enter into that which gives us joy.

Elizabeth Herron, and other members of *The Fierce Beauty Club*,[1] also found this as the answer in their lives. Whether a woman was an artist or an entrepreneur, a home-maker or a savvy businesswoman, when she was doing what really filled her soul, she was at her most attractive. If anything, we would call this process *embracing our light*.

The story of Inanna taught us how we can *embrace our dark*. This is the metaphorical "journey of descent" that many of us undertake — whether or not it plays out as an actual physical journey. Yet all journeys have stages, and all journeys come to an end.

This book started out with the purpose of answering the time-honored question, "What do women want?" Ultimately, we desire to know ourselves, and to cultivate our fullness, richness, and ripeness of being. We found that our full "who-we-are" sense is complex, but can be understood by accessing and integrating several archetypes. Although we've examined and correlated several systems, ranging from the four archetypes identified in Antonia Wolff's *Structural Forms of the Feminine Psyche* to those enumerated in Myers-Briggs Type Inventory (MBTI), we've found that what author Rachel Pollack defined as the *Worldly Sequence*, encompassing the first seven Major Arcana, offers us a useful encapsulation. These seven Arcana also show us that our first major adult task is one of *integration*. It often takes us many years to effectively *integrate* our various modes or archetypes. As we do this, it helps to remember that our real goal is not to be any one mode, or even any combination, but to move towards personal freedom.

The very last Major Arcana card is the *World*,[2] which we can also call the *World Dancer*. The classic iconography of this card shows a beautiful woman, naked save for a long veil, dancing in the center of a wreath of laurel leaves. From this wreath, four heads (three animal, one human) face outwards, towards each of the four directions. The dancer holds the scrolls of knowledge in her hands, symbolizing the completion of her quest. She is dancing in a magical space; there is no earth in sight. She represents not only completion, but also the "pure joy" that Anahid described.

A person reaches the state depicted in this card only after going three stages of evolution. Between the youthful enthusiasm and naiveté of the *Fool*, and the "pure joy" of the *World Dancer*, lie not only challenges, but huge shifts in how we deal with life and events. Beyond the *Worldly Sequence* lie two other seven-card sequences, each of which represents a major adult "life journey."

Even if we have never studied the Major Arcana's symbols, their various meanings so permeate our culture that they form part of our mental fabric. For example, who does not know of the image of seated *Justice* (Card XI), with her sword and scales? Although originally a depiction of the Greek goddess Themis, this image has evolved into the "blind Justice" that we see depicted in courthouses throughout the country. Similarly, we all have a "felt-level" understanding of the *Hermit* (Card IX), where a person separates himself (or herself) from society to seek a mountaintop experience of insight and illumination. In short, the *Major Arcana pre-inform us about the meaning of life*. Our journey through the twenty-two Major Arcana is as much a part of our cultural landscape as is the descent of Inanna, or the journey of Odysseus.

As we completed the *Worldly Sequence*, we became more confident in not just knowing our inner "selves," or inner aspects or archetypes; we became more adroit in bringing together the strengths of each. This became our personal *Winged Victory*. As we noted earlier, this card is followed by *Strength*, which shows a beautiful young woman, with flowing hair and garbed in a white robe, gentling a ferocious beast to the ground. She is not using *Strength* in the classic sense of dominance or force. Rather, she is easing the wild beast into submission.

So, from completing the *Worldly Sequence*, we moved on to *Turning Inward*, the second major seven-card sequence. This becomes a crucial turning point; we went from how *Winged Victory* directs her chariot through force of will to how the *Strength Maiden* achieves similar goals, but through *softening* and gentling her inner beast! Many of us have already accomplished this transition in our lives. Indeed, we may have done this many times, learning the same lesson in different layers or ways. We may not have shifted from martial arts to Oriental dance, but we may have made enormous changes in how we deal with people and life situations.

For many of us, this alone would have been a life-journey culmination. Yet, our inner tradition is much richer and deeper. The transition to real, gentle *Strength* is simply the beginning of our inner work. We noted, in *Chapters 13* and *29*, how the *Turning Inward* sequence came to completion with another strong female archetype: *Temperance*.[3] This is one of the more "magical" Major Arcana cards. By the time that we are at the *Temperance* stage of our journey, we are beginning to do "magical" work on a regular basis. Things are happening for us that go well beyond coincidence. It is at this stage that we begin to do the kinds of "energy work" (or *Level 3* and *Level 4* training) described in *Chapter 29*.

Inanna's descent to the Underworld contained the full range of *Turning Inward* experiences, encompassing the eighth through the fourteenth Major Arcana. She was already a Goddess; she was acclaimed for her feminine *Strength* (Card VIII). She had to draw into herself, re-evaluating her relationship with her husband (*Hermit*, Card IX). She recognized that she needed a change (*Wheel of Fortune*, Card X), because she wanted to see the truth for what it was (*Justice*, Card XI). To do this, she was willing to yield herself completely (the *Hanged Man*, Card XII). Her willingness to "die for the truth" in order to enact the change was (for her) a literal reality (*Death*, Card XIII). Inanna came out of this experience with knowledge of her dark side, and was able to access and blend all of her energy and power together (*Temperance*, Card XIV, and the last in the *Turning Inward* sequence).

As we progress in our inner journey, the way in which we use dance (if that is our chosen art) changes over time. At first (and this may take years), we use dance to discover and cultivate our *Hathor* and *High Priestess* essences. We may start with *Hathor* (some of us never get beyond her), although finding "stillness" within our dance is a wonderful discovery! Once we make this discovery, we often spend time learning how to bring together both qualities. For example, we may use a veil routine to express our succulent, ripe, rich *Hathor*-ness, and then, as the music shifts to a single instrument *taxim* (improvisational solo), we might move into a very quiet, internal dance.

We may even bring our *Amazon* natures into our dance, much as Marlene Dietrich played off her inner masculine when she famously wore a man's tuxedo to a formal gathering. In dance, we may do this via a sword dance or cane dance, or with a firm, emphatic drum solo. And yes, we integrate our *Isis* also. We nurture our audience through eye contact. We help them heal by allowing them to tap into our released and connected energy and body-states.

Over time, though, we change our relationship with our art. We move on from the *Worldly Sequence,* in which we may have come to know our inner *Hathor* and *High Priestess*. We enter a time in which our core desire is to know ourselves more deeply. In so doing, we enter the *Turning Inward* sequence. This is a transformational time, as we release our attachment to normal, daily affairs. It also prepares us to create that which many philosophers, artists, writers, and composers will refer to as their *Magnum Opus,* or *Great Work*. This is the final stage of our journey.

As we start *Turning Inwards,* we use our dance as the vehicle for knowing ourselves. We start by becoming more attuned to our bodies, and focus more on releasing tension and emotional blockages. We begin letting the dance simply flow through us. Both our choreographies and improvisations change. We find that our *taxims* (slow improvisational sections) suggest an inner journey.

Now, as I teach choreographies to my intermediate and advanced students, I encourage them to notice how the music (and their dance) before the central *taxim* is a bit structured. In fact, prior to the *taxim,* the dance movements might even be a bit predictable. Then, both the music and the dance after the *taxim* become more free and spontaneous. During the *taxim,* the dancer metaphorically goes through a journey to the Underworld. When she returns, she is no longer as bound by conventions; she can express herself with greater release and passion. This sense of release, of being less bound by expectations, and being much more able to blend our various energies at will, ties in again with the final card of the *Turning Inward* sequence, *Temperance*.

From this wonderful and exalted place, the next several cards – initiating the final sequence, the *Great Journey* – are both scary and challenging. Immediately following *Temperance*, and starting the *Great Journey*, is a card called the *Devil*.[4] A great horned goat figure presides over two bound persons; a man and a woman. This card refers not just to encountering our baser natures, though. Yes, we do confront our *dark side*; of the many steps in this journey, this is one of the deepest and most direct encounters. However, to unleash our full potency, we must tap into our sexual energy in a new way. We must turn this energy into life force. This is where using the pure, raw power of our energy in our dance-art, and in life, becomes truly available.

The *Devil* card is the moment where we break out of inhibitions – even releasing how we may have accepted cultural conditioning. From this point, we may start gaining true energetic release. However, these new energies, or new realizations, mean that our predictable, comfortable lives no longer work for us.

The next card, the *Tower*, is where life as we've known it disintegrates. In the *Tower*, everything is coming apart and is being destroyed by forces ranging from violent waves to lightning to fire.[5] Anything that disrupts – not so much our lives, but our beliefs about how our lives should be – qualifies as a *Tower*. *Tower* experiences always involve a "breaking down," not only of our life-structures, but also our expectations; about ourselves, about others. Yet our *Tower* experiences are essential to moving forward. We truly have brought the "new wine" into our lives, and the "old wineskins" will no longer hold up. However our *Tower* comes about, our ego takes a massive beating. Whatever we have used to "shore up" our ego is destroyed.

The purpose of the *Tower* moments is not to leave us shattered, but to open us up to greater freedom. We can have many different *Tower* moments in our lives, but when we are older, and when these moments are big ones, they serve an essential purpose. In Innana's life, her *Tower* moment was when she came back from the Underworld and saw her husband sitting, unmoved and unmoving, on the throne. *That* was the moment in which her marriage came crashing down.

Each of us can very likely point to one or more major *Tower* experiences in our lives. I have gone through *Tower* episodes many times. One of my biggest *Tower* moments dealt with a major corporate transition. I had to learn to confront my own fears, and instead of retreating within myself, to work steadily and deliberately with others. While there was much work that had to be done on the overt and practical levels, the deepest change – the deepest "deconstruction" – was in my attitudes about men and my relations with them. I learned a valuable lesson in reclaiming personal power. However, this time was also scary; I "felt" as though I was experiencing all the thunder, fire, and crashing waves of a true *Tower* moment. The value of such *Tower* times in our lives is that they force us to move forward.

Once we have gotten past the worst of a *Tower* experience, we are free to notice the world around us once again. In becoming free of our old structures and constraints, we gain remarkable peace and serenity. Moreover, we start being open to what we might call Divine Inspiration or guidance about our next great purpose in life. This corresponds to the next Major Arcana, the *Star* (Card XVII). The drawing for this Arcana typically shows a naked woman, whom I call the *Star Maiden*, kneeling on one knee by a stream. One foot lightly enters the water (much like how the *Temperance Angel* gently touches one foot into the water). Again, like the *Angel* of *Temperance*, she holds two pitchers; one in each hand. Instead of pouring one into the other (*contained* transformation), she is pouring outwards from each of them; one onto the water, the other onto dry land.

We get the feeling, on seeing this picture, that the flow is unceasing. The pitchers are not being emptied, even though they are constantly gushing forth. This is a time of not only insight, but great creativity. Further, the ability to constantly "flow" our creative passions outward indicates that prior to this time, we have already achieved the *ch'i* access and circulation described in *Chapter 29*.

This theme of creative "gushing forth" is reinforced by the presence of a little bird in the bushes beside the *Star Maiden*. This bird is an ibis; a symbol of the Egyptian god Thoth, who was considered the inventor of all arts, from poetry to pottery.[6] In many symbolic ways, this card also links back to *Strength* (Card VIII), taking the feminine archetype of gentling the inner beast into a higher level of bringing forth insight, inspiration, and creativity.

Just as many of us can (perhaps all too vividly) recall the *Tower* episodes of our lives, we can also most likely recall the creative freedom that has followed. The corporate transition just described was a *Tower* experience for me, as was losing an important person in my life. However, these times were followed by insights, or a *Star* time. These insights were not just into new technical innovations, or even the realizations that have been subject matter for this book. They've also included understanding my own internal processes at a deeper level, coupled with the means to move beyond the old and into better overall life patterns. *Star* times are the times of our "great awakening." Under the calm light of the *Star*, we are open to not only new insights, but also to new ventures. From turmoil and drama, we move on to calm lucidity.

Following the *Star* insights in the *Great Journey*, we encounter the *Moon* (accessing our subconscious for visions, myths, and images), the *Sun* (energizing our creative process), and *Judgment* (responding to an angelic trumpet; literally a call to becoming a "Higher Self"). This sequence culminates in the *World Dancer* (Card XXI), which completes the Major Arcana.

Thus, as we clear out old beliefs, structures, and limitations, we open up to what is often described as our *Great Work*. For men, this is a common theme. For women, especially in our more mature years, this is also important. By the time that we have successfully completed our education, launched our children, and stabilized our careers, we are often at the age where our hormones change. Estrogen levels drop, and our minds and bodies enter a calmer time. Our thoughts are less caught up in the needs and demands of others, and we are less distracted. We are more able to allow our own insights and wisdom to emerge. Far from "retiring," this is often a time of profound generativity, creativity, and leadership.

In their more mature years, each one of my master teachers has produced performance works and shows that are (to date) the highest points of their creative genius. As an example, as Anahid Sofian continued to grow her company and studio, she produced more and more sophisticated programs and dances, and even created major shows for places such as Town Hall in New York City and the Cleveland Museum of Art. In 2005, she created her most ambitious work to that date, *Marrakesh: Inside the Magic Circle*, an off-Broadway production which included a cast of 26 dancers, musicians, acrobats, and a story-teller.

2009 was significant year for Anahid; it was the 37th year for her studio, which she celebrated with a studio recital involving all of her students. More significantly, it was the 35th anniversary of her company, which she celebrated with another major performance at the Lincoln Center Library for the Performing Arts, where her shows had been featured for the past fifteen years. Finally, in the same year, she presented her first one-woman show, which went beyond Oriental dance and circled back to her roots in modern dance. As this book came to completion, Anahid was producing another major show, focusing on her Armenian heritage and roots. This project had been percolating within her for fifteen years.

Similarly, I have seen Elena Lentini and Dalia Carella (naming only two dancers whose works I have respected and followed) create works of ever-increasing richness, depth, and meaning.

On my own *journey*, I have recently passed through a number of *Tower* experiences. Now, I am getting insight (*Star*), more connection with my intuition and inner sense of knowing (*Moon*), and greater creative generativity (*Sun*). New inventions are coming in, and I'm getting the insights needed to complete major works. As just one example, I have been receiving the final insights and connections needed to complete this book!

Still, life is never simple. We always circle back to learn the lessons that we've already encountered, albeit in a different way or to gain a deeper understanding. In this sense, our *pathworking* is much more like a spiral than it is a straight line. As we complete our *journey* in one sense, we often embark on a new *journey* – often overlapping with the one that we are just completing! We may, in fact, be going through more than one life-stage or journey-aspect at once, although these will be in different areas of our lives.

As I complete my own *unveiling journey* by finishing this book, I am finding that both new ideas and new people are coming into my life. They are great people, and like begets like. I see evidence of new energy, and new directions, all around me. At the same time, a new realm of *core wounds* is surfacing. I'm a bit more aware of how "veiled over" I've been, and how much I've used barriers to preclude real intimacy. So while I am approaching the *World Dancer* in one sense, I'm also the *Fool* in another, just beginning the *journey* of allowing intimacy.

It is good for us to take careful note: Our own *Great Work* can indeed be supporting the *Great Work* of another. We, as women, have a profound ability to nurture genius – to ennoble and inspire. As we grow in our own depth, this ability only becomes more profound. Our personal *integration* need not manifest in our own works; it can be seen in the lives of those whom we touch and influence the most. Thus, our *integration* need not result in achievements measured by the *Amazon* yardstick; we may indeed feel that our life's purpose is best served through nurturance. We may also find that our *Great Work* is to develop our own inner peace and serenity – perhaps even answering a call to a more contemplative practice. This is a very personal choice.

One of the clearest signs that any one of us has made progress is that while we are still active, and still very much "engaged" with what is going on, we begin feeling as though we are working with less "effort." This doesn't mean that the days are any shorter, or that the actual work is any less. But rather, we may start feeling that we are not straining so much inside to do the work. Our level of "franticness" diminishes, and our sense of calmness begins to increase. We do the work as needed, while at the same time knowing that as we are guided by our inner awareness, all things will indeed work out to our greatest benefit.

We may find that as we connect with our *High Priestess*, we begin to spontaneously do things that don't quite make sense initially. Then, these actions put us in exactly the right place at the right time. These may be very small, almost to the level of insignificance; but they greatly increase the synchronicity and flow in our lives, making it much easier to simply "be." For example, I recently came in from a round of errands, and for some reason just dropped things on the table and almost ran upstairs to my library and computer desk. I started checking emails, thinking that there was something in there that needed my attention. Within moments, the desk phone rang; it was a colleague who wanted to connect with me. As soon as I had that conversation, I knew that the "inner prompting" that had pulled me upstairs had been satisfied. I was free to go back downstairs and put things away.

Most of all, as we progress through our inner *journeys*, we will notice that with less and less effort on our part, things start to move towards us as we desire, and that even the timing of events gets easier. We begin listening to our intuition more

– about both big things and little. We find that our decisions are easier. We even find that stressful situations are simply less: both less stressful, and less frequent.

Our day-planner may be as full as ever, but our sense of striving and pushing is reduced. We notice that our lives are unfolding more and more as we desire them to be. We are straining and stressing much less. Things simply *happen* for us. We have become *attractors*. Each of us begins practicing our gifts with joy. Each of us becomes, regardless of our roles in life, a *World Dancer*!

CREDITS

GRATEFUL ACKNOWLEDGEMENT IS MADE TO both publishers and authors who have graciously given permission to have their copyrighted work reprinted in *Unveiling: The Inner Journey*. Every effort has been made to contact copyright holders. My special thanks go to:

- ➢ Connell Cowan and Gail Parent, for an excerpt from *The Art of War for Lovers*, copyright © 1998 by Connell Cowan and Gail Parent; reprinted with the permission of Pocket Books, a division of Simon & Schuster, Inc.

- ➢ Stephani Cook (August, 1986), excerpt from "What Men Want," originally published in *Gentlemen's Quarterly*, copyright © 1986 by Stephani Cook and Condé Nast Publications; used with the permission of Condé Nast and the author.

- ➢ David Deida, for excerpts from *The Way of the Superior Man: A Spiritual Guide to Mastering the Challenges of Women, Work, and Sexual Desire*, copyright © 1997, 2004 by David Deida. All rights reserved. Used with permission from Sounds True, Inc., Boulder, CO, www.SoundsTrue.com.

- ➢ Kent Hieatt and Constance Hieatt, for excerpts from "The Wife of Bath's Tale, taken from *The Canterbury Tales*, edited by Kent Hieatt & Constance Hieatt, copyright © 1964 by Bantam Books, an imprint of The Random House Publishing Group, a division of Random House, Inc. Used by permission of Bantam Books, a division of Random House, Inc.

- ➢ Patricia Hopkins and Sherry Ruth Anderson, for excerpts from *The Feminine Face of God*, by Patricia Hopkins and Sherry Anderson, copyright ©1991 by Patricia Hopkins and Sherry Anderson. Used by permission of Bantam Books, a division of Random House, Inc.

- ➢ Jacqueline Magness, Ph.D., and Elizabeth Roslewicz, Ph.D., for excerpt from a letter to Alay'nya, October 4, 2010. Reproduced with permission.

REFERENCES
INTRODUCTION

[1] Campbell, Joseph, *The Hero with a Thousand Faces* (Bollingen Series), 3rd Ed. (San Francisco: New World Library, 2008). (See an online summary of the steps in the *Hero's Quest* at http://www.mcli.dist.maricopa.edu/smc/journey/ref/summary.html, accessed on July 17, 2010, as part of a website devoted to how *The Hero's Quest* can inspire creative works of a mythic scope.)

[2] John Grey, *Men are from Mars, Women are from Venus* (New York: J.G. Productions-HarperCollins, 1990).

[3] Dan Millman, *Way of the Peaceful Warrior* (Novato, CA: H.J. Kramer-New World Library, 1980, 2000).

[4] Toni Grant, *Being a Woman: Fulfilling Your Femininity and Finding Love* (New York: Avon, 1988).

[5] Antonia Wolff, *Structural Forms of the Feminine Psyche* (Trans. P. Watzlawik) (Zurich: C.G. Jung Institute, 1956). According to Dr. Toni Grant, in *Being a Woman*, Ms. Wolff's original work was originally read in 1934 in the Pyschological Club in Zurich, with a more detailed version presented in 1948 at the C.G. Jung Institute in Zurich. The first appearance in print was in *Der Psychologe*, Heft 7/8; Heaugeber: Dr. Phil., G.H. Graber, Bern. A cogent summary appears in Ann Belford Ulanov, *The Feminine in Jungian Psychology and in Christian Theology* (Evanston, IL: Northwestern University Press, 1971), available through Google Books, accessed July 16, 2010. See also a discussion in Patricia Monaghan, *Encyclopedia of Goddesses and Heroines: Volumes I & II* (Santa Barbara, CA: Greenwood Press, 2010), *lviii*.

[6] Karl Pribram, *Languages of the Brain: Experimental Paradoxes and Principles in Neuropsychology* (New York: Brandon House, 1971), see e.g. Chapter Nine, "Feelings," pp. 167-183, ff.., and *Brain and Perception: Holonomy and Structure in Figural Processing* (Hillsdale, NJ: Lawrence Erlbaum Associates, 1991), see e.g. pp. 10-11, ff. For a complete listing of all of Dr. Pribram's books and over 700 research articles, see www.KarlHPribram.com.

PART I: THE AGES-OLD QUESTION

CHAPTER 1: WHAT DO WOMEN REALLY WANT?

[1]   A. Kent Hieatt & Constance Hieatt (Eds.), "The Wife of Bath's Tale," in *The Canterbury Tales by Geoffrey Chaucer* (New York: Bantam Classic–Random House, 1981), p. 223.

[2]   Ibid, p. 229.

[3]   Ibid, p. 229.

[4]   Ibid, pp. 229.

[5]   Ibid, pp. 237-239.

[6]   Ibid, p. 239.

[7]   Ibid, p. 239.

[8]   Ibid, p. 239.

[9]   David Deida, *The Way of the Superior Man: A Spiritual Guide to Mastering the Challenges of Women, Work, and Sexual Desire* (Boulder, CO: Sounds True, Inc., 2004), p. 122.

[10] Ibid, p. 79.

[11] Julia Cameron, *The Artist's Way: A Spiritual Path to Higher Creativity* (New York: Jeremy P. Tarcher–Perigee Books, 1992), pp. 9 ff.

CHAPTER 2: WHO ARE WE, *REALLY?*

[1]   Alison Lurke, *The Language of Clothes* (New York: Vintage-Random House, 1981), p. 227.

[2]   Stefan Bechtel, Larry Steins, & Laurence Roy Steins, and the editors of *Men's Health* books, in *Sex: A Man's Guide* (Emmaus, PA: Rodale Press, 1996), p. 183, quoting from an informal survey conducted by newspaper columnist Ann Landers, done in 1985, on the question of whether women would prefer "cuddling" to sex. According to Ms. Landers, about 72% of the 90,000 female survey respondents preferred "cuddling."

[3]   Stephani Cook, "What men want," *GQ* (August, 1996).

[4]   Desmond Morris, *The Naked Man: A Study of the Male Body* (New York: St. Martin's Press-Macmillan, 2008), p. 202.

[5]   A. Lurke, pp. 243-244.

6   Karen Karbo, "The Secret Economy of Women," in H. Black (Ed.), *The Secret Currency of Love: The Unabashed Truth about Women, Money, and Relationships* (New York: William Morrow-Harper Collins, 2009), p. 12.

7   Ibid, p. 12.

8   Abby Ellin, "Tool Belts, not Tuxes," in H. Black (Ed.), *The Secret Currency of Love: The Unabashed Truth about Women, Money, and Relationships* (New York: William Morrow-Harper Collins, 2009), p. 63.

9   Louise Story, "Many Women at Elite Colleges Set Career Path to Motherhood," *New York Times* (Sept. 20, 2005). (See online version at: http://www.nytimes.com/2005/09/20/national/20women.html?pagewanted=print, accessed on July 11, 2010.)

10 Kerstin Uvnas Moberg, "The Integrative Function of Oxytocin in Motherhood," published online. (See http://www.borstvoedingblijft.nl/artikelen/tysklandborn-morskor%20-%20Kerstin%20Uvnas%20Moberg.pdf, accessed Nov. 12, 2010.) See also D.K. Shahrokh, T.Y. Zhang, J. Diorio, A. Gratton, & M.J. Meaney, "Oxytocin-Dopamine Interactions Mediate Variations in Maternal Behavior in the Rat," *Endocrinology*, **151** (5), 2276-2286.

11 Mika Brzezinski, *All Things at Once* (New York: Weinstein, 2010), pp. 93 ff.

12 Pamela Stone, *Opting Out* (Berkeley, CA: University of California Press, 2007), p. 19.

13 Karine Moe & Dianna Shandy, *Glass Ceilings & 100-Hour Couples* (Athens, GA: University of Georgia Press, 2010), Chapter 4, "Glass Ceilings and Maternal Walls," section on "The Ideal Woman," pp. 54 ff.

14 Carol Evans, *This Is How We Do It: The Working Mothers' Manifesto* (New York: Hudson Street Press-Penguin Group, 2006).

15 Matt Ridley, *The Red Queen: Sex and the Evolution of Human Nature* (New York: Penguin, 1993), pp. 212–244. See also Jan Havlicek, S. Craig Roberts, & Jaroslav Flegr, "Women's preference for dominant male odour: effects of menstrual cycle and relationship status," in *Biol. Lett.* (2005; received 14 March 2005; accepted 4 April 2005). (Article published online as: http://www.natur.cuni.cz/flegr/pdf/domin.pdf , accessed on July 11, 2010.)

CHAPTER 3: BEDTIME STORIES

1   Janice Radway, *Reading the Romance: Women, Patriarchy, and Popular Literature* (Chapel Hill: The University of North Carolina Press, 1984).

2   The "Smithton women" were a group of women from the mid-western community of Smithton who began following a review of romance fiction published by Dorothy Evans, thus forming a cohesive group who could be interviewed on the subject by Janice Radway, author of *Reading the Romance* (1984).

3   Kathleen E. Woodiwiss, *The Flame and the Flower* (New York: Avon-HarperCollins Publishers, 1972).

4   According to an obituary published online, Kathleen E. Woodiwiss published twelve historical romance novels, with a total of over 36 million copies in print. (See http://www.strikefuneral.com/2007/07/07/kathleen-e-woodiwiss/, accessed on July 28, 2010.)

5   Nora Roberts' website provides information about the extensive list of novels that she has authored. (See http://www.noraroberts.com/, accessed on July 11, 2010.)

6   Nora Roberts, *Born in Fire* and *Born in Ice* (New York: Jove-Penguin, 1994 and 1998, respectively).

7   Nora Roberts, *Hidden Riches* (New York: Jove-Penguin, 1998).

8   K. E. Woodiwiss, p. 228.

9   Connell Cowan & Gail Parent, *The Art of War for Lovers* (New York: Pocket Books-Simon & Schuster, 1988), p. 35.

10 Mary Stewart, *Thornyhold* (North York, Ontario, Canada: General Publishing Company, Ltd., 1990).

11 Danielle Steel, *The House* (New York: Dell-Random House, 2007).

12 Top magazine circulation figures are provided by the Magazine Publishers of America. (See http://www.magazine.org/CONSUMER_MARKETING/CIRC_TRENDS/ABC2009TOTALrank.aspx, accessed on July 29, 2010.)

13 Douglas A. McIntyre, "The Sun Sets on Business Week, Forbes, and Fortune," in *24/7 Wall Street* (an online journal, posted May 3, 2009). (See http://247wallst.com/2009/05/03/the-sun-sets-on-businessweek-forbes-and-fortune/, accessed on July 11, 2010.)

14 Jon Fine, "Forbes: Circulation Woes, But at Least They're Not Alone," in *Bloomberg Business Week* (an online journal, posted Dec. 27, 2005). (See the online version at http://www.businessweek.com/innovate/FineOnMedia/archives/2005/12/forbes_circulat.html, accessed on July 11, 2010.)

15   Stephanie Clifford, "For Magazines, the Down Days Continue," in *The New York Times* (August 31, 2009). (See the online version at http://www.nytimes.com/2009/09/01/business/media/01adco.html, accessed on July 11, 2010.)

16   Warren Farrell, *Why Men are the Way They Are* (New York: Berkley, in arrangement with McGraw-Hill, 1986), pp. 18-22.

17   *The Revised Standard Version Bible*, Isaiah 40:11.

18   Louann Brizendine, *The Female Brain* (New York: Broadway-Random House, 2006), see Chapter 5: "The Mommy Brain," pp. 95 ff.

19   Abraham Maslow, "A theory of human motivation," *Psychological Review.* 50(4) (1943), pp. 370-396. (See the online summary at http://en.wikipedia.org/wiki/Maslow's_hierarchy_of_needs, accessed on July 11, 2010.)

CHAPTER 4: PLAYTIME FOR GROWN-UP GIRLS

1   Carole Jackson, *Color Me Beautiful* (New York: Ballentine-Random House, 1987).

CHAPTER 5: CREATING STARDUST IN OUR LIVES

1   Laura Esquivel, *Like Water for Chocolate: A Novel in Monthly Installments with Recipes, Romances, and Home Remedies* (New York: Vintage/Anchor-Random House, 1995).

2   Laurell K. Hamilton, *Guilty Pleasures* (and others following in the series) (New York: Berkley Books/Penguin Group, 1993, 2004).

3   E. Linguanti, F.M. Casotti, & C. Concilio, (Eds), *Coterminous Worlds: Magical Realism and Contemporary Post-colonial Literature in English* (Selected papers from a conference held in Pisa, Nov. 21-22, 1996).

4   Alison Flood, "Potter Tops 400 Million Sales," from *The BookSeller* (www.thebookseller.com, an online journal for the book publishing industry, posted on June 17, 2008). (See http://www.thebookseller.com/news/61161-potter-tops-400-million-sales.html, accessed on July 12, 2010.)

5   Data for the *Twilight* book series circulation obtained from *Publishers Weekly*. (See http://www.publishersweekly.com/pw/by-topic/childrens/childrens-book-news/article/42636-new-stephenie-meyer-novella-arriving-in-june.html, accessed July 28, 2010.) A 2009 article published in *USA Today* compares sales of the *Twilight* and *Potter* book series.

(See http://www.usatoday.com/life/books/news/2009-08-03-twilight-series_N.htm, accessed on July 28, 2010.)

6 Nora Roberts, *Key Trilogy (Key of Light, Key of Knowledge, Key of Valor)* (New York: Jove Books/Penguin Books, October, November, and December 2003, respectively).

7 Rhonda Byrne, *The Secret* (New York: Atria Books-Simon & Schuster, 2006). (See also the movie at http://www.thesecret.tv/, accessed on July 12, 2010.)

8 Joe Vitale, *The Attractor Factor: 5 Easy Steps for Creating Wealth (or Anything Else) from the Inside Out* (New York: Wiley, 2005).

9 One source reporting that *Charm* was incorporated into Glamour is Bob Feldman's blog, "Newhouse Dynasty's Vogue/Conde Nast's Garfinkle Connection Historically," in *Bob Feldman 68: Alternative historical information and alternative news about Columbia University and other U.S. power elite institutions* (May 3, 2009). (See original blog at http://bfeldman68.blogspot.com/2009/05/newhouse-dynastys-vogueconde-nasts.html, accessed on July 12, 2009.)

10 Definition for the word "glamour" (Etymology: Scots "glamour") from the online *Merriam-Webster Dictionary*. (See http://www.merriam-webster.com/dictionary/glamour, accessed July 28, 2010.)

PART II: A WOMAN'S PATH

CHAPTER 6: THE HERO'S QUEST – AND THE HEROINE'S AS WELL!

1 Joseph Campbell, ibid.

2 *The Magic Flute (Die Zauberflöte)* is an opera composed by Wolfgang Amadeus Mozart in 1791, and was first premiered in Vienna of that year. For more details, see M.F.M van den Berk, *The Magic Flute: Die Zauberflote. An Alchemical Allegory* (Leiden, The Netherlands: Koninklijke Brill, NV, 2004).

3 Maureen Murdock, *The Heroine's Journey* (Boston: Shambhalla, 1990), p. 2.

4 L. Brizendine, op. cit.

5 Caroline Myss, *Sacred Contracts: Awakening Your Divine Potential* (New York: Harmony Books, 2001), pp. 134-141.

6   George Lucas (Movie Producer), *Labyrinth* (1986).

7   Philip Pullman, *The Golden Compass (His Dark Materials, Book 1)* (New York: Del Rey-Random House, 1997).

8   L. Frank Baum, with W. W. Denslow (illus.), *The Wonderful Wizard of Oz* (Chicago: George M. Hill Company, 1990).

9   Isabelle's adventures are still under development. For the introductory story, see R. Nicole Cutts, "The Adventures of Isabelle Book I: The Embryo Goddess and the Morpho," in Phyllis Wilson (Ed.), *Many Paths, Many Feet: An Anthology of Women's Stories* (2010). (Book available through www.ManyPathsManyFeet.com, accessed July 11, 2010.)

10   Valerie Estelle Frankel, *From Girl to Goddess: The Heroine's Journey Through Myth and Legend* (Jefferson, NC: McFarland & Co., 2010). (See an excellent reading list associated with this book at http://frankelassociates.com/calithwain/HeroineReading.htm, accessed Oct. 4, 2010.)

11   Kirene, personal conversation followed by email summary, September 18, 2010. Used with permission.

CHAPTER 7: A "REAL" WOMAN'S PATH (REALLY *DOES* EXIST!)

1   The Shaolin monastery, located in the Henan district of China, was strongly active in the seventh century ACE. (For more online information, see http://www.shaolin.com.au/history.htm, accessed July 12, 2010.)

2   Barbara Frale (translated from the original Italian by Gregory Conti), *The Templars: The Secret History Revealed* (English-language edition published in New York: Arcade Publishing, Inc., 2009). The Knights Templar organization was formed during the twelfth century ACE, and was active up until the late 1200's, until it was dissolved by order of Pope Clement V in 1310, following political pressure from Philip IV ("Philip the Fair") to destroy the order.

3   The fictional Jedi Knights are part of the futuristic (fantasy-historical) mythology created by George Lucas as part of the *Star Wars* saga.

4   "Wise blood" is a term used in certain North American Native People's Tribes, referring to women who have gone through menopause. Having ceased menses, they keep their blood inside themselves, for their own nurturance and purposes; it has

thus come to be called "wise blood." See: Susun S. Weed, *New Menopausal Years: The Wise Woman Way* (Woodstock, NY: Ash Tree Publishing, Rev. Ed. 2001), Chapter 3: Post-Menopause: She-Who-Holds-the-Wise-Blood-Inside, pp. 181 ff., and Normandi Ellis, *Feasts of Light: Celebrations for the Seasons of Life Based on the Egyptian Goddess Mysteries* (Wheaton, IL: Quest Books, 1999. (For an online excerpt, see http://www.shamanicjourneys.com/articles/feastsoflight.php, accessed July 16, 2010, and see also a relevant essay by Gina Cloud at http://www.shemiranibrahim.com/menstruation-the-sacred-cycle/, accessed on July 16, 2010.) Note that Christiane Northrup also speaks to this in *The Wisdom of Menopause: Creating Physical and Emotional Health and Healing During the Change* (New York: Bantam-Random House, 2001).

[5]   The situation has been very different in other parts of the world, e.g., India, where recognition and worship of the "Mother Goddess" has continued for millennia, see, e.g., Linda Johnson, *The Living Goddess: Reclaiming the Tradition of the Mother of the Universe* (St. Paul, MN: Yes International Publishers, 1999).

[6]   Hildegard of Bingen (1098 – 1179, ACE) was a medieval Christian mystic, an abbess of the German Benedictine order, and a renowned scholar, herbalist, and composer of music. (See Fiona Maddocks, *Hildegard of Bingen: The Woman of Her Age* (New York: Doubleday-Random House, 2001).)

[7]   Julian of Norwich (1342 – 1416, ACE) was a medieval Christian mystic, and an anchoress (someone who lived enclosed in a small room attached to a church, and was devoted to contemplative prayer) at the Church of St. Julian of Norwich. Her actual name has been lost to history. She is renowned for having and recording her visions (as the *Short Text* and the *Long Text*), along with authoring her major work, the *Sixteen Revelations of Divine Love*. (See Grace Jantzen, *Julian of Norwich: Mystic and Theologian* (London, Great Britain: SPCK, Holy Trinity Church, 1987, 2000).)

[8]   Christiane Northrup also speaks to this in *The Wisdom of Menopause: Creating Physical and Emotional Health and Healing During the Change* (New York: Bantam-Random House, 2001).

[9]   Sherry Ruth Anderson & Patricia Hopkins, *The Feminine Face of God: The Unfolding of the Sacred in Women* (New York: Bantam Books-Doubleday, 1991), pp. 3-4.

[10] Quote from Kurt Lewin (1890 – 1947) taken from *Kurt Lewin: Groups, Experiential Learning, and Action Research*, a biographical summary with links to articles by Dr. Lewin, on a website hosted by infed, a non-profit organization. (See http://www.infed.org/thinkers/et-lewin.htm, accessed July 12, 2010.)

---

[11] T. Grant, *Being a Woman: Fulfilling Your Femininity and Finding Love* (New York: Avon, 1988).

[12] Antonia Wolff, *Structural Forms of the Feminine Psyche*, Trans. P. Watzlawik. (Zurich: C.G. Jung Institute, 1956).

[13] Ann Belford Ulanov, *The Feminine in Jungian Psychology and in Christian Theology* (Evanston, IL: Northwestern University Press, 1971), pp. 195-196.

[14] Shelley E. Taylor, *The Tending Instinct: Women, Men, and the Biology of Relationships* (New York: Times Books-Henry Holt & Co., 2002), see pp. 26, 82-83, and others for descriptions of the oxytocin influence, and p. 64 for discussion of dopamine, together with references at the end.

[15] L. Brizendine, Chapter 5: "The Mommy Brain," pp. 95 ff.

[16] Shelley E. Taylor, *The Tending Instinct*, see also L. Brizendine, p. 42.

[17] Marnia Robinson, with foreword by Douglas Wile, *Cupid's Poisoned Arrow: From Habit to Harmony in Sexual Relationships* (Berkeley, CA: North Atlantic Books, 2009).

[18] Tracey A. Baskerville & Alison J. Douglas, "Dopamine and Oxytocin Interactions Underlying Behaviors: Potential Contributions to Behavioral Disorders," *CNS Neuroscience & Therapeutics*, Wiley Online Library, 16 (3), e92-e123, DOI: 10.1111/j.1755-5949.2010.00154.x (June 2010, first published May 06, 2010). (See http://onlinelibrary. wiley.com/doi/10.1111/j.1755-5949.2010.00154.x/full, as accessed on Nov. 11, 2010.) See also references cited therein.

[19] Meg Daley Olmert, *Made for Each Other: The Biology of the Human-Animal Bond* (Cambridge, MA: Da Capo Press, 2009).

[20] Melanie Phillips, *The Ascent of Woman: A History of the Women's Suffrage Movement* (London, UK: Little, Brown Book Group, 2005).

[21] C. Northrup, p. 122.

[22] Dan Brown, *The Lost Symbol* (New York: Doubleday, 2009), and *The Da Vinci Code* (New York: Doubleday, 2003).

[23] Allen Newell & Herbert Simon, "GPS: A Program that Simulates Human Thought," in E.A. Feigenbaum & J. Feldman (Eds.), *Computers and Thought* (New York: McGraw-Hill, 1963).

[24] Carl Jung, *Psychological Types,* in *Collected Works of C.G. Jung Vol. 6* (Revised Edition; Princeton, NJ: Princeton University Press; 1976); see the online extract of the crucial

Chapter 10 at http://psychclassics.asu.edu/Jung/types.htm, developed by Christopher D. Green, accessed on July 12, 2010.)

[25] Rachel Pollack, *Seventy-Eight Degrees of Wisdom. Part I: The Major Arcana* (Newburyport, MA: Weiser Books, 2007), pp. 21 ff.

[26] Sallie Nichols, with introduction by Laurens van der Post, *Jung and Tarot: An Archetypal Journey* (York Beach, Maine: Samuel Weiser, Inc., 1980).

[27] Corinne Heline, *The Bible & the Tarot* (Marina del Ray, CA: DeVorss & Co., Publishers, 1969).

[28] George Miller (1956). "The magical number seven, plus or minus two: Some limits on our capacity for processing information," *Psychological Review* 63 (2): 81-97. (For an online version, see http://psychclassics.yorku.ca/Miller/, accessed Oct. 1, 2010.)

[29] Stuart R. Kaplan, *The Encyclopedia of Tarot, Vol I*, (Stamford, CT: U.S. Games Systems, Inc., 1978), pp. 65, 327.

[30] R. Pollack, pp. 40 ff.

[31] Gareth Knight, *Evoking the Goddess* (Rochester, VT: Destiny Books, 1985, 1993), p. 37.

[32] Ibid, p. 33. See also S. Kaplan, pp. 40, 68, 89.

[33] S.R. Kaplan, *The Encyclopedia of Tarot, Vol. 1*, p. 40, "The Tarocchi of Mantegna Cards" (illustration); circa 1470, the card for Venus shows a naked Venus bathing in a stream; her blindfolded son Cupid stands on the right bank, bow and arrow in hand, and three other persons stand on the left bank. Many of the earliest cards, e.g., the Visconti and the Visconti-Sforza decks (each circa about 1450), show the "Goddess of Love" as Cupid presiding over a couple, presumably (given the detailed facial depictions on each) of the patrons of the particular deck, as illustrated on pp. 36. The Tarochhini of Mitelli deck (circa 1664) shows a solo Venus on an elegant chariot, p. 54.

[34] S. Kaplan, *The Encyclopedia of Tarot, Vol. 1*, see p. 36, and pp. 37 & 40, for depictions of the *Chariot* being driven by a winged goddess, from the Visconti & Visconti-Sforza decks and the Tarocchi of Mantegna cards, respectively. Vol. 2, p. 15, similarly has an illustration of the Chariot, taken from the Lombardi I deck, timeframe possibly early 1900's, potentially as copies of an earlier deck.

[35] G. Knight, p. 34. See also S. Kaplan, p. 68.

[36] Norma Lorre Goodrich, *Priestesses* (New York: HarperPerennial-HarperCollins, 1989), p. 54.

[37] Ibid, p. 55.

38 Israel Regardie, *The Middle Pillar: The Balance Between Mind and Magic*, Ed. by Chic Cicero & Sandra Tabitha Cicero (St. Paul, MN: Llewellyn Press), Chapter One: "The Two Pillars of the Temple," pp. 3 ff.

39 S. Kaplan, op. cit.

40 C. Heline, *The Bible & the Tarot*, Part I: Basic Principles (pp. 1-49) offers reasonable logic to suggest that the Tarot derives logically from the early Judaic Kabbalistic system, up through its more formal definition in the 1100's and beyond. She further shows how the concepts for the Major Arcana can be "derived" from the Hebrew alphabet, which in itself has a strong Kabbalist connection. Note that the term "Kabbalah" refers to earlier Judaic esoteric traditions, and "Qabalah" to the more recently-developed European esoteric traditions.

41 Sofia is identified in various passages in the Old Testament and other historical works. See Caitlin Matthews, *Sophia: Goddess of Wisdom, Bride of God* (New Revised Ed.) (Wheaton, IL: Theosophical Publishing House, 2001). (For an online resource, see Katia Romaoff (with Mark Raines), "Sophia: Goddess of Wisdom and God's Wife," a web-based article, at http://www.northernway.org/sophia.html, accessed July 12, 2010.)

42 T. Grant, pp. 33-34, pp. 89 ff.

43 Desmond Seward, *Eleanor of Aquitaine: The Mother Queen* (New York: Barnes & Noble, 1978), p. 8.

44 Aspasia (5th century, BCE) was born in the Asia Minor city of Miletus (now in Turkey), and moved to Athens as a young woman. She was renowned as a hetaera of great accomplishment, and was educated in philosophy and elocution. She was the companion of Pericles, and hosted a salon that was one of the intellectual centers of Athens. (See Madeleine M. Henry, *Prisoner of History: Aspasia of Miletus and Her Biographical Tradition* (Oxford, Great Britain: Oxford University Press, 1995), and also H.J. Mozans, *Woman in Science* (Cambridge, MA: MIT Press, 1913, 1940, 1974), pp. 12-17.)

45 Diana Robin. *Publishing Women: Salons, the Presses, and the Counter-Reformation in Sixteenth-Century Italy.* Women in Culture and Society Series (Chicago: The University of Chicago Press, 2007). (See online review by Elizabeth H. D. Mazzacco, on The Free Library, at http://www.thefreelibrary.com/Publishing+Women:+Salons,+the+P resses,+and+the+Counter-Reformation+in...-a0177102198, accessed July 12, 2010.)

46 R. Schwart, "The Salons of the Enlightenment," from web-based course notes for *France in the Age of Les Misérables.* (See http://www.mtholyoke.edu/courses/rschwart/

hist255-s01/paris_homework/Enlightenment_salon.html, accessed July 12, 2010.) An online essay by Whitwell, "Women of the 18th Century Salons," provides more information. (See http://www.whitwellessays.com/docs/DOC_765.doc, accessed July 12, 2010.) Marie-Claude Canova-Green reviews Faith Beasley's *Salons, History, and the Creation of Seventeenth-Century France: Mastering Memory* (Part of the Women and Gender in the Early Modern World series, published in Farnham, Surrey, the United Kingdom, by Aldershot-Ashgate, 2006.) (See the online review at http://findarticles.com/p/articles/mi_7026/is_4_102/ai_n29464239/, accessed July 12, 2010.) Faith Beasley responds to a review of her work by Katherine J. Hamerton (see http://www.h-france.net/vol7reviews/hamerton2.html, accessed July 12, 2010), in an online article. (See http://www.h-france.net/vol7reviews/beasley.html, accessed on July 12, 2010.). Katelyn Ludwig writes about both British and French literary salons in the 18th century in her website; *Reinventing the Feminine: Bluestocking Women Writers in 18th Century London.* (See http://www.katelynludwig.com/masters/the_literary_salon/a_brief_history/index.html, accessed July 12, 2010.)

[47] Betsy Prioleau, *Seductress: Women Who Ravished the World and Their Lost Art of Love* (New York: Penguin Group, 2003), p. 120.

[48] Alison Roberts, *Hathor Rising: The Power of the Goddess in Ancient Egypt* (Rochester, VT: Inner Traditions-Bear Books, 1997), Carolyn Graves-Brown, *Dancing for Hathor: Women in Ancient Egypt* (New York: Continuum International. Publishing Group, 2010), C.J. Bleeker, *Hathor and Thoth: Two Key Figures of the Ancient Egyptian Religion* (Netherlands: Bril Academic Publishers, 1973), and Zachary Gray, *The Intrepid Wanderer's Guide to Ancient Goddesses* (Zachary Gray, 2008). (Hathor, the Egyptian goddess of sexuality and love, as well as pleasure and all forms of the arts, is also described in various online resources. See www.ancientegyptonline.co.uk/hathor.html, http://www.egyptartsite.com/hathor.html, http://www.thekeep.org/~kunoichi/kunoichi/themestream/hathor.html, all accessed on July 12, 2010.)

[49] Iris J. Stewart, *Sacred Woman, Sacred Dance: Awakening Spirituality Through Movement and Ritual* (Rochester, VT: Inner Traditions, 2000), pp. 20-21.

[50] R.E. Witt, *Isis in the Ancient World* (Baltimore, MD: Johns Hopkins University Press, 1971). Isis, one of the most central of the Egyptian god/goddess pantheon, is credited with being the "Great Mother." She is described in several online resources. (See http://www.goddessgift.com/goddess-myths/egyptian_goddess_isis.htm, http://www.touregypt.net/ISIS.HTM, http://www.shira.net/egypt-goddess.htm, all accessed on July 12, 2010.)

51   G. Knight, p. 37.

52   M. Murdock, p. 2.

53   C. Jung, op. cit.

54   Isabel Briggs Myers, *Gifts Differing: Understanding Personality Type* (London & Boston: Davies-Black Publishing-Nicholas Brealey Publishing, 1995). The Myers-Briggs Type Indicator (MBTI) is a psychometric questionnaire, developed by Katharine Cook Briggs and her daughter, Isabel Briggs Myers.

55   W. Kirby, in course notes for a class on Intrapersonal Psychology, "Personality Variables," provides an excellent online summary. (See http://www.uwsp.edu/education/wkirby/ntrprsnl/personalityvariables.htm, accessed July 12, 2010.) *All Experts* (a web-based encyclopedia-style resource) provides a description of the MBTI types, along with their statistical distribution. (See http://en.allexperts.com/e/m/my/myers-briggs_type_indicator.htm, accessed July 12, 2010.) A *Functional Analysis* organizes the sixteen MBTI Types into eight different functional groups. (See http://typelogic.com/fa.html, accessed on July 12, 2010, which describes how Introversion/Extroversion pair with other dominant functions to give eight "faces.")

56   The website offered by *Coaching for New Women Managers* presents online resources, showing how the MBTI is a useful tool for interpersonal work. (See http://www.coaching-for-new-women-managers.com/Myers-Briggs-Type-Indicator.html, accessed on July 12, 2010.) The Center for Applications of Pyschological Type also provides useful online material. (See http://www.capt.org/mbti-assessment/type-descriptions.htm, accessed July 12, 2010.) Each of these online sources provides a good summary of each of the sixteen different Myers-Briggs "Types."

57   David Keirsey, *Please Understand Me II: Temperament, Character, Intelligence* (Del Mar, CA: Prometheus Nemesis Book Company, 1998), with the various temperaments described throughout. For online resources, see BSM Consulting, *The Four Temperaments*, an online description of David Kiersey's work. (See http://www.personalitypage.com/four-temps.html, accessed on July 12, 2010, and also http://www.keirsey.com/handler.aspx?s=keirsey&f=fourtemps&tab=4&c=overview, accessed September 21, 2010.)

58   Dion Fortune, *The Mystical Qabalah* (San Francisco, CA: Weiser Books, 1935, 1998).

59   Louis Herbert Gray, *Introduction to Semitic Comparative Linguistics* (Piscataway, NJ: Gorgias Press: 2006); John Courtenay James, *The Language of Palestine and Adjacent Regions* (Edinburgh, UK: General Books LLC-Clark Publishing, 2010), and also S. Kaplan, op. cit. For an interesting description of a tomb discovery of proto-Semitic

text, see Mati Milstein, "Ancient Semitic Snake Spells Deciphered in Egyptian Pyramid," *National Geographic* (Feb. 5, 2007). (See online version at http://news. nationalgeographic.com/news/2007/02/070205-snake-spells.html, accessed August 10, 2010.) See also Donald M. Kraig, *Modern Magic: Eleven Lessons in the High Magickal Arts, 2nd Ed.* (Woodbury, MN: Llewellyn Press, 1988), pp. 245-249, or comparable charts in the forthcoming *Modern Magic: Twelve Lessons in the High Magickal Arts* (Woodbury, MN: Llewellyn Press, 2010).

[60] Powerpoint™ is a registered Trademark of Microsoft Corporation.

[61] D. M. Kraig, pp. 51 ff. See also S. Kaplan, p. 15, and C. Herrine, op. cit.

[62] D. Keirsey, p. 2.

[63] Isabel Briggs Myers & Mary H. McCaulley, *Manual: A Guide to the Development and Use of the Myers-Briggs Type Indicator* (Palo Alto, CA: Consulting Psychologists Press, Inc., 1985).

[64] Jacqueline Magness, Ph.D., and Elizabeth Roslewicz, Ph.D., letter to Alay'nya, October 4, 2010. Reproduced with permission.

[65] Ross Reinhold presents an excellent, short online summary that gives a much richer, deeper understanding than is typical; *Personality Pathways: Exploring Personality Type and Its Applications.* (See http://www.personalitypathways.com/faces.html, work dated Feb. 14, 2006, accessed on July 12, 2010.)

[66] Gary Hartzler presents an excellent historical online overview of Jungian Personality Types; *History of Type Development Theory* (2001). (See http://www.8functions.com/Articles/History.htm, accessed on July 12, 2010.) See also Ross Reinhold's work (http://www.personalitypathways.com/faces.html, accessed on July 12, 2010.)

CHAPTER 8: THE ESSENCE OF STILLNESS

[1] Fatema Mernissi, *Scheherezade Goes West: Different Cultures, Different Harems* (New York: Washington Square Press, 2001).

[2] The apocryphal story of Esther (born approximately 522 BCE) is found in several sources; historical research identifies her as the wife of Ahasuerus (often identified as Xerxes I), King of Persia. (See Sidnie Ann White Crawford, "Esther," in Carol A. Newsom and Sharon H. Ringe (Eds.), *Women's Bible Commentary, Expanded Edition with Apocrypha* (Louisville, KY: Westminster John Knox Press, 1992, 1998), pp. 131 ff., and

for an online resource visit http://www.hyperhistory.net/apwh/bios/b1esther_p1mw. htm, accessed July 12, 2010.)

3   Scheherazade is the heroine of the *Tales of a Thousand and One Nights*. One version of this book, by an anonymous (original historical) author, is available with illustrations by William Harvey, and translated by N.J. Dawood (New York: Penguin Classics-Penguin Books, USA, 1973).

4   S. R. Anderson & P. Hopkins, pp. 1-2. (See also http://www.northernway.org/ Shekhinah.html, accessed July 12, 2010.)

5   Caitlin Matthews, *Sophia: Goddess of Wisdom, Bride of God* (New Revised Ed.) (Wheaton, IL: Theosophical Publishing House, 2001). (For an online resource, see Katia Romaoff (with Mark Raines), "Sophia: Goddess of Wisdom and God's Wife," a web-based article, at http:// www.northernway.org/sophia.html, accessed July 12, 2010.)

6   Lynn Picknett & Clive Prince, *The Templar Revelation: Secret Guardians of the True Identity of Christ* (New York: Simon & Schuster, 1997), pp. 104-105, ff.

7   Linda Johnsen, *The Living Goddess: Reclaiming the Tradition of the Mother of the Universe* (St. Paul, MN: Yes International Publishers, 1999).

8   Marija Gimbutas, *The Living Goddesses* (Berkeley, CA: Univ. of California Press, 2001).

9   Eckhart Tolle, *A New Earth: Awakening to Your Life's Purpose* (New York: Penguin Books, 2005), p. 140.

10   May Sarton, *Journal of a Solitude* (New York: W. W. Norton & Company; reissue edition 1992).

11   Joan Anderson, *A Year by the Sea: Thoughts of an Unfinished Woman* (New York: Broadway Books-Random House, 2000).

12   Joan Anderson, *A Weekend to Change Your Life: Find Your Authentic Self after a Lifetime of Being All Things to All People* (New York: Random House; Broadway Books, 2007).

13   The Dominican Retreat House in McLean, VA, offers weekend and week-long retreats, for a wide range of (frequently non-denominational) purposes. (See their website at www.dominicanretreat.org, accessed on July 12, 2010.)

14   I. J. Stewart, op. cit.

PART III: RIGHT HERE, RIGHT NOW

CHAPTER 9: THE ART OF VENUS

[1] F. Hollaender & S. Lerner, "Falling in Love Again" (sequenced by Margi Harrell), sung by Marlene Dietrich in *Der Blaue Engel* (*The Blue Angel*), directed by Josef von Sternberg (1930). English lyrics were created later by Sammy Lerner. (See lyrics at http://smickandsmudew.com/lyrics/falling.htm, accessed July 12, 2010.)

[2] Frank Farley, "The Type T personality," chapter in L.P. Lipsett & L.L Mitnick (Eds), *Self-regulatory behavior and risk taking: Causes and consequences*. (Norwood, NJ: Ablex Publishers, 1991). See especially pp. 371, 374, 375, and 378. See also an early article by John Leo, Ruth Mehrtens, & Galvin Madison, "Behavior: Looking for a Life of Thrills," *Time* (April 15, 1985). (See online version at http://www.time.com/time/magazine/article/0,9171,966190,00.html, accessed on July 30, 2010.)

[3] Scott Peck, *The Road Less Traveled: A New Psychology of Love, Traditional Values and Spiritual Growth* (New York: Arrow, 1978, 1992), p. 117.

[4] Marnia Robinson, *Cupid's Poisoned Arrow: From Habit to Harmony in Sexual Relationships* (Berkeley, CA: North Atlantic Books, 2009).

[5] Morocco, one of New York City's greatest Oriental dancers, and a world leader in terms of her knowledge and depth of cultural understanding, has written about childbirth and Oriental dance. (See http://www.casbahdance.org/CHILDBIRTH.htm, accessed Oct. 7, 2010.) Delilah, an internationally-recognized performer and teacher based in Seattle, has written an article about doing a "Dance to the Great Mother" when she was eight months pregnant. (See http://visionarydance.com/store/belly-dancing-as-birth-dance/, accessed Oct. 7, 2010.)

[6] C. Northrup, *The Wisdom of Menopause*, pp. 52-53, 70-75.

[7] Suzanne Somers, *The Sexy Years: Discover the Hormone Connection: The Secret to Fabulous Sex, Great Health, and Vitality, for Women and Men* (New York: Three Rivers Press, 2005). (See also her other books and other resources at http://www.oprah.com/showinfo/Suzanne-Somers-The-Bioidentical-Hormone-Follow-Up_1, accessed July 12, 2010.)

[8] L. Brizendine, pp. 135-136.

[9] Veronica Franco (1546 – 1591) was a Venetian "honored courtesan" and poet. She published a volume of poetry in 1575, the *Terze Rime*, of which 17 of the 25 poems are of her authorship. The 1998 movie, *Dangerous Beauty*, is a semi-biographical account

of her life, in which the Franco role is played by Catherine McCormack. (See http://www.lib.uchicago.edu/efts/IWW/BIOS/A0017.html, accessed July 12, 2010.) She is also the subject of *The Honest Courtesan*, by Margaret Rosenthal (Chicago, IL: Univ. Chicago Press, 1993).

10 Aspasia of Miletus (470 – 400 BCE) was an intellectual force in Athens, and the companion (and later the wife) of Pericles.

CHAPTER 10: SELF IMAGE: BELIEVING IN OURSELVES

1 C. Northrup, *The Wisdom of Menopause*, op. cit. See Chapter 2: "The Brain Catches Fire at Menopause," a section entitled "Embracing the Message Behind Our Menopausal Anger," pp. 53 ff.

CHAPTER 11: SHIFTING STATE

1 W. Timothy Gallwey, E. Hanzelik, & J. Horton, *The Inner Game of Stress: Outsmart Life's Challenges and Fulfill Your Potential* (New York: Random House, 2009), p. 15.

2 Don Miguel Ruiz, The *Four Agreements: A Practical Guide to Personal Freedom (A Toltec Wisdom Book)* (San Rafael, CA: Amber-Allen, 1997).

3 E. Tolle, op. cit.

4 Gallwey et al., p. 15.

5 Gallwey et al., pp. 16-19.

6 Jonathan Van Meter, "Her Brilliant Career," in *Vogue* (December, 2009), pp. 246-257, see p. 248 for specific "mastery of issues" quote.

7 Ibid, p. 252.

8 Ibid, p. 249.

9 Ibid, p. 253.

10 Anne E. Kornblut, *Notes from the Cracked Ceiling: Hillary Clinton, Sarah Palin, and What It Will Take for a Woman to Win* (New York: Crown Publishers-Random House, 2009), p. 59.

11 A.E. Kornblut, p. 59.

12 Ross Reinhold, Myers-Briggs Type Inventory (MBTI) expert, presents an overview at http://www.personalitypathways.com/faces.html (accessed July 30, 2010).

13 Hillary Rodham Clinton, *It Takes a Village* (New York: Simon & Schuster, 1996).

14 Otto Kroeger with Janet M. Theusen and Hile Rutledge, *Type Talk at Work: How the 16 Personality Types Determine Your Success on the Job* (New York: Dell, 2002), p. 279.

15 For some media coverage of Hilary Clinton's "charm offensives," see: http://blogs.reuters.com/frontrow/2009/02/05/clinton-goes-on-charm-offensive-with-french/, http://www.newsmax.com/us/hillary_state_dept/2009/01/28/175874.html, and http://www.dnaindia.com/india/report_hillary-woos-india-with-charm-offensive_1275883 (all accessed July 30, 2010).

16 For some media coverage describing Hilary Clinton's travels in terms of "listening tours," see: http://www.cbsnews.com/stories/2009/02/20/politics/washingtonpost/main4815167.shtml and http://www.cnn.com/ALLPOLITICS/stories/1999/07/09/senate.2000/hrc.senate/ (all accessed July 30, 2010).

17 Drs. Jacqueline Magness and Elizabeth Roslewicz; personal communication. For their study of Myers-Briggs Type distributions in a college senior-level Capstone course, see J.B. Magness & E.A. Roslewicz, "An Innovative Myers-Briggs Type Indicator Educational Experience Used in an Information Technology Capstone Course," *SIGITE '09* (Oct. 22-24, 2009, Fairfax, VA, USA). See also Kroeger et al., pp. 246-247.

18 Madeleine Albright with Bill Woodward, *Memo to the President: How We Can Restore America's Reputation and Leadership* (New York: HarperCollins, 2008), and *The Mighty and the Almighty* (New York: HarperCollins, 2006).

19 The quotation from an interview with Madame Albright is taken from http://www.blackdresstraveler.com/politics/ (accessed July 30, 2010), which quotes a transcript based on an interview with Madame Albright presented on **Real Time with Bill Maher**. (HBO; http://www.hbo.com/billmaher/, March 20th, 2009). (See video clip at http://guerillawomentn.blogspot.com/2009/03/madeline-albright-on-bill-mahers-real.html, accessed Oct. 2, 2010.).

20 Madeleine Albright, *Read My Pins: Stories from a Diplomat's Jewel Box* (New York: Harper, 2009). (See also http://www.stylelist.com/2009/09/30/madeleine-albright-book-read-my-pins-exhibit/, accessed July 30, 2010).

21 Ibid, p. 17.

22 Julia Cameron, *The Vein of Gold: A Journey to Your Creative Heart* (New York: Tarcher/Putnam, 1996).

CHAPTER 12: BE, DO, HAVE:
THE WAY TO GET FROM "HERE" TO "THERE"

1   Peter Ralston, the renowned martial artist, has founded both a style and a school called Cheng Hsin. (See http://www.chenghsin.com, accessed July 30, 2010.)

2   Peter Ralston, *Cheng Hsin: Principles of Effortless Power* (Berkeley, CA: North Atlantic Books, 1999). (See also http://www.chenghsin.com/book-principles.html, accessed July 30, 2010.)

3   Anthony Robbins, *Unlimited Power: The New Science of Personal Achievement* (New York: Free Press-Simon & Schuster), 1997).

CHAPTER 13: THE GENTLE ART OF RECEIVING

1   Julia Cameron, *The Artist's Way*, pp. 21-23.

2   S.R. Anderson & P. Hopkins, p. 19.

3   Robert Fusaro, as of this writing is 7th Dan (seventh-degree black belt) in Shotokan karate, and is founder of the Midwest Karate Association, with headquarters in Minneapolis, MN. (See his website at http://www.midwestkarate.org/, accessed August 24, 2010.)

4   Cassandra, an internationally recognized teacher and performer of Oriental dance, has studio headquarters in Minneapolis, MN, which is also the location of her dance troupe; the *Jawaahir Dance Company*. (See her website at http://www.jawaahir.org/, accessed August 19, 2010.)

5   Robert Fusaro Sensei, telephone conversation, July 25, 2010. Used with permission.

6   Suzanna del Vecchio's *Dances from the Heart I & II* (in DVD format) are available online. (See http://www.suzannadelvecchio.com/, accessed Oct. 7, 2010.)

7   Cassandra, personal email communication, August 21, 2010. Used with permission.

8   197 Maria Strova, *The Secret Language of Belly Dancing: Symbols, Sensuality, Maternity, Forgotten Roots* (Cesana Torinese: Macro Edizione, 2006), p. 33.

9   Stella Grey, one of the most intelligent and insightful commentators on Oriental dance, now writes occasionally for her website, "Age of Iron." (See http://www.ageofiron.net/, accessed September 16, 2010.) She has also reactivated her New York dance-scene website. (See http://www.bellydanceny.com, accessed Oct. 2, 2010.)

[10] Louann Brizendine, *The Male Brain* (New York: Broadway Books-Random House, 2010), Chapter 2: "The Boy Brain," pp. 9 ff.

[11] Anne Thomas Soffee, *Snake Hips: Belly Dancing and How I Found True Love* (Chicago, IL: Chicago Review Press, 2004).

[12] Amustela is a leading Oriental dancer in the Northern Virginia/Greater Washington DC Metro Area. (See her website at http://www.amusteladance.com/, accessed September 16, 2010.)

[13] The Washington Area Mid-Eastern Dance Association (WAMEDA, Inc.) is a non-profit, 501 (c)(3) organization dedicated to serving dancers in the Greater Washington DC Metropolitan Area. (See their website at www.wameda.org, accessed September 16, 2010.)

[14] Nimeera is both an accomplished performer and instructor in the art of Oriental dance. She additionally owns and operates Cleo's Closet, a dance supply company. (See her website at http://www.nimeera.com/, accessed September 16, 2010.)

[15] Dan Brown, *Angels and Demons* (2000), *The Da Vinci Code* (2003), and *The Lost Symbol* (2009) (all New York: Doubleday).

[16] R. Pollack, pp. 64-65, ff.

[17] R. Pollack, pp. 95-98.

[18] Margaret Starbird, *The Woman with the Alabaster Jar: Mary Magdalen and the Holy Grail* (Rochester, VA: Bear & Co., 1993), Chapter 3: "The Blood Royal and the Vine," pp. 49 ff.

[19] *The Revised Standard Version Bible*, John, 11:1-2, and 12:1-8.

[20] *The Gnostic Gospels: Including the Gospel of Thomas {&} the Gospel of Mary Sacred Wisdom* (New York: Watkins-Dunkin Baird Publishers, distributed in the US by Sterling, 2006).

[21] *The Revised Standard Version Bible*, Mark, 14:9.

[22] G.R.S. Mead (Trans.), *Pistis Sophia: The Gnostic Tradition of Mary Magdalene, Jesus, and His Disciples.* (Mineola, NY: Dover Publications, 2005); Samael Aun Weor, *The Gnostic Bible: Pistis Sophia Unveiled* (Brooklyn, NY: Glorian Publishing, 2005).

[23] L. Picknett & C. Prince, *The Templar Revelation*, pp. 48-49; see also Michael Baigent, Richard Leigh, & Henry Lincoln, *The Holy Blood and the Holy Grail* (New York: Delacorte-Random House, 1982) for predecessor work. (For an interesting online summary, see http://www.thestarhouse.org/MMWho.html, accessed July 30, 2010.)

24 Savina J. Teubal, *Sarah the Priestess: The First Matriarch of Genesis* (Athens, OH: Ohio University Press: 1984).

25 *The Revised Standard Version Bible*, Numbers 31:17-18, Judges 21:11; see also Deuteronomy 20:13.

26 *The Revised Standard Version Bible*, Exodus, 22:18.

27 Tikva Frymer-Kensky, *In the Wake of the Goddesses: Women, Culture and the Biblical Transformation of Pagan Myth* (New York: Fawcett Columbine-Ballentine, 1992), Chapter 7: The Marginalization of the Goddesses, pp. 70-80.

28 *The Revised Standard Version Bible*, Timothy 2:11

29 Peter Brown, *The World of Late Antiquity, A.D. 150-750 (Library of World Civilization)* (London & New York: W. W. Norton & Company, 1971), p. 82. (See also an online summary citing Brown's book at J. Beardsley, "Christ and Civilization," Part 3, *The Trinity Review*, February 2003, pp. 2-4, with excerpts presented at http://www.rap-idnet.com/~jbeard/bdm/Cults/Catholicism/ch-state.htm, accessed on July 14, 2010.)

30 M. Starbird, p. 158.

31 Tucker Malarkey, *Resurrection* (a novel) (New York: Riverhead Books-Penguin Group, 2006).

PART IV: IN OUR BODIES

CHAPTER 14: LOCKING OUR MINDS OUT OF OUR BODIES

1 James Weinstein, "Absent from Work: Nature versus Nurture" (Editorial), *Annals of Internal Medicine*, 140 (2) (January 20, 2004), pp. 142-143.

2 A.K. Burton et al., on behalf of the COST B13 Working Group for Guidelines for Prevention in Low Back Pain, *European Guidelines for Prevention in Low Back Pain* (November, 2004), at http://www.backpaineurope.org/web/files/WG3_Guidelines.pdf

3 Cyndi Dale, *The Subtle Body: An Encyclopedia of Your Energy Anatomy* (Boulder, CA: Sounds True, 2009).

Chapter 15: Softening:
Beginning to Break Through

1. Myron Sharaf, *Fury on Earth: A Biography of Wilhelm Reich* (Cambridge, MA: Da Capo Press, 1994), p. 4.

2. Ida P. Rolf (1896 – 1979) pioneered what came to be known as *Rolfing®*, or *Structural Integration*. She wrote her magnum opus, summarizing her life's work, in 1977; *Rolfing: Reestablishing the Natural Alignment and Structural Integration of the Human Body for Vitality and Well-Being* (Rochester, VT: Healing Arts Press, Revised Ed. 1989). For additional insights, see a collection of very heartwarming recollections edited by Rosemary Feitis and Louis Schultz, *Remembering Ida Rolf* (Berkeley, CA: North Atlantic Books, 1997).

3. The Rolf Institute of Structural Integration hosts a website with substantial information. (See www.rolf.org, accessed August 2, 2010.)

4. I. Rolf, *Rolfing: Reestablishing the Natural Alignment and Structural Integration of the Human Body for Vitality and Well-Being* Revised Ed. (Rochester, VT: Healing Arts Press, 1989), p. 21.

5. P.Ralston, op. cit.

6. E. Tolle, *A New World Order*, pp. 144-145.

7. The "King Baby" term was coined by Tom Cunningham to describe a person who has reached adulthood without developing emotional maturity. This work was first put forth in a pamphlet: Tom Cunningham, *King Baby* (Pamphlet) (Center City, MN: Hazelden, 1987).

8. Starhawk, *Truth or Dare: Encounters with Power, Authority and Mystery* (New York: HarperOne-HarperCollins, 1988). (See also: http://www.starhawk.org/writings/truth-dare.html, accessed August 2, 2010.)

9. Starhawk, op. cit.

Chapter 16: Unsticking: Releasing Resistance

1. Wen Zee, with a Foreword by Andrew Weil, *Wu Style Tai Chi Chuan: Ancient Chinese Way to Health* (Berkeley, CA: North Atlantic Books, 2002), p. 7.

2. J. Cameron, p. 44.

3   Esther Hicks & Jerry Hicks, *Ask and It Is Given: Learning to Manifest Your Desires* (Carlsbad, CA: Hay House, 2004), p.25.

4   Bartholomew, *"I Come As a Brother": A Remembrance of Illusions* (Carlsbad, CA: Hay House, 1985).

5   Dr. Phil McGraw, in an article on Relationships/Sex, on the topic: "Calling It Quits: Are You Ready for Divorce?" (See article online at http://www.drphil.com/articles/article/23; accessed August 2, 2010.)

6   C.W. Leadbeater, *The Chakras* (Wheaton, IL: The Theosophical Publishing House, originally published in 1927; third edition published in 1980), see diagram on page inserted between pp. 40 & 41. For more basic information on the chakras (energy centers in our body), see Harish Johari, *Chakras: Energy Centers of Transformation* (Rev. & Expanded Ed.; Rochester, VT: Destiny Books, 2000).

7   E. Tolle, p. 147.

8   Esther Hicks & Jerry Hicks, *The Vortex* (Carlsbad, CA: Hay House, 2009), *The Amazing Power of Deliberate Intent: Living the Art of Allowing* (Carlsbad, CA: Hay House, 2006), and other works by the same authors.

PART V: THE RITUAL: PREPARING TO DANCE

CHAPTER 17: WE'RE WORTH THE EFFORT!

1   Donald S. Lopez, *Prisoners of Shangri-La: Tibetan Buddhism and the West* (Chicago: University of Chicago Press, 1998), pp. 126 ff.

2   Ibid, p. 133.

3   June Campbell, *Traveller in Space: Gender, Identity, and Tibetan Buddhism* (London: Continuum, 1992; Rev. Ed. 2002), p. 64.

4   Ibid, p. 64.

5   D. Deida, p. 114.

6   The song "Tradition" in the *Fiddler on the Roof* was composed by Jerry Bock, with lyrics written by Sheldon Harnick, and first produced on Broadway in 1964. *Fiddler on the Roof*, one of Broadway's longest-running musicals, was based on a book by Joseph Stein, and adapted from Sholom Aleichem's stories by special permission

from Arnold Perl. (For the lyrics, see http://www.stlyrics.com/lyrics/fiddlerontheroof/tradition.htm, accessed August 6, 2010.)

[7] Laren Stover & Kimberly Forrest, with Nicole Burdette & Randi Gollin, *The Bombshell Manual of Style* (New York: Hyperion, 2001), pp. 22-23.

[8] *The Revised Standard Version Bible*, Matthew 7:16, 20.

[9] Carole Jackson, *Color Me Beautiful* (New York: Ballantine, 1987) (See also http://www.colormebeautiful.com/seasons/colormebeautifulbook.html for a newer book, *Reinvent Yourself with Color Me Beautiful* by Joanne Richmond, offering similar themes and an online color analysis quiz, accessed Oct. 3, 2010.)

[10] Suzanne Caygill, *Color: The Essence of You* (Berkeley, CA: Celestial Arts, 1980). (See also an excellent online summary at http://en.wikipedia.org/wiki/Color_analysis, accessed August 6. 2010.)

[11] S. Caygill, op. cit. (See quote presented in context in an online overview of color theory and personal style at http://www.rochelehirsch.com/coloredgesuzannestheory.htm, accessed August 6, 2010.)

[12] Denise Linn, *Altars: Bringing Sacred Shrines into Your Everyday Life* (New York: Ballantine, 1999).

[13] Donald J. Trump with Meredith McIver, *How to Get Rich* (New York: Random House, 2004), "Reflect for Three Hours a Day," pp. 91-92.

Chapter 18: The Ritual – and Why We Need It

[1] Rabbi Harold White, Georgetown University, personal communication, July 21, 2010.

[2] I. J. Stewart, op. cit.

[3] G.R.S. Mead (Trans.), *Pistis Sophia: The Gnostic Tradition of Mary Magdalene, Jesus, and His Disciples.* (Mineola, NY: Dover Publications, 2005); Samael Aun Weor, *The Gnostic Bible: Pistis Sophia Unveiled* (Brooklyn, NY: Glorian Publishing, 2005).

[4] Francis Legge, *Forerunners and Rivals of Christianity: From 330 BC to 330 AD* (Whitefish, MT: Kessinger Publishing, 2010).

[5] Joe Williams teaches the Delsarte Method, with background and workshop information available at www.delsarteproject.com (accessed August 16, 2010).

CHAPTER 19: A SACRED TIME, A SACRED SPACE

[1] Richard J. Curry, S.J., Ph.D., preaching the *Mass of the Holy Family*, Holy Trinity Church, December, 2009.

[2] L. Brizendine, p. 145.

[3] D. Deida, p. 193.

[4] Eva Cernik, personal communication via e-mail, August 21, 2010. Used with permission.

[5] Videos of Eva Cernik's performances are available from online resources. (See http://home.earthlink.net/~evacernik/video.htm, accessed August 6, 2010.)

[6] Artemis Mourat offers both instructional and performance DVDs and videos. (See http://www.serpentine.org/video/video.html, accessed August 6, 2010.)

[7] Dalia Carella offers both instructional and performance DVDs and videos. (See http://daliacarella.com/cube/ and also her solo dances, presented in *Festival of the Nile*, see http://www.baladiboutique.com/Videos.html, both accessed on August 6, 2010.)

[8] For two excellent yearly dance camps, see http://www.folktours.com and http://www.middleeastcamp.com/general.htm, and also http://www.alaynya.com/community.htm, with links to current camps.

CHAPTER 20: THE POWER OF SCENT

[1] Edwin Morris, *Fragrance: The Story of Perfume from Cleopatra to Chanel* (London: Dover, 2002), p. 44. (See also a lovely summary and discourse on the role of scent at http://www.american-buddha.com/lit.naturalhistsenses.smell.htm, accessed August 16, 2010.)

[2] Charlotte-Anne Fidler, "Scents of Desire," *British Elle*, December 1996, p. 172, and also cited in Michelle Kodis, David T. Moran, & Deborah Houy, *Love Scents: How Your Natural Pheromones Influence Your Relationships, Your Moods, and Who You Love* (New York: Dutton-Penguin Books, 1998). Also, in Celia Lyttleton, *The Scent Trail: How One Woman's Quest for the Perfect Perfume Took Her Around the World* (New York: New American Library-Penguin Books, 2007), the author describes how Serge Lutens, a *hauts perfumeur*, notes that the Chinese were the first to develop the pattern of feeding the courtesans "bland food laced with musk" so that when they made love, "their consorts could enjoy the scent of their bodies as they sweated pure perfume," p. 74.

CHAPTER 21: DRESSING THE PART

1   Rosina-Fawzia Al-Rawi, *Grandmother's Secrets: The Ancient Rituals and Healing Power of Belly Dancing* (Northampton, MA: Interlink Publishing, 2000), see pp. 42-46, & pp. 126-128, describing the Ouled Nail, a Berber tribe in North Africa.

2   Guillermo De Osma, *Fortuny: The Life and Time of Mariano Fortuny* (New York: Rizzoli International Publishers, 1980).

3   Julie Rahm, "America's Mindset Mechanic." See http://www.americasmindsetmechanic.com/ (as accessed on March 7, 2011).

PART VI: THE RITUAL: PREPARING TO DANCE

CHAPTER 22: LOOKING LIKE A DANCER (EVEN IF YOU'RE NOT!)

1   Suhaila Salimpour offers DVDs, music downloads, and online classes. (See http://www.suhailainternational.com/, accessed August 17, 2010.) Dalia Carella similarly offers both online classes and DVDs. (See http://daliacarella.com/cube/, accessed August 17, 2010.)

CHAPTER 23: IN PRAISE OF A FEW GOOD MEN

1   Esther Hicks & Jerry Hicks, op. cit.

2   Peter Ralston, *Integrity of Being: The Cheng Hsin Teachings* (copyright © Peter Ralston, 1983); this book, now out of print, was a predecessor text to P. Ralston, *Cheng Hsin: Principles of Effortless Power*, 2nd Ed. (Berkeley, CA: North Atlantic Books, 1999).

3   Napoleon Hill, *Think and Grow Rich* (New York: Ballantine, 1937, 1987), Chapter 12, *Sexuality*.

4   S. R. Anderson & P. Hopkins, pp. 1-2, 99, and 162. (For a relevant online source, see also the *Jewish Encyclopedia (online)* at http://www.jewishencyclopedia.com/view.jsp?letter=S&artid=588, accessed July 14, 2010.)

5   D. Deida, p. 143.

6   Joanna Barsh & Susie Cranston, *How Remarkable Women Lead: The Breakthrough Model for Work and Life* (New York: McKinsey & Co., Inc.-Random House, 2009).

7   S. R. Anderson & P. Hopkins, p. 4.

CHAPTER 24: MEN: A SHORT OWNER'S MANUAL

1   Tom Cunningham, *King Baby* (Pamphlet) (Center City, MN: Hazelden, 1987).

2   John Eldredge, *Wild at Heart: Discovering the Secret of a Man's Soul* (Nashville, TN: Thomas Nelson, 2010), Chapter 1: "Wild at Heart," pp. 1-18.

3   D. Deida, p. 27.

4   R. Pollack, pp. 88-91.

5   Daniel Levinson, *The Seasons of a Man's Life* (New York: Ballentine-Random House, 1986).

6   Regina Thomashauer, *Mama Gena's School of Womanly Arts* (New York: Simon & Schuster, 2002) and *Mama Gena's Owner's and Operator's Guide to Men* (New York: Simon & Schuster, 2003).

7   D. Deida, p. 70.

CHAPTER 25: SEX "SECRETS" OF BELLY DANCERS

1   Carmine D. Clemente, *Clemente's Anatomy Dissector*, (Philadelphia, PA: Lippincott Williams & Wilkins-Wolters Kluwer Health, 3rd Ed., 2010), see "Dissection 18: The Male and Female Pelvis".

2   For a good diagram of this, I recommend C. Harbut, *Pelvic diaphragm Powerpoint: Muscles of the Pelvic Floor* (MS Powerpoint presentation). (See www.cerritos.edu/charbut/AP150/lec_otl/Pelvic%20diaphragm.ppt, accessed Oct. 7, 2010.)

3   Mantak Chia, *Awaken Healing Energy Through Tao* (Santa Fe, NM: Aurora Press, 1983); Mantak Chia & Maneewan Chia, *Healing Love Through Tao: Cultivating Female Sexual Energy* (Huntington, NY: Healing Tao Books, 1986).

4   Helen O'Connell, Anatomical Relationship between Urethra and Clitoris, *Journal of Urology*, 159 (June, 1998), see also *New Scientist* (1 August 1998), pp. 34-35, and for an online summary with anatomical diagrams, http://www.enhancedorgasms.com/clitoris.html, accessed Oct. 7, 2010.)

[5]   Natalie Angier, *Woman: An Intimate Geography* (New York: Anchor-Random House, 1999), pp. 62 ff.

[6]   Gerson Kuhr, *Core Training for Belly Dancers* (2006); DVD is available through Amazon.

[7]   Napoleon Hill includes a section on transmuting the emotion of sex energy in each of his books; you might start with *Think and Grow Rich* (New York: Ballantine-Random House, 1987), Chapter 12, and *Grow Rich! With Peace of Mind: How to Earn All the Money You Need and Enrich Every Part of Your Life* (New York: Fawcett Crest, 1967), Chapter 8: "How to Transmute Sex Emotion into Achievement Power," pp. 101-110.

CHAPTER 26: UNVEILING: SELECTIVE REVELATION

[1]   Sun Tzu, a Chinese general and military strategist, supposedly wrote *The Art of War* sometime between 476–221 BC; a period which included commentaries made by other strategists on his original work. This work has undergone numerous translations and commentaries. For a recent edition with commentary, see Mark McNeilly, *Sun Tzu and the Art of Modern Warfare* (Oxford, England: Oxford University Press, 2001).

[2]   For information on the Abraham-Hicks materials, visit the website www.abraham-hicks.com, accessed August 17, 2010.

PART VII: THE RITUAL: PREPARING TO DANCE

CHAPTER 27: LETTING GO: THE INANNA STORY

[1]   Diane Wolkstein and Samuel Noah Kramer, *Inanna: Queen of Heaven and Earth* (New York: Harper & Row, 1983).

[2]   Thorkild Jacobsen, *The Treasures of Darkness: A History of Mesopotamian Religion* (New Haven: Yale University Press, 1976), pp. 135-140.

[3]   Betty De Shong Meador, personal communication via P.L. Gough, University of Texas Press. Material used with permission.

[4]   Betty De Shong Meador, *Inanna Lady of the Largest Heart: Poems of the Sumerian High Priestess Enheduanna* (Austin, TX: University of Texas Press, 2001), p.11

[5] Diane Wolkstein, a New York City-based storyteller, has skillfully translated and presented numerous world stories. (See http://dianewolkstein.com/, accessed on March 7, 2011.)

[6] Wolkstein & Kramer, p. 12.

[7] Ibid, pp. 16-18.

[8] Ibid, pp. 14-15, 21.

[9] Ibid, p. 53.

[10] David Adams Leeming & Jake Page, *Goddess: Myths of the Female Divine* (Oxford: Oxford University Press, 1994), p. 63.

[11] Wolkstein & Kramer, p. 65.

[12] Debbie Ford, *The Dark Side of the Light Chasers: Reclaiming Your Power, Brilliance, Creativity, and Dreams* (New York: Riverhead Trade-Penguin Group, 1999).

[13] Wolkstein & Kramer, pp. 158-160.

[14] Ibid, pp. 61, 62.

[15] Ibid, p. 64.

[16] Ibid, pp. 67-68.

CHAPTER 28: GOING DEEPER

[1] D. Wolkstein & S.N. Kramer, pp. 69-70.

[2] Ibid, p. 71.

[3] Ibid, p. 45.

[4] Ibid, p. 40.

[5] Ibid, p. 48.

[6] Ibid, p. 49.

[7] Ibid, p. 45.

[8] Ibid, p. 162.

[9] *The Revised Standard Version Bible*, Isaiah 53:3.

[10] Wolkstein & Kramer, p. 77.

[11] John Milton, *Paradise Lost* (Cambridge: University Press, 1918; first edition 1892), Book I, 240-330. (See http://www.authorama.com/national-epics-41.html, for an online version, accessed August 18, 2010.)

[12] D. Deida, p. 77.

[13] Mary Batten, *Sexual Strategies: How Females Chose Their Mates* (New York: Tarcher, 1992), p. 22.

[14] De Shong Meador, op. cit.

CHAPTER 29: PRAGMATIC ESOTERICS

[1] Cassandra, an internationally recognized teacher and performer of Oriental dance, has studio headquarters in Minneapolis, MN, which is also the location of her dance troupe; the *Jawaahir Dance Company*. (See her website at http://www.jawaahir.org/, accessed August 19, 2010.)

[2] *The Revised Standard Version Bible*, Numbers 20:8. (See an online version end exposition at http://www.ohrtorahstone.org.il/parsha/5761/chukat61.htm, accessed August 19, 2010.)

[3] Peter Ralston, an internationally-acclaimed martial artist, has developed his own style of martial arts, which he calls Cheng Hsin. (See his website at http://www.chenghsin.com/, accessed August 19, 2010.)

[4] Ron Sieh, *T'ai Chi Ch'uan: The Internal Tradition* (Berkeley, CA: North Atlantic Books, 1993).

[5] Israel Regardie, *The Middle Pillar: The Balance between Mind and Magic*, edited and annotated with new material by Chic Cicero & Sandra Tabatha Cicero (St. Paul, MN: Llewellyn Publications, 2003).

[6] Mantak Chia and Maneewan Chia, *Healing Love Through the Tao: Cultivating Female Sexual Energy* (Huntington, NY: Healing Tao Books, 1986), pp. 60 ff.

[7] Mantak Chia, *Awaken Healing Energy Through Tao* (Santa Fe, NM: Aurora Press, 1983).

[8] R. Sieh, p. 22.

[9] Kathryn Ferguson has an excellent DVD that I recommend to all my beginner students; Kathryn Ferguson, *Mid-Eastern Dance: An Introduction to the Belly Dance*. (For ordering the DVD, see http://www.bastetproductions.com/mideast.htm, accessed August 19, 2010.) Suhaila Salimpour also offers a wide range of useful DVDs, some

are particularly appropriate for Beginners. (See http://www.suhailainternational. com/, accessed August 19, 2010.)

10   Sri Swami Sivananda, *The Science of Pranayama* (Thousand Oaks, CA: BN Publishing, 2008; First Ed., copyright The Divine Life Society, 1935), pp. 8 ff.

11   Peter Ralston, *Integrity of Being: The Cheng Hsin Teachings* (1983), notes from his private manual, pp. 29-30.

12   Mantak Chia & Maneewan Chia, *Cultivating Female Sexual Energy,* op. cit.

13   Alma Daniel, Timothy Wyllie, and Andrew Ramer, *Ask Your Angels* (New York: Wellspring/Ballentine-Random House, 1992).

14   D.M. Kraig, *Modern Magick: Eleven Lessons (2nd Ed.),* Chapter 2, pp. 33 ff.

15   The spiritual exercises of St. Ignatius of Loyola are described in various works, one instance is Anthony Mottola, *Spiritual Exercises of St. Ignatius* (New York: Image-Doubleday, 1989).

16   S. Viraswami Pathar, *Gayatri Mantra* (Gayatri Mantra, 2006). The musical duo Rasa has included the Gayatri Mantra on one of their CDs; *Saffron Blue* (New Earth Records, 2007).

17   Dan Brown, *The Da Vinci Code* (New York: Random House, 2003), pp. 142-143, 307-309.

18   Richard Wilhelm, with commentary by Carl Jung, *The Secret of the Golden Flower: A Chinese Book of Life* (New York: Mariner Books, 1962).

19   Donald Michael Kraig, *Modern Sex Magick: Secrets of Erotic Spirituality* (Woodbury, MN: Llewellyn Publications, 2002), and see also *Modern Magick: Twelve Lessons in the High Magickal Arts* (Woodbury, MN: Llewellyn Publications, 2010).

20   Louis Culling, *Sex Magick* (St. Paul, MN: Llewellyn Press, 1988), pp. 25 & 39.

21   Ibid, p. 51.

22   D. Deida, pp. 166, 170.

23   D. Deida, pp. 72.

24   Napoleon Hill, *Think and Grow Rich* (New York: Ballantine, 1937, 1987), p. 236

25   Examples of these works include Napoleon Hill, *Think and Grow Rich* (New York: Ballantine-Random House, 1937, 1987), Chapter 12: "Sexuality," and *Grow Rich! With Peace of Mind: How to Earn All the Money You Need and Enrich Every Part of Your*

Life (New York: Ballantine, 1967), Chapter 8: "How to Transmute Sex Emotion into Achievement Power," pp. 101-110.

CHAPTER 30: PLAYING WITH YOUR EDGE

1   Peter Ralston, *The Book of Not Knowing: Exploring the True Nature of Self, Mind, and Consciousness* (Berkeley, CA: North Atlantic Books, 2010), p. 2.

2   Julia Cameron, *The Artist's Way: A Spiritual Path to Higher Creativity* (New York: Tarcher, 1992).

3   R. Thomaschauer, *Mama Gena's Guide to the Womanly Arts*, op. cit.

4   I.J. Stewart, pp. 164-173.

CHAPTER 31: FOR ALL OF US (SPIRAL PATHWORKING)

1   Elizabeth Herron, *The Fierce Beauty Club: Girlfriends Discovering Power and Celebrating Body and Soul* (Boston, MA: Houghton Mifflin, 2000).

2   R. Pollack, pp. 124-127.

3   R. Pollack, pp. 95-98.

4   R. Pollack, pp. 101-105.

5   R. Pollack, pp. 106-110.

6   R. Pollack, pp. 110-112.

INDEX

Made in the USA
Lexington, KY
03 September 2011